Praise for
THE BERLITZ TRAVELLERS GUIDES

"Aimed at educated, experienced travellers, the [Berlitz Travellers] Guides capture the flavor of foreign lands."
—*Entrepreneur*

"Filling a needed niche in guidebooks ... designed to eliminate the cumbersome lists of virtually every hotel and restaurant .... Special out-of-the-way places are detailed.... The books capture the personality and excitement of each destination."
—*Los Angeles Times*

"There's a different tone to these books, and certainly a different approach ... information is aimed at independent and clearly sophisticated travellers.... Strong opinions give these books a different personality from most guides, and make them fun to read."
—*Travel & Leisure*

"Aimed at experienced, independent travellers who want information beyond the nuts-and-bolts material available in many familiar sources. Although each volume gives necessary basics, the series sends travellers not just to 'sights,' but to places and events that convey the personality of each locale."
—*The Denver Post*

"Just the right amount of information about where to stay and play."
—*Detroit Free Press*

"The strength of the [Berlitz Travellers Guides] lies in remarks and recommendations by writers with a depth of knowledge about their subject."
—*Washington Times*

"The most readable of the current paperback lot."
—*New York Post*

"Highly recommended."
—*Library Journal*

"Very strong on atmosphere and insights into local culture for curious travellers."
—*Boston Herald*

"The [Berlitz Travellers Guides] eliminate cumbersome lists and provide reliable information about what is truly exciting and significant about a destination.... [They] also emphasize the spirit and underlying 'vibrations' of a region—historical, cultural, and social—that enhance a trip."
—*Retirement Life*

"Information without boredom.... Good clear maps and index."
—*The Sunday Sun* (Toronto)

CONTRIBUTORS

BERNARD SHARE, formerly the editor of *Cara,* the in-flight magazine for Aer Lingus, writes frequently on travel and Irish history. Author or editor of several books, he has recently completed an anthology of 1,500 years of travel writing by Irish men and women. He is also a regular broadcaster for RTE-Irish radio and is the editorial consultant for this guidebook.

VINCENT CAPRANI, a lifelong resident of Dublin, is the author of numerous magazine articles on the city, and has written a number of fiction and nonfiction books, including the best-selling Dublin guidebook *A View from the DART.*

MARY DOWEY is editor of the Aer Lingus in-flight magazine *Cara,* for which she undertakes regular travel assignments. She also contributes articles to newspapers and magazines in Britain and Ireland, including the *Sunday Times, Country Living,* and the *Irish Times.* She has north Donegal roots—and a cottage there to go with them.

WILLIAM MAXWELL, a resident of Dublin and a literary critic for the *Irish Independent,* was for 30 years the press-division manager at Aer Lingus, Ireland's national airline. A longtime journalist, he contributes articles to many travel magazines.

SAM McAUGHTRY is a native of Belfast and the author of six books, including three collections of short stories. He is a former award-winning columnist for the *Irish Times,* and is well known as a radio and television scriptwriter and broadcaster both north and south of the border.

JOHN O'DONOGHUE has been a freelance journalist for many years, working mainly for the *Irish Times.* He is also a senior staff reporter at the Irish National Broadcasting System covering a wide range of topics and events in Ireland, and has written and presented documentaries for the BBC.

LORCAN ROCHE, a descendant of the Roches who arrived in Wexford in 1167, is a freelance writer and a drama critic for the *Irish Independent,* and has been associate editor of *Travel-Holiday* magazine in the United States.

LORNA SIGGINS is an Irish journalist whose itchy feet have taken her through Europe, parts of the Middle East, India, and Japan. She has contributed to numerous publications, and is now a staff reporter in the Dublin office of the *Irish Times.*

COLM TOIBIN was born near Dublin and works there as a journalist and broadcaster. He has edited both of Ireland's current affairs magazines and is the author of a novel, *The South,* and a travel book, *Walking Along the Border.*

THE BERLITZ
TRAVELLERS GUIDES

AUSTRALIA

CANADA

THE CARIBBEAN

ENGLAND & WALES

FRANCE

GERMANY

GREECE

HAWAII

IRELAND

LONDON

MEXICO

NEW YORK CITY

NORTHERN ITALY AND ROME

PORTUGAL

SAN FRANCISCO &
NORTHERN CALIFORNIA

SOUTHERN ITALY AND ROME

SPAIN

TURKEY

THE BERLITZ TRAVELLERS GUIDE TO IRELAND 1993

ALAN TUCKER

General Editor

BERLITZ PUBLISHING COMPANY, INC.
New York, New York

BERLITZ PUBLISHING COMPANY LTD.
Oxford, England

THE BERLITZ TRAVELLERS
GUIDE TO IRELAND 1993

Berlitz Trademark Reg U.S. Patent and Trademark Office
and other countries—Marca Registrada

Published by Berlitz Publishing Company, Inc.
257 Park Avenue South, New York, New York 10010, U.S.A.

Distributed in the United States by
the Macmillan Publishing Group

Distributed elsewhere by Berlitz Publishing Company Ltd.
London Road, Wheatley, Oxford OX9 1YR, England

ISBN 2-8315-1773-7
ISSN 1057-4719

Designed by Beth Tondreau Design
Cover design by Dan Miller Design
Cover photograph by Anthony Edgeworth/The Stock Market
Maps by David Lindroth
Illustrations by Bill Russell
Fact-checked in Ireland by Orla Nolan
Copyedited by Cynthia Sophiea
Edited by Julia Hubbard

Printed in the United States of America
1 3 5 7 9 10 8 6 4 2

THIS GUIDEBOOK

The Berlitz Travellers Guides are designed for experienced travellers in search of exceptional information that will enhance the enjoyment of the trips they take.

Where, for example, are the interesting, out-of-the-way, fun, charming, or romantic places to stay? The hotels described by our expert writers are some of the special places, in all price ranges except for the very lowest—not just the run-of-the-mill, heavily marketed places in advertised airline and travel-wholesaler packages.

We indicate the approximate price level of each accommodation in our description of it (no indication means it is moderate in local, relative terms), and at the end of every chapter we supply more detailed hotel rates as well as contact information so that you can get precise, up-to-the-minute rates and make reservations.

The Berlitz Travellers Guide to Ireland 1993 highlights the more rewarding parts of the country so that you can quickly and efficiently home in on a good itinerary.

Of course, this guidebook does far more than just help you choose a hotel and plan your trip. *The Berlitz Travellers Guide to Ireland 1993* is designed for use *in* Ireland. Our writers, each of whom is an experienced travel journalist who either lives in or regularly tours the city or region of Ireland he or she covers, tell you what you really need to know, what you can't find out so easily on your own. They identify and describe the truly out-of-the-ordinary restaurants, shops, activities, and sights, and tell you the best way to "do" your destination.

Our writers are highly selective. They bring out the significance of the places they *do* cover, capturing the personality and the underlying cultural and historical resonances of a city or region—making clear its special appeal.

The Berlitz Travellers Guide to Ireland is full of reliable and timely information, revised and updated each year. We would like to know if you think we've left out some very special place. Although we make every effort to provide the most current information available about every destination described in this book, it is possible too that changes have occurred before you arrive. If you do have an experience that is contrary to what you were led to expect by our description, we would like to hear from you about it.

A guidebook is no substitute for common sense when you are travelling. Always pack the clothing, footwear, and other items appropriate for the destination, and make the necessary accommodation for such variables as altitude, weather, and local rules and customs. Of course, once on the scene you should avoid situations that are in your own judgment potentially hazardous, even if they have to do with something mentioned in a guidebook. Half the fun of travelling is exploring, but explore with care.

ALAN TUCKER
General Editor
Berlitz Travellers Guides

Root Publishing Company
330 West 58th Street
Suite 504
New York, New York 10019

CONTENTS

MAPS

THE
BERLITZ
TRAVELLERS
GUIDE
TO
IRELAND
1993

OVERVIEW

By Bernard Share

Bernard Share, formerly the editor of Cara, the in-flight magazine for Aer Lingus, writes frequently on travel and Irish history. The author or editor of several books, he has recently completed an anthology of 1,500 years of travel writing by Irish men and women. He is also a regular broadcaster for RTE-Irish radio and is the editorial consultant for this guidebook.

The image of Ireland: a green, somnolent land over which there linger the still-pungent odors of battles long ago; a self-regarding community that has somehow contrived to sidestep the grosser manifestations of modern affluence; a concatenation of tight-knit factions none of which will give an inch and from which the more harassed or more adventurous escape to zigzag round the globe with, as the poet Louis MacNeice put it a generation ago, "... a gesture and a brogue/And a faggot of useless memories."

Like all reflective images, it is to be read backwards. Ireland today produces as many electronic components as cattle, imports its potatoes, and sends its army on United Nations missions and its elite rock groups everywhere. It is still green—a maritime location in the path of the Atlantic weather systems sees to that. And it is still, in spite of its membership in the European Community, the United Nations, and a clatter of other international conspiracies (always excluding military alliances), inward-looking. It is, its philosophers will tell their less percipient co-citizens, still in search of an identity. This in spite of having recivilized Europe in the Dark Ages by means of a shock wave of monks and having contributed again in

5

this century through the impact of a pantheon of such major literary figures as Joyce, Yeats, Beckett, Synge, Wilde, and O'Casey. None of this the alert visitor will miss, as it is constantly being brought to the attention of a public that is probably, at any given time, more interested in the British soccer results, American TV soaps, or the price of drink. Should the visitor be from another English-speaking country, even if his name be Katzentraum or Ng, he automatically will be assumed to be of Irish descent, because the extended Irish diaspora is the one significant external factor to which this self-absorbed society will readily admit. There are nevertheless many Irelands, some of them existing simultaneously in the same place, even in the same area of national consciousness, and the ones you will remember may not necessarily be those that your camera records.

The particular Ireland you choose to pursue in the space of a short visit will, of course, depend upon your individual taste and inclination; but this is a small and compact country (32,595 square miles, or a little smaller than the U.S. state of Maine), and you will not find difficulty in combining within the confines of a two-week vacation the Dublin theater with hill walking, genealogical research with canal cruising, the brooding Celtic past with the rocking present.

Excluded by geography from the simplistic appeal of a sun destination, Ireland has developed its own highly individualistic attractions that are governed not so much by the temporalities as by temperament. This is not to say that the weather is a negative factor: The succession of changes within the course of a single day may serve to illumine quite an ordinary event or introduce into even the best-laid plans a piquant element of challenge. The weather, you will discover, is a topic of diurnal speculation in a way it would never be in, say, Los Angeles or Sydney. Some say that its rapidly changing moods account for the perceived volatility of the Irish character. You may make up your own mind on that.

Whatever you feel about the weather—and Ireland, in a good summer, can be hotter than Spain—you will probably discover in the Irish people a quality of individuality that has resisted the stereotyping imposed by concentrated urban living and the uneasy suspicion of one's fellow man that it engenders. Thus it is rare to pass someone on the road—whatever your mode of travel—without a greeting, which may vary from a curt nod or a hand salute from the wheel of a car (the variation of gesture from county to county is a study in itself) to a "Grand evening" or more ample and leisurely exchange in a shop or a pub. People in Ireland talk to one another—on trains, in buses, in the street, at the racetrack—as a matter of course and because there is a perennial interest in other people's occupations and preoccupations. And that holds for the visitor as well. "The Irish are very fond of strangers," observed a French traveller in 1644—a conclusion to which the more commercial aspects of tourism have done little to give the lie.

In very simple terms Ireland is a flat saucer rimmed with modest mountains. The greatest concentration of population—and prosperity—is on the eastern seaboard and centered upon the county and city of Dublin, which accounts for nearly one-third of the total population of some 3.5 million. Administratively the island is divided into 32 counties, of which 26 constitute the Republic of Ireland ("The South") and six form the area of Northern Ireland, an integral part of the United Kingdom of Great Britain and Northern Ireland. These six counties also constitute six-ninths of the Province of Ulster, one of four (the others are Leinster, Munster, and, in the west, Connacht, also given as Connaught) that were defined in Ireland's early history. In spite of more recent political divisions, they retain a strong sense of identity and still play Gaelic and Rugby football against each other. There are many other ways in which the whole island of Ireland functions as an entity: Both the Roman Catholic and Episcopalian (Church of Ireland) churches recognize no internal frontier. In many sports Ireland fields 32 county teams. The car rally known as the Circuit of Ireland is just that. And the Railway Preservation Society of Ireland, based just north of Belfast, sends its steam specials to any place on the island where the rails still run.

The partition of the island into Northern Ireland and the Republic occurred in 1922 as a result of the largely Protestant north opting out of a state that had achieved its independence from Britain after some 700 years of colonial rule. There were those who bitterly opposed and continue to oppose this solution to what used to be known as The Irish Question—hence what are euphemistically known as "The Troubles" that manifest themselves in the form of continuing civil strife in parts of Ulster. It must immediately be said, however, that as a visitor you may pass freely and safely in any part of Ireland, you will be welcomed by all regardless of your or their religious and political conviction, and you are more than likely to remain totally unaware of any military or paramilitary presence—unless, of course, you go looking for it. Northern Ireland, under the guidance of its tourist board, has developed the many natural and man-made attractions of the region to a level that at least equals and sometimes excels that of the rest of the country. Whatever the present political realities, *as a visitor you would be well advised to think of Ireland as one nation and to plan accordingly.*

Change is not something that this country is inclined to embrace for its own sake. Because of demographic and geographic constraints Ireland has always been slow to ape the initiatives of richer, more populous societies, and has thus preserved evidences of many eras of its history, from the prehistoric to the postbellum. There was, for instance, no industrial revolution here, and hence, in contemporary terms, no deserted wastelands, no gaunt-eyed factories, no—or very few—inherited urban slums. Ireland today is an industrial nation, but that industry is very much the creation of the last three or four decades. Its tools are electronic, its products high tech, its markets global.

Because there was no industrial revolution many of the old craft-based occupations survived to assume a new dimension in a push-button world. Many countries have developed crafts industries under the impetus of the tourist trade, but some, structured more or less from scratch, have lacked the traditional resonance that gives them real validity. In the West of Ireland they still build—and use—*curraghs* (a form of rowboat) in the style of that which may have taken Saint Brendan to America in the sixth century. The Irish, it may be asserted with some confidence in the face of Scottish protest, invented whiskey. Aran sweaters, from the islands of that name off the west coast, were knitted in distinctive patterns to facilitate the identification of fishermen drowned at sea. There is frequently a story behind such traditional occupations, and usually someone willing to tell it . . . in English, the second official language. Irish, sometimes called Gaelic, is recognized as the nation's first tongue, and is taught in all the schools. You will hear it on the radio, on television, but infrequently as the common language except in the West, where it still thrives. It is said, however, that the largest Gaeltacht (Irish-speaking area) is now located in Brussels.

The oldest recognizable Irish civilization dates from

around 3500 B.C. From that era onward the country saw a succession of invasions, each of which made its own distinctive contribution to the modern nation. The Celts, the Normans, and the British constitute the main streams, but Ireland has at different times given shelter and welcome to French Huguenots, Russian Jews, Chilean exiles, and Vietnamese boat people. So have many countries, but because the population of Ireland has always been small in relation to the number of its immigrants these later comers have created a more tangible impact than they might have done in a larger, more cosmopolitan society.

It is thus possible in Ireland to make giant leaps, both in time and in cultures, with a minimum of geographical displacement: from Neolithic monuments to Celtic churches to medieval monasteries to Georgian great houses, from 17th-century battlefields to Europe's largest lead and zinc mines, all within, say, the modest counties of Louth and Meath. One of the prime attractions of the country is this ease of access, this possibility of doing something quite different every day without having to travel inordinate distances. There are some happenings, of course, that are at best annual events, as anywhere. But with a little careful reading of this book supplemented by informed inquiry of tourist offices it should be possible to include the Wexford Opera Festival, the Dingle Curragh Races, the Irish Derby, the Dublin Theatre Festival, Kilkenny Arts Week, the Ould Lammas Fair at Ballycastle, the Yeats Summer School, or whatever attracts you within your planned program and itinerary.

Some of these events, together with others you have heard about, you may *not* find in this book. To avoid presenting a mere catalog we have chosen to be selective rather than inclusive, leaving you a certain amount of discovering to do on your own. We suggest, therefore, nine main areas of interest, each with its own appeal, each a distinctively colorful piece of the patchwork that is Ireland.

Dublin is an obvious starting point, not only because it is a 1,000-year-old capital city with all that implies in terms of cultural, recreational, and historical attractions, but because in its corporate identity there are subsumed the many discrete elements of the wider Irish society: Norman and Gael, Catholic and Protestant, unrepentantly urban and but recently rural. With Dublin as a base it is easy to expand into the environs—**"The Pale"** that was historically the limit of the occupying power for several centuries. More than a hinterland, it embraces the evocative emptiness of the Wicklow Mountains, the Neolithic mega-monuments of the Boyne Valley, and many civilized pleasures in between.

Kilkenny, Ireland's jewel among medieval cities, suggests an ideal center from which to explore the sunny **Southeast** ("sunny" usually being a relative adjective in Ireland, but here deployed with some confidence), with its rich Norman and Viking associations, good fishing, fine beaches, and a tapestry of intriguing towns and villages.

From there it is a simple move to the wilder **Southwest** and **West**, through the cultured, quasi-Continental city of **Cork** with its lilting speech to the fjords and mountains of **West Cork** and **Kerry.** Come here to enjoy gourmet food, to hear Irish spoken and traditional music played, and to wonder at the landscape. Northward into Clare and Galway this latter changes as subtly as the speech.

In **Clare** you'll find, perhaps, the best traditional music anywhere—though this would be hotly contested from Kerry to Donegal—set against the stark backdrop of the Burren, a limestone plateau like a life-size model of the moon. **Galway City** has absorbed in its time many influences (not for nothing does it boast a Spanish Arch) but its eyes are to the west: to the **Aran Islands** and Irish-speaking **Connemara,** to the finest fishing lakes you'll find anywhere.

Wherever you choose to begin your Irish journey, in the course of your travels you will at some stage find yourself crossing **The Midlands**—the string of counties more or less contiguous to the River Shannon. The Midlands are often overlooked in the desire to visit such better-known areas as Killarney and Donegal. But this very fact has made them something special, with many simple and even secretive pleasures well worth seeking out. You could, of course, spend a whole holiday on the river itself, as many do. But even if you never become waterborne you will find much to absorb and intrigue you in its islands and monuments, its bankside villages and historic river crossings, its many moods and manifestations, and in the life that goes on along and around it.

Northward again, **Mayo, Sligo,** and **Donegal,** all rugged, Atlantic-rimmed counties where life has never been easy, offer the kind of peace and easy-paced daily life that present an unspoken challenge to urban values. There is much to do in the **Northwest** (golf, pony trekking, fishing, eating, drinking, talking), but many will rejoice in the fact that there is also a lot *not* to do.

The last two areas we cover embrace the politically divided **Northeast**: Northern Ireland. For the visitor, however, the division will remain largely a line on the map— though Derry, Enniskillen, and, of course, Belfast, will make you aware of the alternative Irish tradition: Protestant and planter rather than Catholic and Gael. For a rich amalgam try the **Border Counties**, where the national frontier disappears beneath the placid waters of Lough Erne, which glitter, happily, neither orange nor green. After this disarming baptism you will be all the more ready to appreciate the sharp contrasts, and sharper wit, of Antrim, Down, and Armagh, where the welcome will be at least as warm as anywhere else on the island and the wit, the "crack" . . . well, that we leave you to discover for yourself.

Some attractions, of course, are common to the island as a whole. Golf in Ireland, of outstanding appeal to visiting players, is a very democratic sport: few elaborate clubhouses, associated facilities or frills. But the prices, including those for caddies and lessons, are surprisingly agreeable, as is the accessibility of the more than 230 courses to choose from, ranging from the justly famous (Portmarnock or Royal Portrush) to seaside links (the biggest distraction is the scenery) and friendly local courses in Midland towns. All welcome visitors, but it is advisable to call beforehand, particularly on weekends. Local tourist offices will put you in touch.

Finally, a word on the travel itself—the mechanics, the pleasures, and, sometimes, the frustrations. Do not plan to drive from one side of the island to the other in a day, unless you really have to. In this country there are few long stretches of nothing, and, even where there are, the *néant,* or nothingness, possesses its own elusive appeal, as in the case of the Midland bogs. Do not confine yourself, if driving, to the major, N-class roads. Much of the hidden Ireland lies down the back roads: the pubs where, if you have a mind to, you really will meet the locals; the towns that rarely or never see bus tours and where you may thus observe their people going naturally about their daily business. Few of these places do not boast some antiquity, often taken so much for granted by the natives that they are unable to account for it, or some claim to fame, if only for having nurtured a famous son. Take your time—an art not altogether lost in rural Ireland. Remember, too, that driving motor vehicles is not entirely the well-regulated business that it may be in other parts of the world, and that such matters as double yellow lines and other parking prohibitions, bus lanes, traffic lights, and the laws relating to drunken driving are more frequently honored in the breach.

The intercity trains, on the other hand, travel at an air-conditioned 90 m.p.h. And from the smallest village on the remotest peninsula you may call, if you have to, the other side of the world. You may fly by regular scheduled services to Dublin from four airports west of the Shannon: Knock, Galway, Shannon, and Sligo, as well as from Kerry. In Ireland it is true to say that you are never very far from anywhere else, distance being, in this context, as much a temporal as a linear measure. Enjoying yourself as a guest for an evening in an 18th-century mansion or sitting with a fishing line on the end of a deserted pier watching the sun going down over Galway Bay you will, if you are lucky, experience an otherness that few tourist destinations can still provide.

Ireland, it has been said, is a state of mind—a fact that has been acknowledged by visitors to her shores for at least half a dozen centuries. As the Irish writer Oliver Goldsmith put it in the 18th century: "The natives are peculiarly remarkable for the gaiety and levity of their dispositions; the English, transplanted there, in time lose their serious melancholy air, and become gay and thoughtless, more fond of pleasure and less addicted to reasoning." *Caveat viator!*

USEFUL FACTS

Getting There

By Air. Aer Lingus has the most comprehensive year-round schedule from New York, Chicago, and Boston to Shannon and Dublin. Delta serves Shannon and Dublin. The only direct flights from Canada are charters.

From Britain, Aer Lingus serves Dublin, Cork, and Shannon; British Midland Airways flies from London to Dublin; Ryanair flies from Luton and Stansted to Dublin; Ryanair also serves Knock Airport, Cork, and Sligo; and Aer Lingus has daily commuter flights to Sligo, Knock, Farranfore (Kerry), Cork, Shannon, and Galway, all via Dublin. Passengers from European cities and beyond have a wide choice of direct flights on Aer Lingus, Air

France, Lufthansa, and SAS; for details consult your travel agent.

By Sea. B. and I. ferry services operate daily from Holyhead and Pembroke (Wales) to Dublin and Rosslare, respectively; Tel: (01) 679-7977, Fax: (01) 77-81-46. The Sealink Stena line operates between Holyhead and Dún Laoghaire, and between Fishguard (Wales) and Rosslare; Tel: (01) 280-8844. Swansea-Cork ferries make daily trips between Swansea (Wales) and Cork; Tel: (021) 37-80-36; and Irish Ferries sails from La Havre and Cherbourg in France to Rosslare every other day. Brittany Ferries sails from Roscoff (France) to Cork once a week; Tel: (021) 27-78-01. Isle of Man car ferries sail between Douglas and Dublin three times a week. As schedules change, passengers should consult a local travel agent.

Entry Documents

All visitors except British citizens require up-to-date valid passports. U.S., Canadian, and Australian citizens do not requre visas. Ireland has strict regulations regarding importation of livestock, foods, and agricultural produce, so check with your local airline or commerce department before you leave.

When to Go

The most abused facet of Ireland is its weather. It follows one of the best Irish euphemisms: "not too bad and not too good"—which means, bring a raincoat and a heavy sweater, even in summer, to cater to sudden changes. The best time to go is between April and October, but the Gulf Stream does have an effect year-round: Ireland never gets heavy snowfalls, and it is not so much cold in the winter as damp from the rain—which, after all, keeps the grass green.

Local Time

Ireland, like Britain, operates on Greenwich mean time; western European time is one hour ahead of GMT. New York and Toronto are five hours behind GMT. Irish clocks move to daylight saving time for the summer months.

Telephones

The country code for the Republic of Ireland is 353; for Northern Ireland it is 44. The city code for Dublin is 01. When phoning Ireland from outside the country, drop the zero from all city codes.

Currency

The unit of currency in Ireland is the Irish pound, sometimes called the punt, which is divided into 100 pence. The British pound sterling and U.S. dollars are accepted in many Irish stores, but other currencies should be converted at banks. Major credit cards—American Express, Diners Club, Visa, and MasterCard—are accepted almost everywhere. There are coins for 1p, 5p, 10p, 20p, 50p, and £1, and notes in denominations of £5, £10, £20, £50, and £100. At press time the rate of exchange was U.S. $1.00 to £.52.

The official currency in Northern Ireland is the pound sterling, although the Irish pound is generally accepted in border areas.

Electric Current

The standard is 220 volts, so North American appliances require converters and adapter plugs. Hotels and guest houses usually have dual 220/110 sockets for razors and other portable electrical equipment.

Business Hours

Business hours are from 9:00 A.M. to 6:00 P.M., with late nights on Thursdays and Fridays. There is some Sunday shopping in Dublin, but you should check with your hotel. (Outside Dublin, shops and many restaurants almost always are closed on Sundays.) Banking hours are generally 10:00 A.M. to 3:00 P.M., Monday through Friday; museums generally open from 10:00 A.M. to 6:00 P.M., but are closed Mondays.

Health Care

E.C. visitors are entitled to medical care in Ireland under reciprocal agreement. U.K. travellers should pick up a brochure on their entitlements from local GP or social security offices before travel.

Staying in Ireland

Hotel and other accommodation rates are quoted *per person* for a double room (per person sharing, pps): For two people the price is roughly double. A room for a single occupant costs more. Rates do not include breakfast or other meals unless otherwise stated, although many of the smaller hotels and all bed-and-breakfast establishments include a full Irish breakfast in the price.

Self-catering cottages throughout Ireland can be rented

by the week or for the weekend. Information is available from any Irish tourist office, which will also take your booking. Prices range from £150 to £550 per week for cottages that accommodate six to eight adults.

The term "high season" refers to the main tourist months, roughly June to the end of September, but it should be noted that public holidays, such as Easter and St. Patrick's weekend, rate as high season even though they fall outside this period, and specific local events (the Dublin Horse Show, Galway Races, etc.) attract high-season rates.

Finally, prices quoted for 1993 are *projections* only. Always check on actual rates before booking.

Getting Around

The national transport service includes buses and trains. Dublin Bus serves the city, Bus Eireann serves the provinces, and Irish Rail runs the railways. Dublin City has the DART (Dublin Area Rapid Transport system), which provides a rail link around the city from Howth to Bray, with feeder buses linking in. Pick up a bus and train schedule from your local tourist office (see below).

In Northern Ireland, Northern Ireland Railways and Ulster Bus provide services.

Taxis are supposed to be metered, and should not be employed if they are not. Apart from local journeys to hotels or airports, taxi drivers are prepared to make extended trips, but the price should be agreed upon beforehand.

All major car-rental companies—Avis, Budget, Dan Dooley, and Irish Car Rentals—have offices at airports and points of entry in Ireland. Rates are posted publicly.

Ireland has two major inland waterways, the 210-mile-long River Shannon, which flows through County Cavan and County Limerick to the Atlantic, and the 80-mile-long Grand Canal, which links Dublin with the River Shannon and the River Barrow. You can cruise these scenic waterways by renting a cabin cruiser from one of nine outfits approved by the Irish Tourist Board. All of the boats have cooking facilities and showers, and sleep from two to eight people. Operators must be at least 21 and prove they can handle the controls. Rates run from £300 to £1,700 a week, depending on the size of the craft and the season.

For rentals on the River Shannon, contact: **Carrick Craft**, P.O. Box 14, Reading RG3 6TA, England, Tel: (0734) 42-29-75, Fax: (0734) 45-14-73; **Emerald Star Line Ltd.**, 47

Dawson Street, Dublin 2, Tel: (01) 679-8166, Fax: (01) 679-8165; **Athlone Cruisers Ltd.**, Shancurragh, Athlone, County Westmeath, Tel: (0902) 728-92, Fax: (0902) 743-86; **SGS (Marine) Ltd.**, Ballykeeran, Athlone, County Westmeath, Tel: (0902) 851-63, Fax: (0902) 854-31; **Shannon Castle Line**, Dolphin Works, Ringsend, Dublin 4, Tel: (01) 60-09-64, Fax: (01) 68-90-91; **Derg Line Cruisers**, Killaloe, County Clare, Tel: (061) 37-63-64, Fax: (061) 37-62-05. Boats can also be rented for travel on **Lough Erne**. See the Border Counties chapter for details.

To rent a boat on the **Grand Canal**, contact: **Celtic Canal Cruisers Ltd.**, Tullamore, County Offaly, Tel: (0506) 218-61, Fax: (0506) 512-66; or **Lowtown Cruisers**, Robertstown, County Kildare, Tel: (045) 604-27, Fax: (045) 603-72.

Irish Tourist Offices

These are exceptionally good in terms of providing literature, advice, and information on local events such as theater, musical evenings, the best singing pubs, where to go and what to do. The staff are courteous and go out of their way to be helpful. No visitor should fail to drop in on them. They are located in virtually every town and are extremely well stocked with free literature; books, cassettes, and records are for sale. Ask for a copy of their illustrated guide to hotels and guest houses, updated annually. In Dublin the Irish Tourist Board (Bord Fáilte) is located at 14 Upper O'Connell Street; Tel: (01) 74-77-33 and the Northern Ireland Tourist Board is at 16 Nassau Street; Tel: (01) 679-1977. In Belfast the Northern Ireland Tourist Board is at 59 North Street; Tel: (0232) 23-12-21 or 24-66-09.

Outside of Ireland you may contact offices of the Irish Tourist Board at: 757 Third Avenue, New York 10017, Tel: (212) 418-0800; 160 Bloor Street East, Suite 934, Toronto M4W 1B9, Tel: (416) 929-2777; 150 New Bond Street, London W1Y 0AQ, Tel: (03071) 493-3201; 36 Carrington Street, 5th Level, Sydney NSW 2000, Tel: (02) 299-6177.

For information on Northern Ireland contact: Northern Ireland Tourist Board, 276 Fifth Avenue, Suite 500, New York, NY 10001, Tel: (212) 686-6250, Fax: (212) 686-8061; Northern Ireland Tourist Board, 111 Avenue Road, Suite 450, Toronto, Ontario M5R 3J8, Tel: (416) 925-6368, Fax: (416) 961-2175; Northern Ireland Tourist Board, 11 Berkeley Street, London W1X 5AD, Tel: (071) 493-0601, Fax: (071) 499-3731; and British Tourist Authority, Midland

House, eighth floor, 210 Clarence Street, Sydney NSW 2000, Tel: (02) 267-4666, Fax: (02) 267-4442.
—*William Maxwell*

BIBLIOGRAPHY

General and Literary

MAURICE CRAIG. *The Architecture of Ireland*. A comprehensively illustrated account from the beginnings to 1880.

Facts About Ireland. This official publication of the Department of Foreign Affairs will settle most arguments.

CHRISTOPHER FITZ-SIMON. *The Irish Theatre*. Traces the colorful history of drama in Ireland from miracle plays to Beckett and after. Illustrations include playbills, productions, protagonists.

R. F. FOSTER. *Modern Ireland 1600–1972*. The best general history available, it is incisive and eminently readable.

Gasaitéar nah Éireann (*Gazeteer of Ireland*). An official bilingual listing of place names with linguistic and grammatical information.

PETER HARBISON. *Guide to the National and Historic Monuments of Ireland*. Covering all 32 counties, it is the work of one of the country's leading archaeologists.

LORD KILLANIN AND MICHAEL V. DUIGNAN. *The Shell Guide to Ireland*. Revised and updated by Peter Harbison, this is an excellent one-volume guide with archaeological and historical emphases.

SALLY AND JOHN MCKENNA. *The Bridgstone Irish Food Guide*. A complete compendium of cheese makers, bacon curers, oatmeal makers . . . and, or course, restaurants big and small throughout the North and South.

JOHN FITZMAURICE MILLS. *A study of the Noble Dwellings of Ireland*. A study of the human faces behind the Palladian façades. Color illustrations.

FRANK MITCHELL. *The Irish Landscape*. From 2,000 million years ago to today. Comprehensive and highly readable.

T. W. MOODY AND F. X. MARTIN (EDS.). *The Course of Irish History*. (Revised and enlarged ed., 1984.) The best one-volume account for the general reader.

JAN MORRIS. *Ireland—Your Only Place*. Evocative essay with superb photographs.

SEAN O'FAOLAIN. *The Irish*. A "character study" by the distinguished short-story writer and critic of social mores.

MICHAEL RICHTER. *Medieval Ireland: The Enduring Tradition*. A Continental scholar discusses the island's history and religious and intellectual life from the early years of the Christian Era to the founding of Dublin's Trinity College in 1591, to show how the Learned Tradition of Ireland set it apart from England and the Continent for a millennium.

AIDRIAN ROOM. *A Dictionary of Irish Place Names*. A key to the meaning of many names still recognizable in their original form, in spite of often crude "anglicizing," with apposite background information.

KATHLEEN JO RYAN AND BERNARD SHARE (EDS.). *Irish Traditions*. Essays by several hands on distinctive aspects of the Irish experience, from sports to suburbs, from Neolithic artifacts to neighbors. Color photographs.

DARAGH SMYTHE. *A Guide to Irish Mythology*. A competent and informative introduction to "forms more real than living men."

ANTHONY WEIR. *Early Ireland: A Field Guide*. A site-by-site listing of everything prehistoric worth seeing, with map references.

KEN WHELAN. *The Sea Angler in Ireland; The Coarse Angler in Ireland; The Game Angler in Ireland*. All the keen fisherman needs to know, and a good deal more.

MICHAEL WYNNE. *National Gallery of Ireland: Fifty Irish Painters*. A succinct introduction to Irish art through three centuries.

The volume and richness of Irish literature must restrict us to a few general indications. For Dublin, see the works of James Joyce, Brendan Behan, Sean O'Casey, Flann O'Brien (Myles na Gopaleen), James Plunkett, George Moore *(Hail and Farewell)*, Oliver St. John Gogarty, Jonathan Swift's pamphlets. For Cork: Sean O'Faolain, Frank O'Connor; for County Clare: Edna O'Brien; for Kerry and the west in general: J. M. Synge, John B. Keane, Liam O'Flaherty, W. B. Yeats, Lady Gregory; for Donegal: Patrick McGill, Peadar O'Donnell; for the Midlands: John Broderick, John McGahern, Patrick Kavanagh; for the north: John Hewitt, Seamus Heaney, Sam Hannah Bell, Brian Moore, Forrest Reid. Browsing in the bookshops of Dublin, Cork, and Belfast will add many more, and Kenny's of Galway in particular offers excellent service to visitors. The magazine *Ireland of the Welcomes,* published six times a year by the Irish Tourist Board, is consistently interesting and informative.

Dublin and Environs

DOUGLAS BENNETT. *Encyclopedia of Dublin.* Comprehensive and rich in fascinating detail.

HENRY BOYLAN. *This Arrogant City: A Reader's and Collector's Guide to Books about Dublin.* An excellent guide to a wide range of further reading.

VINCENT CAPRANI. *A View from the DART.* Dublin and suburbs from the coastal rapid-transit system. Witty and informative.

CON COSTELLO. *Looking Back. Aspects of History, Co. Kildare.* Informative illustrated guide.

MAURICE CRAIG. *Dublin 1660–1860.* The authoritative architectural history of the city's golden age.

PAT LIDDY. *Dublin Be Proud.* Drawings of the city's more interesting details, with background information.

FRANK MCDONALD. *The Destruction of Dublin.* The ravages of the planners and "developers" in the recent past and the present and the threat to the future. Timely and caustic.

E. E. O'DONNELL. *The Annals of Dublin.* From 4.5 million years ago to date. A must for fact fanciers. Fine old photographs.

MICHAEL J. O'KELLY. *Newgrange: Archaeology, Art and Legend.* The definitive work on one of the most important and impressive prehistoric sites in Europe.

ALFRED P. SMYTH. *Celtic Leinster.* Life in the Pale and beyond, A.D. 500–1600. A fascinating perspective on the social and political role of the great boglands.

PETER SOMERVILLE-LARGE. *Dublin: The First Thousand Years.* The best one-volume social, political, and cultural history.

J. M. SYNGE. *In Wicklow and West Kerry.* An account of his travels rich in poetic insight and shrewd observation.

The Southeast

GERALDINE CARVILLE. *The Heritage of Holy Cross*. The history and restoration of 12th-century Tipperary Abbey.

R. H. HYLAND. *The History, Topography and Antiquities of the County and City of Waterford*. A compendious record first published in 1824 and still well worth consulting.

KATHERINE M. LANIGAN AND GERALD TYLER (EDS.). *Kilkenny: Its Architecture and History*. A comprehensive account of the sixth-century foundation from a conservationist standpoint.

DERVLA MURPHY. *Wheels Within Wheels*. The distinguished travel writer's childhood in County Waterford.

HUMPHREY O'SULLIVAN. *The Diary of Humphrey O'Sullivan*. A fascinating account of 19th-century life in County Kilkenny, written in Irish between 1827 and 1835.

RICHARD ROCHE AND OSCAR MERNE. *Saltees, Islands of Birds and Legends*. An account of these offshore islands, breeding ground for more than 200 species of birds.

Cork and Kerry

T. J. BARRINGTON. *Discovering Kerry*. The most comprehensive study of the kingdom's history, heritage, and topography available, with illustrations and maps. Exhaustive and exhausting.

T. CROFTON CROKER. *Legends of Killarney* and *Legends of the Lakes*. Rich local lore—to be taken with a grain of salt.

ROBERT GIBBINGS. *Lovely Is the Lee* and *Sweet Cork of Thee*. Headily atmospheric accounts adorned with the author's own fine woodcuts.

DES LAVELLE. *Skellig—Island Outpost of Europe*. The two remarkable islands off the Kerry coast examined in detail, with historical background.

MUIRIS MACCONGHAIL. *The Blaskets, A Kerry Island Library*. The definitive book on the area.

DAPHNE POCHIN MOULD. *Discovering Cork*. A historical and topographical survey by Ireland's first female flying instructor.

SEAN PETTIT. *The Streets of Cork* and *My City by the Lee*. Good walking guides.

PEIG SAYERS. *Peig.* Renowned autobiography, written originally in Irish, of life on the now-abandoned Blasket Islands.

CHARLES SMITH. *The Ancient and Present State of the County of Kerry.* The classic 1761 account.

PETER SOMERVILLE-LARGE. *From Bantry Bay to Leitrim.* An evocative journey in the footsteps of O'Sullivan Beare on his retreat from the battle of Kinsale in 1601.

JOAN AND RAY STAGLES. *The Blasket Islands.* The community that once formed "the next parish to America" in words and pictures.

Clare and Connemara

GEORGE CUNNINGHAM. *Burren Journey West.* The flora and fauna of the area.

RUTH DELANY. *By Shannon Shores.* Not just those of Galway and Clare, but the full length of the great waterway. Read this before you cruise the river.

JOHN M. FEEHAN. *The Secret Places of the Burren.* Observations of a perspicacious and disputatious traveller.

JAMES HARDIMAN. *The History of the Town and County of Galway.* First published in 1820 but still a standard work.

BRIAN MERRIMAN. *The Midnight Court.* Ribald poem, originally in Irish, set in County Clare in the late 18th century. Frank O'Connor's translation is the best.

J. W. O'CONNELL AND A. KORFF (EDS.). *The Book of the Burren.* Contributions by several hands on this enduringly fascinating area. Finely illustrated.

PEADAR O'DOWD. *Old and New Galway.* A comprehensive, illustrated reference.

RICHARD POWER. *Apple on the Treetop.* A novel based on a year among the Aran islanders.

TIM ROBINSON. *Stones of Aran.* A poetic journey with insights into the history and folklore of the islands; included are his two large-scale, annotated maps of Aran and the Burren.

COLIN SMYTHE. *A Guide to Coole Park, County Galway.* Lady Gregory's house, destroyed in 1941, was the "headquarters" of the Irish literary revival and the setting for several of Yeats's poems.

J. M. SYNGE. *The Aran Islands*. An account of the islands, the source of much of the author's achievement as a writer. Includes his original photographs.

Donegal, Sligo, and Mayo

ROBERT BERNEN. *Tales from the Blue Stacks*. Stories by a New Yorker who settled on a derelict Donegal sheep farm in 1970.

BRIAN BONNER. *Our Inis Eoghain Heritage*. First of three books dealing with the life and traditions of the Inishowen Peninsula.

DESMOND FENNELL. *A Connacht Journey*. A fine contemporary travel narrative that probes the reality behind the myths of the west of Ireland.

T. A. FINNEGAN. *Sligo: Sinbad's Yellow Shore*. A prospect of Sligo and environs from the vantage point of Coney Island (the original one).

SHEELAH KIRBY. *The Yeats Country*. The places associated with the life and writings of the poet.

H. T. KNOX. *The History of the County of Mayo*. Covers the period up to 1700 in absorbing detail.

ALAIN LE GARSMEUR AND BERNARD MCCABE. *W. B. Yeats— Images of Ireland*. Superb photographs with accompanying poetic text.

T. O'RORKE. *The History of Sligo, Town and County*. A 19th-century work of scholastic devotion, but very readable.

LORD SLIGO. *Westport House and the Brownes*. Family history writ large: a lively account of 12 generations.

DOROTHY HARRISON THERMAN. *Stories from Tory Island*. Oral history from the islanders themselves.

DAVID THOMSON. *Woodbrook*. Life in a Sligo "big house" between the two world wars. Brilliant re-creation of the end of an era.

The Border Counties

POLLY DEVLIN. *All of Us There*. A beautifully written re-creation of a childhood on the shores of Lough Neagh in the 1940s and 1950s.

HENRY GLASSIE. *All Silver and No Brass*. The Christmas mummers of County Fermanagh and the authentic tang of Ulster speech.

EUGENE MCCABE. *Heritage*. Short stories dealing with the peculiar ferocity of the sectarian divide on the border.

MARY ROGERS. *Prospect of Fermanagh*. The history, archaeology, and folklore of the county, described with great enthusiasm and local knowledge.

————. *Prospect of Tyrone*. The history and legends of the county examined with the same affection.

COLM TOIBIN. *Walking Along the Border*. A journey by foot from Derry to Warrenpoint, crossing and recrossing the border.

Antrim, Down, and Armagh

J. C. BECKETT ET AL. *Belfast: The Making of a City*. A comprehensive and concise survey from the beginnings in 1800 to 1914.

JOHN BROOKS. *Ulster's Heritage* (Irish Heritage Series). A tour of the properties of the National Trust in Northern Ireland.

ROBERT BROWN. *Strangford Lough*. The wildlife of a beautiful County Down sea lough.

LYNN DOYLE. *An Ulster Childhood*. Growing up in County Down at the end of the last century.

ALAN GAILEY. *Ulster Folk Ways* (Irish Heritage Series). An introduction based on the collections of the Ulster Folk and Transport Museum, Cultra.

JOHN HEWITT. *Rhyming Weavers*. Country poets of Counties Antrim and Down. Includes samples of their styles.

MICHAEL J. MURPHY. *Mountain Year*. Life on the slopes of Slieve Gullion, County Armagh.

JOHN PEPPER. *John Pepper's Ulster Phrase Book*. A humorous guide to the intricacies of Ulster speech (Sotsotis— "the weather is very warm").

—*Bernard Share*

DUBLIN

By Vincent Caprani

Vincent Caprani, a lifelong resident of Dublin, is the author of numerous magazine articles on the city, and has written a number of fiction and nonfiction books, including the best-selling Dublin guidebook A View from the DART.

If Dublin has, over the past quarter century, paid a high price for its efforts to become a modern industrial and commercial capital, it is nonetheless one of the few cities that is preferred by its citizens to any other. The natives remain—and the visitors come—for a variety of reasons:

- To immerse themselves in one of the great literary capitals of the world
- To take advantage of its location as the gateway to rural and ancient Ireland
- To sample a sporting town's wealth of golfing, fishing, and equestrian and aquatic pastimes
- To experience a sense of distant history as close as yesterday
- And to find quaint pubs, colorful characters—and even more colorful talk.

Above all, Dubliners are talkers and, by extension, writers. Dubliners have a constant need to "discuss" their city, as is evidenced by the annual output of about 25 books on Dublin written and published by Dubliners for the city's one million inhabitants, and the numerous albums and cassettes recorded by local ballad groups and solo artists extolling the city's charms and culture. No other city has produced three Nobel Prize winners for literature (George Bernard Shaw, William Butler Yeats,

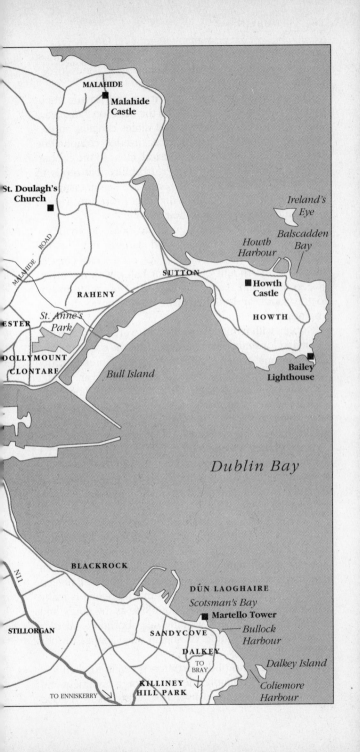

and Samuel Beckett) and given modern literature its most famous day: June 16, 1904—Bloomsday, in James Joyce's *Ulysses*.

The citizens love chatting, writing, and singing about their city and its characters. Even the occasional disparaging note in their discourses and ditties contains an element of wounded pride or a backhanded compliment. Dubliners' humor is earthy, satirical, close to the cobblestones, and with a racy imperturbability that tends to deflate the pompous. Their songs are sentimental and nostalgic, covering an absurdly kind heart and a stern pride in the superiority of their town.

And Dubliners do have much to boast about. Their city—the country's capital and largest city in the Republic—occupies a beautiful site on the east coast of Ireland at the mouth of the River Liffey, with the broad sweep of Dublin Bay to the east, the Dublin Mountains to the south, and rolling plains extending to the west and north.

Dublin, with its many separate and overlapping districts, is a marvelous mix of the parochial and the cosmopolitan, the traditional and the modern. Many of its present problems stem from half-hearted efforts to contain an elegant 18th-century core within the rapidly expanding 20th-century sprawl of satellite towns, industrial parks, housing developments, and motorways that has almost entirely swallowed up the pleasant rural villages that formed the city's periphery less than a quarter of a century ago. Yet vestiges of these villages remain because, above all, Dublin is still a place of contradiction rather than conformity. Its citizens revel in controversy, not consensus, in myth rather than method.

One such myth is that the city is more or less divided between wealthy, erudite, and sophisticated inhabitants south of the River Liffey, and shabby, impecunious, and unlettered denizens on the North Side. Statistical data certainly indicates a preponderance of the well-heeled south of the river, yet also shows that there are as many low-income families on the South Side as the north, and the latter area contains wealthy neighborhoods such as Howth, Sutton, Malahide, Glasnevin, and Clontarf, further confounding the issue.

So, if some form of demarcation is required, then it is perhaps better to ignore the north–south argument and to plump for a more realistic east–west divide. A good rule of thumb is to seek the better-class districts close to the sea and more or less contiguous to the DART rail line. (With the advent of easy rail travel in the mid-Victorian era, Dublin merchant and professional classes hastened to the maritime suburbs for the cleaner air, hence a spread of upmarket housing adjacent to the railway. The trend has never really abated.) The southern section of the line in particular, say Sandymount to Killiney, runs through a pleasant area full of Victorian terraces, graceful mansions, and charming single-story cottages. The modest homes, many with pretty little gardens, are gracefully built on the principle of the rural cabin, and are said by some experts to be the single and most distinctive Irish contribution to architecture.

By the same token of contradiction, however, many of the rail lines today pass through enclaves of dingy streets and poor housing, and the newer and predominantly working-class locations lying in a vast semicircle to the west and north of the city are liberally dotted with fine old mansions, parklands, and modern villas.

Dublin is a place that can be evoked but rarely summed up, a solid harmony of granite, warm brickwork, harsh concrete, trees, canal water, wrought iron, macadam, cobblestones, bright sunlight, misty rain—in short, depicting it is as easy as capturing a few blobs of mercury with the prongs of a table fork. Like the vast majority of its citizens who so frequently criticize their mother town—and then immediately combine in argumentative opposition to the foreigner who has the impudence to agree with them—it is a contradiction.

It is also an adventure and a voyage of discovery. We cover ancient Dublin first, at the center—mostly on the South Side of the Liffey, where the major interests for most visitors lie. Then, after a foray into the southern suburbs and the South County beyond, we return to the North Side, move into the northern suburbs, and end in the North County.

MAJOR INTEREST

St. Patrick's and Christ Church cathedrals
Dublin Castle
Street life in the Liberties
Marsh's Library
The pubs of Dublin

Irish Museum of Modern Art

Trinity College (and Long Room, with the *Book of Kells*)

Grafton Street shopping

Merrion and Fitzwilliam squares and Georgian Dublin

National Library (first editions of Irish writers)

National Museum (Irish antiquities)

National Gallery (Irish, English, and European masterpieces)

Beatty Library and Gallery of Oriental Art (Egyptian papyruses)

The Martello tower at Sandycove (Joyce's *Ulysses*)

Municipal Gallery of Modern Art (Impressionists)

Malahide Castle

Dublin owes its existence to the Liffey. Viking and Danish pirates sailed up this river more than a thousand years ago (the city celebrated its millennium in 1988), liked what they saw, and decided to stay. That decision meant laying waste to the tiny Celtic settlement huddled about the ford of the river. Though few Dubliners today know where the ford stood, it is not too difficult to locate this cradle of early Dublin: about midway along Usher's Island (on the south bank of the river) and facing the spot where Blackhall Place exits onto the north bank of the river at Ellis Quay. Blackhall Place leads to Stoneybatter ("batter" comes from the Irish *bothar,* a road); this ancient thoroughfare was called Bothar-na-gloch (the road of stones), and was part of the second-century highway from the royal Hill of Tara to Wicklow. It crossed the Liffey near that early Celtic settlement known—as Dublin is still called in Gaelic—as Baile Átha Cliath (pronounced ball-*ya* aw klee-a), or "town of the ford of the hurdles." Both the name and the settlement were quickly supplanted by the Norse Dyfflin (from the Irish Dubh Linn, meaning "black pool"). In time the tiny riverside Norse hamlet became a Norman fortress, then an Elizabethan citadel, then the elegant Georgian "second city of the Empire," before slipping back a little into a mixture of Victorian slums, factories, and warehouses surrounded by the suburban mansions and villas of its rich merchants. And that, in a sentence, is the history of Dublin.

Scandinavian Dublin

There are three spots where Dublin is reputed to have begun, all three with Scandinavian connections. Take your pick of (1) Wood Quay, lying in the riverside shadow of Christ Church Cathedral and the controversial modern "pepper-and-salt-canister" municipal buildings; (2) the high ground at the junction of Suffolk and Andrew streets and Church Lane near Trinity College, now occupied by St. Andrew's Church, which is built on the ancient mound of the Thingmote, where early Norse Dubliners held their great outdoor assemblies and crude parliaments; or (3) the little grass triangle at the northern side of Trinity College, just a truncheon's throw from the door of College Street police station—which, with typical Dublin idiosyncrasy, isn't actually in College Street but at the western end of Pearse Street. The stone ornament in the grassy triangle marks the position of the ancient Steyne, or great stone, around which those first Viking invaders beached their fearsome dragon-prowed longships.

In those days—more than a thousand years ago—the Steyne and the Thingmote stood well outside the little wattled hamlet of Dyfflin. From this embryonic Dublin the Norsemen made inland raids on their Gaelic neighbors, routing them and exacting tribute—the *nosegelt,* so called from the penalty for default, namely cutting off the offender's nose. Those early Norse Dubliners also traded in metals, skins, timber, fish, and wines with their kinsmen along the coasts of western Europe. Relics of this buried past may be viewed in the National Museum (discussed at greater length below) in Kildare Street.

Norman Dublin

There was a thriving and settled community at Dyfflin by the time the mail-clad Norman horsemen came riding down on the little township in the 1160s. Warlike, though cultured, the Normans under Richard de Clare (known as Strongbow) quickly took the town and the surrounding countryside and inaugurated profound changes in Irish life. The Norman method was to conquer, build stout and graceless defensive towers, have vassals and villeins work the captured land, and then make an endowment to the Roman church in thanksgiving to the Almighty for having

blessed the bloody work of sword and longbow. Their architectural genius was expressed in immense grim castles and noble abbeys, giving Dublin three of its most ancient and impressive buildings: Christ Church Cathedral (1172), St. Patrick's Cathedral (1191), and Dublin Castle (1205). All three are inextricably interwoven into the story of Dublin, and all are within easy walking distance of one another and well worth visiting.

St. Patrick's Cathedral (in Patrick Street, several blocks west of St. Stephen's Green) once stood on an island encircled by two branches of the River Poddle, long since confined underground. A trace of the island is still discernible in the attractive little park adjoining the present cathedral, which dates from 1370 and was erected with many of the stones and on the site of the original cathedral of 1191. Visitors with a literary bent will undoubtedly recall Jonathan Swift's incumbency as dean of St. Patrick's from 1713 to 1745, and will be attracted to the Swift memorabilia here in the form of his pulpit, table and chair, a collection of his works, and his scroll as a freeman of the city. Swift's bust, epitaph, and tomb, "where savage indignation can no longer lacerate his heart," lies close by that of his beloved "Stella" (Esther Johnson) in the west end of the nave. There, too, is the medieval Chapter House door with a curious hole cut in it. This is the "door of reconciliation," which gave the phrase "chancing your arm" to the English language. In 1492 the earl of Kildare cut the hole and through it stretched his arm to clasp the hand of his archenemy, the earl of Ormonde, who had taken refuge in the Chapter House. By this gesture peace and reconciliation were restored.

For those interested in military history, the cathedral's nave contains a Roll of Honour listing the names of 50,000 Irishmen who fell in the First World War, and the sad, tattered flags of the many Irish regiments who served on the battlefields of Europe and the British Empire still hang above solemn aisles where Cromwell's Roundheads contemptuously stabled their horses during the wars of the 17th century. The place abounds in memorials and monuments—from the black marble over the grave of the duke of Schomberg, who fell at the battle of the Boyne in 1690 (the monument contains an inscription by Swift), to the impressive Baroque monument to the Boyle family erected by the first earl of Cork. The visitor should note the effigy of a little boy in the center of the lowest tier: It represents Robert Boyle (1627–1691), later a famous chemist and physicist. Today St. Patrick's is the national cathedral of the Church of Ireland (Protestant).

(A general rule in the exploration of old churches: Where inscribed stones are found on the floor an actual tomb is indicated, but in the case of a wall tablet there may be a coffin or an urn of ashes underneath, or the wall tablet may be only a cenotaph, that is, a memorial to a person or persons buried elsewhere.)

Christ Church Cathedral, built at what is now the western end of Dame/Lord Edward streets on the site of the original wooden cathedral founded in 1038 by Sitric Silkenbeard, the first Christian king of the Dublin Norsemen, took more than 50 years to complete. In addition to its historical significance and fine architectural qualities, the cathedral—which since the Reformation has belonged to the Anglican Communion—stands as a kind of memorial to its founder, Richard de Clare, the Norman overlord who had Sitric's simple wooden structure torn down and then rebuilt in stone at the behest of Saint Laurence O'Toole, archbishop and patron saint of Dublin.

Christ Church's range of monuments, memorials, and memorabilia equals that of St. Patrick's, but to some Dubliners its greatest treasures are the heart of Saint Laurence O'Toole (died 1180), which is encased in an iron heart-shaped receptacle in a little chapel to the right of the high altar, and the crusader-like monument to Richard "Strongbow" de Clare in the south aisle. Incidentally, some authorities claim that the time-honored Dublin penchant for bestowing nicknames dates from the coming of the Normans and especially Strongbow. The dockside area of Ringsend (known generally as Raytown from the fish originally unloaded there) boasts that it is the world capital of nicknames. One of Raytown's pubs, the **Oarsman**, at the bridge, proudly displays on its barroom wall a chart listing more than 500 of the most colorful local nicknames.

The romance of **Dublin Castle** is a microcosm of the city's history since 1205, when Henry II wrote to his chief lieutenant in Ireland, Myler FitzHenry: "You are to erect a castle at Dublin, as well to curb the city as to defend it . . . and with strong fosses and walls. . . ." There was need of such a fortress in those days. The regular forays from the Wicklow Mountains of the hardy clansmen of the O'Byrnes and O'Tooles made life in Norman Dublin exciting, even precarious. The castle was quickly built and just as quickly besieged by the mountain marauders. By 1228 the archbishop of Dublin had to build a bigger and better castle. There then followed bigger and better sieges. By 1361 the entire fortress had to be rebuilt.

Within the massive new walls were the Mint and the Courts of Justice. These latter saw the occasional "trial by ordeal," one as late as 1528, in which Teig MacGilpatrick O'Conner, charged with murder, and his accuser fought with sword and shield like gladiators of old. This "trial" took place before a distinguished assembly, and O'Conner was vindicated: He shortened the prosecutor's stature by lopping off his head and presented it ceremoniously, as proof of his innocence, to the lords of justice, by whom he was immediately acquitted. Perhaps the Irishman's distrust of "castle justice" was nurtured on such events. The main entrance today occupies the site of the old gate on which the heads of many rebellious Irish chiefs were exposed on spikes. To the leaden statue of Justice surmounting the entrance (the work of Van Nost, 1752), the political climate of the 18th century caused Dubliners to add the slogan,

> "Statue of Justice, mark well her station
> Her face to the Castle, her back to the Nation!"

At the commencement of the 1916 Easter Rising a band of two dozen Irish Citizen Army men made an unsuccessful effort to capture the castle. Their surprise attempt to rush the Upper Yard was foiled by an elderly policeman, who managed to get the iron gate shut and locked just in the nick of time. The insurgents then occupied the nearby City Hall and other buildings opposite the castle entrance and, like their O'Toole and O'Byrne ancestors 700 years before, put up a fierce fight for three days before being repulsed with heavy casualties.

Less than six years later, on January 16, 1922, Michael Collins (as chairman of the new Irish Free State government) entered the castle's council chamber and presented a copy of the Anglo-Irish treaty to the last of Britain's viceroys, Lord Fitzalan. In return the castle was formally surrendered to the Irish government.

For Collins it was only his second visit to the castle. Two years before, with a price on his head, he had entered the castle in the guise of a grimy-faced coal-cart driver in order to make contact with his own agents inside.

The chapel in the Lower Yard dates from 1814 and is

the work of Francis Johnston. It is a fine Gothic edifice with a ceiling of groined arches supported by beautiful pillars, and its stained-glass windows depict the coats of arms of all the viceroys from 1814 to 1922.

Dublin Castle also houses the sumptuous 18th-century State Apartments, which, since 1938, have been the scene of the inaugurations of Ireland's presidents. Guided tours of the apartments and the "Under Croft," including the base of the Powder Tower, part of the 12th-century city walls, the moat, the postern gate to the original castle, the chapel, and more, are available. Because the State Apartments are occasionally closed to the public during important state functions, however, visitors are advised to check in advance (Tel: 01/77-71-29 or 77-75-80).

The Liberties

Situated near the castle and the two cathedrals are a number of other historic buildings—St. Audoen's Church (1171), the Tailor's Guild Hall (1706), Marsh's Library (1702), and the Brazen Head Inn (1668). Life is lived lustily in this South Side district west of the castle, once the "Liberties of the Abbey of St. Thomas à Becket," then the domain of the earl of Meath—and thus largely outside the legal jurisdiction of the city's lord mayor and sheriff (hence, "the Liberties"). No trace of the abbey exists today. At the Reformation its lands and rights were granted to the earl of Meath. Dubliners visiting the Liberties do so rather as explorers, in a spirit of adventure, seeking some experience not readily obtainable elsewhere. They are lured by the old antiques and bric-a-brac shops in Francis Street and to the pubs, market stalls, and huckster shops. Not many of the Liberties people know or care how this place got its name and distinctive character, or that many of them are descendants of French Huguenot refugees and silk weavers who fled from Catholic persecution after the Edict of Nantes was revoked in 1685.

St. Audoen's Church, across from Christ Church and the oldest of Dublin's many parish churches, is named after the patron saint of Rouen, France, who was held in special veneration by the Normans. Three of the bells in the tower were cast in 1423 and are the oldest in Ireland. **St. Audoen's Arch** (1275) is the sole surviving gate of medieval Dublin.

The **Tailor's Guild Hall**—open to the public from Monday to Friday, and entered from the narrow, cobbled

Back Lane (off Nicholas Street near Christ Church) through a quaint stone archway dating from 1714—has been the headquarters of An Taisce (pronounced un tashk), the Irish National Trust since 1983. An Taisce is a voluntary watchdog organization concerned with environmental matters, the preservation of Ireland's historical and architectural heritage, and the restoration of buildings and sites that represent that heritage.

Despite inadequate funding and severe financial constraints, An Taisce has carried out much needed refurbishment to many buildings, such as the Tailor's Guild Hall. One example of the task confronting the organization involves the original marble fireplace in the guildhall's general assembly room. Some years ago, when the building was unoccupied and in a near ruinous condition, the fireplace was crudely ripped out of its setting by scavenging junk dealers and broken into four or five separate pieces, which wound up in a number of junkyards in different parts of the city. A small group of An Taisce enthusiasts tracked down the scattered portions and then painstakingly repaired, reassembled, and relocated the fireplace in its original setting.

Tailor's Hall is the last surviving guildhall in Dublin. Its assembly room contains a fine 18th-century musicians' gallery from which the patriots Wolfe Tone and Napper Tandy are known to have addressed the members of the revolutionary "Back Lane Parliament" with rousing speeches that helped kindle the flames of the subsequent 1798 Rising. Also in Back Lane, and directly opposite Tailor's Guild Hall, is **Mother Redcap's Tavern**. Converted from a disused shoe factory, it provides lunches, midday snacks, and music most evenings; it's also something of a hangout for An Taisce activists, inner-city conservationists, ballad singers, and traditional reciters.

Just to the east of St. Patrick's Cathedral stands **Marsh's Library**, the oldest public library in Ireland. Bequeathed to the city by Archbishop Narcissus Marsh in 1702, it contains all his books and Edward Stillingfleet's vast and priceless collection of early printed books from the 15th century, rare manuscripts, and the autographs of many of the famous people from the 15th to the 17th century. The library fittings are still as they were in the 18th century (a major restoration of the interior funded by the American Irish Foundation was completed in 1986) with tiny reading cells of decorative woodwork, the hefty and valuable tomes secured against possible theft by lengths of heavy

Recommended B + B
Gerard + Liz Christie
17 Lorcan Drive
Santry
Dublin 9
Phone - 01 - 8 429364
(Near shopping and just
off the bus line for a
nice ride downtown)

Irish telephone Directory
www.goldenpages.ie
www.smarttravels.com
TV.

the Captains House B + B Dingle
52 pubs in Dingle

Stay in Kenmare near the
Ring of Kerry— less Touristy!
(per Rick Steves)

Dingle Peninsula is just as pretty
as the Ring of Kerry

chain. Also dating from the 18th century is the legend that the ghost of Dr. Marsh wanders from shelf to shelf each night in a vain search for some long-lost family document. The library is closed to visitors on Tuesdays and public holidays.

If all the foregoing historical names and dates require the flavoring of the romance—and the liquid refreshment—of an ancient hostelry, then the visitor should explore the **Brazen Head** in Lower Bridge Street, just a few minutes' walk from Tailor's Guild Hall. There is nothing manicured or sanitized about the back streets of the Liberties, and this gem of a tavern is the sole survivor of the numerous inns that stood here in Norman, Tudor, and Stuart times, eras of lusty revelries and the brutal sports of cockfighting and bullbaiting. Though it is mentioned in Joyce's *Ulysses,* and Brendan Behan was one of its habitués, visitors to the Brazen Head may be disappointed by its lack of literary memorabilia and the confession-box dimensions of its old taproom. This bar parlor nonetheless contains a motley collection of prints and mementos of Irish history; an upstairs room (open to visitors) contains a table, chair, and desk reputed to have belonged to the romantic and tragic young patriot Robert Emmet.

The Brazen Head served as a kind of unofficial headquarters for the United Irishmen, some of whose leaders were arrested here in 1798. In addition to the 350-year-old oaken beams supporting the low ceilings and the upper portions of the inn, a small but interesting feature is the mid-18th-century graffito cut with a diamond ring into one of the original bottle-glass panes of the first-landing window. Impromptu but authentic ballad sessions by some of Dublin's leading traditional singers and musicians are a frequent occurrence here most Sundays at midday. But now a word on our pubs in general.

The Dublin Pub

There are about 700 pubs—give or take a few—in the greater Dublin area, and that doesn't include hotel and theater bars, army messes, or private "members only" sports clubs and the like. The pubs are liberally scattered about the city and suburbs and range from the grotty and unpainted to the brass-and-glassy glitter of Victorian emporiums, such as the **Long Hall** in South Great George's Street and the **Stag's Head** in Dame Court, a little alley off the south side of Dame Street. The pub remains virtually unchanged since its gala opening in 1895. Practically all of the slicker type provide tasty pub grub of the soup-salad-hot-pot variety.

Many of the center-city pubs have in recent years mildly offended old-style Dubliners by dropping the traditional family name over the shop front in favor of tourist-slanted though tenuous—or even spurious—associations with the city's historic and literary personages of the past; hence a plethora of the "Oscar Wilde," "Daniel O'Connell," "Robert Emmet" nomenclature on the fascia board.

Nearly all Dublin pubs are "winter" drinking holes rather than "summer" ones; that is, their decor is generally polished wood and suggests warmth rather than the coolness imparted by tiled patios or leafy beer gardens. Most have their own distinct type of loyal clientele— newspapermen, firemen, actors, sportsmen, students, or whatever—though all have the ubiquitous floaters and, periodically, the trendies who, like a swarm of chattering starlings, suddenly descend on the latest "in" place. Except for some of the latter, Dublin pub patrons have never acquired the habit of cocktails; regulars will tell you that the pint (by which they mean Guinness, though there are at least ten different brands of draught beers and lagers generally available) is the only true beverage.

A lot of Dublin's social life revolves around the pub scene, which helps nurture one's sense of priorities: convivial conversation, griping about politicians, gossiping about sports, and breaking into impromptu singsongs. Nightlife tends to reach its crescendo about pub-closing hours (11:30 P.M. in winter, and midnight during the summer), maintaining the tempo through the last-bus curfew and diminishing a little as the under-21s seek out the discos (weekends mainly) and the older crowd hits the Leeson Street nightclub strip.

Many of the pubs provide good music; *In Dublin* magazine regularly lists about 120 venues, from "trad" at the **Béal Bocht** (Charlemont Street, south of St. Stephen's Green) to jazz at **Slattery's** (Capel Street) and the **Waterfront** (Sir John Rogerson's Quay, east of City Quay) to Irish music and step dancing at **Hughes's** (Chancery Street). The music and the musicians vary greatly, as do the patrons and the venues—"Jazz when I'm happy, trad when I'm sad," seems to be a fairly good guide to Dublin preferences.

For the best in authentic traditional singing try **An**

Góilín (pronounced un *go*-leen, which can be roughly translated from an old Mayo Gaelic dialect as either "an inlet" or "Have you been singing lately?"), an informal club that welcomes foreign folk singers and instrumentalists as well as natives. It meets on Friday evenings (9:00 P.M. September through July) in the back bar at the Brazen Head (see The Liberties section, above). But come early (around 9:30 P.M.) as it's always packed with enthusiasts; admission is one punt.

In addition to a variety of music, many pubs display all manner of odds and ends: old prints, brass, framed news clippings, crockery, pewter, weird bottles, fancy mirrors—most of these items are authentically old, others specially manufactured for today's taverns. This is a gallant attempt to reverse the 1960s trend of plastic-and-veneer modernization, when the Victorian legacy of mahogany and brass fittings were widely discarded. Ironically, many of the very same pubs that modernized are now leading the way in restoring old-style qualities and craftsmanship to their premises, often turning them into mini-museums in the process. **Kitty O'Shea's** (Upper Grand Canal Street, near Lansdowne Stadium), named after Parnell's paramour and a favorite with rugby football fans—the pub, not the lady—has many items of Parnelliana displayed on its walls, while **The Bailey** (Duke Street) has Michael Collins's revolver, as well as the hall door rescued before the sad demolition of 7 Eccles Street, Leopold Bloom's fictional home and once a city landmark.

Almost every Dublin street has its own pub, if not several, each with unique qualities of character or entertainment—and their resident personalities, some of whom are only too willing to explain the particular pub's wall charts, mementos, pictures, historical bric-a-brac, or whatever. Of course, the more garrulous and "helpful" the character, the more he may expect to be treated to a pint for his trouble. (Later in this chapter, the Bars and Nightlife section provides a roundup of more Dublin pubs.)

But back to the area around the Brazen Head.

The North Quays

Normans, Huguenots, Flemings, Walloons—Dubliners have a varied ancestry. But what of those Dublin Norsemen so abruptly displaced by the Norman newcomers of the late 1160s? Only a few paces from the Brazen Head stands the Father Mathew Bridge (formerly the Whitworth Bridge), which occupies the site of the ancient and sole bridge built by those Scandinavian Dubliners.

They were sent scurrying across their narrow wooden bridge by the arrival of the first Normans, vanquished and banished to the near north side of the river and the areas now known as Smithfield and Oxmantown (the latter deriving from Ostman, or Eastmen, a name given to all Scandinavians, Danes, and Norsemen originating from east of Dublin). As recently as the early 20th century—and despite nearly a thousand years of cosmopolitan admixture—residents of the Smithfield and Oxmantown areas retained to a remarkable degree the flaxen-haired and blue-eyed characteristics of their ancestors. Even today the astute observer can spot the occasional Scandinavian type among the burly fruit porters and denizens of the Green Street market area.

The visitor with an ear finely attuned to the nuances of accent and remote dialect may also catch the odd word of an indecipherable argot that is neither Dublin slang nor a western Ireland Gaelic importation. Throughout the year, on the first Sunday of every month, horse dealers throng into Smithfield (just in off Arran Quay and sandwiched between Queen Street to the west and Bow Street to the east), among them members of Ireland's itinerant or "travelling people" clans with their own secret language, Shelta. Shrewd judges of men, money matters, and markets, the travelling people—an Irish equivalent of gypsies, though they are not a Romany breed—use a strange coded language when they wish to communicate among themselves in matters of horse dealing and cart buying.

Mysterious words like *vardy* (a caravan, or cart), *gathkane* (pub), and *shades* (police) are whispered amid the palm-spitting, hand-slapping ritual of unwritten contracts and the clatter of horse hooves over the broad, elongated square of Smithfield—for centuries a hay market and in the 1960s the cinematic location for the Berlin Wall environs in the Richard Burton film *The Spy Who Came in from the Cold*.

Smithfield is also the headquarters of the Irish Distillers Group. While once it boasted a half dozen distilleries, Dublin no longer has any, and nationwide only two remain of the thirty-odd active breweries of a century ago. Since the closure of the Jameson distillery in 1972, the old spirit store in Smithfield has been converted for use as the distillers group's administrative center, and an old warehouse has been adapted with imagination and care as an intriguing **Whiskey Museum**. On display are many articles associated with the old craft, a working model of the distilling processes, plus an audiovisual presentation and commentary. Here visitors are given a thoroughly enjoyable introduction to the subject of the "best whiskey in the world." Public tours are conducted Monday through Friday at 3:30 P.M.; Tel: (01) 72-55-66.

The origins of whiskey distilling are shrouded in the past, although the Irish boldly claim to have discovered it, subsequently exporting it along with Christianity and Gaelic music to the western isles of Scotland. The Scots dispute this, but they are content that their commercial product outstrips the Irish brand of whiskey on world markets. However, it is clear that the word "whiskey" is an English corruption of *uisge beatha,* the Gaelic for aqua vitae—the water of life. The Irish maintain that their version is the true source and that it dates to Tudor times, when invading English troops took a fancy to the local women and to the drink, but pronounced *uisge* as "whiskey."

Just to the east of Smithfield are the ancient thoroughfare of Church Street and **St. Michan's Church** (founded in 1095), the oldest building on the north side of the river; the tower and some portions of the church are original. The vaults are celebrated for the antiseptic qualities of dry air, constant temperature, and chemical properties exuding from the limestone walls and the subterranean bog that contains the foundations. This combination operates wonderfully to preserve, in mummified form and in uncovered coffins, some 300-year-old corpses with features such as skin, fingernails, teeth, and veins clearly discernible.

Few places in Dublin more fully maintain the city's contrasting traditions than this area of largely run-down and derelict sites on and behind the north quays. The rough-and-ready monthly horse fair at Smithfield has its daily counterpart in the early morning bustle of the Dublin Corporation's **Fruit and Vegetable Market**, housed in a Late Victorian red- and yellow-brick building with its main entrance on Mary's Lane. A produce clearing center for the nation, the place is thronged from dawn light with vehicles bearing the exotica of imported fruits and the produce of Ireland's rich market gardens, orchards, and fields. This hurly-burly is in marked contrast to the late-morning pomp and dignity of the law at **Green Street Courthouse** (1797) north of the market and the **Four Courts** building at Inns Quay to the south, with judges and lawyers in their black robes and wigs toing and froing between chambers and courts.

Another Dublin idiosyncrasy: There were actually five courts—Chancery, King's Bench, Common Pleas, Exchequer, and Rolls Court—originally housed in James Gandon's magnificent 18th-century building that fronts the river and splendidly counterbalances his other masterpiece, the Custom House (1792), three-quarters of a mile east down the quays on the same side of the river. Both buildings were extensively damaged during "The Troubles." In 1922 the Four Courts was seized by the Irregular (anti-Treaty) forces, who used it as their headquarters for two months during the uneasy peace that followed the evacuation of British troops from Ireland. Its shelling by the National (pro-Treaty) army on June 27 of that year precipitated the Irish Civil War. An explosion set off by the Irregulars before surrendering almost completely destroyed the building's interior—along with the priceless documents, many of them public records dating back to 1174.

A similar thing happened at the **Custom House**, one of the chief centers of British administration in Ireland until the Dublin Brigade of the old IRA carried out its destruction in May 1921; here, too, the interior and a vast quantity of valuable books, records, and documents were destroyed.

Poor Gandon—all his fine interiors were either bombed, burned, or blasted in the cause of Irish freedom. The only one to survive is the dining room at the **King's Inns**, Gandon's final public building a few blocks north of the Four Courts on Henrietta Street. That dining room is still the venue for a 400-year-old custom whereby barristers-to-be, notwithstanding their successes at law studies, must partake of a certain number of dinners at the Inns before qualifying. The Society of King's Inns assumed that title in 1542—about the time lawyers were acquiring the land and property of the dissolved monasteries. Such legal centers were called "inns" because members took up residence there, and "inns of court" because of their ancient association with the judiciary.

Henrietta Street, Dublin's oldest Georgian thoroughfare, was once one of Europe's most elegant and fashionable streets. At the height of its fame in the mid-1700s it

contained the residences of four bishops, a duke, four
earls, a viscount, and an assortment of lesser knights and
nobles. Luke Gardiner—who laid out many North Side
streets on the sequestered lands of St. Mary's Abbey, and
founded the Mountjoy and Blessington dynasty—had the
German architect Richard Cassels design the houses, including Gardiner's own residence, number 10. Here the
family resided for over a century, and here too was held
"the grandest wake ever seen in Dublin" when, in 1814,
the 103-year-old countess of Blessington (said to have
died as the result of a fall from an apple tree in the back
garden of number 10) was laid out in state. The doors of
the house were thrown open to all, and lavish fare to the
tune of £4,000 was provided for any who cared to enter
and pay their last respects. Moves are afoot for the preservation and renewal of Henrietta Street and North Great
George's Street, another almost intact period street with
several houses still used as private residences.

Phoenix Park

To the west of Smithfield lies **Collins Barracks** and then
Phoenix Park. Formerly the Royal Barracks (and built in
the year of Blenheim, 1704), Collins is believed to be the
world's oldest military barracks built for that purpose in
continuous occupation. At one time it was also the
world's largest, accommodating a total of 5,000 British
troops. Dubliners said of such garrisons that they were
"useless in times of war and dangerous in times of
peace."

West Dublin has in recent years become a crowded,
sprawling region of suburban housing developments and
industrial parks, but when the city had earlier put space
aside for leisure and recreation it did so on the grand
scale. Phoenix Park is Europe's largest enclosed urban
park. Dublin being a city of misnomers, the park got its
name, like whiskey, from another curious corruption of
the Irish word *uisge,* in this case *fionn uisge,* meaning
"clear water."

The then duke of Ormonde had the park walls erected
in 1671 for the purpose of confining a deer herd within
its precincts. Today some 300 fallow deer move freely
among the trees flanking the park's main thoroughfare.
Always a popular place with Dubliners, the park contains,
among other things, the People's Gardens, the official
residences of the Irish president and the U.S. ambassador,

the papal nunciature, the Irish Army general headquarters, a hospital, the lofty 205-foot Wellington obelisk, the typically misnamed Fifteen Acres (formerly the city's dueling ground and now an extensive plain of sports fields), and the **Dublin Zoo** (dating from 1831). The zoo has attracted worldwide attention for its success in breeding certain animals in captivity, most notably lions, one of which became the famous MGM motion-picture mascot.

Kilmainham

For the energetic walker wishing to return to the south bank of the Liffey, Islandbridge Gate is perhaps the best exit from the park. This leads across the river to Kilmainham with its Royal Hospital (1680) and Kilmainham Jail (1796). The long, tree-lined approach to the **Royal Hospital** gives an excellent view of Ireland's first classical building, the one that ushered in the architectural development of Dublin. It was originally an institution for wounded army pensioners and, as such, the first of its kind in the British Empire. Over the centuries the building has seen many uses but was permitted to fall into a near-ruinous state after it was closed in 1928. The efforts to restore it between 1980 and 1984 earned the prestigious European NOSTRA award for "distinguished contribution to the conservation of Europe's architectural heritage." Its magnificent apartments (open to the public on Sundays from 2:00 to 5:00 P.M.) contain exhibits from the National Museum; a new gallery of modern and contemporary art; and a permanent exhibition of Hogarth, Rembrandt, and Dürer engravings. In addition to offering various entertainments, exhibitions, and guided tours, the Royal Hospital also hosts many important state and private functions and is now the home of the **Irish Museum of Modern Art**.

Ireland's first-ever museum of modern art was officially opened by the Irish prime minister, Charles J. Haughey, in May 1991 with the intention of presenting, through its permanent collections and temporary exhibitions, international and Irish art of the 20th century underpinned by a strong community and education program. Artists represented in the inaugural exhibitions ranged from Picasso, Miró, and Mondrian to LeWitt, Judd, Serra, Mullican, and Haacke, and from Jellet and Yeats to Doherty, Cross, Maguire and Lennon.

Plans for 1993 and beyond include IMMA's own growing

collection of Irish and international works in regular rotation with temporary exhibitions and projects by Terry Atkinson: "Grease Works"; Duane Hanson: "New Sculpture"; Gilbert and George: cosmological pictures; Lee Jaffe: "Recent Works"; and a John Heartfield retrospective.

Open hours are Tuesday through Sunday 10:00 A.M. to 5:30 P.M.; admission is free. The museum restaurant opens for lunch and refreshments from 10:00 A.M. to 5:00 P.M. every day. The Royal Kilmainham Bookshop, specializing in art, architecture, and design is open during museum hours.

Nearby, on the corner of South Circular Road and Inchicore Road, and in stark contrast, stands **Kilmainham Jail**, Ireland's Bastille. The prison's story closely reflects the turbulent history of Ireland from the time it was founded just prior to the 1798 Rising until the end of the Civil War in 1923. Each succeeding generation of rebel and patriot provided guests for its dark dungeons and punishment cells—United Irishmen, Young Irelanders, Fenians, Land Leaguers, Parnellites, Sinn Feiners, and IRA men. Many were executed in its gaunt prison yard, including the Phoenix Park "Invincible" assassins of 1882 and the signatories of the 1916 Proclamation of the Republic, Padraig Pearse and James Connolly being among the latter. The very last prisoner to be held in Kilmainham (and not released until 1924) was Eamon de Valera, a leader in Ireland's struggle for independence who later became president of the Irish Free State (1932–1937), chairman of the Council of the League of Nations (1934–1935), taoiseach (prime minister, pronounced *Tee*-shock) three times, and president of Ireland from 1959 to 1973.

In 1960 a group of voluntary workers began restoration work on the jail, and the resultant and ever-expanding museum reflects the Irish struggle for independence and the prominent part played by the various inhabitants of Kilmainham Jail in that struggle. This historical resource center provides guided tours every half hour and audiovisual presentations from October through May on Wednesdays and Sundays (2:00 to 6:00 P.M.) and from June through September seven days a week (11:00 A.M. to 6:00 P.M.). Also featured during the summer months are various art and sculpture exhibitions related to the theme of Irish nationality and identity. Admission is £1.50 for adults, 60p for children and students. Tel: (01) 53-59-84. Take bus 23, 24, 51, 51B, 78, or 79 from the city center.

A little to the east of Kilmainham and across from Heuston Station—right back in the Liberties area, to be exact—lies a city within a city, the centerpiece of which is a tapering 150-foot tower crowned with a strange, onion-shaped cupola visible for miles. This is no weird Muscovite importation but a massive windmill, now shorn of its giant vanes, standing in the heart of the 234-year-old **Guinness Brewery**.

Legend has it that the first Arthur Guinness acquired the secret of his distinctive dark brew through the accidental burning, or roasting, of some barley, and that the popularity of this blackish beer among the hefty market porters of the 18th century earned for it the name of "stout porter" beer. Occupying 64 acres in the center of Dublin, Guinness's is not only Europe's largest brewery but is also the largest single beer-exporting company in the world, with some 300 million pints annually shipped abroad in the company's own tankers. But Dubliners, and visitors for that matter, need not be alarmed at such a huge drain on the lifeblood of the nation. The brewery is capable of producing two and a half times that a year, which is just as well considering the avidity with which the Irish lower the drink.

The brewery's former hop warehouse in nearby Crane Street was completely refurbished in recent years, and is now used as an exhibition center. Open to visitors on weekdays, the Hop Store provides a film presentation every 20 minutes and houses the brewery's extensive archival and museum collections.

From Guinness's and St. James's Gate it is no more than a brisk 20-minute stroll back to the city center in an almost straight line past the Tailor's Guild Hall, Christ Church Cathedral, and Dublin Castle—almost, because in Dublin straight lines invariably contain a wobble or two. The locals are fond of quoting such Irish bulls as "the farther one walks a straight line the sooner one makes a detour." The detours in this case are slight: perhaps a visit to the foyer of the City Hall on Cork Hill (beside Dublin Castle) or to the Olympia Theatre almost directly opposite it, or a stroll through the warren of old, narrow streets lying between Dame Street and the river and known as the Temple Bar area, Dublin's newly discovered and self-proclaimed Left Bank—even though it is, in fact, the Right! (The Temple Bar area and Olympia Theatre are discussed below.)

The **City Hall** is worth a visit to see the frescoes, mosaics, and sculptures that decorate its interior rotunda. The hall, which was built as the Royal Exchange, dates from 1769, and the Dublin City Council meets in what were once the coffee rooms of the old merchant guilds that effectively ran the city back in the 18th century. The City Council, somewhat facetiously and unfairly described as an "elected group of men with no money who meet each week to distribute it," handles an annual budget of over £330 million and governs a population of about 503,000; the combined population of both Dublin city and county is in excess of one million.

The mosaic on the floor of the City Hall's rotunda shows the city's coat of arms—three castles with flames issuing from their towers to symbolize the citizens' readiness to defend Dublin—and the city's motto *Obedentia Civium Urbis Felicitas,* which may be roughly translated as "Obedient citizens make for a happy city," a pious aspiration with which generations of disobedient and not-too-happy Dubliners have periodically taken issue.

Temple Bar

Though facing out onto Dame Street, the modern **Central Bank** building (not to be confused with the nearby historic Bank of Ireland) more or less dominates Temple Bar, a district fast becoming a popular place for restaurants, crafts centers, recording studios, and theater workshops. While not yet a Covent Garden, Greenwich Village, or the Left Bank of Dublin, Temple Bar nonetheless is being developed along similar lines. It is part of an extended pedestrian link that runs through Crown Alley, under Merchant's Arch—a favorite place for street musicians and buskers—and over the Liffey Bridge (Ireland's oldest metal bridge and formerly a toll bridge, hence its more commonly used nickname, Ha'penny Bridge) to a similar pedestrian shopping area on the North Side comprising Liffey, Henry, and Mary streets.

If the Abbey Theatre (on the North Side; discussed below) is Ireland's national theater, then the **Olympia Theatre**, on the western end of Dame Street, may be termed the city's national playhouse, where everything from the Irish equivalent of vaudeville, dramatic works, and revues to concerts, one-man shows, and pantomime are performed. Deceptively diminutive from the outside, the 1870s Olympia, with its genuine Victorian music-hall decor, has actually a hundred more seats than the better-known **Gaiety** (South King Street off St. Stephen's Green West), which, in addition to providing much the same type of theatrical fare as the Olympia, regularly asserts its superiority by hosting visiting repertory companies, ballet, and the Dublin Grand Opera Society's spring season (with important European stars in the leading roles).

While Dublin has had numerous theaters since the opening of the first one in Werburgh Street in 1637, and has produced a continuous supply of internationally acclaimed playwrights, actors, and actresses since William Congreve (1670–1729), Spranger Barry (1719–1777), and Peg Woffington (1720–1760), it has no readily identifiable theater district corresponding, say, to New York's Broadway or to London's West End. Its present-day professional theaters are dotted indiscriminately about the city: the Gate on Cavendish Row on the North Side (at the northern end of O'Connell Street, just past the Parnell monument), the Peacock, a downstairs adjunct to the more prestigious Abbey, also in the north, the above-mentioned Olympia and Gaiety theaters on the South Side, and about a dozen fringe theaters. Various other halls and venues are pressed into service for performances during one of the city's chief cultural events, the **Dublin Theatre Festival**, held annually around the end of September to early October.

For details of venues and times for all theater, cinema, concert, poetry reading, and art and photographic exhibitions, purchase the biweekly information magazine *Around Town* from almost any newsagent shop or newspaper seller.

For spotting actors and show-biz personalities—homegrown as well as visiting international stars like Eric Clapton, Sting, and Shirley Bassey in their moments of relaxation—perhaps there's no better place than **Bad Bob's Backstage Bar** at the corner of Sycamore and East Essex streets, virtually sandwiched between the Olympia's stage door and the Project Art Centre's 150-seat **pocket playhouse**. The Back Stage Bar provides live music seven nights a week—jazz, ballads, rock, or traditional—and its **Granary Buffet** restaurant, specializing in home-style food, is one of the most popular places for theater suppers. The bar is also a regular launching pad for events associated with the theater festival and the **Dublin Film Festival**, which follows about a week or two later in October each year. Near the playhouse you'll also find the **Project Gallery**, featuring mainly young, modern, innovative artists and sculptors. Open 11:00 A.M. to 6:00 P.M., Monday to Saturday; admission is free.

Dubliners hear much but see little of Ireland's financial market, and very few are aware of the location of the Stock Exchange in Anglesea Street. No spot in the city exhibits such a contrast in population as the picturesque streets surrounding the Central Bank. At noon on a week-day it is a teeming hive, its pavements thronged, its narrow roadways reverberating with the buzz of traffic and business activity; in the evening the same streets give over to leisurely promenaders and strolling lovers.

College Green

College Green—not to be confused with "the Green," which to Dubliners signifies St. Stephen's Green, the delightful center-city park—is the broad area in front of Trinity College and the Bank of Ireland where lower Grafton Street, Westmoreland Street, College Street, and Dame Street converge.

Big business has its aristocracy, and this district is devoted to the upper circles of commerce. Clothes tend to be more formal here; even the liveried bank porter has not quite disappeared from this stronghold of wealth. Because of the tendency of Dubliners to emphasize the elegance of their Georgian streetscapes and squares, Dublin's Victorian buildings are often overlooked or even criticized. Take, for example, the row of banking and insurance offices on the south side of College Green and facing the Bank of Ireland. While the overloaded detail of some of these buildings—mock turrets and conical towers—may be displeasing, many of the individual conceptions repay examination, particularly the interior ceiling work and decor of the Northern Bank building.

To be seen to best advantage, the **Bank of Ireland** would probably require an elevated site and some surrounding gardens or parkland, but even in its low-lying, mid-city situation it is still a magnificent building. It was built in 1739, but at various times over the following 60 years all the leading architects of the era—Lovett Pearse, James Gandon, Robert Parke, and Francis Johnston—had a hand in its design. It was formerly the House of Parliament, unique perhaps among the world's parliaments in that it was the only one ever to vote itself out of existence, and famed for its learned debates and the oratorical skills

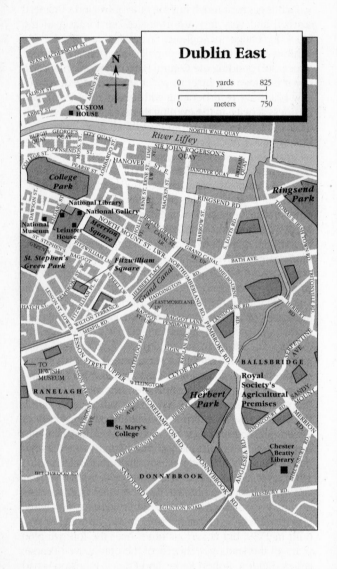

of such men as the patriot Henry Grattan (his statue on College Green displays a raised, declamatory hand).

After the Act of Union in 1800, the building was adapted by Francis Johnston for the sole use of the bank; the cannon and sentry boxes outside date from that time, when it was deemed necessary to form a militia guard for the bank's protection.

During normal business hours the bank's old House of Lords, displaying the speaker's mace and two large 1735 tapestries illustrating the battle of the Boyne and the siege of Derry, is open to the public and worth visiting; on Tuesdays well-known Dublin historian Eamon Mac Tomáis gives free lectures.

Trinity College

The Bank of Ireland is one of two great showpieces in College Green. Trinity College's west front is the other.

Each of Dublin's three universities enjoys a particular prestige and position: Dublin University (Trinity), University College, Dublin (a constituent college of the National University), and the new Dublin City University—the latter two located in the suburbs. Of these three, Trinity has the most atmosphere, which is another way of saying that it has an older and greater tradition. That tradition can be detected in campus meetings, conversations, clubs, some 200 societies, two pubs, and the writings, acting performances, and debate it engenders—a kind of liberal (and Protestant) ethos, which until about 20 years ago was so frowned upon by the Catholic hierarchy that members of the flock had to seek special permission from Dublin's archbishop to study here. And it is probably for that reason that this 40-acre, open-to-the-public oasis of gardens, playing fields, cobbled quadrangles, and old buildings has until quite recently retained a slightly forbidding air of "excommunication" for Dublin's predominantly Roman Catholic population.

The cultural and recreational pursuits of Trinity's 7,000 students proclaim themselves from the myriad posters on the notice boards at the College Green and Nassau Street entrances, many of which invite the participation of the general public. Undergraduate life is particularly festive and raucous on occasions such as the annual Rag Week and Trinity Ball in May.

Founded by Queen Elizabeth I—the carved royal arms of Good Queen Bess near the exit of the library is the only remaining relic of the original building—Trinity is Ireland's oldest university. Most of its present buildings, however, date from the early 18th century, though the ancient cobblestones, the cast-iron bollards and lamps, and a leisurely Old World air that gives no hint of the turmoil that marked the college's early history heighten the sense of antiquity within its precincts.

In 1643 the college had to pawn its silver, and most of the fellows were expelled by Cromwell's officers; subsequently, others were excluded in a tit-for-tat reprisal by the monarchy; and all—fellows and students alike—were sent packing when James II turned the place into an army barracks in 1689. The following century witnessed periodic town-versus-gown riots.

Yet those centuries also witnessed an age of ardent learning and wide-ranging scholarship that produced such Trinity men as Ussher the biblical scholar, Marsh the Orientalist, Dodwell the historian, and Stearne, who founded the Irish College of Physicians. Most of the outstanding Irishmen of the 18th century, including Molyneux, Berkeley, Grattan, Tone, Burke, and Goldsmith— the last two commemorated by fine statues outside the main entrance—were Trinity men, and the influence of their alma mater is discernible in their writings and speeches. Also educated here were writers such as Jonathan Swift, Oscar Wilde, and Samuel Beckett, and scientists such as Rowan Hamilton of quaternions fame and E. T. S. Walton, who won the Nobel Prize for his work on the atom. The college further distinguished itself by admitting female students to degrees as early as 1903.

To appreciate the wealth and variety of Trinity, a detailed guidebook and ample leisure are required; Trinity students conduct tours of the college that leave every 15 minutes from inside the main gate. If you are pressed for time, however, a visit to the old library should suffice. Its famous **Long Room** on the first floor (for North Americans, second floor) is said to be the largest single-chamber library in Europe. Its 200,000 volumes and 5,000 manuscripts—Greek, Latin, Egyptian papyruses, etc.—are the college's oldest and most-prized possessions. Among its principal treasures are eighth- and ninth-century Irish ecclesiastical manuscripts including the books of Durrow, Dimma, and Armagh, and the magnificently illuminated copy of the Gospels, the **Book of Kells**. Since 1801, under various copyright acts, the college has been entitled to receive one copy of every work published in Ireland and Britain, so it now requires seven additional buildings, and a half-mile increase in bookshelves every year, to contain a collection exceeding two and a half million volumes.

The 1760 Provost's House (to the left of the main entrance and facing onto lower Grafton Street; not open to the public) is the oldest continuously inhabited house in Dublin. Of its many prominent tenants perhaps the most colorful was Dr. John Mahaffy, professor of Greek, sportsman, social snob, and wit. "In Ireland the inevitable never happens, but the unexpected often occurs" is one of his better-known quips. Mahaffy impressed on the young Oscar Wilde the importance not of being earnest but of making bons mots and the right social contacts. It was Mahaffy who, on being shown a sample of Joyce's work, snorted contemptuously, "the inevitable result of extending university education to the wrong sort of people." It need hardly be added that Joyce was a graduate of University College, Dublin, not of Mahaffy's beloved Trinity.

Grafton Street

Dublin's main shopping area lies along and near O'Connell and Grafton streets, which run north and south through the city center across the Liffey, O'Connell to the north of the river, Grafton to the south—although almost every side street and outlying suburb has its boutique, antiques store, or crafts shop. Dubliners like to hint or boast of little places in the quieter districts where all sorts of bargains supposedly can be unearthed; these places are not closed or out of bounds to the visitor—he or she has only to find them.

Grafton Street, which is closed to automobile traffic, and the side streets, interconnecting lanes, shopping malls, and alleys linking it with South Great George's Street to the west and Dawson Street to the east, is *the* shopping strip in Dublin. Side streets contain everything from the Westbury Hotel, the Hibernian Shopping Arcade, the Civic Museum, and the **Bruxelles Music Pub**, to Lord Powerscourt's 200-year-old town house, where a delightful enclosed courtyard and balcony have been converted into a modern shopping center, the **Powerscourt Townhouse Centre**, with everything from designer shoes and handbags to Irish linen and lace.

Grafton Street's leading department stores, **Switzers**

and **Brown Thomas**, almost rival the nearby bookshops of **Waterstone**, **Hodges Figgis** (both on Dawson Street), and **Fred Hanna** (Nassau Street) in their encyclopedic range, while the neighboring streets are havens for print and antiques shops and boutiques. Shoppers here should concentrate on the Irish products of exceptional quality, such as Belleek china, Waterford and Galway crystal, woollens, and tweeds.

The **Sweater Shop** (Wicklow Street) is tops for Aran hand-knits, kilts, lamb's-wool sweaters, and the like, and **Weir's Jeweller's** (Grafton Street) gives good value for leather, gold, and silver items, and offers one of the finest selections of Claddagh rings, those distinctive, old "hands-clasping-a-crowned-heart" Irish wedding tokens. At the top of Grafton Street, where it ends in a kind of dramatic flourish opposite the Fusiliers Arch (a memorial to the officers and men of five battalions of the Royal Dublin Fusiliers who died in the Boer War), stands Dublin's largest retail development, the St. Stephen's Green Centre (see Shops and Shopping, below).

Westward from O'Connell Street on the North Side runs Henry Street, a busy shopping area with popular department stores such as Arnotts, Roches, and the modern ILAC (Irish Life Assurance Company) Centre, and just around the corner from the famous Moore Street shops and stall holders. **Moore Street** provides one of the briskest scenes of general barter in the city. Fruit, vegetable, and fish stalls crowd the pavements, and nowhere are the vendors more pressing in their invitations to buy. Keen bargain sleuths who are not averse to poking through tatty junk piles laid out on the sidewalks of seedy North Cumberland Street (a few minutes' walk to the east side of O'Connell Street's northern end, taking the first right after the Gresham Hotel into Cathal Brugha Street) may occasionally unearth treasures from among the oddments of chinaware, pottery, brasswork, old picture frames, coins, military bric-a-brac, old household appliances, rusty garden implements, carpet scraps, and toys found here. The **Cumberland Market** is a once-a-week, Saturday morning affair—arrive very early, six to seven—in a very unprepossessing area that is best avoided at any other time, especially at night. (Shopping throughout Dublin is covered later in this chapter.)

Dawson Street
and St. Stephen's Green

Back to the Trinity College area: Trinity's Lincoln Place gate leads southeast to Merrion Square, its Nassau Street gate south to Dawson Street and the Green. St. Anne's Romanesque-fronted church, the Royal Irish Academy, and the Mansion House are cheek by jowl in Dawson Street.

It has been said that Dublin almost rivals Rome in the number and variety of its churches. A sprinkling of Jewish, Greek Orthodox, and Moslem congregations augment all the Protestant denominations in this city whose population is about 90 percent Roman Catholic and which has, in addition to its secular clergy, well over a hundred separate religious orders of priests, nuns, monks, and brothers.

St. Anne's, one of the most beautiful of these churches, is known to a small group of Dubliners of all religious persuasions for the excellent lunchtime musical and cultural activities that take place here every Thursday. Visitors to St. Anne's should note the wooden "bread" shelves behind the altar. In the 1720s one of St. Anne's first parishioners made a bequest of £13 per annum in perpetuity to provide weekly loaves of bread for the poor of the parish. The custom of laying out loaves for distribution continues to the present day, although the original handsome bequest must now be supplemented by donations.

The Royal Irish Academy, next door to St. Anne's, publishes major reference works of scholarly interest—its library contains an extensive collection of ancient Irish manuscripts—and holds a leading place among the learned societies of Europe. It is not open to the public. Nor is the Mansion House, except for group visits by prior arrangement. The Mansion House, essentially a town house of the Queen Anne period (1710) with Victorian embellishments added later, has been the official residence of the lord mayor of Dublin since 1715 and thus predates its London counterpart by about 30 years. Its principal interior apartment is the Round Room, built expressly for the reception of George IV in 1821 but much better known as the assembly room of the first Dáil Eireann (the parliament of the Irish people) where, in

1919, in defiance of Westminster, the Declaration of Independence was ratified.

The clean atmosphere of the Irish capital is doubtless largely due to its proximity to the sea and the mountains, and also due to its many fine parks and open spaces. One of these, **St. Stephen's Green**, is everything a center-city park should be. An air of subdued holiday spirit pervades its wooded walks (it's a mile-long walk around its four sides), formal lawns, fountains, and duck ponds. It also contains a bandstand, a pavilion, a children's playground, and 15 monuments and statues. Lord Ardilaun (Sir Arthur Edward Guinness) had the park laid out in its present form in the 1880s, at which time he also established a decoy pond for wildfowl, a source of much entertainment to generations of Dubliners and visitors.

The buildings surrounding the Green include (south side) Iveagh House, now the Department of Foreign Affairs, and University Church with its narrow, fussy entrance leading into the nearest thing Dublin has to a Byzantine-type church; (west side) the Unitarian Church, containing a striking collection of stained-glass windows (French, Flemish, English, and the main window, a splendid example of the revived Irish style), the College of Surgeons (1806), and the St. Stephen's Green Centre (Dublin's largest retail development), which opened in 1988 at a cost of £60 million plus and contains a wide range of Ireland's most exclusive department stores; and (north side) the Adam Salesrooms and the Shelbourne Hotel.

The **College of Surgeons** was built on the site of an old Quaker cemetery, and when it was extended by William Murray in 1825 care was taken to retain the two narrow lanes (Goat Alley and Glovers Alley) flanking the building that originally facilitated the nocturnal activities of the body snatchers—known locally as "Sack 'em up men"—whose business it was to discreetly deliver their macabre bundles to the college's dissecting room. During the 1916 Rising the college was commandeered by the Irish Citizen Army led by Michael Mallin and with the colorful and tempestuous Constance Markievicz as second-in-command.

The north side was the former "Beaux Walk," the 18th-century center of fashion and dandyism, and the haunt of such notorious rakes as the inveterate gambler Buck Whaley, who once walked to Jerusalem and back to win a bet, and "Sham Squire" Francis Higgins, who, for 1,000 pounds, betrayed his friend, the patriot Lord Edward

Fitzgerald, to the authorities before the 1798 Rising. To-day what remains of Victorian and Edwardian club life still flourishes on this side of the Green.

The **Adam Salesrooms** on this side provide a happy hunting ground for dealers and collectors interested in period furniture, paintings, glass, silver, porcelain, china, books, manuscripts, and wine. To witness an auction here is first-class entertainment. Not that there is much visible excitement. An air of laid-back ennui appears to prevail as first editions and rare documents go under the hammer and change hands, often for considerable sums. Dublin-ers, from plebeian ex-tenement dwellers to shabby gen-teel suburbanites and a few faded remnants of the Anglo-Irish ascendancy class, have in recent years taken to rummaging through their attics and cellars for forgotten valuable heirlooms or quaint family bric-a-brac to sell at the salesrooms.

The **Shelbourne Hotel**—known to upper-class globe-trotters of every continent—dates back to 1824 and pos-sesses the hallmark of approval of royalty and nobility, as well as millionaires, literary personalities, and stars of stage and screen. Thackeray stayed here in 1842, describ-ing it as a "respectable old edifice" and exclaiming over its "copious breakfasts," and George Moore wrote parts of his novels *A Drama in Muslin* and *The Bending of the Bough* in a front bedroom commanding a splendid view of the Green. The late Princess Grace of Monaco appreciated its elegance and the fact that she could take quiet early morning walks in the Green away from the usual hordes of international press photographers and reporters. The Irish Constitution of 1922 was drafted in Room 112, now called the Constitution Room. The Shelbourne's Lord Mayor's Lounge, with leaf-green silk-lined walls, swag and tail drapes, and a splendid chandelier, is a toney reflection of the leisurely Victorian age and the perfect setting for relaxed morning coffee and the 150-year-old tradition of afternoon tea. Like the famous Horseshoe Bar, this cele-brated tearoom is popular with discerning Dubliners and visitors alike as an ideal place to meet or to relax after shopping or sightseeing forays. (The Shelbourne Hotel is discussed further in the Accommodations section, below.)

Directly opposite the Shelbourne's front entrance, illu-minated at night by a brace of lanterns held aloft by statues of two nubile slave girls with fettered ankles, stands a modern commemorative statue to the patriot Wolfe Tone. Tone's statue, against a background of giant granite plinths, was no sooner unveiled when some Dublin wag christened it "Tone-henge" (the nicknaming of the city's statues being something of a traditional pastime).

Georgian Dublin

Few European cities offer the same scale and scope of 18th-century elegance as the area of Dublin bordered by Trinity College and the east side of St. Stephen's Green on the one side, and the Mount Street and Leeson Street bridges of the Grand Canal on the other. Its Georgian buildings give it nobility; its bosky squares, tree-lined canal, and broad thoroughfares (as far back as 1768 the city had a special Wide Streets Commission to give muscle to its plan for spaciousness) make it a district of openness, light, and air. It is also the district of museums, art galleries (public and private), little parks, historic houses, government offices, nightclubs (Leeson Street), and even the occasional fine restaurant or ballad pub. Though the interiors of what were formerly residences have largely been converted into offices, consulting rooms, and private apartments, a sober austerity of old-style Anglo-Irish Protestantism lingers about these buildings, an overall unity of design relieved by the constant variety of detail in doorways, fanlights, and ornamental balconies.

The Anglo-Irish—a rather loose term for all those well-to-do Protestants who, over about three centuries, owed their cultural and even political allegiance to London and to their British cousins—haven't really had very good press in recent years. This generic term usually refers to someone who isn't Gaelic, Catholic, or Nationalist in background and outlook, though like everything else in Ireland there are contradictions and notable exceptions.

The original Norman invaders of 800 years ago, aristocratic in their ambitions at least, had little difficulty in assimilating with a native Gaelic order that itself was inherently aristocratic in character. By the time of Elizabeth I these Hiberno-Normans (or "Olde English," as the London court termed them) had become more Irish than the Irish themselves, and the Virgin Queen considered it most politic to plant "New English" in the rich pasturelands of Munster and the Pale.

Elizabeth's successor, James I, went much farther when

he literally sowed the entire province of Ulster with Scottish Protestants after the exodus of the Gaelic chiefs in 1603. The subsequent wars and the political ferment of the 17th century brought new strains of Englishness. Cromwellian troopers were rewarded with vast tracts of land, and, similarly, William of Orange, after he became William III of England, Scotland, and Ireland in the Revolution of 1688, paid off many of his English and Dutch officers by creating a new landed gentry on the forfeited estates of those who had sided with his Catholic rival, James II. The less turbulent years of the 17th and 18th centuries saw the peaceful infiltration of many English and Scottish merchants into the life of the country. Out of this essentially Protestant and British oligarchy grew the term "Anglo-Irish."

If history can accuse this class of having perfected the art of skimming the cream off Ireland, then it can also credit the same people with having created the Augustan era of Georgian Dublin and of having laid the groundwork for much that is elegant and erudite in Ireland today. In addition to producing everything from profligate rakes, cruel landlords, proud soldiers, gentle scholars, and altruistic women, the Anglo-Irish class has provided Ireland with such names as Swift, Berkeley, Goldsmith, Burke, Shaw, Wilde, and Yeats, together with patriots such as Grattan, Emmet, Butt, Davis, and Parnell.

The Georgian district also contains a famous collection of institutions devoted to educational, artistic, and scholarly interests. In **Kildare Street**, parallel to and east of Dawson Street, the National Museum and the National Library flank the forecourt and "town house" façade of Leinster House, the seat of Dáil Eireann (House of Representatives) and Seanad Eireann (Senate).

The **National Library** entrance hall frequently displays small exhibitions—Irish bookbinding, prints, political tracts and posters, famous Irish letters, and the like— while the Reading Room (scene of the literary debate in Joyce's *Ulysses*) preserves a representative collection of first editions and works of such Irish writers as Swift, Goldsmith, Yeats, Shaw, Joyce, and Beckett. The library's need for additional space for its ever-increasing collection of books, maps, and newspapers led to the recent acquisition of the adjoining Kildare Street Club premises, a Venetian-style brick "palazzo" at the northern, or Trinity, end of the street that now houses the Heraldic and Genealogical Museum—of particular interest and help to those tracing ancestral roots. Both buildings are closed on Sundays.

The **National Museum** houses an outstanding collection of Irish antiquities, some of which are among the finest examples of Early Christian art in Europe. Exhibits cover a period from roughly 6000 B.C. to modern times, with everything from costumes, silver, medals, and weapons to photos, letters, and military memorabilia of the 1916 Rising.

The museum's **Treasury Gallery** is inspired by the great cathedral galleries of Europe and illustrates the pagan pre-Celtic and Celtic background of Early Christian Irish art, including stunning gold masterpieces—gorgets, torques, lunulae—from pre-Celtic times as early as 1800 B.C., and from the Celtic pre-Viking zenith. An audiovisual presentation, which explains the historical and archaeological context of the exhibition and gives guidance on how to appreciate the major masterpieces, is presented in a specially designed theater with informal tiered seating and selected exhibits, including sculptures, which are linked to the on-screen program. Centerpieces of the display itself include the eighth-century A.D. **Ardagh Chalice** and **Tara Brooch, St. Patrick's Bell**, the **Cross of Cong**, and the **Moylough belt shrine**, together with book shrines, croziers, crosses, and other priceless items. To these are added the fruits of intensive collecting over the past decade, including the recently discovered "Derrynaflan hoard" and six other recently acquired silver hoards from the Midlands containing over 30 kilograms of silver objects. An exquisitely worked chalice is the most important item among the eighth- and ninth-century religious artifacts in the Derrynaflan hoard, discovered in February 1980 near a ruined fifth-century abbey in County Tipperary.

The **Music Room** contains some 70 musical instruments, mostly Irish made, with *uilleann* pipes, harps (one ascribed to the great Carolan), pianos, harpsichords, and experimental stringed instruments. The Art and Industrial Division comprises Irish glass, furniture, costumes, coins, stamps, ceramics, and medals. In addition to Greek, Roman, Egyptian, and Oriental antiquities, the museum's Ethnographical Collection contains much material originating from Captain Cook's voyages of discovery.

The **National Museum Annexe**—around the corner in

Merrion Row, just past the Shelbourne Hotel—contains numerous Viking artifacts discovered during the almost continuous excavations between 1962 and 1981 in the city's Christchurch Place, Winetavern, and Wood Quay sites, among Europe's largest and richest urban digs. Exhibits on display here include 11th-century bone-and-antler combs and carrying cases, iron swords, polished bone pins, scales for weighing precious metals, hundreds of lead weights all conforming to units based on the Carolingian ounce, and an iron saw shaped to resemble a Viking longboat and used to cut antler and bone.

Both the library and the museum are open to the public, as is Leinster House when the parliament is not sitting. **Leinster House** (1745) was originally the town house of the duke of Leinster, who, on being reminded of the folly of building his mansion in what was then rural countryside when the fashionable side of the city was clearly on the north side of the Liffey, declared that fashion would follow him across the river. The accuracy of his forecast was quickly proven.

The opposite side of this sprawling educational and legislative complex is on Merrion Square and contains the National Gallery and the Natural History Museum. Like their Kildare Street counterparts, they flank Leinster House, in this case the rear, "country house" façade, with its lawn and obelisk commemorating the founders of the Irish Free State: Arthur Griffith, Michael Collins, and Kevin O'Higgins, a tragic triumvirate, all of whom died within five years of each other, the last two by bullets.

The **Natural History Museum** holds a valuable collection of the remains of extinct and prehistoric animals and birds, together with mounted and preserved representatives of the world's fauna.

Outside the entrance to the **National Gallery** are statues of George Bernard Shaw, who claimed that he owed his education to the gallery and bequeathed a third of his estate to it, and the Irish railway pioneer William Dargan, who was the prime mover in its establishment. One of the best "small" galleries in Europe—Irish painters, Dutch masters, English watercolorists, 17th-century French, Italian, and Spanish schools, and French Impressionists, amounting to more than 2,000 works on view—the building also houses an extensive art reference library, lecture theater, and, on the ground floor, **Fitzer's**, one of Dublin's most popular and inexpensive restaurants.

In all there are about 40 galleries in the center-city

area—a dozen of them in the Merrion-Fitzwilliam-St. Stephen's Green district—and every Saturday and Sunday an ongoing open-air exhibition takes place in **Merrion Square** park (opposite the National Gallery), with paintings, prints, drawings, and lithographs festooning the park railings and clustered about the Rutland Fountain (1791). The park, once the scene of distressed and starving hordes surrounding the soup kitchens of the famine era (1845–1847), is now one of the most beautiful and most popular of center-city retreats. Plaques on the walls of the surrounding mansions recall famous occupants— the Wildes, Daniel O'Connell, W. B. Yeats, George Russell (AE), and Sheridan Le Fanu—and the view from the south side of the square, looking toward Upper Mount Street and crowned by the "pepper canister" cupola of St. Stephen's (1825), offers what is possibly the finest Georgian vista in the city. **Fitzwilliam Square** to the south, on the other hand, is the smallest, latest (1825), and best preserved of Dublin's Georgian squares.

Dublin's Canals

Just as Londoners born within hearing of Bow Bells are said to be the true Cockneys, so too are the "rale Dubs," or Jackeens, said to be born within the confines of the city's Royal and Grand canals.

The Liffey divides old Dublin into two nearly equal portions, the North Side and the South Side. Until the advent of the railways—and, indeed, for almost a century after, it might be argued—the river acted as a kind of natural frontier between North Siders and South Siders. Well into this century, and in addition to the separate and distinct classes of citizens based on social and religious differences, there was this geographic division too. To the majority of North Siders the south city and its environs were almost as foreign as the Sahara and Timbuktu; and north of the river, as far as most South Siders were concerned, might well have been Ultima Thule or Alaska. Villages such as Irishtown and particularly its sister parish of Ringsend (then almost entirely surrounded by the waters of the Liffey, the River Dodder, and the sea) were remote and distinct places. The building of the canals in the late 18th century added a further clannish frontier on both sides of the Liffey: Everyone outside the canals was said to be a "hazeler," so-called from the hazel sticks the rural drovers used to guide their cattle into the Dublin markets.

The South Side **Grand Canal** was constructed in 1772 to provide a passenger link between Dublin, the midland towns to the west, and the River Shannon. (Its most attractive urban setting is the tree-lined stretch between Leeson Street Bridge and the picturesque Huband Bridge at Upper Mount Street, near the "pepper canister" church.) Tens of thousands of passengers travelled annually along this 90-mile stretch prior to the introduction of the railways in the 1850s. Thereafter passenger traffic deteriorated, but freight barges continued working the canal right up to the middle of the present century.

Like so many things in Ireland, the building of the rival North Side **Royal Canal** grew out of personal pique and a subsequent feud. John Binns (there's a canal bridge named after him in Drumcondra) quarreled with his fellow directors on the Grand Canal board, resigned, and angrily vowed to build a bigger and better canal on the opposite side of the city. He commenced the Royal Canal in 1790, but, alas, lack of sufficient passengers and freight kept his venture only limping along until the advent of the steam locomotive. It was the extensive network of Ireland's 19th-century railways (with their ability to transport many more passengers and much more freight and mail in far quicker time, and at cheaper rates, over all manner of boggy lowland and hilly terrain) that ushered in the steady decline of the slower, more leisurely canal traffic.

The Royal Canal's subsequent fate accurately mirrored that of its South Side rival: It was closed to traffic in the early 1960s. In 1986 the Office of Public Works was vested with ownership and both canals are now entering a new era as sites for water cruising. Today the canals (thanks to the Trojan efforts of a handful of waterway enthusiasts, who have painstakingly rebuilt old lock gates and removed debris, silt, and weeds) provide a "romantic" and slower mode of inland exploration with the provision of leisure and pleasure craft.

The South Side Suburbs

A suburb may have its charm no less than a historic city center. East of St. Stephen's Green along Baggot Street, or east of Merrion Square along Mount Street/Northumberland Road, **Ballsbridge**—containing the Berkeley Court and Jury's hotels, most of the foreign embassies, the Royal Dublin Society (R.D.S.) Showgrounds, and the Chester Beatty Library—stands for elegance, even luxury. A century ago it was the Belgravia of Dublin. At the time, the residents of Ballsbridge regarded themselves as more than members of Dublin's respectable Victorian society—they *were* that society. Their rules of behavior were not formulated in written codes, their social regulations being governed by nothing more than an innate awareness that things were either "done" or "not done." This sense of refinement still exists, displayed in a succession of tints: neat rectangles of lawn fringed with flowers, painted wrought iron, the mica-glint of granite on steps and lintels, broad leafy avenues, and sturdy mansions.

Topography confines Ballsbridge to the district that is bounded on the north by the Grand Canal, on the south by Donnybrook, on the west by Ranelagh, and on the east by Sandymount. Socially, however, it may be said to extend much farther afield and to include most of its bordering districts. Although the professions and business interests have secured a footing in Ballsbridge, the area is still mainly occupied by the wealthy and the fashionable. Superior hotels, high-class restaurants, and diplomatic missions are interspersed among luxury apartments, suburban villas, and mansions. The centerpiece is undoubtedly the extensive R.D.S. Showgrounds. The **Royal Dublin Society**—the first of its kind in Europe, and with over 250 years of promoting improvements in agriculture, veterinary science, and stock breeding—is renowned worldwide for its two great annual events: the **Spring Show** (May) and the **Dublin Horse Show** (August). The former is primarily an agricultural produce/machinery/livestock exhibition and includes equestrian events; the latter is devoted to premier show jumping competitions. The Dublin Horse Show still attracts the best jumpers in the world to compete for the supreme equestrian prize, the Aga Khan Trophy. The society's Simmonscourt Extension is the venue for many indoor exhibitions, concerts, and shows throughout the year.

Nearby, in Shrewsbury Road—a delightful, wooded road—is the **Chester Beatty Library and Gallery of Oriental Art**. There is not a student of the Near and Far East in the world today who does not owe something to Chester Beatty, a New Yorker who roughed it in the mining camps of the Wild West as a mining engineer with a six-gun strapped to his waist. A millionaire at 40, he took to wintering in Africa to ease the chronic chest ailment brought on by silicosis, the miners' respiratory disease. The African continent brought him into contact with the world of ancient Egyptian manuscripts written on papyrus. Over the next 50 years he sought, acquired, and assembled the most remarkable collection of papyruses and Oriental art in the world. In 1950 Beatty came to live in Dublin, bringing his priceless collection with him. When he died in 1968 he bequeathed his vast collection to the Irish nation. Highlights include items dating back as far as 2500 B.C., biblical papyruses, Persian and Turkish paintings, Qur'ans, Japanese and European wood-block prints, and Chinese jade books (closed Sundays and Mondays).

Ireland's Jewish community numbers only about 2,000 members but has contributed in no small measure to the cultural and business life of the city since the arrival of the first group of Jews about 300 years ago. This contribution is well recorded in an absorbing collection of Jewish and Dublin memorabilia on display in the **Irish Jewish Museum**, in what was once the old Walworth Road Synagogue off Victoria Street in the Portobello district bordering on the Grand Canal. Israel's then-President Chaim Hertzog—himself a "Dub" who once lived in nearby Bloomfield Avenue—officially opened the museum. It is open Tuesdays, Thursdays, and Sundays from May through September, and on Sunday mornings only the rest of the year.

SOUTH COUNTY

DART (Dublin Area Rapid Transport) runs from Howth (North Side) through the city center to Bray (South Side), a distance of about 25 miles. For the visitor the DART is best travelled from the city center southward (with the exception of an excursion to Howth and neighboring Sutton), where the stretch of line from Merrion to Dún Laoghaire seems to run almost along the sands and offers a panoramic view of Dublin Bay. En route, high walls front the public bathing places at Blackrock and Salthill, a legacy of Victorian prudery and railway stipulations preventing "such bathing places and the persons bathing therein from being exposed to the view of passengers on the said railroad." The final southern stretch of the DART line—exiting from the Dalkey hilltop tunnel and running through Killiney to Bray—possesses a touch of the Mediterranean. The view of the bay and the gentle curve of Killiney beach is said by many to rival the glories of Naples and Sorrento. Some, in fact, would claim that the bay is a gentler, prettier, less cluttered, and more nearly perfect crescent than its better-known rival. (The weather is a different matter.) See Getting Around, below, for more information about using the DART.

Dún Laoghaire

Dubliners "discovered" Dún Laoghaire (formerly Kingstown) with the coming of the railways in the 1830s and the simultaneous introduction of the world's first suburban railroad.

The place still retains a certain 19th-century charm along with its modern shopping complex, humble artisan dwellings, busy harbor, resort-type hotels and boarding-houses, regal promenade, and quaint side streets. Gothic church spires punctuate the predominantly horizontal rows of solid, comfortable bourgeois terraces (groups of row houses). Here and there the stately exclusiveness of some of its tree-lined avenues suggests the superiority of a minicapital city. Dún Laoghaire is unashamedly Victorian, a vivid expression of the twin 19th-century virtues of business acumen and social respectability.

Yet for all its "gem of the period" Victoriana, the township retains a salty tang. Dún Laoghaire is preeminently a sailors' town, for more than 150 years the exit and entry point for the main sea route between Ireland and Britain. It is still the home port of a busy commercial sea fishery, the mail boat terminal, the Sealink car-ferry service terminal, the base for Irish lightships, and Ireland's premier yachting center, the site of such famous and ancient clubs as the Royal St. George, the Royal Irish, the National, and the Motor Yacht Club alongside one another on the harbor front. It also is headquarters for the Irish Yachting Association and the National Maritime Museum, the latter housed in what used to be the Mariner's Church.

Dún Laoghaire is well supplied with restaurants and cafés, the most notable being **Restaurant na Mara**, located at the DART station and overlooking the harbor. *Na mara* means "of the sea" in Gaelic, and, as the name suggests, the place specializes in seafood (Tel: 01/280-6767 or 0509). Also on the seafront, at Windsor Terrace, are **Steers Steak House** (Tel: 01/280-6535) and **Digby's** (Tel: 01/280-4600), both offering fresh seasonal food. The **Salty Dog** at

3A Haddington Terrace (Tel: 01/280-8015) prepares Indonesian as well as European dishes.

Sandycove

A brisk 20-minute walk from Dún Laoghaire's east pier around the rim of Scotsman's Bay takes you to Sandycove and the **James Joyce Museum**. The museum, open May through September, is housed in a Martello tower, one of the 20-odd squat military fortifications resembling foreshortened butter churns that dot County Dublin's coast. These towers, modeled and named after a similar defensive tower at Cape Mortella in Corsica, were built in 1804 to withstand a Napoleonic invasion that never materialized.

Joyce set the opening chapter of *Ulysses* in the Sandycove tower, where he lived for a week in 1904 with his friend Oliver St. John Gogarty, whom he later immortalized and mercilessly portrayed in his masterpiece as the flippant Buck Mulligan. Sandycove has since become a mecca for Joyce enthusiasts, and today the ever-growing collection of Joycean memorabilia at the tower—letters, manuscripts, paintings, photos, rare and early editions of the author's work, his guitar, piano, waistcoat, and walking stick—is viewed by thousands of visitors each year.

Like many places on this stretch of coastline, Sandycove is a popular spot for Windsurfing, canoeing, and water-skiing. Frequent aquatic displays of a different sort take place year-round at the renowned Forty Foot bathing place, a secluded and picturesque seawater retreat for hardy swimmers. The Forty Foot was until quite recently the exclusive preserve of male bathers, many of whom enjoy swimming and sunbathing in the nude. The advent of the feminist movement, however, inevitably brought a determined invasion of this bastion of male chauvinism by some activists.

Dalkey

Dalkey, farther down the coast from Sandycove, is a place of weathered old stones, a village with a Continental flavor because of its narrow streets and fine villas. The old stones are evident in the main street at **Archibold's Castle**, a reminder that Dalkey was once a walled medieval town designed to persuade the warlike O'Toole and O'Byrne clansmen outside that the garrison inside was stronger in number than it really was. Across the street from the castle a restored 16th-century castellated stone house is now the Town Hall. Then there are the stones of the seventh-century **St. Begnet's Church** on **Dalkey Island**, an example of early Irish ecclesiastical architecture; the massive shards of granite that hem in and seem to dwarf tiny Coliemore Harbour; and the stones of neighboring Bullock Harbour and castle. On the slopes of Dalkey Hill—great views here of the entire sweep of Dublin Bay, Dublin, and distant Howth—is **Torca Cottage**, where Shaw resided as a boy. (He claimed later that he was "a product of Dalkey's outlook.") Dalkey Hill is connected by a saddleback ridge to nearby Killiney Hill, together laid out as a public park complete with nature trail, the remains of an ancient church, and the prehistoric arrangement of stones known as the Druid's Chair. Killiney Hill affords similarly fine views of Killiney Strand, Bray Head, and, inland, the Dublin and Wicklow mountains.

Small boats are available at Bullock and Coliemore harbors for the sea angler, and at the latter harbor for the short trip to barren Dalkey Island, which, apart from St. Begnet's ruined church and a locked-up Martello tower, contains nothing of interest. Off Dalkey Island and the Muglin rocks (where, at one time, the bodies of pirates hung in chains and clanked their ominous warning to other nautical lawbreakers) there is fishing for coalfish, pollack, tope, skate, and conger. Farther out, on the Burford and Kish banks, blond and thornback ray, turbot and brill, plaice and dab are among the more common species taken on the hook. In fact, the whole coastal area from Dún Laoghaire, where fishing from the rocks and piers is free, to Killiney and the County Wicklow resort town of Bray, where boats may be hired, abounds in bass, flounder, codling, and sea trout.

Bray

The massive promontory of **Bray Head** covers the southern extremity of Dublin Bay. Behind it lies the wild moorlands of the Wicklow Mountains, below it one of Ireland's premier seaside resorts, Bray. From Bray Head the views of the mountains inland, or back toward Killiney, Dalkey Island, and across the bay to Howth, are among the most spectacular on the east coast, while the narrow cliff walk around the shoulder of the Head—precipitously high above the single track of main-line railway, it is not a hike for anyone suffering from vertigo—offers breathtaking views of misshapen crags, coves, and rocks carved out by the eternal tides.

The town of Bray itself is a conglomerate of tiny fishing harbor, holiday resort, shopping center, elegant Victorian and Edwardian terraces and squares, lowly cottages, restaurants, boardinghouses and hotels, ballrooms, discos, and fast-food joints—a hodgepodge of the graceful and the garish, redeemed by a stony beach under a stout sea wall and a broad, mile-long esplanade. Bray is perhaps too near Dublin to be considered a part of County Wicklow (which of course it is), and that proximity to the capital has always made it popular with Dubliners.

Inland from this coastal area—in a rough arc from east to west—lie the mountain hamlets and wooded hills of southern County Dublin, an area of numerous nature trails, forest walks, pony-trekking centers, picturesque golf courses, and secluded picnic sites. All are within an hour's bus journey of the city center (see Getting Around, below).

DUBLIN'S NORTH SIDE

With a few notable exceptions, the city area north of the Liffey offers little of interest in comparison with the South Side. The shift of fashion south across the river inaugurated by the duke of Leinster was followed by a general exodus of the nobility in the wake of the Act of Union (1800), when London became the legislative and social hub of the British Isles. The inevitable result was that the fine Georgian terraces surrounding and radiating from places like Rutland (now Parnell) and Mountjoy squares soon degenerated into Victorian slums, a condition that lasted well into this century. Even today the area has a seedy, run-down appearance despite the best efforts of Dublin Corporation, the municipal authority, to revitalize it with attractive housing and miniparks.

The area's—and the city's—main street is the north–south **O'Connell Street**, Ireland's best-known thoroughfare. It is the venue for parades, political rallies, and kindred demonstrations, which usually take place outside the historic and impressive **General Post Office**. This building (1816) is, of course, hallowed as the improvised headquarters of the insurgents at the time of the 1916 Rising. It was from the post office portico that Padraig

Pearse first read out the words of the Proclamation of the Irish Republic.

O'Connell Street is reputed to be one of the widest main streets in Europe. Statues of famous local sons—Catholic emancipator Daniel O'Connell, labor leader Jim Larkin, temperance monk Father Mathew, parliamentarian Charles Stuart Parnell, et al.—line the center of the thoroughfare, and, together with Clery's department store, Eason's bookshop, British Home Stores, the Gresham and Royal Dublin hotels, and a few remaining Victorian façades, enhance a street that has more or less given up the struggle in the rearguard action against the ravages of hamburger bars, jukeboxes, and fast-food joints. The street's newest statue—a 1988 Millennium presentation to the city by well-known local businessman Michael Smurfit—is an elongated female figure representing the mythical river Liffey and reclining in a bubbling fountain; the wags quickly christened it "the floozie in the Jacuzzi."

The other statues on the street are also not without interest. The quartet of buxom angels seated at the corners of the O'Connell monument contain visible bullet holes in breast, arm, and neck—grim reminders of the 1916 Rising and the fierce street fighting that occurred then and during the subsequent Civil War of 1922 to 1923. At the opposite, or northern, end of the street stands the triangular obelisk of polished Galway stone commemorating Parnell. Emblazoned on the obelisk are Parnell's oft-quoted words, "No man has a right to fix the boundary to the march of a nation," and as one arm of his life-size effigy appears to be pointing directly at the Rotunda Maternity Hospital, the irony of the words is not lost on those Dubliners who are aware that their city has one of the fastest-growing populations in western Europe.

The **Rotunda Hospital** (1752), the first purpose-built lying-in, or maternity, hospital in Europe, was the brainchild of Dr. Bartholomew Mosse, a barber-surgeon who also practiced what was then considered to be the lowly profession of midwifery. Concerned about the high rate of infant mortality and childbirth deaths, Mosse funded his venture by organizing everything from fancy dress balls to concerts and recitals (the premiere of Handel's *Messiah* in the Fishamble Street Music Hall was one such), and by opening first pleasure grounds behind the hospital and later the Rotunda Room (which gives the hospital its popular name) and the Assembly Rooms as income-generating entertainment centers.

Although technically under the same roof, the modern hospital and the former Assembly Rooms are now separate entities—the latter housing the now-closed Ambassador Cinema in the Rotunda Room, the old circular assembly room, and the Gate Theatre in what was the adjoining assembly supper room. The hospital chapel is an exquisite example of Austrian-style Baroque craftsmanship and as such represents Ireland's only essay into that Flamboyant Rococo genre on such a grand scale, making it one of Dublin's most unusual places of worship. It is open to the public daily between 9:30 A.M. and 8:30 P.M.

The Rotunda Room witnessed the formation of the modern Irish resistance movement in November 1913, when 4,000 men enrolled at the inaugural meeting of the Irish Volunteers. Little remains of the former pleasure grounds except the excellently maintained Garden of Remembrance (1966), which was built to honor the memory of all those who died in the struggle for Irish independence. Its location has a kind of poignant appropriateness: close to the Rotunda, site of the Volunteers' foundation, and directly on the open space where many of the same volunteers, as rebel prisoners, were stockaded overnight following the surrender that marked the end of the 1916 Rising.

A focal point of the garden is a bronze sculpture by the Irish artist Oisin Kelly, which shows four human figures being transformed into swans (a link with the mythological Children of Lir), symbolizing rebirth and victory. Enclosed by a marble wall at the rear, the Garden of Remembrance contains attractive sunken walkways and a shallow pool. Visitors should note the mosaic of blue-green waves interspersed with weapons from Ireland's Heroic Age (300 B.C.–A.D. 300) at the bottom of the pool; the broken spears recall the ancient Celtic custom of discarding weapons and throwing them into water at the cessation of hostilities.

Close by are the Municipal Gallery of Modern Art (Parnell Square, north side) and the **National Wax Museum** (just around the corner in Granby Row), featuring wax figures of personalities from over 200 years of Irish history: writers, statesmen, sportsmen, and many contemporary world figures.

Charlemont House (1762), the former town house of the earl of Charlemont, was once regarded as the showpiece of the fashionable Dublin that the duke of Leinster wrenched southward to the Merrion fields. It is now the **Municipal Gallery of Modern Art**, converted to such use in 1908 largely through the generosity of Sir Hugh Lane, a wealthy collector who perished when the *Lusitania* was torpedoed in 1915. Lane's collection of French Impressionists forms the nucleus of the gallery's display, which also includes many 20th-century Irish and European masters, but because of a compromise resulting from a disputed codicil to his will his pictures alternate between galleries in London and Dublin.

Almost next door to the Municipal Gallery, at 18 Parnell Square North in an 18th-century town house that still retains the best of its Georgian features, is the **Dublin Writers Museum**. Opened in November 1991 by the then-taoiseach Charles Haughey, the museum's permanent display illustrates the city's rich literary heritage and history from earliest times to the present. Thirty-two panels of text together with letters, photographs, rare books, first editions, literary periodicals, paintings, death masks, busts, and memorabilia (including Joyce's piano, Kavanagh's old typewriter, and St. John Gogarty's aviator goggles) help to place the galaxy of writers and their immortal works in a tangible and lively context. The most recent additions are a bronze bust of Christy Brown, author of *My Left Foot* and *Down All the Days,* and the work of U.S.-based sculptor Peter Lipman-Wulf. The Gallery of Writers salon, the entrance hall, and the fine ceiling of the Gorham Library display the original plasterwork of Dublin's most famous 18th-century stuccadore, Michael Stapleton.

The museum's bookshop, beside the coffee shop in the modern annex at the rear of the building, contains a vast range of Irish and Irish-interest titles in addition to a unique out-of-print/antiquarian book-search service, and its **Chapter One** restaurant specializes in the best of Irish cuisine. Since its inception the museum has regularly mounted exhibitions of special interest, and continues to provide a varied program of readings, musical recitals, and lectures.

Next door at number 19 (and still very much a part of the museum complex and the literary ethos) is the **Irish Writers' Centre**, which provides an informal and friendly environment for contemporary Irish writers to meet and work in a relaxed, congenial atmosphere. All writers, aspiring and established, are always welcome.

Hours for the Writers Museum and Irish Writers' Centre are Monday through Saturday, 10:00 A.M. to 5:00 P.M.; Sundays and bank holidays, 2:00 to 6:00 P.M.

Within easy walking distance to the north of the Municipal Gallery is Temple Street and Hardwicke Place, site of **St. George's Church** and what is thought by many to be the city's most beautiful and elegant spire (1814). It was at St. George's in 1806 that the duke of Wellington—after a protracted and lackluster engagement—married Kitty Pakenham. The Iron Duke deprecated his Dublin birthplace and denied his Irishness with the remark, "Being born in a stable doesn't make one a horse"—which probably accounts for O'Connell's description of the blunt and unbending old soldier as possessing "all the qualities of a poker except that of its occasional warmth." Be aware however, that St. George's is in a neighborhood notorious for purse snatching and mugging.

Also within easy walking distance—a minute or so from the Wax Museum—is the **Black Church** (at St. Mary's Place off Dorset Street), where Dublin urchins, up until the 1960s, ran the "gauntlet of youthhood" by sprinting around its high-railed perimeter on the stroke of midnight, at which hour one was supposed to encounter Satan in person. That deliciously terrifying sprint was mercifully of short duration because the Black Church—like its contemporaneous "pepper canister" cousin St. Stephen's in Mount Street—is built on what might be described as a traffic island. Local lore has it that these Protestant churches of the 1820s were designed and situated this way so that their congregations could easily turn them into defensive fortresses in the event of a popular Catholic uprising. A glance at the high, narrow, musket-slit windows and the slender main door, said to be built to permit the entrance of only a single mounted rider bearing siege provisions, would seem to support the legend. The Black Church, no longer in use as a place of worship, earns its name not from any association with the Devil but from the calp stone from which it was built and which turns a blackish hue in the rain.

It is curious that Dublin, arguably the most Catholic capital in Europe, does not possess a Roman Catholic cathedral per se. **St. Mary's Pro-Cathedral** ("pro-cathedral" refers to a kind of stand-in or substitute cathedral) dates from the pre-Catholic Emancipation era of 1815 to 1825, when such churches were generally confined to back streets in a desire to avoid offending the Protestant powers that be with too great a display of confidence or ostentation. To this day no Roman Catholic archbishop of Dublin has petitioned the pope to revoke the cathedral status of Christ Church, which has belonged to the Church of Ireland, or Anglican Communion, since the Reformation.

The design for the pro-cathedral (in Marlborough Street, which runs parallel to and just to the east of O'Connell Street) was submitted by a brewer named Sweetman who had no formal training as an architect and who worked on its detailed plans in Paris while serving 18 years of political exile for his part in planning the events leading to the 1798 Rising. In 1902 the pro-cathedral's famed Palestrina Choir helped launch the singing career of John McCormack, the tenor who subsequently toured the world and became one of the richest and most successful recording artists of the early phonograph era. The choir can be heard any Sunday morning at the 11:00 mass.

South along Marlborough Street toward the Liffey, at the corner of Lower Abbey Street, stands Ireland's national theatre, the **Abbey**. Opened in 1904 by such stalwarts of the Irish literary and cultural revival as Yeats, Lady Gregory, and Edward Martin, and famous for its production of their early plays and the launching of Sean O'Casey's "triptych" of early-20th-century Dublin revolutionary working-class dramas, *The Plough and the Stars, Juno and the Paycock,* and *The Shadow of a Gunman,* the Abbey's original building was destroyed by fire in the early 1950s. The present plain but ultramodern structure dates from 1966.

Other notable buildings on this side of the Liffey, both on the quays, are Gandon's Custom House and the city's first skyscraper, Liberty Hall, on the former site of the Northumberland Chop House, later headquarters of "Larkin's Union" and the place where the Proclamation of the Irish Republic was printed on the eve of the 1916 Rising. It is also where the Irish Citizen Army assembled for battle on Easter morning, 1916.

The **Custom House** is partially obscured by the ugly Loopline railway bridge and is best viewed from George's Quay on the opposite, or south, bank of the river. It stands today almost as much a memorial to political chicanery and property speculation, on the grand 18th-century scale, as to the architectural genius of James Gandon and the sculptural skills of Edward Smyth.

When in the 1770s John Beresford (chief commissioner of revenue) and his landholding crony Luke Gardiner set about wrenching the commercial axis of Dublin from the castle and Capel Street district to the new area in and around the present O'Connell Street, they used the arguments favoring the building of a new customhouse as the means of doing so. There was immediate opposition—parliamentary petitions, complaints, even mob violence—which was just as suddenly replaced by guffaws when it was realized that the Beresford-Gardiner clique had the harebrained scheme of erecting their massive edifice on a quagmire of river mud. But Gandon conceived an ingenious and innovative method of constructing the building's foundations on a vast raft of fir planks. The plan worked, establishing Gandon's reputation beyond all doubt. The decoration of the Custom House also established the reputation of the hitherto unknown Dublin sculptor Edward Smyth, who until then had spent his talents on nothing more exciting than modeling ornaments for chimneypieces and the odd tombstone.

The greatest of all Smyth's achievements (his later work can be seen in the statues surmounting the pediment of the General Post Office and the stone carvings on the Casino in Marino) is reckoned to be the riverine heads, the river gods of Ireland, used as keystones for the arches of the Custom House. There are 14 in all, each emblematic of a major Irish river—though one of them is curiously entitled "The Atlantic"—and distinguishable by means of the produce of their various riverbanks. The Liffey, as Anna Livia Plurabelle, is the only female head. (In Joyce's *Finnegans Wake,* Earwicker's wife, Ann, is symbolized in a dream as Anna Livia Plurabelle, signifying her beauty and plurality, containing the essence of all rivers and all women.)

The Custom House is the gateway to Dublin's dockland and harbor to the east—or, rather, what's left of the old dockland in an age of container traffic and jet travel. The stevedores, bargees, crane drivers, and lightermen have virtually disappeared, and the 27-acre site of derelict warehouses at the Custom House and St. George's Docks is the site of the city's most significant development of this century. With 450,000 square feet currently under construction and another 750,000 earmarked for further phases, development of Dublin's International Financial Services Centre is ahead of schedule. To date more than 200 companies have applied to set up in the IFSC, and many senior foreign financiers are already in Dublin to set up an eventual pool of 2,500 banking, brokerage, and insurance executives and an expected total workforce of about 7,000 people. The accompanying salaries and lifestyles—and the commercial and cultural activity emanating from such an influx—is expected to have a considerable impact on many aspects of Dublin life, and, by regenerating the use of prime, serviced land on the north quays, to reverse decades of neglect and decay. In addition to the huge financial service center and offices the site will include apartments, shops, an art gallery, a riverfront luxury hotel, and a multipurpose convention center-cum-leisure area. Some existing cranes, hoists, capstans, cobbles, cut stone segments, and brickwork will be retained to maintain the original character of the district.

Dublin's extensive harbor dates from the 18th century, when a "ballast of stones" was built to confine the sprawling river and create today's quays. In 1800 Captain William Bligh, of *Mutiny on the Bounty* notoriety, carried out a detailed survey of the mouth of the river and made certain valuable recommendations.

The North Side Suburbs

Dublin's North Side inner suburbs contain the Botanic Gardens (Glasnevin), the Casino (Marino/Donnycarney), St. Anne's Park (Raheny/Dollymount), and Bull Island.

The **Botanic Gardens** date from 1795, a time when the curative properties of many plants were recognized by the medical profession and accordingly cultivated. The gardens' layout is formal and orderly, with 20,000 different varieties of plants, rare shrubs, and trees (the giant California redwood is one). There are separate gardens for roses and vegetables as well as individual sections for dwarf conifers, cacti, Oriental shrubs, houseplants, and so forth. The magnificent curvilinear range of glasshouses dates from the mid-19th century, when the gardens shared in the great discoveries brought back from voyages to every corner of the globe, and when Dublin's Botanic Gardens were noted for such fine achievements as the earliest reported attempt to raise orchids from seed. Take bus 13 or 19 from O'Connell Street, or 34 or 34A from Middle Abbey Street.

The **Casino** (1762–1771; restored in 1984) is acknowledged to be one of the finest examples of Palladian architecture in Europe. Lord Charlemont, an aesthete who (in Macaulay's words) "gave the tone to the Society of the age," returned from his grand tour of Europe

determined to build a palatial villa with a gallery to house
his priceless collection of paintings and to have its accompanying gardens set off with a temple, or "casino," such as
he had seen in Italy. The design was entrusted to Sir
William Chambers, the leading Palladian expert of the
day.

The result was a delightful masterpiece containing a
subtle optical illusion: Viewed from a distance the Casino
seems small, pretty, and one-roomed, whereas in fact it has
three stories, 16 rooms, and such trick features as balus-
trades concealing the upper windows and classical urns
serving as chimneys. The cost of building the Casino—and
also that of the now demolished Marino House, of which
the masons estimated each carved stone at "the value of a
townland"—crippled Lord Charlemont's estate. Visitors
journeying by bus to the Casino should take an upstairs
right-hand window seat to try to catch a glimpse, too, of
Marino Crescent, at the corner where the bus turns from
Fairview into the Malahide road. Once known locally as
"Ffolliot's Revenge," the crescent was built by a painter of
that name, who, having some disagreement with Lord
Charlemont, built this row of houses in order to effectively
shut out the view of the sea from Marino House. Ffolliot's
masterstroke of spiteful revenge was to build the rear of
the crescent-shaped terrace of houses—and therefore the
view presented to Lord Charlemont's outraged eye and
aesthetic sensibilities—as a terrible hodgepodge of asym-
metrical chimneys, crooked roof lines, unaligned windows, and jutting and irregular outhouses. Take bus 42 or
43 from Beresford Place, opposite the Custom House
lawn, or 20A, 20B, or 24 from Eden Quay.

St. Anne's Park, formerly owned by the Guinness family, has a mile-long, tree-lined drive leading to the spot on
which the Guinness mansion once stood. There are now
playing fields, wooded walks, a pond, a number of "fol-
lies" (those 18th- and 19th-century minitowers, obelisks,
temples, and gazebos with which the aristocrats and nouveau riche of the era vied with each other), and an
internationally renowned rose garden. Take bus 29A or
30 from Lower Abbey Street.

Bull Island (or Dollymount Strand, as it is popularly
known), with its miles of sand dunes and gently sloping
beach, is the seaside area most frequented by Dubliners.
In 1981 UNESCO designated it Ireland's first Biosphere
reserve (one of only 220 such nature reserves in the
world, along with places such as Yellowstone National

Park in the United States and La Camargue in southern France). Greater Dublin, in fact, is probably unique among the metropolitan areas of western Europe in that it includes within its boundaries two extensive wildlife sanctuaries, Bull Island and the much smaller South Side **Booterstown Marsh**. These provide roosting areas for thousands of birds that use the mud flats of Dublin Bay as a source of food, and have one of the greatest densities in Europe of overwintering waders and wildfowl. Bird-watchers are at their busiest in the winter months, when about 30,000 birds of various species settle on the mud flats after migrating from the Arctic.

Bull Island—actually a constantly growing, low-lying sand spit of about 3,469 acres—is linked to the mainland by an 80-year-old open-latticework wooden bridge, and, 1 km (½ mile) north of it, a modern four-lane causeway road. A new interpretive and exhibition center on the island end of the causeway road acts as a kind of watch-tower for the region, and, in addition to providing infor-mation leaflets, videos, and exhibitions, has facilities for the study of the flora and fauna of the island. Here, less than 3 km (2 miles) from the center of a modern capital city, are more than 30 types of grass and vegetation, almost every form of indigenous salt-marsh and sea crea-ture, plus mainland animals such as the rabbit, hare, rat, field mouse, and the occasional fox, stoat, pygmy shrew, and badger. Many land birds—owls, kestrels, sparrow hawks and peregrines—can also be seen, with increasing frequency.

NORTH COUNTY

North of Phoenix Park is the **Dunsink Observatory** (1785), one of the world's oldest astronomical/meteorological re-search centers, with a small collection of exhibits relating to astronomy and famous personalities of the astronomical world, including William Rowan Hamilton (1805–1865). As Astronomer Royal of Ireland he was its first director and the first-ever Foreign Associate of the American National Academy of Sciences (1863). The observatory is open on the first and third Saturday of each month from September to March. Admission is by ticket only; for information, Tel: (01) 38-79-11 or send a note specifying the date you want to visit and a stamped, self-addressed envelope to the

Secretary, Dunsink Observatory. (There is no charge.) Take bus 40A from Parnell Street.

Continuing in a rough west-to-east arc: The **Boot Inn**, behind Dublin Airport, has a skull-scraping low ceiling and old oak bar and, outside, the ancient mounting stone where bygone boozing pals helped the highwaymen Jack Clinch and Collier the Robber into the saddle. Claiming to be Ireland's oldest inn (1604), it's still a fine pub, with good grub. Take bus 60 from Eden Quay.

About 2 km (1¼ mile) to the north, on the main Belfast motorway, is **Swords**, the overnight resting place of the slain Brian Boru after the battle of Clontarf, with its 13th-century castle and its round tower slap up against the square tower of a 14th-century Norman church. Take bus 33, 41, or 41B from Eden Quay. Farther north is **Lusk** (more round towers, plus a "rural life" museum) and the seaside resort of **Rush** with its Good Old Days exhibition bringing alive the folk life of the last century. Take bus 33 from Eden Quay. Finally, at Donabate, there's the stately **Newbridge House** (1740s), with its ornate Red Drawing Room (unaltered in furnishings, paintings, and drapes since 1820), its magnificent kitchen displaying the full range of cooking and household appliances of three centuries, and its courtyard exhibiting a representative selection of horse-drawn carriages, including Lord Chancellor "Black Jack" Fitzgibbon's magnificent state coach of 1790. Take bus 33B from Eden Quay or the outer suburban train from Connolly Station.

Southeast of Donabate on the sea about 16 km (10 miles) from the city center is the pretty village-cum-dormitory suburb of Malahide, and to the south and at the head of Dublin Bay just east of Bull Island is the Howth Peninsula. **Malahide**, a consistent winner of the Irish Tidy Town competition and recipient of the prestigious European Entente Floreale Award in 1990, has a broad, shallow river estuary excellent for dinghy sailing and wind-surfing training. The marshy fringes of the river (like the Bull Island and Booterstown mud flats) are designated as a wildlife sanctuary for migratory birds. **Gibney's**, the village's oldest pub (dating from 1740), still retains the original well from which successive publicans have drawn their supply of fresh spring water.

Howth, with its steep old streets and fair-sized harbor, was originally intended as the main port for mail and passenger transport between Ireland and England until its harbor began to silt up in the 1820s. Thereafter the town reverted to being a mere fishing village, a character it more or less retained well into the latter half of this century. Both Malahide and Howth have perfectly preserved and romantically storied castles (see below). The outer suburban railway runs from the city center to Malahide, Donabate, and points farther north, such as the steadily developing dormitory suburbs growing up around the former rural and fishing villages of Rush, Skerries, Gormanston, and Balbriggan. DART goes from the center up to Howth.

Malahide

The oldest part of **Malahide Castle** dates from about 1174, when the surrounding countryside was seized by the Norman knight Richard Talbot in the second wave of the Norman invasion of Ireland.

First as a graceless defensive tower, then with the additions of battlemented walls and turrets to awe the natives and to command a wide view of the sea, and later as a stately mansion with a mock-Gothic porch, Malahide Castle remained in the continuous possession of Richard Talbot's heirs and descendants for 800 years (the last Lord Talbot died in 1973). It is everything a castle should be: impressively old, picturesque, historic—and haunted. The spectral form of Puck (a dwarfish medieval family retainer) roams the castle's passageways, and in the past his nocturnal appearances were said to presage a death in the Talbot family. A somewhat more romantic ghost is that of the White Lady, who is reputed to step out of her portrait in the great hall and to glide about the dark corridors at night.

In the 1640s the castle was briefly occupied by Oliver Cromwell and his Roundhead officers, and it figured prominently in the later Williamite wars. The castle, which was acquired by the state and which now houses the **National Portrait Gallery**, possesses a wealth of historical, architectural, and artistic items. The splendid Banqueting Hall dates from 1475, the wainscoted Oak Room from the 17th century, the Small Drawing Room from about 1750, and the Large Drawing Room from the early 19th century. The castle is set in some 260 acres of picturesque wooded grounds. The castle parklands also contain the Fry Model Railway (a large working model), exotic gardens, and a cottage museum maintained and

staffed on a voluntary basis by members of the Old Malahide Society. The museum's exhibits include numerous
artifacts from local archaeological digs, including the
second-oldest stone axhead ever discovered in Ireland,
dating from 2000 B.C.

About 5 km (3 miles) south of Malahide (on the main
Dublin road) is St. Doulagh's, a charming, stone-roofed
ninth-century church claiming to be the oldest still in use
in Ireland (take bus 42 or 43 from Beresford Place, opposite the Custom House lawn).

Howth

The area of Howth, southeast of Malahide, is a treasure
house of legend, myth, and history. At the dawn of Irish
history, the Parthalons and the Firbolg peoples lived on
this peninsula, mining for copper, until they were con-
quered over the course of the fifth to first century B.C. by
the Celtic Gaels, who, with their great iron swords, were
not long in hacking through the light copper-made weapons of the Firbolg. Criomthain, the first Gaelic chieftain of
the locality (a cairn on the summit is said to cover his
remains), had his fortress near the site of the present
Bailey lighthouse. From here he sailed with his warriors
to Roman Britain to pillage and to do battle, returning
with vessels laden with plunder and slaves. Finn mac
Cumhail's band of Celtic warriors, the legendary Fianna,
ever on the lookout for approaching war vessels, had a
military post here in ancient times; the summit commands an extensive view not only of Dublin Bay and the
Wicklow Mountains but also of the peaks of the Mournes
more than 60 miles to the north and, in favorable conditions, the distant Welsh mountains across the Irish Sea.

From this summit were first glimpsed the dreaded
Viking longships of the eighth century. For more than two
centuries these northern pirates plundered Ireland and
in the process established their colonies along the coast
in places like Howth. They in turn watched fearfully as the
mail-clad Norman horsemen rode out from Dublin—a
new breed of ruthless adventurers, aristocratic in their
pretensions, skilled in the arts of the new warfare—led
by the fearless Sir Almeric Tristram. With his men-at-arms
and bowmen Sir Almeric slaughtered the Norsemen of
Howth near a brook on the hillside that still bears the
awesome name of the Bloody Stream. When the lands of
Howth, thus acquired by the sword, were confirmed by

England's King John, Sir Almeric thereupon assumed the surname St. Lawrence, the name borne by his descendants at Howth to this day.

The splendid **Howth Castle** of his descendants, 15 minutes from the DART station or the number 31 bus stop, is a Norman keep consisting of battlements flanked by towers with some 18th-century additions and modifications. Its armory contains Sir Almeric's massive two-handed sword, an 800-year-old weapon he brought from a shrine in Normandy for the purpose of wresting half an Irish county from its warlike inhabitants. The grounds of the castle—famous for their 2,000 species of rhododendrons—are equally a reminder of Howth's turbulent past. A dolmen there is said to be the burial place of Aideen, who died of grief when she learned of the death of her princely husband, Oscar, slain in battle in A.D. 248. And because the gates of the castle were once locked against the Gaelic pirate-queen Grace O'Malley (who sought shelter and sustenance after a stormy sea voyage from England), she later kidnapped the son and heir of the St. Lawrences and held him prisoner until the lord of Howth gave a written pledge never to close the gate again at suppertime. This condition was observed faithfully by generations of St. Lawrences for more than 200 years, and then was modified by the present custom of always setting an extra place at the dinner table for any "unexpected guest."

The castle's present occupant, Christopher Gaisford St. Lawrence, is a descendant in the female line of the original Sir Almeric and thus represents the present generation of a family that has played a central role in the history of the Howth Peninsula for more than 800 years. He has opened up the estate—but not the castle—to the public with a 31-room hotel, the **Deer Park**, and an 18-hole golf course, both in picturesque settings and offering magnificent views out over the isle of Ireland's Eye toward the Mountains of Mourne. (See Accommodations, below, for more information on the Deer Park Hotel.)

A mile northeast of Howth Harbour—and forming a natural breakwater—lies the picturesque and uninhabited island of **Ireland's Eye**, about 60 acres of rocky, mountainous land mostly covered by tall ferns and with only two buildings: a deserted Martello tower and the ruins of Saint Nessan's sixth-century monastic church. Boat trips from Howth Harbour to the island in summertime have always been popular with day visitors from the city, as has been fishing from the harbor piers or waiting for the herring boats to come in with their catch on Thursday evenings. (The 40-odd boats of the fishing fleet pull in to the west pier anytime between 6:30 and 10:00 P.M. Local fish merchant Mick Wright welcomes visitors to his premises to see the process of "salmon smoking" and to enjoy a tasting of this Irish delicacy.)

The footprint of King George IV can still be seen on the jetty at the end of Howth's west pier, where he landed unexpectedly in 1821, much to the surprise of the local fisherfolk—and to the chagrin of the civic dignitaries and populace of Dún Laoghaire, on the southern side of Dublin Bay, who had been expecting him and who had provided a brand-new royal slipway, a band, a pavilion, a guard of honor, and countless flags and buntings. (He made amends a month later at the conclusion of his visit by departing from Dún Laoghaire, allowing the citizens to rename their harbor village Kingstown and to erect a George IV Testimonial Obelisk, which Thackeray later described as "hideous ... an obelisk stuck on four fat balls and surmounted with a crown on a cushion ... the latter were not bad emblems perhaps of the monarch in whose honor they were raised." The obelisk can still be seen at Dún Laoghaire, minus one of its balls, the result of a Republican bomb attempt to remove this royal reminder.)

While in Howth be sure to take in the fishing fleet (Thursday evenings, mentioned above); the new Marina and Yacht Club House; the cliff walks from Balscadden to the Bailey lighthouse; Howth's Tram and Transport Museum (Howth Castle Estate, open Saturdays, Sundays, and bank holidays from 2:00 to 5:00 P.M.; for further information contact Liam Kelly, Tel: 01/848-0831; and the **Abbey Tavern**, Abbey Street, with its warm turf fires, original stone walls, flagged floors, and gaslights. The Abbey Tavern specializes in fish dishes and traditional ballad entertainment nightly. Reservations are essential; Tel: (01) 39-03-07. Boats for hire and fishing parties can be arranged through Laurence Hudson, East Pier, Tel: (01) 32-42-55.

St. Mary's Abbey (14th century) in Howth Village, though roofless, is still a reasonably well preserved ruin containing the 1462 altar tomb of Sir Christopher St. Lawrence and his wife, Anne. The abbey was once used by smugglers for storing their contraband.

GETTING AROUND

Simple—just walk.

Not from Dublin Airport or the ferry terminals, of course; there are bus and train link services to those two Dublin gateways from the city center. Bus service between the center and Dublin Airport runs approximately every 25 minutes from Busaras, the central bus station in Store Street. The 41A Dublin city bus service also runs between Eden Quay (off O'Connell Street on the north bank of the river) and the airport. There is taxi service, but unfortunately it can be a shock to the purse when you look and sound like a foreigner fresh off the plane. Any taxi you use should have a meter. The fare from the airport to the city center should be about £10 to £12.

Though the city center is best seen on foot, you can also travel by public transport, by rental car, or by bicycle—the last for the city area, perhaps, and a car when you intend to move farther afield into the countryside. You can get details about renting both from tourist information offices. Car-hire (rental) firms, as usual, have desks at the airport. Note that signposting in Dublin city leaves a lot to be desired, so drive with a navigator and a good map.

CIE (Coras Iompair Eireann) is the umbrella semi-state body for three transport companies: **Dublin Bus** (serving Dublin; Tel: 01/73-42-22), Bus Eireann, a.k.a. **Irish Bus** (serving provincial areas from Dublin; Tel: 01/36-61-11), and **Irish Rail**, including DART suburban rail (Tel: 01/36-62-22). Hours for all three information offices are 9:00 A.M. to 7:00 P.M. weekdays and 10:00 A.M. to 7:00 P.M. on Sundays and holidays. Timetables, including details of money-saving commuter tickets, can be purchased from newsagents and bookshops.

Bus drivers won't be too impatient if you don't have the exact change on entry, or if you aren't sure where you are going. However, look closely at the numbers on the stop and ask someone in line, if possible. Destinations (and numbers) are usually written in Irish and English on the bus itself. Don't rely on the service running on time; it won't. Depending on your destination, the fare will range between 55p and 110p.

The efficient DART suburban rail service, which runs from 6:30 A.M. to 11:30 P.M., goes overland around Dublin Bay, linking Howth on the North Side to Bray on the South Side, via the city center. The neighborhoods of all DART stations are fairly well signposted with directional aids sporting the distinctive DART livery of light green and dark green and its logo. Timetables can be obtained free of charge at all stations, tourist-information offices, and most local travel agents. Tickets can be purchased and information acquired regarding times, destinations, and the like at each station's manned ticket office. A special Dublin Explorer ticket that leaves you change out of a £10 note offers unlimited bus and rail (including DART) transport in Dublin city *and* county within a 20-mile radius. Special concessionary tickets on bus and train services are worth inquiring about at the Dublin Tourism Office, 14 Upper O'Connell Street (Tel: 01/74-77-33), as terms and rates can vary from year to year.

Opposite the tourism office at 59 Upper O'Connell Street is the Dublin Bus office, where you can make reservations for city or south and north Dublin coastal tours that run in open-deck buses during the summer (Tel: 01/73-42-22). Dublin Bus also runs Heritage Trail tours of the city from May 1 to September 30, with continuous commentary by an experienced driver/guide. The £5 "all day" ticket allows you to hop on and off the buses as often as you wish from the ten strategically located Heritage Trail bus stops, near sites such as the Garden of Remembrance, Writers Museum, Trinity College, and Dublin Castle. If you intend to travel out of the city, the Irish Rail/Irish Bus Rambler ticket is a very good value, allowing you unlimited travel by rail, express buses, and local services for £78 for 8 days or £115 for 15 days.

Getting out of Dublin

Apart from the DART and coastal commuter train stations—Connolly Station (Amiens Street), Tara Street, and Pearse Street are the main ones—the two main railway stations linking Dublin to the rest of the country are **Heuston Station** off Parkgate Street in the west and, again, **Connolly Station** on Amiens Street.

There are interconnecting buses between Connolly and Heuston stations, and from the latter to the city center (by O'Connell Bridge) or to Busaras, the central provincial bus station in Store Street. For special excursions and weekend tours, inquire at the Dublin Tourism Office on Upper O'Connell Street or phone Irish Bus and Irish Rail (see above for the numbers).

ACCOMMODATIONS

A well-known London art critic came over to Ireland a few years ago to give a lecture at Trinity College, Dublin. An Irish friend recommended that she and her husband stay in the Royal Hibernian Hotel in Dawson Street, as she was on an expenses-paid trip. Later the friend asked her what she thought. Her reply was ecstatic—not because of the luxurious rooms, the silver service, or the fact that her presence was mentioned in the Social and Personal column of the *Irish Times* the following day. Rather, what tickled the art critic was the advice that she and her husband received when ordering sandwiches at midnight. The obliging waitress offered a choice of ham, cheese, beef, or chicken. "Oh, and there's turkey," the young woman added. The couple ordered turkey, and the waitress protested. "You see," she explained to them, "if you order chicken, you are going to get turkey anyway. And chicken's a lot cheaper."

It's that sort of thoughtful touch that has given Irish hospitality a good name abroad. Sadly, the Royal Hibernian Hotel has been demolished and Dublin has taken on some of that impersonal air that you might find in any European city. *Some,* anyway. Dublin accommodation may be expensive, but it still has a charming informality about it.

Basically there are two types: hotels and guest houses. Hotels, generally providing meals as well as sleeping quarters and bar service, are graded by Bord Fáilte, the Irish Tourist Board, into A*, A, B*, B, and C. Guest houses vary from the purpose-built to the period-style residences, their main attraction being the personal attention and informal atmosphere therein. Bord Fáilte also grades guest houses into A, B*, B, and C. To find out precisely what these gradings mean, consult the *Ireland Guest Guide* published annually by Bord Fáilte, which can be purchased from most of their information offices or direct from Bord Fáilte, Baggot Street Bridge, Dublin 2, Ireland; Tel: (01) 76-58-71 or 61-65-00. This guide, which is simply a list, not a critical review, also gives rates for those hotels and guest houses that offer room only or bed and breakfast, while reserving another section for a scale of maximum charges for overnight and inclusive accommodation.

Three things to note: First, as a rule there is a big jump between first- and third-class hotel accommodation. Secondly, staying in Dublin can be expensive, by European standards at least. Lack of competition here, especially during the off-season, can be blamed for the fact that even less-central premises will happily charge you £40 a night, and more. And lastly, the national telephone network is being overhauled. As of April 1993 all Dublin six-digit telephone numbers beginning with 60, 61, 63, 64, and 68 will be preceded by a seventh digit, "6"; those six-digit numbers beginning with 90, 92, 93, 94, 96, and 97 will be preceded by a "4."

Bord Fáilte has a Central Reservation Service for booking accommodations at the Dublin Tourism Office at 14 Upper O'Connell Street, Dublin 1 (Tel: 01/74-77-33; Fax: 01/78-62-75—for bookings with Access, MasterCard, and Visa). Bord Fáilte also has a desk at Dublin Airport and Dún Laoghaire ferry port, and there are regional tourism offices throughout the country. **The Hidden Ireland** is a private organization offering accommodations in private country houses that possess architectural character and merit (and, they say, owners to match); Tel: (01) 68-64-63; Fax: (01) 68-65-78. You may also book directly or through your travel agent, of course, or through the nearest Irish Tourist Board office in your country.

First of all, decide where you want to be: Dublin is not a sprawling city, and the suburbs are within easy reach. Therefore, if you have a car or if you yearn for more relaxed surroundings, there are a number of competitively priced hotels and guest houses outside of the city center.

Note that the South Side area is in demand during the Royal Dublin Society's Spring Show in May and the Horse Show in August; weekends of international rugby matches can also be hectic.

Tipping is low in Ireland, at 10 percent. Before booking, check that your hotel doesn't run discos and conferences too frequently for your comfort. And be prepared for the hearty Irish breakfast of juicy pork sausages, rashers (bacon), fried eggs, tasty black pudding—and good strong tea that you could trot a horse and four over.

The hotels and guest houses discussed below are presented geographically, generally from the most expensive to the least. Note that the rate ranges given here are for the low and high seasons in 1993; for up-to-the-minute rate information it is always wise to telephone before booking. Unless otherwise indicated, rates are per person sharing and do not include meals or service.

The telephone country code for the Republic of Ireland is 353; the city code for Dublin is 01.

City Center and Immediate Environs

Within the city center itself, the **Shelbourne Hotel** on St. Stephen's Green has to be one of the most elegant accommodations—and most expensive. Statues of two nubile slave girls guard the entrance to the mid-19th-century building, where the Irish Constitution was drafted in 1922. It has welcomed, and continues to receive, many celebrated guests. Looking out onto landscaped parkland that was donated to the capital by the Guinness family, the hotel is a few minutes' walk from shops, theaters, and the important sights of the city. Politicians fresh from Dáil Eireann down in Kildare Street frequent the bar; it has a fine restaurant, and afternoon tea in the high-ceilinged parlor overlooking the Green is an experience.

27 St. Stephen's Green, Dublin 2. Tel: 76-64-71; Fax: 61-60-06. £97.50.

The **Westbury Hotel,** in Clarendon Street, west of Grafton, is one of the city's most luxurious hotels, with spacious bedrooms of mahogany and brass. Its elegant upper foyer of marble, wood paneling, and Chippendale leads to bars and a restaurant, and is the haunt of public-relations consultants promoting blockbuster authors—but even they may find the room rates a mite expensive.

Grafton Street, Dublin 2. Tel: 679-1122; Fax: 679-70-78; in U.S., Tel: (800) 223-6800 or (212) 838-3110. £75.

The **Central Hotel** on Exchequer Street might not seem very central, but it is in fact in an ideal location—just three minutes' walk up Wicklow Street from Grafton Street. It is comfortable, efficient, unpretentious, and imaginative. Who would ever guess from its restrained exterior that it has earned a reputation for one of the most unusual bridal suites in the city. Ask for a peep into the Rooster Room while you are there.

Exchequer Street, Dublin 2. Tel: 679-7302; Fax: 679-7303. £35–£47.50.

Buswell's, close to the Irish parliament in Molesworth Street south of Trinity College, is very cozy and genteel, with a loyal political clientele and a family-run atmosphere.

25–26 Molesworth Street, Dublin 2. Tel: 76-40-13; Fax: 76-20-90. £41–£43.

Blooms Hotel in Anglesea Street, near Trinity College and behind the Central Bank, is convenient and comfortable. It is in the "A" category, though at the less expensive end of the spectrum. It has a popular restaurant, and its noisy bar attracts a young after-work clientele on Fridays.

Anglesea Street, Dublin 2. Tel: 71-56-22; Fax: 71-59-97; in U.S., Tel: (800) 223-0888 or (212) 545-2222. £50–£55.

The **Clarence Hotel** on Wellington Quay, overlooking the Liffey, has been a favorite with Irish visitors to the capital for many years. Within sight of the Ha'penny Bridge, it has a Regency air and a friendly atmosphere. Not what you would call elegant or luxurious, but homey. It has two restaurants and bars and is very close to the Olympia Theatre and the Project Arts Centre behind.

6–8 Wellington Quay, Dublin 2. Tel: 77-61-78; Fax: 77-74-87. £27.50–£34.50, breakfast and service included.

The **Harcourt Hotel** on Harcourt Street is worth mentioning for its lack of pretension as well as its location; it is within five minutes of Grafton Street shopping, and close to St. Stephen's Green and the city center. Reasonably priced, it is popular with jazz aficionados on Sunday evenings.

60 Harcourt Street, Dublin 2. Tel: 78-36-77; Fax: 78-36-77. £35, breakfast and service included.

A plethora of small, comfortable hotels have opened in the city center in recent years in response to the Irish government's introduction, for a limited period, of tax incentives. **Longfields** in Fitzwilliam Street, between Baggot Street and the Georgian elegance of Merrion Square, is a good example. It has period furnishings, a well-regarded restaurant, and warm service, while being close enough to government buildings, the National Gallery, and the administrative heart of the city to do a brisk business in both accommodation and meals.

9–10 Lower Fitzwilliam Street, Dublin 2. Tel: 76-13-67; Fax: 76-15-42. £49.50, breakfast included.

Similarly, **The Grey Door Rooms** is round the corner from Merrion Row in Upper Pembroke Street. Handsomely furnished, the seven spacious rooms are an extension of an excellent and established restaurant (see Dining, below).

23 Upper Pembroke Street, Dublin 2. Tel: 76-32-86; Fax: 76-32-87. £42.50.

Just east of St. Stephen's Green, the extremely comfortable **Georgian House** on Lower Baggot Street above the Ante Room restaurant offers restrained luxury in a 200-year-old house.

20–21 Lower Baggot Street, Dublin 2. Tel: 61-88-32; Fax: 61-88-34. £24.40–£36, breakfast included.

Ten minutes away from the center-city bustle in the business and diplomatic area of Dublin, the tree-shaded **Berkeley Court** in Lansdowne Road, Ballsbridge is the haunt of film stars, rock stars, and any other stars that shoot into Dublin. This hotel, with its own restaurant, grill, and bar, attracts interesting and affluent guests.

Lansdowne Road, Ballsbridge, Dublin 4. Tel: 60-17-11; Fax: 61-72-38; in U.S., (800) 223-6800 or (212) 838-3110. £75.

Similarly high on the reputation and price list are **Jury's Hotel and Towers**, which moved from College Green in the heart of the city to Ballsbridge in 1972 and has recently undergone an impressive extension, and the luxurious **Burlington Hotel**, with its brash mock-palatial façade looking out onto Upper Leeson Street. Both—like the Berkeley Court—are large, modern international hotels south of the Grand Canal in the suburbs, though still within walking distance of the center. They are popular with large tour groups, and both have cabarets in the summer season. The bar at Jury's is very popular among Dubliners, and its 23-hour coffee shop is a regular haunt for night-owls with an appetite.

Jury's Hotel and Towers, Pembroke Road, Ballsbridge, Dublin 4. Tel: 60-50-00; Fax: 60-55-40; in U.S., Tel: (800) 843-6664; in Canada, Tel: (800) 268-1133; in London, Tel: (81) 569-5555 or (71) 937-8033; in U.K., Tel: (0345) 01-01-01. £57.50–£87.50.

Burlington Hotel, Upper Leeson Street, Dublin 4. Tel: 60-52-22; Fax: 60-84-96; in U.S., Tel: (212) 593-4220. £47.50–£52.50.

The **Mount Herbert** on Herbert Road, Ballsbridge, is only a few minutes' walk down Landsdowne Road from big hotels such as Jury's, but its rates are much lower. The hotel, a section of which was once the home of a lord, is popular with visitors from Northern Ireland during Horse Show Week and during international rugby matches in the Lansdowne Road stadium just around the corner.

Mount Herbert, Herbert Road, Ballsbridge, Dublin 4. Tel: 68-43-21; Fax: 60-70-77. £24.95, including breakfast and service.

On the North Side, also central, the **Gresham Hotel** on O'Connell Street has been graced by the likes of Ronald Reagan, General Eisenhower, Elizabeth Taylor, Marlene Dietrich, and Danny Kaye. Founded in 1817 and rebuilt after damage in the 1916 Rising, it retains some Old World style, despite recent refurbishment. Be prepared, however, to share the hotel with innumerable tour groups.

23 Upper O'Connell Street, Dublin 1. Tel: 74-68-81; Fax: 78-71-75; in U.S., Tel: (800) 221-4832. £55–£70.

The generally high standard of guest-house accommodation in Dublin makes it almost unfair to single out particular establishments. **Kilronan House**, however, is worth mentioning; it is well established, well run, and located south of University College (below St. Stephen's Green), within walking distance of all major sites.

70 Adelaide Road, Dublin 2. Tel: 75-52-66; Fax: 78-28-41. £26–£35, breakfast included.

Such are Dublin hotel rates that it is good to know about such less expensive alternatives as hostels. **An Oige's Dublin International Youth Hostel** at 61 Mountjoy Street on the North Side (Tel: 30-17-66) has cheap dormitory-style accommodations. From £7–£9 for IYHA members (the membership fee of £7.50 allows use of all hostels). The **Dublin Tourist Hotel** at 2–5 Frenchman's Lane, also on the North Side, is next to the central bus station at Store Street, and offers dormitory-, double-, or single-room accommodations in a converted wine warehouse at very low rates. £5.50–£12.50. Tel: (01) 36-38-77. **Kinlay House** at 2–12 Lord Edward Street, on the South Side just up from the Olympia Theatre and close to Christ Church Cathedral and Viking Dublin, offers hostel-style bed and breakfast and is highly recommended. Tel: 679-6644; Fax: 679-7437. £8.50–£10.50, breakfast included.

Farther Out

Overlooking Dublin Bay, the suburb of Dún Laoghaire on the South Side has some fine hotels and guest houses— as befits its former name of Kingstown—such as the **Royal Marine Hotel**, which combines Victorian elegance with 20th-century comforts. It commands an imposing view of the ferry port and the yachting activity. There's plenty of walking out on the extensive piers, built by convicts to shelter the 240-acre harbor.

Marine Road, Dún Laoghaire, County Dublin. Tel: 280-1911; Fax: 280-1089. £45–£60.

Farther down the coast, the **Killiney Court Hotel** has an irresistible location overlooking Killiney Bay. The breathtaking panoramic view to sea has often been compared to the Bay of Naples, and the hotel itself is right next to the DART suburban rail station. Unfortunately, the Killiney

Court is very popular for wedding receptions and conferences.

Killiney, County Dublin. Tel: 285-1622; Fax: 285-2085. £31.50–£34.50.

Howth Harbour, the North Side fishing port, is similarly blessed with the DART suburban railway service and excellent walks. The comfortable **St. Lawrence**, facing the fishing harbor, and the intimate **Howth Lodge Hotel** are two good choices for those who wish to amble along Howth Head every morning before breakfast and take in the fine views of Dublin Bay to the south.

St. Lawrence Hotel, Harbour Road, Howth, County Dublin. Tel: 32-26-43; Fax: 39-03-46. £26 (breakfast included).

Howth Lodge Hotel, Howth Road, Howth, County Dublin. Tel: 32-10-10; Fax: 32-22-68. £24.50–£29.50.

For golfers, the **Deer Park Hotel and Golf Courses** is a must, a comfortable, modern hotel overlooking Howth Castle, on extensive grounds. Many of its rooms have stunning views—on clear days—of the island known as Ireland's Eye and, beyond, of Lambay Island. The hotel offers golf packages and residents have access to its three courses.

Howth, County Dublin. Tel: 32-26-24; Fax: (01) 39-24-05. £26, breakfast included.

—Lorna Siggins

DINING

Travel and travellers have been the savior of the Irish restaurateur. Without both, the Irish would still be completely oblivious to the delight of good food. For, apart from the time of the famine that decimated the Irish population in the last century, food has always been plentiful, and few really appreciate or, some say, know how to cook the materials that abound. But there's still nothing like brown soda bread; the Irish breakfast of bacon, eggs, and sausages is a hearty one; and traditional dishes, when cooked properly, are something to be proud of. That's not just Irish stew and bacon and cabbage.

Food is important to Dublin's restaurant clientele, but atmosphere ranks higher. We're not talking about a physical location but ambience. Restaurants come into fashion for no particular reason, and some make their exits just as quickly. Others work hard to keep their regular, influential customers. Dublin has no shortage of restaurants, but eating out is not cheap.

Note that "full licence" entitles the restaurant to provide a full range of alcoholic drinks, while "wine licence" means just that. New legislation has extended full licensing to more restaurants.

We've taken Dublin by area, rather than by type of cuisine—but you can get a taste of everything here, from Italian to Japanese. Phone numbers are given where reservations are advisable.

O'Connell Street/Westmoreland Street Area

Bewley's Oriental Café on Westmoreland Street on the South Side is one of the four famous coffeehouses in the city center founded by the Quaker Bewley family, and it serves a hearty breakfast. Once frequented by James Joyce, it has wood-paneled walls and marble-top tables and is popular with the literati, but it has undergone a few changes since its opening in 1916. Open from 7:30 A.M. to 7:30 P.M. Monday through Saturday and from 10:00 A.M. to 6:00 P.M. on Sundays. The first Bewleys Hotel is due for completion here in early 1993. **Middays** in the Peacock Theatre (below the Abbey Theatre) in Lower Abbey Street is a popular self-service lunchtime restaurant, ideal if you are in the area to buy theater tickets. The homemade fare has a healthy vegetarian emphasis. No credit cards.

Temple Bar

Off Westmoreland Street, across the Liffey, Temple Bar (an extension of Fleet Street, past Bewley's side entrance) is the home of an interesting selection of lunchtime/ evening restaurants in an area that has been designated an inner-city renewal project. The **Pizzeria Italia** at 23 Temple Bar fills up quickly when it opens at noon, and at night the waiter will take your name and point you toward the local pub while you wait. A small high-stool, checkered-tablecloth establishment, it is relatively cheap. Closed Sundays. No credit cards. A couple of doors away is **Gallagher's Boxty House** at 20–21 Temple Bar. This is the nearest you'll get to an "Irish ethnic restaurant." The emphasis is on the "boxty," or potato cake, stuffed with a variety of delicious fillings. Not to everybody's taste, but definitely worth trying once. There's a friendly atmosphere, and the background music (Irish traditional) is usually good.

Next door at number 22 is **Le Restaurant Casablanca**. As the name suggests, the menu is Moroccan. Both Gallagher's and Le Restaurant are a little overshadowed by the fashionable **Elephant & Castle**, a little farther up the street. This American-style restaurant renowned for its healthy portions has a Caesar salad that would feed a Roman army! The restaurant is clean, the staff friendly and efficient, the coffee good, and the prices reasonable. Breakfast is served from 8:00 A.M.

Still in the warren of little streets running down to the Liffey in the Temple Bar area, the **Well-Fed Café** at the Dublin Resource Centre, 6 Crow Street, adjoining a worker's co-op, is a good place for lunch, offering vegetarian fare, including soups, salads, lasagne, and quiche. Open until 4:30 P.M.; cash only.

Tante Zoe's at 1 Crow Street offers Cajun-Creole cuisine, with fish claws 'n' tails as a typical appetizer. Open for lunch and dinner six days, for dinner only on Sundays.

College Green West to Christchurch Hill

Little Lisbon, a Portuguese restaurant beside the Central Bank at the junction of Dame and Fownes streets, makes the most of Irish fish. You can bring your own wine— unusual for Dublin restaurants. No credit cards.

Caesar's at 18 Dame Street and **Nico's** at number 53 are lively, well-established Italian restaurants, moderately priced and close to the Olympia Theatre, while the **Lord Edward** at 23 Christchurch Place, named after Lord Edward Fitzgerald who led the United Irishmen in the abortive 1798 Rising, excels in fish. The Lord Edward is quite expensive, but worth it for the service and attention to detail. Closed Sundays and Mondays; Tel: (01) 54-24-20. At **Burdock's**, next door in 900-year-old Werburgh Street, people come from all over Dublin to wait in the rain for a special. Burdock's is a fish-and-chips take-away, one of the best in the city (or *the* best, according to your source).

The **Old Dublin** at 90–91 Francis Street is right in the heart of medieval Dublin, near Dubh Linn (Black Pool), one of the city's first settlements. The Old Dublin excels in Russian and Scandinavian cuisine served in a reserved atmosphere, and the prices reflect it; fish is a forte. It's advisable to book in advance; Tel: (01) 54-20-28.

South Great George's Street/Camden Street

The **Marks Brothers** on 7 South Great George's Street on the South Side has some of the best sandwiches in town, great dishes for vegetarians, and is popular with students—thus the long lines. Lunch only. Farther south, at 31 Upper Camden Street, **Oisin's Irish Restaurant** serves what one critic describes as "indigenous food":

Irish stew, bacon and cabbage, spiced beef, and the infamous Dublin coddle, a mixture of potatoes and other vegetables, sausage, bacon, and additional ingredients, depending on where you eat it. Expect a throat-scorching sup of *poitín,* that devilish Irish firewater, when you arrive. Tel: (01) 75-34-33; open for group bookings only on Sundays, and closed Monday nights.

The Kapriol at 45 Lower Camden Street has a reputation for serving some of the best regional Italian food in Dublin—and that's with quite a bit of competition from compatriots of the Peruzzi family. Prices are on the high side; however, you should find that one course makes a filling meal. Make sure to splurge on one of their irresistible desserts (try the crème caramel if you can be tempted). Closed Sundays; Tel: (01) 75-12-35.

La Fiesta at number 41 is an intimate family restaurant as well, but the accents are Irish and the menu is best described as Mediterranean. La Fiesta is run by the ever-efficient Fitzer family, who know how to knock off some of the best salads in Dublin. Closed Sundays; Tel: (01) 75-31-09.

Grafton Street/Nassau Street
There are plenty of interesting little tributaries off of Grafton Street itself. This main shopping street is in effect a southern extension of O'Connell and Westmoreland streets. Starting with Andrew Street, at the Trinity College end, there's the intimate and friendly **Trocadero**, with realistic prices. The "Troc," as it is fondly known among theatergoers and others who like it for its night-owl hours, has an atmosphere described as "stagey"; its walls are festooned with photos of familiar faces from the acting profession. Booking is strongly advised; Tel: (01) 77-55-45. Opposite the Trocadero is the **Cedar Tree,** a Lebanese restaurant with a large fountain and delicious food that is deservedly popular with those many Irish who have worked in the Middle East. Tel: (01) 77-21-21.

The **Old Stand** in Exchequer Street and the **Stag's Head** in Dame Court are two of many pubs in the area known for a good lunch, while the pricey **Radjoot Tandoori** at 26–28 Clarendon Street—near the Westbury Centre—is one of Dublin's finest Indian restaurants; Tel: (01) 679-4274. There are plenty of dining spots within and around the Powerscourt Townhouse Centre in South William Street. Try the excellent **Periwinkle** seafood bar tucked away on the ground floor of the Centre, with its sumptuous chowder, for lunch. In Johnston's Court, linking the Clarendon Street entrance to Grafton Street, the **Wildebeest** (formerly known as the Colony) is very "in," serving everything from pasta to steak to fish à la carte at student prices, and with live music at night; open for lunch and dinner Monday through Saturday. The **Cornucopia**, at 19 Wicklow Street, has been awarded the title of best vegetarian restaurant in the country, with a breakfast menu from 8:00 A.M. (Saturdays 9:00 A.M.) that offers vegetarian sausages and scrambled free-range eggs. For those eating on the premises, seating is on cramped stools. Open till 9:00 P.M. six days, closed Sundays.

In Grafton Street itself, there's a refurbished branch of **Bewley's Oriental Café** for breakfast or lunch seven days a week, with a waitress-service mezzanine level overlooking the street and lots of the popular sticky buns. Monday to Saturday 7:30 A.M. to 10:00 P.M., Sundays 9:30 A.M. to 7:00 P.M. **Captain America's**, also in Grafton, was the first of its type to hit Dublin: inexpensive hamburgers, Tex-Mex, and barbeque, with loud music and a fully licensed bar.

Such is the Irish climate that street cafés appear only during warm summer weather, between showers. For a street-side version of Café Costes on the Place des Innocents in Paris, try the **Buttery Brasserie** on the Royal Hibernian Way, which links Dawson Street to Grafton Street via Duke Street. Full bar, coffee, tea, and lunchtime salads—and it becomes a trendy pub at night.

Everybody who is anybody in Dublin has supped at one time or another in **George's Bistro** at 29 South Frederick Street, off Nassau. Its late opening hours and its proximity to the Irish parliament help to attract what one reviewer describes as "the most powerful in the land"— depending on your point of view. A resident team of musicians provides the "bistro" bit on two floors. Closed Sundays; Tel: (01) 679-7000.

In Nassau Street along the southern side of Trinity College, the **Kilkenny Kitchen** within the Kilkenny Shop— itself very interesting for regional crafts—is always bustling, daytime only, while the nearby **Coffee Bean** at lunch becomes **Gastrognome** in the evening, one of the city's finest health food and vegetarian restaurants, specializing in salads, quiches, and lasagne; reasonably priced with a good view of the playing fields in Trinity. Closed Sunday and Monday; no credit cards. Tel: (01) 679-5123.

St. Stephen's Green Area

The Commons at 86 St. Stephen's Green is definitely not common. Housed in the basement of Newman House, an 18th-century university establishment built by Robert Chappell Whaley (father of Buck), it is very European in style. The one clear concession to dear old dirty Dublin is the Joycean theme in the art collection. Smart, efficient, and pricey, it offers nouvelle cuisine *bien sûr*. Tel: (01) 75-25-97. Open Monday through Friday for lunch, and Monday through Saturday for dinner. **Mitchell's**, in the cellar of its own wine shop in Kildare Street, is an expensive lunch venue for the captains of industry—and of politics, Mitchell's being within spitting distance of the Irish parliament.

Merrion Row/Baggot Street/Merrion Square

The **Grey Door** at 23 Upper Pembroke Street off Baggot is a cozy, exquisite dining room within the former drawing room of a Georgian house. It specializes in Russian and Scandinavian cuisine and is quite expensive. Closed Sundays; Tel: (01) 76-32-86.

The **Unicorn** at 12 Merrion Court off Merrion Row is a favorite of the aspiring and actual intelligentsia, who also frequent Doheny and Nesbitt's pub nearby. One of Dublin's established Italian restaurants, with a lovely seafood pizza, Unicorn is particularly lively during Saturday lunch hours. Closed Sundays; Tel: (01) 76-21-82.

Turn down into Merrion Square and to the restaurant within the **National Gallery**; run by Fitzer's of Camden Street, it is excellent for lunch, and also is open until 8:00 P.M. on Thursdays. Closed Mondays.

You may need a map to locate 46 St. James's Place and **Patrick Guilbaud** (first locate St. James's Street, off Lower Baggot Street). Serving superb French cuisine in a spacious room with natural lighting, the place has received accolades for "supreme excellence." It's pretentious, pricey, and popular with gossip columnists. Closed Sundays. Booking advised; Tel: (01) 76-41-92.

Off the Beaten Track

You probably have enough restaurant choices in the city itself to keep you from starving, but a few out-of-the-way spots are worth mentioning if you happen to be in the vicinity.

North Side. Out in the fishing port of Howth at the head of the East Pier, the **King Sitric**, named after the first king of Dublin, has a reputation for seafood, with prices on the high side. It's situated in a Georgian house that was once the home of Howth's harbormaster, and serves such delights as Howth crab and lobster, squid, John Dory fish, and black sole. Closed Sundays; Tel: (01) 32-52-35. The **Abbey Tavern** in the village itself is a tourist oriented Old World tavern with stone walls, flagged floors, Irish music, sirloin steaks, and more. It's quite expensive, and reservations are advised; Tel: (01) 39-03-07.

South Side. A good Sunday brunch venue is at the **Royal Hospital**, Kilmainham, to the southwest of the city center. The price covers food, music, and a guided tour of the current exhibitions.

In Ballsbridge, if you tire of **Jury's Coffee Dock** (open 23 hours a day in Jury's Hotel, with a standard menu for both meals and snacks and efficient service night and day) there's the elegant and expensive **Kițe's** at 15–17 Ballsbridge Terrace, serving Cantonese food; Tel: (01) 60-74-15. **Le Coq Hardi**, in a Georgian town house at 35 Pembroke Road, is constantly winning awards for its nouvelle cuisine. It combines the best of French and Irish cooking with such dishes as cabbage with quail and chicken and bacon baked in Irish whiskey. Expensive. Tel: (01) 68-41-30. Middle Eastern *baba ganouj, taramosalata,* and other Mediterranean dishes feature on the versatile menu of **Senor Sassi's**, one of the city's more recent brasseries. It's a little out of the way, down the Grand Canal at 146 Upper Leeson Street; Tel: (01) 68-45-44. A group can eat well here and cross over to O'Brien's pub for a pint afterwards.

On the Grand Canal at Portobello near the suburb of Rathmines, **Locks** at 1 Windsor Terrace has made a name for itself as a provincial French restaurant; expensive and highly recommended. Closed Sundays; Tel: (01) 54-33-91.

Blackrock, a suburb on the South Side coast, can boast the luxury Japanese restaurant **Ayumi-Ya** in Newtownpark Avenue. **Restaurant na Mara** in Dún Laoghaire farther along the coast resides in what was the Kingstown railway terminal building in the 19th century. It's formal and quite expensive, but good for fish. Tel: (01) 280-6767 or 0509.

The **Beaufield Mews** in Woodlands Avenue, Stillorgan (off the Dublin–Wicklow road), is ten minutes south of the city. This 18th-century restaurant claims to be Dublin's oldest, and long-standing trees shelter the original cobbled courtyard. Family-owned, Beaufield Mews is medium-priced with a European menu; it also has an antiques shop in the loft. Open Tuesday to Saturday, 3:00 to 9:00 P.M. Also in Stillorgan at 4 Lower Kilmacud Road is **Chinese Sichuan**. The only restaurant sponsored by the Chinese government in all of Britain and Ireland, it offers fantastic food, excellent service, and incredible value. Booking advised; Tel: (01) 288-4817 or 9560. Next to Chinese Sichuan is **Mr. Hung**, a Thai restaurant opened in 1991 by a Hong Kong restaurateur. It's relatively inexpensive and is open seven days a week. Booking is advisable on weekends; Tel: (01) 288-8727. All three of these restaurants are a taxi ride from the city center.

Really in Wicklow territory, but within driving distance of Dublin—and worth the journey if your credit is good—are three dining spots of note. **Tinakilly House**, a restored Victorian country house in Rathnew and the former home of Captain Robert Halpin, first officer of the *Great Eastern,* who laid the first transatlantic cable, has an extensive wine cellar to accompany an imaginative menu served in peaceful surroundings; Tel: (0404) 692-74. **Hunter's Hotel**, also in Rathnew, is one of Ireland's oldest coaching inns, boasting the best of Irish meat, fish, and vegetables; Tel: (0404) 401-06. Or, on the way back to town, stop at the Greek-Cypriot **Tree of Idleness** on the seafront in Bray (closed Mondays) for what has been described as a "glorious indulgence"; Tel: (01) 286-3498.

—Lorna Siggins

BARS AND NIGHTLIFE

When Bob Hawke, the former Australian prime minister, visited Dublin in 1987, he did not spend every one of his few nights at glittering banquets or shows. This had nothing to do with security. Rather, he gave the security forces a large headache, and lots of overtime pay, when he decided to embark on a tour of Dublin pubs. This, Mr. Hawke recognized, was what the capital was all about.

Despite the stereotype of the drunken redheaded Irishman (with its roots in bigotry), you may spend days in Dublin before encountering an example. In fact, statistics show that Ireland is not a nation of drunkards; it is a nation of pub drinkers.

We are not recommending that you try to take in all 700 or so of Dublin's pubs. The following list is highly selective, and must be, for pubs are a very personal thing. (An earlier section of this chapter provides an overview and highlights of the Dublin pub scene.) By the same "logic" that ignores millions spent on new technology and insists that pulling a pint is *still* an art form, it is often held that the plusher the surroundings the poorer the porter (a.k.a. Guinness). As for the trend toward pub grub at lunchtime, this is anathema to any midday imbiber, who knows that the barman must not be distracted.

You can usually judge a good premises by the crowd within it, rather than by its cleanliness or comfortable decor. Pubs get lively from 9:00 P.M. on, and, under new legislation, "drinking-up" time now extends to midnight, Monday through Saturday between April and October and 11:30 P.M. in winter (on Sundays, year-round, closing is at 11:00 P.M.). The new law also permits full liquor licenses to restaurants. Most people have their "local," where you are expected to join in the chat; you're excused if there's music in session, in which case you may be invited to shake a leg.

You might like to begin on the quays with the oldest pub in Dublin, the **Brazen Head**, at 20 Lower Bridge Street off Merchant's Quay. The site dates as an inn from 1198; the present building is 17th century (15 of the United Irishmen were arrested here in 1798). On a Friday night you may have to struggle to reach the bar, where old copper kettles and bellows hang beside posters for Wills Anchor Navy Cut cigarettes at 5½ old pennies, but there's often good Irish music, an open fire in winter, and that much abused descriptive noun "crack"—untranslatable, with the nearest English word being "fun."

Over on the other side of Bridge Street, past Christ Church Cathedral and opposite the Brazen Head, is the **Merchant**, where you can watch set dancing, which is undergoing a great revival. Set dancing is not the conventional Irish or *ceili* dancing, but was introduced by the Normans and patronized by the landed gentry. The sets, which vary from county to county, derive from the quadrille, or square dance, with much foreign influence. Adapted to the quicker tempo of Irish reels, jigs, hornpipes, and polkas, set dancing spread—with the help of foreign regiments—throughout 19th-century Ireland. A Tipperary man, Connie Ryan, is credited with its revival. For dates and other venues check the listings sections in publications like the fortnightly *In Dublin* magazine.

A brisk walk west to **Ryan's** in Parkgate Street, near Heuston Station (but on the North Side) is worth it for the great character and conversation that can be enjoyed here, even if you have to take a taxi back. Note the mahogany and brass fittings, the Victorian design, and the little pigeonholes and tea drawers behind the counter, a legacy from the days when Ryan's was also a grocery. There is now a restaurant here as well. Sadly, the two front snugs—little cubbyholes where women drank in the days when men preferred to have the bar to themselves—have been removed by the owner to make space for more imbibers.

Back in the center of Dublin, on the South Side off Westmoreland Street, the **Palace Bar** at the Bewley's Café end of Fleet Street, and **Bowe's** at the other, are worth their pints. Both there and in the newer **Doyle's** in nearby College Street you might be drinking elbow to elbow with journalists from the *Irish Times.* (Doyle's, which lacks atmosphere, used to be called the Oscar Wilde, but sadly all reference to the Irish writer has been carefully removed by the new proprietor.)

Scribes from the *Irish Press* tend to frequent **Mulligan's** in Poolbeg Street, between Trinity College and the river, not exactly handsome with its strip lighting, but James Joyce was a patron, and Mulligan's, which has changed little since Joyce's death, has maintained a mixed bag of regulars since it first opened—in 1782.

O'Neill's in Suffolk Street off College Green and the **Stag's Head** in Dame Court south off Dame Street nearby are haunts of students from Trinity College, and of academics who can bear the company of their students. Founded in 1770, the latter's stained-glass skylights, wrought-iron chandeliers, and leather upholstery give it much of its character. The **Old Stand** in Exchequer Street, the **International Bar** in Wicklow Street—good for music—and the **Long Hall** in Great St. George's Street are also recommended.

The **Bailey** and **Davy Byrne's**, immortalized by Bloom's patronage in *Ulysses,* are very "in," both on Duke Street off Grafton. Both have a cosmopolitan singles-bar atmosphere; no spitting on the wood and sawdust floor here, thank you. **Kehoe's** on South Anne Street (parallel to Duke) serves what experts say is one of the best pints in town. **Neary's** in Chatham Street off Grafton is a theater pub, close to the Gaiety, and **McDaid's** on Harry Street just to the north is yet another, where playwright Brendan Behan sunk his black (pints). **O'Donoghue's**, where the Dubliners launched their career in folk music, is still a favorite music pub on Merrion Row just east of St. Stephen's Green North, as is **Toner's**, which is believed to be the only public house in Dublin that Yeats ever visited—and he didn't stay long! Up the road farther east in Baggot Street is **Doheny and Nesbitt's**, fashionably known as Nesbitt's, where civil servants, well-known journalists and campaigners, and musicians gather, and where its own "Doheny and Nesbitt School" of economists agonize over the ills of the country.

Back down by the Liffey, in the South Side dockland area of Sir John Rogerson's Quay, the unassuming **Dockers'** pub is a haunt for those seeking a glimpse of the rock band U2 or newer, "rising" bands recording in studios nearby. It's about a 15-minute walk from O'Connell Bridge along the south bank of the river toward the estuary and Dublin Bay.

On the North Side, in addition to Ryan's, there is also **Kavanagh's** in Aughrim Street, just east of St. Brendan's Hospital, an Old World Dublin pub with plenty of character; the **Meeting Place** in Dorset Street, a well-known Irish folk- and traditional-music venue; and a different **Kavanagh's** in Glasnevin, affectionately known as the "Gravedigger's," at the back gate to Glasnevin Cemetery near the Botanic Gardens. But you have to leave something to the Dubliner. . . .

Dublin is the home of U2, the Hothouse Flowers, Sinéad O'Connor, the Chieftains, and the Dubliners, so the music scene is always fairly lively in the capital. Many of the jazz, folk, and rock gigs are in pubs or late-night venues like **Mother Redcap's Tavern** on Back Lane, opposite Tailor's Guild Hall, near Christ Church Cathedral, and **Bad Bob's Backstage Bar**, beside the Project Arts Centre in East Essex Street, between Dame Street and Wellington Quay. For dates and details refer to *In Dublin,* or to *Hot Press,* the fortnightly music paper. The former also carries theater and cinema listings.

You cannot say you've been to Dublin without going to the theater—though some would argue that the art is alive and well on the city streets and in some of its livelier hostelries. For major works of Irish drama by such writers as Sean O'Casey, J. M. Synge, Samuel Beckett, Brian Friel, and John B. Keane, the **Abbey Theatre** on Lower Abbey Street (Tel: 01/78-72-22) and the **Gate** at the top of O'Connell Street on Cavendish Row (Tel: 01/74-40-45) are the places to go. Major credit cards are accepted; you can book by phone or in person at the theater. Most box offices open at 11:00 A.M.

You'll find everything from opera to pantomime and

midnight comedy at the grand old houses: the **Gaiety** in South King Street off St. Stephen's Green (Tel: 01/77-17-17) and the **Olympia** in Dame Street (Tel: 01/77-77-44). Productions at smaller, "alternative" venues like the **Project Arts Centre** on East Essex Street (behind Dame Street; Tel: 01/71-23-21) and the **Focus** on 6 Pembroke Place off Pembroke Street (Tel: 01/76-30-71) are always stimulating. A particularly noteworthy theater among the many in the city is the **Tivoli** in the Liberties on Francis Street; Tel: (01) 54-44-72. The new **Andrew's Lane Theatre**, off College Green/Dame Street, is also worth checking out; Tel: (01) 679-5720.

And what is there after pub closing time? If you're looking for nightclubs try the big hotels and the **Leeson Street** strip for late-night disco music and wine that can cost an arm, if not a leg. **Suesey Street**, 25 Lower Leeson, and the **Pink Elephant**, South Frederick Street, are among the trendy spots. For many, the Pink Elephant is the place to try to spot U2—music people and people-who-wish-they-were or like-to-be-seen-with-music-people are among its clientele. On the Leeson Street strip, nightclubs with ever-changing names are generally located in basements, guarded by big doormen who don't look for a cover charge. The sting is the wine—usually plonky and very pricey from at least £15 a bottle—and the fact that after all that you have to take a taxi home.

For post-nightclub recovery, try **Jury's Coffee Dock**, which is open 23 hours a day, in Jury's Hotel and Towers, Ballsbridge.

—*Lorna Siggins*

SHOPS AND SHOPPING

Aran and tweeds, linen and lace, a bit of Waterford crystal—it is a commonly held belief that that is all visitors are interested in when it comes to buying Irish. We know that this isn't true, or at least that it doesn't have to be. The Irish clothing industry, for example, has undergone a revolution in recent years, and no longer are chunky Aran sweaters and tweed caps for the North American tourist the standard fare. Sweater shops in Wicklow Street, Powerscourt Townhouse Centre, Nassau Street, and beyond have plenty of big, bright, colorful machine-made and hand-knit articles designed with an eye to fashion. Dublin is a walking city—although it won't be for much longer if motorway-mad Dublin city councillors have their way. Though it no longer has its weaver streets and tallow-chandler streets and barber streets (the guild system finally broke up in 1840, after about 600 years), such is its geographical layout that shopping here becomes an adventure.

Remember shop hours are usually 9:00 A.M. to 5:30 P.M. Monday through Saturday, and until 8:00 P.M. on Thursdays; some shops—apart from weekend markets—are now open on Sundays. For details of VAT (value-added tax) refunds, and a guide to sizes, weights, and measures, ask for a Bord Fáilte shopping brochure, which also lists shopping venues by item.

Grafton Street Area

Grafton Street, Dublin's version of Bond Street, and named after an 18th-century viceroy, is closed to automobiles. It is famous for its century-old department stores **Switzers** and **Brown Thomas**, both of which are good for tweeds. **Weir's Jewellers** (expensive) was founded by a Glasgow goldsmith in 1869 and stocks everything from antique silver to leather-bound hip flasks. Principles, Benetton, and Laura Ashley are among the international outlets that have opened here in recent years. The refurbished Bewley's Oriental Café on Grafton, dating from 1927, is famous for its sticky buns and Jersey milk; many cups of its coffee have been sipped by Dublin's cognoscenti.

Off Grafton, Wicklow Street, characterized by leather, sheepskin, and shoe shops, winds on up to South Great George's Street, where there is another branch of Bewley's. Wend your way back down Wicklow Street to South William Street and take the front entrance into the **Powerscourt Townhouse Centre**, built in 1774 for Lord Powerscourt and now sensitively refurbished for commerce. Here you can buy handmade shoes (men's) at Tutty's, or a Persian carpet, or jewelry to match a dress from the major Irish clothing designers. Or eat or drink.

Back on Grafton Street, via Johnson's Court, amble down Duke Street and South Anne Street, havens for antiques and curio hunters. **Cathach Books** at 10 Duke Street has antiquarian printed matter. The **Royal Hibernian Way** links Dawson Street to Grafton Street, via Duke Street. This sophisticated shopping mall was formerly the site of the much-mourned Royal Hibernian Hotel, demolished in 1984.

The **Westbury Mall**, off Harry Street, adjoins the luxurious Westbury Hotel. Not the place to go looking for your pair of Wellington boots for bog trotting, but there's the **Best of Irish** shop for knitwear, crystal, china, Belleek porcelain, and jewelry. Yet another new shopping mall, the **St. Stephen's Green Centre**, has transformed the more genteel face of the Green, on the corner of St. Stephen's Green West and South King Street.

Walk up Dawson Street, bustling with designer boutiques, passing **Waterstone** and **Hodges Figgis** (with its excellent Irish section) bookshops on the way. **Fred Hanna,** another good bookstore around the corner in Nassau Street, also deals in secondhand volumes. Farther along on Nassau you'll find good tweeds, linens, and woollens at **Blarney Woollen Mills** and the **Kilkenny Design Centre**, formerly a state-sponsored outlet for the best of Irish design and workmanship.

If you continue straight east along Nassau Street, with the grounds of Trinity College on your left, you will come to tiny Clare Street and the inimitable **Greene's** bookshop, which has two floors full of secondhand books spilling out onto trays in the street, and a post office downstairs to boot.

Also near this area—within walking distance of the National Gallery of Ireland on Merrion Square West—are commercial art galleries, but call ahead to check open hours. The **Gorry Gallery** at 20 Molesworth Street stocks mainly Irish artists of the 18th, 19th, and 20th centuries (Tel: 01/679-5319).

Central Bank Area

Known as Dublin's Left Bank—or Marais for those who know what Paris is like now—the Central Bank area is neither. A warren of streets here lead down to the Liffey on the South Side near the bank, where jewelry, lace, secondhand linen, fireplace surrounds, Victorian dressers, music, and science-fiction books can be rooted out around Crown Alley, Merchant's Arch, Temple Bar, and East Essex Street. In **Rory's Fishing Tackle**, 17A Temple Bar, there's everything from fly rods to flasher rigs, and lots of maggots.

As you walk up College Green toward the Central Bank, look for **Books Upstairs** (opposite Trinity College and the Bank of Ireland) at number 36, open late in the evenings and also Sunday afternoons. Farther up at 56 Dame Street is the **Alchemist's Head** bookstore, for science fiction and the occult.

The **Temple Bar Gallery** and studios at 4–8 Temple Bar

welcomes visitors who wish to view local artists' work from 11:00 A.M. to 5:30 P.M. weekdays and from noon to 4:00 P.M. on Saturdays (Tel: 01/71-00-73). Farther up, across Parliament Street, **Cathair Books** at 1 Essex Gate claims to be the city's oldest bookshop—and bookselling here does date as far back as the 1690s. Their stock includes antiquarian and contemporary books, prints, newspapers, and postcards. Walk down Parliament Street away from the Liffey and toward the City Hall and you'll see the **Riverrun Gallery** on your left. The spacious, well-lit restored premises exhibit a good representation of contemporary Irish art. Open from 10:30 A.M. to 5:30 P.M. Monday to Saturday (Tel: 01/679-8606).

Henry Street District

On the South Side of the Liffey, look for the **Gallery of Photography** at 37 Wellington Quay, which houses exhibitions of international and Irish photography and sells a selection of posters, postcards, prints, and books (Tel: 01/71-46-54). Up toward O'Connell Bridge on Crampton Quay is **George Webb**'s bookshop, a renowned secondhand dealer now owned by Hanna's of Nassau Street. North across the Liffey by the Ha'penny Bridge, linking Crampton Quay to Bachelor's Walk, antiques shops predominate along the quays. You'll also see **Dublin Woollen Mills**, good for chunky knits, while the **Winding Stair** bookshop beside it, at 40 Lower Ormond Quay, is a heavenly retreat from the city bustle. Named after a poem by W. B. Yeats, it occupies two floors and has a fine selection of rare and secondhand titles in addition to contemporary publications, with poetry a specialty. Very lively, with coffee and homemade cakes for browsers.

Crossed by the north–south Liffey Street, the pedestrianized **Henry Street** is the more concentrated shopping area of the city, where the *real* Dubliners can be found. There are plenty of department stores here, such as Arnott's, Marks and Spencer, Roches stores, and Penneys, as well as boutiques. The ILAC (Irish Life Assurance Company) Centre is a lively shopping mall, but it has detracted from Moore Street, running north of Henry, which was once a bustling market area. Up in O'Connell Street itself, awash with discount stores and fast-food shops and described as a "honky-tonk freeway," the saving graces are **Clery's** department store, where you can buy linen, crystal, and Belleek, and **Eason's** bookshop, both dating from the 19th century and both ravaged by the 1916 Rising hostilities around the nearby General Post Office. **McDowell's Jewellers**, also destroyed in 1916, recently has been elegantly refurbished and has antique silver, Waterford crystal, and Claddagh rings.

Off the Beaten Track

Irish craft and design is well represented in the city center, but if you have the time it is worth venturing a little farther afield. The **Tower Design Centre** is in the IDA Enterprise Centre, Pearse Street. To reach it on foot take the College Street turn off Westmoreland Street (down the other side of Trinity College) and keep walking down Pearse Street until you come to a canal bridge. Buses 1, 2, and 3 from Clery's department store in O'Connell Street will also take you there. If you're travelling by DART train, get off at the Pearse Street station and walk toward Ringsend. The tower building, constructed in 1862, has housed a sugar refinery, a distillery, and an iron foundry; in 1978 the Industrial Development Authority (IDA) purchased and restored it. More than 14 craftworkers are based here, and you can buy pewter, silver and gold jewelry, Irish bog oak artifacts, hand-crafted wooden toys, knitwear, hand-painted silks, pottery, and wood carvings. Open 10:00 A.M. to 4:00 P.M. weekdays; Tel: (01) 77-56-55.

The **Marlay Craft Centre** (Tel: 01/94-20-83) in Rathfarnham is a 25-minute drive from the city center south toward the Dublin foothills. In the courtyard you can buy pottery, glass, weavings, and assorted crafts, and there is also a small coffee shop. Open 10:00 A.M. to 5:00 P.M. weekdays, 11:00 A.M. to 5:30 P.M. weekends. After shopping you might take a walk in nearby Rathfarnham Park, one of the city's most magnificent expanses.

Irish Food Specialties

Ireland boasts its own cheese, homemade chocolates, and other delicacies, which can be bought in the city center. For smoked salmon, **Caviston's** of 59 Glasthule Road, Sandycove and **Molloy's** of 47 Donnybrook Road are recommended, while Howth Harbour has **Peter Forman's** on the west pier. Most fish shops close on Sundays and Mondays. Ask whether it is wild or farmed salmon before purchasing, and don't wait to buy at Dublin Airport, where it is grossly overpriced. Remember that there is a significant difference between "smoked Irish" and "Irish smoked"—the latter may have been imported.

—Lorna Siggins

DUBLIN ENVIRONS
THE PALE AND BEYOND

By Bernard Share

You will not hear the word "Pale" used in Ireland now, except in the context of mockery or political point-scoring; but it is a useful enough term to define the area surrounding and contiguous to Dublin, particularly as it has always been rather more a state of mind than a precise geographical definition. First attested historically in 1446, the Pale was that area considered by the Anglo-Norman invaders and their successors, if not by the resident Irish, to be under their occupational control and influence. As the fortunes of the insurgents waxed and waned there were times when it virtually ceased to exist.

In its greatest extent the Pale embraced the present-day counties of Louth (north of Dublin), Meath (to the north and northwest), Dublin, and Kildare (southwest)—the area, in effect, surrounding the capital on all but the southern side to a distance of some 30 miles. Wicklow to the south, mountainous and inaccessible, in marked contrast to the flat plains or gentle hills of the other counties, continued to resist English attempts to include it within their scheme of things. The O'Tooles and the O'Byrnes, from their rocky, boggy fastnesses in Wicklow, continued to harass and provoke the settled citizens of Dublin until modern warfare finally caught up with them. A drive through their territories, even to this day, will quickly reveal what the forces of law and order were up against. On a quiet weekday the countryside is much as the

O'Tooles and the O'Byrnes left it: a starkly beautiful, virtually uninhabited natural wilderness.

Though small in extent (no point on the following itineraries is more than 80 km/50 miles from Dublin), The Pale offers marked and interesting contrasts both in the nature of the countryside and the range of attractions.

Wicklow is dominated by its mountains, which divide the county into the eastern coastal strip, with several attractive seaside towns and resorts, and the sparsely inhabited foothills of West Wicklow, where rural life has changed little in spite of the proximity to the capital. The eastern side is popularly known as "The Garden of Ireland," and the number of fine and historic gardens open to the public here attests to the appropriateness of the description. A **Gardens Festival** is held in June.

Louth and Meath, to the north, are largely composed of good farming lands intersected by myriad intriguing by-roads, modest but—given the flat nature of the country—commanding hills, and the beautiful valley of the Boyne, with its remarkable richness of prehistory.

Kildare, Ireland's flattest county, makes up in cultural and sporting attractions for what it lacks in contours: It offers the excitement of the Mondello motor-racing circuit as well as leisurely fishing and cruising on its canals. From the mountain summits of Wicklow, where the deer, if not the antelope, play, to the civilized pleasure of a good dinner in a 12th-century castle keep (Barberstown, between Celbridge and Clane in County Kildare), the Pale offers much within a small compass.

The people of the Pale reflect both its geography and its complex and at times convoluted history. In Wicklow they are "mountainy men," small farmers fighting a running battle with nature, their domain increasingly eroded at the edges by suburban sprawl and the value system that it implies. On the other sides of the city (the east, of course, is all water) the suburbs straggle out perhaps even less entrancingly, but you can still be clear of them in half an hour. The north Kildare people love horses—and look it. Meath is rich pasture and prosperous farms. Louth, boasting the Boyne Valley, is otherwise a little down on its luck. But closeness to the capital means that there is a wide range of amenities developed for percipient city dwellers, which visitors will also appreciate.

MAJOR INTEREST

Boyne Valley (stone monuments older than the
   Pyramids of Egypt)
Hill of Tara and the other two Celtic royal hills
Great houses (some of Ireland's finest 18th-century
   mansions)
Bog of Allen (peatlands rich in botanical interest)
Wicklow Glens (rural solitude within a stone's
   throw of the city center)
Glendalough (Early Christian Ireland at its most
   evocative)
Well-run restaurants in appealing locations
Good pubs
Fishing
Horse racing

Before the Pale

Irish history did not, of course, begin with the arrival of the
Anglo-Normans in A.D. 1169. Antedating this admittedly
pivotal event were centuries of Celtic and pre-Celtic civilization, all amply exemplified in the larger surroundings of
Dublin. The great prehistoric chambered tomb at Newgrange in the Boyne Valley dates most probably from 3000
B.C. There is evidence of Bronze Age cultivation (2000 to
500 B.C.) on the slopes of the Wicklow Mountains. The date
of the arrival of the Celts themselves is still the subject of
learned controversy, as is their provenance, but a date of
1500 B.C. meets with general support. At the great Celtic
sites—the Hill of Tara, seat of the high kings, and the Hill
of Allen, associated with the legendary Finn mac Cumhail
(MacCool) and his band of warriors known as the Fianna
(hence the modern term Fenian)—little or no visible
evidence remains of the glory of the Celts. The informed
imagination must do the work, reclothing these unremarkable eminences with the panoply of a culture that flourished when the rest of Europe was immersed in darkness,
producing exquisite gold artifacts and, in the leanest period of the Christian era, illuminated manuscripts associated with long-established centers of learning such as
Ceanannas Mór (Kells) and Cill Dara (Kildare). The original Celtic place-names, many rendered unlovely by insensi-
tive anglicizing (Kill, County Kildare is an example; the
original is Cill, "a church"), can provide an insight into a

world long gone. Those with a linguistic bent will find further-reading suggestions in the Bibliography.

King and Castle

Territory wrested from the inhabitants by force of arms must be constantly defended. The fortified castle, a form of architectural expression unknown to the native Irish, thus became the Anglo-Norman trademark, and 500 years of castle building has left the Pale rich in examples, ranging from the almost perfectly preserved specimen to the shattered single bastion marooned in a boggy meadow. Most may be visited quite informally; others are in the care of a local custodian, who will provide a key.

The Norman legacy is more than a sermon in stone. The great Norman names—the Fitzgeralds, earls of Kildare, for example—have resounded down the centuries, having, in the course of time, become "more Irish than the Irish." But many strands are woven into the past and present culture of the Pale, as the literary associations attest: Jonathan Swift (Celbridge and Laracor, County Meath); the poet Francis Ledwidge (Slane); and, more recently, the fragmented but revealing glimpses of the Wicklow landscape in the work of Samuel Beckett. Other talents thrive: The colorful race meetings at the Curragh, Punchestown, Naas, Laytown, and Fairyhouse proclaim the kingdom of the horse; breeding, training, racing, and selling constitute a major business, mirrored in the pub talk of counties Kildare and Meath.

COUNTIES
LOUTH AND MEATH:
THE BANKS OF THE BOYNE

Take the N 1 northward from Dublin to Drogheda (follow the signs for Belfast); at Gormanston, some 11 km (7 miles) before Drogheda, you will pass—or stop at, as you feel inclined—**The Cock**, reputedly the oldest pub in Ireland, with origins in the 14th century, the property of one family for most of its recorded history. A beer garden here is an added attraction on sunny days. **Drogheda**— Droichead átha (the Bridge of the ford)—is situated at the mouth of the Boyne, circled by commanding hills on the north and south. It was established by invading Vikings under Thorgestr, alias Turgesius, in A.D. 911, though there were already separate native settlements on each side of the River Boyne, early indications of a rivalry that was to persist. Then the Normans under Hugh de Lacy built a castle at Millmount, which has all but vanished, but the military barracks that succeeded it (left at the traffic light immediately after the railway bridge, then right at the top of the hill) have been transformed very imaginatively into the **Millmount Craft and Cultural Centre**, where you may choose from pottery, jewelry, and other crafts produced on the premises. It incorporates an excellent town museum, which is strong in local interest. Call to check opening hours; Tel: (041) 363-91. A good, moderately priced wine bar and restaurant here, **The Buttergate**, offers dramatic views over the town, and the **Sennhof Gourmet Restaurant** in the Boyne Valley Hotel features Swiss specialties.

In 1649 Cromwell, the lord protector of England, breached Drogheda's walls, the town having declared for the Royalists, and in a crime against humanity spectacular even by modern standards butchered, on his own admission, 2,000 people and deported the remaining citizens to Barbados. The "curse of Cromwell" is still a vivid folk memory; there are few names more universally execrated in Ireland.

Visible relics of a turbulent past include the head of Saint Oliver Plunkett in St. Peter's Church (West Street), who was hanged, drawn, and quartered in London in 1681; and, in Protestant St. Peter's (Magdalene Street), the graves of Isaac Goldsmith, uncle of Oliver (whose country lies westward of our area in Longford/Westmeath) and Bartholomew Van Homrigh, father of Swift's Vanessa (see below, Celbridge). St. Laurence's Gate barbican is all that is left of the town walls.

The most prominent architectural feature in Drogheda, and one that adds a certain aerial dimension to a low-lying town, is the high railway viaduct carrying the Dublin–Belfast railroad, viewable from The Mall (cross the bridge and take a sharp right), where **Greene's** extensive antiques galleries will detain the lover of period furniture (closed Sundays). Two good places to pause before heading north, still on the N 1, to Monasterboice: **Gleeson's Pub**, with its fine oak ceiling, opposite the Tourist Information Office in West Street (free parking adjacent); and **Weaver's**, another pub in West Street with a good choice of simple food. Drogheda's seaside resort, Bettystown, has a six-mile beach on which a colorful horse-race festival is held, usually in August depending on the tides; call the Drogheda Tourist Office for dates. The **Coastguard Inn** restaurant in Bettystown has a good reputation.

Monasterboice

Continuing on the N 1, take a left 8 km (5 miles) north of Drogheda towards Monasterboice. An ancient monastic settlement, Monasterboice is remarkable for its tenth-century **Muirdeach's Cross**, featuring excellently preserved biblical scenes in sculptured panels on its east and west faces. The adjacent ninth-century round tower is open to visitors (get the key at the house at the gate).

Visit Monasterboice as a side excursion from Drogheda; there is too much in the Boyne Valley proper to include it in a one-day trip. About 5 km (3 miles) west from Drogheda on the N 51 is the site of the **battle of the Boyne**, fought on July 12, 1690, between a Catholic Scot and a Dutch Protestant for the throne of England, an event that has left an indelible mark on Irish history. A right-hand turn from the battle site (it's signposted) leads to **Mellifont Abbey**, the first (1142) Cistercian house in Ireland, founded on the site of a seventh-century convent. Of particular interest are the massive gatehouse, the chapter house, and the octagonal lavabo, of which five walls still stand; the Abbey is open from May through October. The setting, on the banks of the little River Mattock, makes an attractive picnic spot. The Boyne waterway, fallen into disuse, is being restored, and it offers good fishing (some species restricted; inquire at tourist offices in Dublin). The energetic may consider walking all or part of the riverside path from Drogheda to Navan—a leafy stroll through green, placid countryside (about 30 km/19 miles one way along the north bank of the river).

Newgrange

At the precise moment of the winter solstice the sun shines down the long, low passage of the huge prehistoric tomb at Newgrange and strikes a rock face in the cruciform, corbeled inner chamber. Who planned it, all of 4,500 years ago? Was it, in fact, the world's first astronomical observatory? What hands fashioned this fearful asymmetry? Whoever they were, these proto-Irish, they have departed leaving little or nothing but their inscrutable burial monuments. Visit Newgrange—and its companion grave of **Knowth**—at an off-peak time if you can to avoid crowds (especially weekends). A certain solitude is of assistance in adjusting to the time scale and its implications. The construction of Newgrange required, it is estimated, some 180,000 tons of stone. (The façade is a modern restoration.) There is an excellent and unobtrusive information center at the entrance, and a 700-acre National Archaeological Park is being created on a site centered on these remarkable monuments. As in the case of the Australian aboriginal culture, the Neolithic art found at Newgrange in the form of rock carvings is too remote in time to make a large impact on present-day consciousness, though it continues to inspire Irish artists working in a variety of media. The site remained important into Celtic times: The Irish name is Brugh na Bóinne (the Palace of the Boyne). Newgrange is south of the N 51, 18 km (11 miles) west of Drogheda, and is well signposted.

Close by the tumulus is **Newgrange Farm**, where the Redhouse family invites you to sample the flavor of contemporary rural life through guided tours of a functioning farm. Open weekdays from April through September 10:00 A.M. to 6:00 P.M. and Sundays 2:00 to 6:00 P.M. There are picnic areas and a coffee shop.

Slane

You can reach Slane by returning to the N 51 from New-grange and continuing west, but two other possibilities are to approach it from Dublin via the Derry road, N 2 (straightened, according to popular rumor, to permit King George IV of England rapid access to his paramour Lady Conyngham in Slane Castle), or by the picturesque route that skirts the south bank of the Boyne from Drogheda. Slane is a good example of a stone-built 18th-century landlord village, sited at a cross roads and built around a central octagon (inevitably known locally as the Square) with a good eye for symmetry and decorum. The village is largely unspoilt, and several of the buildings on the Drogheda road have been sensitively restored. **Slane Castle**, in the possession of the Conyngham family since 1641, suffered a disastrous fire at the end of 1991, but the earl of Mount Charles (the title borne by the eldest son) plans a full restoration of both the castle and the visitor facilities, which include a restaurant and nightclub. Inquire locally as to progress. Meanwhile, in the village itself, the **Conyngham Arms** provides an all-day buffet featuring a varied and modestly priced menu of roasts, fish, and curried dishes as well as simpler snacks. There is also a more formal restaurant.

Just north of the village on the Derry road is the **Hill of Slane**, upon which Saint Patrick, in the year 433, lit the Paschal fire as a direct challenge to that kindled for older ceremonial purposes by King Laeghaire at his court on the Hill of Tara. The confrontation of the spiritual and the temporal, as Muirchu, Patrick's biographer, tells it in an account written some 200 years after the event, resolved into a competition in prestidigitation, with Laeghaire's wizards gloomily predicting an unfavorable—for the Irish—outcome. Ercc, the first convert, became the first bishop of Slane and is commemorated in the ruins of a Gothic church in the castle Demesne.

Kells

Turn right at Slane Castle to Kells (or Ceanannas; you will see both on signposts), or continue from Slane via Navan (or start from Dublin on the N 3) to investigate the atmosphere, if little else, of the **Hill of Tara**, 9½ km (6 miles) northwest of Dunshaughlin. Teamhair na Ríogh (Tara of the Kings) was an important settlement in the Bronze Age and not finally abandoned until A.D. 1022. Tara's halls are now discernible only as earthen ditches and ramparts, but a major excavation is in progress. There is a visitors' center and guide services. The modern statue of Saint Patrick is best ignored.

Beyond Navan on the Kells road toward the northwest lies the third of the royal hills, the **Hill of Tailte**, where the Irish version of the Olympic Games, Aonach Tailteann, was held from the prehistoric era until A.D. 1168—and revived briefly in the first flush of regained independence in the 1920s. **Kells**, where Saint Colmcille founded a monastery in the sixth century, gave its name to the magnificent gospel manuscript now in Trinity College, Dublin, and recently reproduced in full authenticity by Swiss master craftsmen. An eighth-century building known as **St. Columba's House** (Columba is an anglicization of Colmcille) in Kells is in the style of St. Kevin's Church in Glendalough (see below); there is a 100-foot round tower, unusual in that it boasts five windows, each facing an ancient entrance to the town. Ask Mrs. Carpenter in Church Lane for the key. Close by is the finest of the High Crosses of Kells, rich in sculptured ornament. There are three others; the example in the marketplace was employed as a gallows during the Rising of 1798. Little remains of the town's once-formidable walls and fortifications. The **Headfort Arms Hotel** (owned by Tom and Peggy Duff) is a good base for exploring, fishing, hunting, or shooting.

Leave Ceanannas by the R 163 west for Crossakeel, where you should take the right turn toward Oldcastle. The road runs at the foot of Slieve na Caillighe. Another right turn some 8 km (5 miles) from Crossakeel leads to a remarkable concentration of megalithic tombs, including, on the summit of Carnbane East, a classic example of an Irish cruciform passage-tomb. Entry is possible by obtaining a key from Basil Balfe in the first house on the right as you turn off R 154. A deposit (refundable) is required. From here return to Crossakeel and continue on the R 154 to Athboy and on to Trim, passing the Meath Gaeltacht (Irish-speaking area) of Rathcarn on the left.

Trim

"Whoever stands in King John's city sees/The tide of life for ever ebbing back," wrote the poet Donald Davie of the antiquities of Trim, southwest of Navan, where, to his eye, "Great walls lie beached on fields like bladder wrack." True, certainly, of the remains, imposing even in dereliction, of **Trim Castle**, the largest Anglo-Norman fortress in Ireland, founded in 1173 and the seat of power of the lordship of Meath. The five surviving towers and one of the two gate towers date from 1220. The river that skirts it is the Boyne. The castle, under extensive restoration, is open to the public. Trim has two other fortresses: Nangle's Castle, and Talbot's Castle (1415) off High Street. Transformed into a school, Talbot's provided the early education of the duke of Wellington, Arthur Wesley, or Wellesley, who lived in Dublingate Street (now Patrick Street), where a monument commemorates this somewhat reluctant Irishman. The school had been owned earlier by Swift's Stella (Esther Johnson), who sold it to the dean—at a profit.

The **Wellington Court Hotel** in Trim is family run and has period charm. If you are able to share a more specialized nostalgia, **The Station House** restaurant and hotel in Kilmessan is particularly appealing. (From Trim on the Navan road make a right past Bective Abbey, founded 1146, the present ruins dating from the 12th and 13th centuries.) The Station House occupies the site and some of the buildings of the junction of two long-vanished railroads, and has been most attractively reconstituted by Thelma and Christopher Slattery. The gardens, cuisine, and ambience can be commended.

NORTH COUNTY KILDARE

The sector west and southwest of Dublin bounded roughly by the Dublin–Galway (N 6) and Dublin–Tullow (N 81) roads, though flat and visually undramatic, contains much of interest. **Maynooth**, the former seat of the Fitzgeralds, 32 km (20 miles) northwest of Dublin on the N 4, may also be reached by outer suburban rail from Dublin's Connolly Station or by number 66 or 67A bus. **Carton House**, in Maynooth, is not generally open to the public, however arrangements might be made by calling Tel: 01/628-6250 or 6293. If you strike it lucky, there is some good stucco work by the Francini brothers to be seen in it. Maynooth is a university town, the establishment having grown out of the ecclesiastical (Catholic) seminary founded in 1795 by the British administration to stem the dangerous (to them) practice of priests going for training to the Continent in the wake of the French Revolution. Still the seedbed of the Church in Ireland, it has been an open university since the mid-1960s. The faculty of physics plays a significant role in the European Space Program. Eamon de Valera, the New York–born former president of Ireland, lectured here in mathematics. The **Russell Library** houses an important collection of early Irish manuscripts; it is open by appointment only (Tel: 01/628-5222). A new library was opened in 1984 and memorializes the visit of Pope John Paul II in 1979. There is, intermittently, good music to be heard in the chapel.

The **castle** at the college entrance was probably built around 1176 by Maurice Fitzgerald, an associate of Strongbow, and after a checkered history was dismantled in 1647 by Owen Roe O'Neill. There remain a massive keep, some towers, and fragmentary outworks. (There are ambitious plans for its restoration as a major tourist center.) The pub on the nearest corner, **Cassidy's Roost**, is a remarkable exercise in classical kitsch, with tables out on the sidewalk in summer for drinks and pub snacks. More elaborate fare is available at **Moyglare Manor Hotel** (the Galway side of the town; follow the signs), a finely situated Georgian country-house hotel and restaurant for local gourmets and expense-account diners; no lunch on Saturdays. Moyglare offers luxurious bedrooms, garden suites with noble views, fine antique furniture, and, as the season dictates, log fires and candlelight. The wine list features some remarkable and almost-vanished years of the great names (prices to match) to set against a distinguished cuisine.

From Maynooth the road south to Celbridge crosses the railway and the **Royal Canal**, which was opened as far as Kilcock in 1796, to the Shannon in 1817, and closed to all traffic in 1961. This section has now been reopened for pleasure boating as far as Mullingar.

Celbridge

As you enter Celbridge's main street the gates at the left are those of **Castletown House**, one of the finest Georgian mansions in Ireland and headquarters of the Irish Georgian Society. Castletown was built from 1722 to 1732 for William Conolly, speaker of the Irish parliament, and remained in the family until 1965. Of the 100 or so rooms, the Long Gallery is the most impressive. A cracked oval mirror in the dining room is said to commemorate an unexpected visit by the Devil who, in the guise of a dinner guest, insinuated himself into the company of the then owner, "Tom" Conolly, in the early 1800s. When the visitor refused to leave, the parish priest was summoned and threw a missal at him, which struck a glancing blow on his head and then hit the mirror. Satan decided to call it a day and vanished through the hearthstone—also cracked—in the conventional puff of smoke. Castletown is open to the public; call for opening hours (Tel: 01/628-8252). A restaurant in the basement kitchen offers good value in unusual surroundings. Reservations are essential; Tel: (01) 628-8252. Castletown also hosts cultural events, including Music in Great Irish Houses, an annual series of summer concerts featuring leading international artists. Booking is normally heavy, so it is best to call ahead; Tel: (01) 628-8252. (Another venue—they vary with each series—is Russborough House, County Wicklow; see below.)

Celbridge is the birthplace of Arthur Guinness, generally referred to by Irishmen in terms of respectful gratitude as "Uncle Arthur," and has close associations with Jonathan Swift, dean of St. Patrick's, Dublin: pamphleteer, patriot (of his own kind), and lover—if that is not too unambiguous a word to apply to his relationship with two women, Esther Johnson (Stella) and Esther Van Homrigh (Vanessa). Vanessa's home, **Celbridge Abbey**, was built by her wealthy Dutch father, and is now the property of the St. John of God Brothers, who welcome interested visitors. It is said that Vanessa constructed a bower by the Liffey side for the entertainment of Swift on his rare rides out from Dublin to see her and "drink her coffee"—a locution interpreted by some as a euphemism. The Romantics, led by Sir Walter Scott, who visited Celbridge, believed that Vanessa died of a broken heart—a verdict the dean chose neither to confirm nor deny. Celbridge now hosts an annual Swift Seminar; for details, Tel: (01) 628-8161 through 8163.

Bog Lore

The road from Celbridge to Clane to the southwest, a part of one of the straightest roads in Ireland but otherwise unremarkable, passes a turn (left) to Straffan, where there are several notable attractions (inquire in the village for exact locations). The **Straffan Steam Museum** features a remarkable collection of working stationary system engines housed in a Gothic church removed bodily from Inchicore, Dublin, and painstakingly rebuilt. These, along with an exhibit of very rare early models, are the brainchild of Robert Guiness, who has assembled the whole collection in his spacious grounds. Open July through September. At the **Butterfly Farm** rare specimens, available for purchase, enjoy the freedom of a tropical tunnel, and the **Morell Farm** features unusual farm animals (picnic area and refreshments available). The luxurious and correspondingly expensive **K Club** (Arnold Palmer golf course plus hotel and other facilities, some open to visitors) was formerly the home of "French Tom" Barton, founder of the Bordeaux wine firm of Barton & Guestier. Chateaux Langoa-Barton and Leoville-Barton are still in the family.

James Joyce was educated at Clongowes Wood College, near Clane (not open to the public), and the opening of *Portrait of the Artist as a Young Man* is set there. Onward from Clane the Prosperous road skirts the great **Bog of Allen**, a vast area of peatland. Much of it is utilized for fuel by Bord na Mona, the state peat authority, which has pioneered the relevant technology and advises on peat production as far away as Burundi, Central Africa. The vast yellow peat-harvesting machines are impressive in action, even from a distance, as they creep like lazy mastodons across the golden-brown surface of the bog. The historic and ecological significance of the bog is only now fully coming to be realized as most European deposits are depleted. Historically, the boglands played an important role in the struggle of the Irish against a succession of invaders, because only those with local knowledge were able to move freely in the treacherous terrain over tracks invisible to the inexperienced eye. This information and much more is available at the **Peatland World Visitors' Center** in **Lullymore** (left over the canal about 10 km/6 miles past Prosperous). There are guided bog tours, video shows, and museum exhibits.

The town of **Prosperous** is a popular center for fishing (rudd, tench, bream) on the adjacent **Grand Canal**, opened from Dublin to Sallins for passenger traffic in 1780 and completed to the Shannon by 1803. Trade boats ceased to ply in 1960, and the canal now carries cruising traffic. **Lowtown Cruisers**, based a mile west of Robertstown, offer luxury craft for hire; Tel: (045) 604-27; Fax: (045) 603-72. Though amenities are relatively undeveloped along the canal, there are pleasant waterside pubs at Sallins and at Robertstown, a "canal village" that preserves one of the original hotels built for the 18th-century passenger business. The canal offers much to interest the industrial archaeologist, in particular the **Leinster Aqueduct** (2½ km/1½ miles west from Sallins by water; or follow the towpath), built to carry the waterway across the River Liffey. The French traveller De Latocnaye described it in 1796 as of "really prodigious length and height." A series of brochures mapping canal bank walks in this area is available from County Kildare Sports Advisory Committee, Naas (Tel: 045/970-71) or from local libraries.

Off the Prosperous–Kildare road is the **Hill of Allen**, a modest eminence magnified by its dominance of the surrounding bogland, and the legendary headquarters of the equally legendary Finn mac Cumhail and his warriors, important figures in pre-Christian Irish epics. The hill is an easy climb, but don't expect to see more at the top than an extensive view.

The Curragh

If you are visiting Lullymore the road south via Rathangan, another attractive canal town, will bring you to Kildare. Alternatively you may travel from Celbridge via Clane (left turn at the village) to **Naas** (Nás na Ríogh, "the Meeting place of the Kings"), an attractive county town. There are several interesting shops here, including **Tutty**, at the Dublin end of the main street, purveyor of handmade shoes. Also at this end of the street is an imaginative restaurant, **Batt Mullins**, with a varied, modestly priced menu. The **Manor Inn**, a prime gathering place for the race-going fraternity and almost impenetrable during the three-day Punchestown races in early May, serves an excellent home-made steak-and-kidney pie and a very adequate house wine. The former Garda (police) barracks, in the Scottish baronial style, has been imaginatively converted into the **Naas Court Hotel**, a good base from which to follow the horses. Both accommodations are on Main Street.

Frank Fallon's **Red House Inn**, on the main road between Naas and Newbridge, grows its own vegetables and features a patio bar. Newbridge, a former British garrison town, is on the edge of the **Curragh**, a 5,000-acre grassy plain where horses have been raced for 2,000 years and the center of Irish horse-breeding and training. A race meeting here is recommended, if only for the atmosphere. The **Irish Derby**, run in May or June, is the most important event on the calendar and currently the prize money makes it the second-richest race in Europe. Check with Midlands-East Tourism (Tel: 044/ 486-50) for dates.

Kildare owes its existence to a religious foundation by Saint Brigid in the fifth century. St. Brigid's Cathedral (now Protestant) has recently been extensively restored, and includes a fine specimen of a round tower. At **Tully**, ½ km/1 mile from the town, the National Stud (home of bloodstock breeding) incorporates a Japanese garden of considerable charm, symbolic of the journey through life that is open from Easter through October. The **Silken Thomas** pub on the main street is a good place for a snack and a drink, and for lodging, the adjacent 18th-century **Lord Edward Guest House** is convenient—especially if you are visiting the races.

From Kildare take the Athy road (R 415) south via Fontstown to **Ballitore**, a Quaker village where the statesmen Henry Grattan and Edmund Burke and the churchman Cardinal Cullen were educated. **Ballitore Library and Museum** encapsulates the history of this unusual settlement; open Wednesday, Friday, and Saturday. A short distance away the restored **Crookstown Mill** (1840) preserves the almost-vanished technology of stone milling and extends a friendly welcome. Refreshments are available. Continue south on the N 9 to **Timolin**, where the **Irish Pewtermill** (left at the pub) produces a range of tankards, trays and dishes, flasks, jewelry, and spoons on the premises, and also houses a small pewter museum. A little distance farther is the re-erected **Moone High Cross** (ninth century), which was unearthed in 1835. Its scripture panels are strikingly vivid in concept and execution. Past the site take the signposted right turn to **Kilkea Castle**, the oldest inhabited castle in Ireland (1180) and a now a luxury hotel of great charm set in 200 acres. Reminiscent of the Spanish *paradores,* Kilkea capitalizes successfully on its long tradition and looks to the future: An 18-hole golf course is being developed.

Returning to Timolin a minor road to the right will take you to Dunlavin, passing (or, better yet, with a stop at) **Rathsallagh House**, 12 guest rooms in converted Queen Anne stables described by its genial giant of an owner, Corkman Joe O'Flynn, as "not a hotel." It is that, however, and much more: 500 acres of farmland, a golf range, gardens, hunting country, plus a gourmet restaurant. Very special. Resume the route northeast from Dunlavin to Hollywood to reach the mountains.

COUNTY WICKLOW

"A road still carriageable climbs over the high moorland. It cuts across vast turfbogs, a thousand feet above sea level, two thousand if you prefer. It leads to nothing any more. A few ruined forts, a few ruined dwellings. The sea is not far, just visible beyond the valleys dipping eastward, pale plinth as pale as the pale wall of sky. Tarns lie hidden in the folds of the moor, invisible from the road, reached by faint paths, under high over-hanging crags."

The writer is Samuel Beckett, recalling, in the novel

Mercier and Camier, the Wicklow of his youth. Today, 80 years later, little is changed: It is still a largely uninhabited expanse of rugged, heather-covered mountains, often snow-covered in winter, where a scattering of sheep graze, and, in summer, where people from Dublin city come to engage in the backbreaking business of cutting turf (peat) for their winter fires. Late spring, when the roads leading up into this vastness are ablaze with gorse, is perhaps the best time to enjoy the solitude. Drive up on a weekday in early evening when you could find yourself the monarch of all you survey.

The road to which Beckett refers is the **Military Road**, built by the British in response to the 1798 Rising, and which traverses the mountain system from Kilakee, in the south Dublin suburbs, up to the Sally Gap, a crossroads in the middle of nowhere, and onward to Laragh and Glendalough. A similar route runs from the Dublin–Tullow road, N 81, near Blessington via the Sally Gap to the Dublin–Glendalough road north of Roundwood (the highest village in Ireland).

A third begins at the little village of Hollywood, south of Blessington, and crosses the **Wicklow Gap** to Laragh. This last road is perhaps the most impressive introduction to the pleasures of Wicklow. Lined with state forests (entrance only on foot in most cases; there are picnic tables), the road rises through the valley of the Kings River to the gap (a parking place and lookout with fine views eastward to the sea). At the junction in Laragh turn right for Glendalough, which may also be reached from Dublin via the Bray road (N 11). A private bus service, St. Kevin's, operates to Glendalough from St. Stephen's Green daily at 11:00 A.M., and regular tours depart from Busaras, the central bus station in Dublin's Store Street. There are other alternatives: Ten varied touring routes have been mapped and distinctively signposted. Full details are available from Midlands-East Tourism (see above).

Glendalough

This sixth-century foundation encapsulates Early Christian Ireland, and should not be missed. The setting, in a steep-sided valley (Gleann Dá Locha, "the Valley of the Two Lakes") chosen by Saint Kevin for its remoteness, still preserves something of that quality in spite of its popularity as a tourist attraction. (Avoid weekends if possible, but try to time your visit for late in the evening, when the light is particularly evocative.) Saint Kevin (d. 619?) established a monastic center of learning here that endured until the 16th century. Something of a misogynist, the saint, as legend has it, was pursued by a determined female across the upper lake to a cave where he had taken refuge. (Boats are available for hire to visit the cave.) The settlement was plundered by the Danes in the 11th century and by the English of Dublin in the 14th, but the remains are more than sufficient to convey a vivid impression of the flowering of Irish monasticism. The building known as **St. Kevin's Kitchen** is in fact a two-story oratory in the Celtic manner dating from the ninth century, with a steeply pitched stone roof. St. Mary's Church marks the supposed site of Saint Kevin's grave; its round tower is the fourth highest in the country (after Kilmacduagh, Galway, and Kildare), the conical cap having been reconstructed using the original stones. **Glendalough Craft Centre**, close to the ruins, specializes in weaving and jewelry. A new and comprehensively equipped visitors' center forms the nucleus of a major national park that is being developed in the area.

The Wicklow Way

This is ideal walking country, whether you are a dedicated hiker or have just a day, or half day, to devote to a short ramble. A long-distance path, named the Wicklow Way for one of the ancient roads of Ireland, Slí Cualann, runs from the south Dublin suburbs at Marley Park (buses 74, 48A, and 48B) to Clonegal in County Carlow, a total distance of some 78 miles. It offers a rich variety of scenery and terrain, from barren mountains to lush farmland, with glimpses of wildlife—including red and sika deer, hare, fox, squirrel, and the occasional badger. This is the area that provided the background for several of John M. Synge's plays, including *In the Shadow of the Glen*. Short sections of the Way are perfectly feasible for the inexperienced or for those with limited time. For the more ambitious, bed-and-breakfast accommodations are available at points along or somewhat off the route at places such as Glencree, Roundwood, and Laragh. (To arrange accommodations contact the Wicklow Tourist Information Office; Tel: 0404/691-17 or 18.) A good deal of the Way is, however, at some remove from even the basics of civilization, and all normal precautions associated with hill walking should be taken, particularly in regard to advance planning, suitable clothing and footwear, and information to third parties as to your intentions. Full-scale maps and descriptive details on the Way are available from tourist offices and bookstores. Alternatively, you could joint a six-day guided walking tour. For details contact **Countryside Study Tours**, Knockrath, Rathdrum, County Wicklow; Tel: (0404) 464-65.

Blessington and Russborough

Blessington, a one-street town with a 17th-century church 31 km (19 miles) from Dublin on N 81, is a good starting point for a circular tour of Blessington Lake, which is in fact a man-made reservoir set in attractive countryside in the foothills of the Wicklow Mountains. The reservoir is fed by the circumambient Liffey, which rises near the Sally Gap a bare 12 miles from Dublin but requires nearly eight times that distance to reach the sea. The **Lakeside Leisure Center**, 1½ km (1 mile) from the village, provides a wide range of outdoor pursuits including canoeing and pony-trekking. Go 5 km (3 miles) south from Blessington on N 81 to reach **Russborough House** (to the right; signposted), a fine Palladian mansion built in 1741 by Richard Cassels, or Castle, the German architect also responsible for Castletown and Carton. Russborough, owned by the Alfred Beit Foundation, is open to the public from Easter to October; inquire locally for times. Guided tours reveal such treasures as works by Vermeer, Goya, Gainsborough, Rubens, Hals, and Reynolds; Baroque plasterwork by the Francini brothers; and an abundance of Caribbean mahogany.

On leaving Russborough turn right on the main road for Poulaphouca (Poll a' Phúca, "the Pool of the Pooka," a malignant spirit that takes the form of a black dog). Here, where the Liffey is dammed for hydroelectrical purposes, a sign points left to **Tulfarris Hotel and Country Club**, a Late Georgian country-house hotel and leisure center beautifully situated on the far shore of the lake. It may take a little finding, but it is worth the trouble, with golf, tennis, fishing, sailing, windsurfing, a choice of bars and restaurants, and elegant public rooms. From here you may continue the lake circuit back to Blessington or divert right into the mountains via Valleymount and the Wicklow Gap.

Other Routes through Wicklow

A glance at the map of Wicklow will suggest several round-trip routes from Dublin, some of which, via the Military Road, have already been mentioned. One possibility is to travel out via **Enniskerry**, a pretty dormitory village at the foot of Glencree, through which a scenic road rises to the upland area known as the Featherbed. At the head of Glencree a cemetery holds the remains of German victims of the Second World War, some of whom crash-landed in Ireland and others whose bodies were washed ashore.

Up the hill beyond Enniskerry toward Glendalough is **Powerscourt Demesne**; the gardens here, open to the public, provide a fine view of the two Sugarloaf Mountains. The house (1731–1741) was destroyed by fire in 1974, together with its valuable contents. Just a few miles from the house, Powerscourt Waterfall, which impressed William Thackeray (*Irish Sketch Book,* 1843), is one of the highest waterfalls in Ireland. The Glendalough road climbs up to the Calary Bog and through Roundwood (site of the highest pub in Ireland) and Annamoe to Laragh. If you are not visiting Glendalough turn left here to Rathdrum, but take the right fork up a steep hill, where a beautiful route crosses the hills to Glenmalure, a dead-end valley at the foot of Lugnaquilla (3,039 feet), Wicklow's highest mountain and a challenging, though not difficult, climb. On the outskirts of Rathdrum (also accessible by rail and bus service from Dublin) is **Avondale Forest Park**, centered upon the former home of Charles Stuart Parnell, the charismatic 19th-century political leader. The house is now a museum, and the park contains stands of noble and unusual trees. In Rathdrum, a picturesque hilltop village, **Pierce's Lounge** on the square has attractive Art Nouveau stained glass and serves pub lunches in pleasant surroundings.

From Rathdrum the return to Dublin by road is via Glenealy and Rathnew, where a right turn (Wicklow road) will bring you to the entrance (1 km/½ mile on the left) of **Tinakilly Country House and Restaurant**, the embodiment of Victorian elegance in a fine coastal setting. It was built in the 1870s for Captain Robert Halpin, commander of the *Great Eastern,* the vessel that laid the first submarine cable between Europe and America. In 1991 William and Bee Power, the owners of the inn, won a major award for service, comfort, and hospitality. Go for peace and tranquillity, or for the many adjacent sporting facilities, which include golf, tennis, deer-stalking, and rough shooting.

Back in the direction of Dublin turn left at Ashford to the **Devil's Glen**, "which forms," wrote Thackeray, "a delightful wild walk, and where a Methuselah of a landscape painter might find studies for all his life long. All sorts of foliage and colour, all sorts of delightful caprices of light and shadow—the river tumbling and frothing amidst the boulders. . . ."

On a less dramatic scale, but equally impressive, are the lovely gardens of **Mount Usher** (to the right, just before Ashford, on the main road; open during the Spring and Summer). A right turn at the village (posted) suggests an alternative route to Dublin via the coastal route passing **Hunter's Hotel**, one of Ireland's oldest coaching inns and now in the fifth generation of the same family. The fine gardens are bordered by the River Vartry. Golf, tennis, riding, and sea fishing are available. Alternatively, continue on the N 11 via Newtownmountkennedy, the village with the longest name in Ireland, and through the picturesque Glen o' the Downs, after which, on your left, is the Great Sugarloaf: an extinct volcano, as its form suggests. No immediate eruptions are predicted by *Old Moore's Almanack*.

GETTING AROUND

A glance at the map will reveal that the lines of communication in the area run radially from Dublin, and since the distances are not great and the roads generally adequate most visitors will probably opt to explore on a daily basis from the city, setting off along one of the main arteries— N 1, N 2, etc.—numbered counterclockwise around Dublin. Two important exceptions should be made: The Boyne Valley requires more time—perhaps a circular tour with a night spent in a country hotel—as does the Wicklow region, which would be a pity to dismiss in a day.

Because, it is said, the Irish never really took to living in organized communities until it was forced upon them, these counties constitute a maze of little roads, many of them apparently designed to bring you back to the point from which you set out. This phenomenon is in no way mitigated by the amiable local habit of turning signposts to point to somewhere else altogether. So if you are proposing to travel, for example, from Trim to Kildare Town (a perfectly feasible trajectory), keep a firm hand on the map should your confidence, or your orientation, desert you.

On account of the road pattern and the location of many places of interest well away from main arteries, public transport is by and large not the best method of exploring the environs of Dublin. Exceptions and alternatives are noted. Specialized bus tours do, however, operate to the most popular locations from Busaras (the central bus station, Tel: (01) 30-22-22) in Dublin; details are available from Bus Atha Cliath (Dublin Bus, Tel: (01) 73-42-22) or tourist offices.

ACCOMMODATIONS REFERENCE
The telephone country code for the Dublin environs is 353. When dialing telephone numbers in the Republic from outside the country, drop the 0 in the area code. The rate ranges given below are projections for 1993; for up-to-the-minute rate information it is always wise to telephone before booking. Unless otherwise indicated, rates are per person sharing and do not include meals or service.

County Meath
▶ **Headfort Arms Hotel. Kells,** County Meath. Tel: (046) 400-63; Fax (046) 405-87. £28, breakfast included.

▶ **The Station House. Kilmessan,** County Meath. Tel: (046) 252-39; Fax: (046) 255-88. £25 (breakfast and service included).

▶ **Wellington Court Hotel. Trim,** County Meath. Tel: (046) 315-16 or 311-08; Fax: (046) 363-56. £22, breakfast included.

County Kildare
▶ **Kilkea Castle. Castledermot,** County Kildare. Tel: (053) 4510-56 or 00; Fax: (0503) 451-87; in U.S., Tel: (800) 222-1180. £60–£110.

▶ **Lord Edward Guest House. Kildare,** County Kildare. Tel: (045) 223-89; Fax: (045) 212-64. £16, breakfast included.

▶ **Moyglare Manor Hotel. Maynooth,** County Kildare. Tel: (01) 628-6351; Fax: (01) 628-5405; in U.S., Tel: (800) 223-6510. £55 year-round.

▶ **Naas Court Hotel. Naas,** County Kildare. Tel: (045) 660-73; Fax: (045) 660-72. £37.50–£50, breakfast included.

County Wicklow

▶ **Hunter's Hotel. Rathnew,** County Wicklow. Tel: (0404) 401-06; Fax: (0404) 403-38. £35 year-round.

▶ **Rathsallagh House. Dunlavin,** County Wicklow. Tel: (045) 531-12; Fax: (045) 533-43. Low-season rates vary; high season, £55.

▶ **Tinakilly Country House and Restaurant. Rathnew,** County Wicklow. Tel: (0404) 692-74; Fax: (0404) 678-06. £45–£100, breakfast included.

▶ **Tulfarris Hotel and Country Club. Blessington,** County Wicklow. Tel: (045) 645-74; Fax: (045) 644-23. £40–£62.

THE MIDLANDS

OFFALY, WESTMEATH, ROSCOMMON, LEITRIM, LONGFORD, AND LAOIS

By Bernard Share

Lying at the heart of Ireland, sandwiched between the better-known attractions of Dublin and Wicklow in the east and Connemara and the west, the Midlands area is not spectacular country in any accepted sense. The hills and mountains are modest, the centers of population small, the roads winding and often devious. On the other hand, the Midlands are one of Ireland's least-explored territories, with no massive tourist developments, no crowds, few traffic jams—other than those caused by cows or a couple of motorists pausing to pass the time of day in the middle of a village street—and a way of life that owes little to urban preoccupations. Take your time with it: The pleasure here lies in the detail rather than the broad panorama. The best way of all to slow things down is to undertake a little travel by water, the informing spirit of the Midlands.

The unifying factor in what might at first appear a somewhat random assembly of midland counties is the River Shannon—Ireland's longest (240 miles), most spectacular, and most storied waterway. The suggested itinerary will follow the river, with some substantial deviations, almost to its source in the north and back again; but it is

an itinerary designed to be adaptable. However you approach it, the big river and its influence will never be far away.

MAJOR INTEREST

Castles and museums
The bogland areas
Monastic city of Clonmacnois
Goldsmith Country
Lough Key Forest Park
Unspoilt Leitrim
Cruising on the Shannon and Grand Canal
Riparian towns and villages
The Slieve Bloom Mountains
Fishing and country sports
Walking and rambling

This itinerary assumes you will be travelling by road. If you don't want to drive, there are boats for hire, rail access (see Getting Around), bus tours, and short river trips from Banagher, Athlone, Portumna, and other centers (check with local Tourist Information offices). **Birr**, an attractive, mostly 18th-century town southwest of Dublin in County Offaly, is a good place to start. The town is closely tied to the family of the earls of Rosse. **Birr Castle**, the family seat, originally housed the O'Carrolls of Ely before being granted to Sir Laurence Parsons in 1620, after the death of Sir Charles O'Carroll. Parsons rebuilt the castle (largely as it appears today) and established Parsonstown, which later became known as Birr. The Rosse family inherited the Earldom from an uncle in County Longford, and in the 1840s the third earl of Rosse built a telescope at Birr Castle that was the largest in the world until 1917. Still in use as the family home, the castle is frequently inaccessible to visitors, but the landscaped castle grounds, with their fine trees, shrubs, and waterfalls, are open daily; the present, seventh earl of Rosse is maintaining the family tradition with the establishment of a science museum in some of the outbuildings—he is part of the 14th generation of the Parsons family to live in the castle. The elegantly picturesque All-Ireland Carriage Driving Championships are held on the grounds annually in September.

The town of Birr preserves a good measure of its 18th-century character. The long-established **Dooly's Hotel** (1747) on the main square is a good place for a meal (at the bar, the coffee shop, or in the elegant **Emmet Restaurant**) or for an overnight stay in one of its 18 comfortable rooms if you are spending time in Laois and Offaly.

Northwest of Birr on the R 439 is **Banagher**, a cruising center on the Shannon where, according to local tradition, the river was bridged as early as 1049. The town has several literary associations. The English writer Anthony Trollope found inspiration for his "Irish" novels here and served as Deputy Postal Surveyor in 1841 (his house can still be seen at the top of the town), and Charlotte Brontë spent her honeymoon here. In the summer season Banagher, thanks to the river traffic, has a truly cosmopolitan complexion. Visit the beer garden at the **Shannon Hotel**—close to the waterway, it is a favorite haunt of cruising people from many countries. A little farther up the street Mac and Gerry Crean's **The Old Forge** provides economical and attractive bed-and-breakfast accommodation; included in the room rate is the use of their boat.

A Trip on the Bog

From Banagher head northeast on the Cloghan road; after about 3 km (2 miles) turn left for Shannon Harbour and Clonony, from which another left turn will lead you in the direction of Shannonbridge. On the right the huge **Blackwater bog** stretches to the horizon, an apparently empty world where nothing lives or moves except the huge machines harvesting the peat to fuel the Shannonbridge electric-power station. About 3 km before Shannonbridge, a right turn will bring you to the **Clonmacnois & West Offaly Railway** and an opportunity to travel the bog on the tracks normally reserved for power-station traffic. It is an unusual experience and one not to be missed. The ride, in a specially built passenger car reminiscent of those that traversed the Wild West, is comfortable and leisurely, and the on-board commentary is friendly and informative about the history, flora, fauna, ecology, and archaeology of this impressive russet-brown wilderness. (A 3,000-year-old settlement has recently been excavated in these bogs.) Tel: (0905) 741-14 or 72 for schedules and travel directions.

Shannonbridge itself, as befits a strategic river crossing on the frontier of Connacht, has well-preserved early-

19th-century fortifications. On a good day try a drink in the sun in front of one of several pubs lining the approach to the river.

The monastic city of **Clonmacnois** is about 6 km (3½ miles) from Shannonbridge. If at all possible, arrange to approach this magical place by water, as did Saint Ciaran and eight companions on January 25, 545, when they came downstream from Inis Ainghin (Hare Island) to found a monastery here. (Short boat trips to the monastery are available from Banagher.) Subsequent to Ciaran's death in the following September the site became a center of pilgrimage (Pope John Paul II visited in 1979) and a hotbed of medieval learning: Its scriptorium was responsible for a great deal of important vernacular literature. Attacked, pillaged, and burnt by Vikings, English, and the native Irish over the centuries, Clonmacnois is nevertheless, in its ruined state, potently evocative and rich in artifacts of archaeological and historical interest, including High Crosses from the ninth and tenth centuries. Information is available from the Interpretative Centre at the site, which is best visited on quiet weekdays out of the main summer-holiday season.

Athlone and Lough Ree

From Clonmacnois take the road north to **Athlone**, a rather unattractive historical river crossing commanded by a substantial castle on the County Roscommon side. The present structure dates to 1210 and contains a regional museum and tourist information center; you may park your car at the castle base and walk up. The little streets around the castle shelter a number of appealing pubs and restaurants catering to passing boat people; the **Prince of Wales Hotel** here is a good place to base yourself for a leisurely venture into the region. If you're only looking for a brief respite try the hotel's pleasant coffee lounge, where snacks are available.

Athlone lies at the southern extremity of Lough Ree, one of two major bodies of water that give the Shannon system much of its character and appeal (Lough Derg, farther south near Portumna, is the other). Our route now follows, at a greater or lesser distance, the eastern shore of this lake, passing, on the N 55, through **Glasson**, where Michael Brooks's picturesque **Glasson Village Restaurant** is well worth a visit: The wine list is varied, interesting, and realistically priced (the restaurant is closed Sunday evenings and all day Monday). From here you might follow the **Lough Ree Tour** (signposted) along the lakeshore. Fishing for pike, trout, perch, and bream can be arranged with Mr. **J. P. Nolan** (Tel: 0902/850-41). The N 55 continues through **Goldsmith Country**, an attractive rural area where the author of *The Vicar of Wakefield* grew up and spent half his short life, and which has altered little since his day. Several locations associated with Goldsmith, such as the 3 Jolly Pigeons hostelry that figures in *She Stoops to Conquer,* are clearly signposted. Real enthusiasts may celebrate the connection in the Goldsmith Summer School (usually in June and not as academic as it sounds) centered in Ballymahon.

From Ballymahon a turn left for Lanesborough (at the head of the lough) skirts a large bogland area on the right and a network of minor roads on the left offering another opportunity to explore the shore of Lough Ree and its islands. At Lanesborough the road crosses the Shannon into County Roscommon (this site was strongly defended by the Irish forces under Sarsfield during the Jacobite wars of 1690–1691). Continue on the R 371 north toward Rooskey, turning left onto the N 5 at Scramoge for **Strokestown** and **Strokestown Park House**, a fine Neo-Palladian mansion built in the 1730s by Richard Cassells (or Castle), the architect of Dublin's Leinster House as well as of the mansions of Carton and Russborough. Strokestown Park House has been lovingly and magnificently restored and refurnished by local enterprise, and possesses a lived-in feeling uncommon to such undertakings. The house and a museum devoted to The Great Hunger (the devastating potato famine of the 1840s) are well worth the diversion. Open from June to September, Tuesday through Saturday, afternoons only.

From Strokestown return the short distance on the N 5 to Scramoge and turn left for Rooskey. Here the road climbs high enough to afford expansive views over Kilglass Lough and Lough Boderg before descending once more to the Shannon. **Rooskey** (also Roosky and Ruscaigh—you will encounter all three versions) is half in Roscommon, half in Leitrim, and altogether devoted to the delights of the waterway. **The Crew's Inn** restaurant here, however, extends an equally friendly welcome to landlubbers, and New Zealander Martin Bourke, one of the partner-proprietors, specializes in the outstanding wines of his own country. Apart from the restaurant there is a lounge with an excellent bar menu at modest prices and an open fire in chilly seasons.

Lough Key

From Rooskey return south on the R 371 for about 1½ km (1 mile) and take the first turn to the right, keeping a sharp eye on the map to help you through this network of back roads meandering between river and lake. A right turn at the T-junction on R 368 brings you to **Carrick-on-Shannon**, a major cruising center. Its century-old rowing club produced a world-class oarswoman not long ago who subsequently took over **Cryan's** pub and restaurant. It is on the right after you cross the bridge, and offers good pub food in a friendly atmosphere. About 8 km (5 miles) northwest of Carrick on the N 4 in the direction of Boyle, a signpost on the right indicates the **Arigna Drive**, a circular tour, via Cootehall and Knockvicar, of **Lough Key** and its extensive (850 acres) **Forest Park**, a major leisure center on the grounds of the former Rockingham House, built by John Nash and burnt down in 1957. The Forest Park's amenities include nature trails, a bog garden, relics of the former mansion including an ice house and subterranean passageway, a shop, and a modest restaurant.

Lough Key, one of the loveliest lakes in the Shannon system, was the focus of 1,500 years of colorful history. On **Castle Island** Tadhg Mac Dermot of the ruling Mac Dermot family, lords of Moylurg, feasted the literati of Ireland in 1541, an event that surely prefigured the many summer schools of the present era with its mixture of learning and conviviality. **Trinity Island** holds the ruins of the only surviving monastery of the Irish branch of Premonstratensian Canons, an order founded in France in 1120. One of the sons of the King family, 17th century grantees of the Mac Dermot estates which included Trinity Island, was drowned on a voyage to Dublin. He is commemorated in the poem "Lycidas" by his fellow Cambridge student John Milton.

Due west of Lough Key, the small town of **Boyle** is notable for the ruins of its 12th- to 13th-century **Cistercian abbey**, among the most impressively preserved in the country. The carvings of men and beasts on the capitals of the arcade are remarkable. In the abbey grounds two mews-type houses are available for rental on a self-catering basis by the week or weekend. For details call Martin Mitchell; Tel: (079) 623-85. From here the R 285 northeast leads to **Ballyfarnan**, where a right turn takes you to the village of **Keadew**, final home of the blind harper Turlough Carolan (1670–1738), "the last of the Irish bards." He is buried in the church of Kilronan on the Ballyfarnan road. From Keadew continue northeast to the T-junction with R 320 and turn left (north) along the western shore of **Lough Allen** to **Drumkeeran**. This is wild, empty country; for those who live here it lacks virtually any employment opportunity now that Ireland's only power station using native coal has been closed down, nearby at Arigna. For the fisherman Lough Allen offers good trolling for pike; there is an angling center in Drumshanbo at the southern end.

County Leitrim

About 8 km (5 miles) north of Drumkeeran take a left turn for **Dromahair**. "He stood among a crowd at DrMa-hair/His heart hung all upon a silken dress," wrote W. B. Yeats in "The Man Who Dreamed of Faeryland." But if it's the rare crowd to be encountered in this quiet village these days, there is perhaps still something otherworldly about it. For modest, comfortable, and friendly accommodations here try **Stanford's Village Inn** on the main street of town. In the same family for five generations, it is essentially a bed and breakfast with restaurant and bar, popular with the locals. Ask for a room at the back overlooking the river. Private fishing is available, horse-trekking is by arrangement.

Three kilometers (2 miles) north of Dromahair via the R 288, which skirts Lough Gill on its way to Manor-hamilton, the 17th-century **Parkes Castle** stands on the riverbank, on the site of Breffini Castle. It was from here that Dervorgilla, wife of Tiernan O'Rourke, was abducted by Dermot Mac Murrough, king of Leinster, setting off the train of events that culminated in the Anglo-Norman invasion of Ireland and all that flowed from it. The abduction (some say she arranged it) took place in 1152; O'Rourke got her back the following year. Mac Murrough nursed his desire for revenge until 1166 when, threatened with defeat by O'Rourke, he took ship for England on his way to France to persuade the French/English king Henry II to help him against his rival. Henry agreed . . . and the rest, as they say, is history. Parkes Castle has been splendidly restored as an interpretative center for Leitrim, Sligo, and south Donegal: The great hall was re-roofed with native oak, fastened without the use of nails, and timber also was exclusively employed in the construction of a 17th-century spiral staircase. Outside, the courtyard features cobblestones set in the style of the original period. Open daily from June through September; open days vary the rest of the year. For details, Tel: (071) 641-49.

Manorhamilton has little to detain the visitor. Follow the R 280 north through precipitous mountain country to the town of Kinlough, finely situated on Lough Melvin and close to where a narrow tongue of County Leitrim meets the Atlantic Ocean. Return along R 281, the road skirting **Lough Melvin**, noted for its unique variety of trout, the *giolla rua* ("red fellow," or gillaroo). On an island near the shore are the ruins of the 15th-century **Rossclogher Castle**. In this MacClancy stronghold a survivor of the Spanish Armada, Francisco de Cuellar, found sanctuary before making his way back to Spain to record his not entirely flattering impressions of Ireland and the Irish.

The R 281 connects with R 282, the road back to Manorhamilton, and the R 280, which leads to Killarga and eventually Drumkeeran; from Drumkeeran turn left toward Dowra, with its fine views over the northern end of Lough Allen. Complete the circuit of the lough by turning right at Dowra, where you cross the now-diminutive Shannon very close to its source. Signs here indicate the route of the **Slí Liatroma** walking trail, which can, if time and energy permit, be undertaken in short sections. It combines fairly demanding terrain with easy road stages and is well marked. Maps are available from Tourist Information offices. Otherwise, follow the scenic lakeshore road to Drumshanbo.

The route east (R 208) from Drumshanbo to Ballinamore skirts the northern shores of a series of lakes linked by the **Ballinamore & Ballyconnell Canal**, a waterway with a curious history. Begun in 1840 as a commercial link between the Shannon and Erne rivers, it was finally completed, after multifarious difficulties, on July 4, 1860, only to be abandoned as a technical and commercial failure some nine years later. Only eight boats are known to have passed through the canal during its short working life. Happily, however, the long-neglected channels are close to being fully restored, vastly expanding the potential of the country's inland waterway system and creating one of the finest cruising facilities in Europe. Reopening is scheduled for this year, when **Ballinamore**, an attractive village with modest facilities, will undoubtedly prove popular as a port-of-call. (The **Sliabh an Iarainn** hotel on the main street offers simple accommodation and sustenance.) If you have any ancestral connections with County Leitrim the **Leitrim Heritage Centre**, housed in the County Library on the main street facing the church, offers a professional genealogical service backed by a comprehensive and fully indexed assemblage of source material. Open weekdays; Tel: (078) 440-12.

Leaving Ballinamore, head south on the minor Cloone road beside the church. At Aghoo, where the road crosses the restored canal, **Riversdale** offers attractive accommodations on a working sheep farm owned by Violet and Raymond Thomas; choose between the farmhouse itself, self-catering bungalows, and a fully equipped gate lodge. Leisure facilities include an indoor heated swimming pool, a squash court, and a sauna. If you fancy a little fishing you have a choice of 25 lakes within a five-mile radius: the fishing is free year-round. Riversdale offers full facilities, including storage for tackle, a drying room, and the hire of boats with or without outboards.

County Longford

The area around **Drumlish**, south of Cloone and the R 201, is good for fishing. Pascal and Joan Etienne offer two luxury self-catering apartments here at **"Chez Nous,"** near an 18-hole golf course with horseback riding (the apartments include access to a rowboat). Week-long or weekend rentals are available. From Drumlish take the R 198 south to the town of **Longford**. The County Longford Golf Club offers special "improve-your-golf" classes at a reasonable fee; Tel: (043) 463-10. The main Dublin road (N 4) southeast from Longford brings you to **Edgeworthstown**, otherwise known as Mostrim, home of the novelist Maria Edgeworth (1767–1849), whose work influenced Jane Austen, Walter Scott, and the Russian Turgenev.

Leave Mostrim by the Granard road (N 55) north, turning right almost immediately on R 395 to **Castlepollard**. Just short of this attractively laid-out village is **Tullynally Castle**, known as Packenham Hall from circa 1730 to 1961 and until that latter year seat of the earls of Longford. It is now the home of the author Thomas Packenham, and is open to visitors from mid-July to mid-August. Extended and elaborated upon since the 17th century by succeeding occupants, it is well worth a visit. There are so many rooms in this castle that when Thomas Packenham was writing his book on the Boer War he allocated one per chapter, leaving the finished draft on the floor before moving elsewhere to begin its successor. In Castlepollard itself **The Pollard Arms** on the main square is a congenial pub with character.

Fore

> To Fore next let us go,
> That valley lying low;
> And see the rill
> That through the hill
> To turn the mill
> Saint Feichin caused to flow.

Fore is a miniature fortified town that once marked the frontier of the English Pale and that retains the ruins of its two gateways. It is celebrated for its monastery, founded by Saint Feichin in 639, and for what have become known as its "seven wonders." A devious argument persists locally as to their definitive identity, but they certainly include the two-ton lintel stone that the saint hoisted into position, with divine assistance, over the door of his church; the water that flows uphill; the tree that won't burn, and the monastery built on a bog.

Within Fore's small compass lie the wonders, as well as more reliably attested relics of its monastic age, such as Saint Feichin's church itself, which was possibly the oratory of the original seventh century monastery; the Benedictine priory (largely 15th century); and the Anchorite's cell containing a memorial to the last hermit of Fore, who died in 1616. The modern Fore is a pleasant little village. To reach Fore, take the R 195 Oldcastle Road east from Castlepollard.

To reach tranquil **Lough Derravaragh**, return to Castlepollard either the way you came or around Lough Lene via Collinstown. Then follow the R 394 south to Mullingar, passing on your right signposts indicating the proximity of the lake, where, legend has it, the four children of Aobh and the sea-god Mannanan Mac Lir (after whom is named the Isle of Man in the Irish Sea) spent 300 years of an eternal 900-year cycle, having been changed into swans by Mac Lir's second and jealous wife Aoife, Aobh's sister. You may catch them before they set off for 300 years on the North Channel between Ireland and Scotland and 300 on the Atlantic. If not, enjoy the peace and seclusion of Derravaragh anyway.

County Westmeath

Mullingar, a lively town in the center of Westmeath, has a few good pubs (**Con's,** near the railroad station serves good snacks, too) and **The Greville Arms**, a long-established hotel of some repute—not least because it figures in the works of James Joyce, who rarely looked for inspiration beyond his native Dublin. A lifelike Joyce occupies a quiet corner, and the bar is at least as atmospheric as it was at the time of his visits in the 1890s. South of Mullingar via the Kilbeggan road (N 52), which skirts Lough Ennell, sit the 18th-century mansions of the Rochfort family—Belvedere and Tudenham (formerly Rochfort), situated between the road and the lake and separated by what has become known as the "jealous wall." The story is too complex to tell here; a visit to Tudenham will reveal all. Or pick up a copy of the *Tourist Guide to Tyrrellspass,* available from Tyrrellspass Castle (see below).

Some 5 km (3 miles) beyond Tudenham the left fork at Dalystown leads to Tyrrellspass, named for the Tyrrells who came to Ireland in 1169 and built many castles in south Westmeath. The last of those, **Tyrrellspass Castle**, is just outside the village, and was built circa 1410 to guard the pass between two large stretches of bog and swamp. Meticulously restored in the 1970s and 1980s, the castle includes a very functional *garderobe* (toilet), which relied upon the law of gravity; it now also houses a small museum with a good display of local artifacts and ephemera, an antiques-and-books shop, and a small restaurant. Open daily. Tel: (044) 231-05. Tyrrellspass itself is Georgian, built in 1800 around a village green by Jane, countess of Belvedere, who was responsible for much of its layout and elegant houses. On the corner of the main road, heading west, some of these have been incorporated in **The Village Hotel**, a charming, ten-bedroom establishment with a good restaurant and an open fire in the lounge. The bar-food buffet is open all day.

The N 6 trunk road brings you swiftly west from Tyrrellspass to **Kilbeggan**, where Locke's Distillery, reputed to be the oldest licensed pot-still distillery in the world, was in production from 1757 to 1954. Pending the planned resumption of distilling, Locke's now functions as a maturing facility for a new whiskey company. Much of its machinery, including a huge waterwheel turned by the River Brosna and a massive steam engine, has been restored to working order as the centerpiece of the **Industrial Museum and Craft Enterprise Center**. Coffee, wine, and light refreshments are available, and there is a public bar and *bureau de change*. Guided tours (every half hour from April to October) include samples of the maturing whiskey. From November to March tours must be arranged in advance; Tel: (0506) 321-34 or 15.

Fourteen kilometers (9 miles) farther west on the N 6, in County Offaly, the expansive village of **Moate** takes its name from a substantial prehistoric earthwork situated southwest of the town. As it has not yet been excavated, there is no visible clue as to what lies within. A little farther along the N 6, a turn to the left leads to **Kilcleagh Park Hotel**, a Georgian manor house set in 35 acres. The menu of the restaurant here, a place popular with both residents and locals, usually features freshly caught salmon and trout. You can avail yourself of shooting, golf, fishing, and horseback riding in the vicinity.

From Moate the N 80 will take you south through Clara to **Tullamore**, another town with a long distilling tradition and now the home of Irish Mist liqueur. The premises are immediately on the right as you cross the bridge over the canal, but the complex is not open to visitors. The Grand Canal from Dublin once terminated here (it has subsequently been extended to the Shannon), and the harbor and other buildings are still extant. Cruising on the canal is a pleasant and leisurely pastime, offering the opportunity to visit little villages (and their hostelries) not easily accessible by road. **Celtic Canal Cruisers**, based a short distance east of town on the Daingean road, can arrange hire. Call Mike and Heather Thomas; Tel: (0506) 218-61. Tullamore, the county seat of Offaly, is largely an 18th-century creation, with some good surviving architecture of the period. The Catholic church, rebuilt after a fire in 1982, now contains some fine stained glass by Harry Clarke.

The Slieve Bloom Mountains

Mountmellick, south of Tullamore on the N 80, was an early (1600s) settlement of the Quakers (Society of Friends) in Ireland; their original meeting house and school remain, though not as Quaker establishments.

From Mountmellick turn right on the R 422 to **Rosenallis,** a name which derives from the Irish Ros Fhionn-ghlaise, (the Wood of the Bright Stream), but which was popularly assumed locally to commemorate two Quaker ladies, the misses Rose and Alice. This road skirts the little-travelled **Slieve Bloom Mountains**, a miniature range on the Laois-Offaly border rich in unspoilt solitude and expansive vistas. Continue from Rosenallis to Clonaslee, where a left turn will take you up through The Cut. From the other side of the pass you may descend by a variety of routes to Kinnitty or drop down to Mountrath and the main road (N 7) to Dublin and Limerick. For those with time and energy the **Slieve Bloom Way** offers a 32-mile circular walking trail through deep glens and past waterfalls and large forestry plantations, rising to a height of 1,509 feet. The trail is well marked, and may be joined at many points on the circuit by car (ample parking is available). Camping is possible, but forbidden near the state forests that clothe large areas of the Slieve Blooms. Maps and information sheets may be picked up at Tourist Information Offices. If you complete the circuit of the mountains to Kinnitty, you are only a short distance from Birr, the starting point of this Midlands circuit.

GETTING AROUND

The Midlands area is easily accessible by car from all directions. From Shannon via Limerick and Killaloe to Portumna; from Dublin via N 6 to Kinnegad and Athlone; from Belfast via M 1 and A 4 to Enniskillen and then north County Leitrim—there are many possibilities, which a glance at a map will reveal.

Boyle, Carrick-on-Shannon, Longford, Roscommon, Mullingar, Athlone, and Tullamore are served by rail from Dublin; these and many other cities are also on express and local bus routes. By air, Sligo and Galway are practical starting points.

Boat Rental

Cruisers may be rented at various locations, from Portumna and to the north, for periods ranging from a weekend to a lengthy vacation. Because of the popularity of water travel in the Midlands you should book as far in advance as possible if you are planning a trip in July or August. Boats, suitable for parties of two to eight people are plentiful, and because the Shannon system is extensive you'll never really feel crowded on the rivers. You can learn to handle a Shannon cruiser in 20 minutes; however, if you'd rather not be at the helm but would nevertheless like to enjoy the waterways, you can book a day trip on the comfortable hotel-barge **Tristan**, based in the new harbor at Portumna. (There are two harbors: this is the one near the main street and signposted.) Call Brian Kelly of the Tristan at Tel: (088) 56-79-11 or fax him at (0509) 414-59 for bookings and directions.

ACCOMMODATIONS REFERENCE

The telephone country code for the Midland area is 353. When dialing telephone numbers in the Republic from outside the country, drop the 0 in the area code. The rate ranges given below are projections *for 1993; for up-to-the minute rate information it is always wise to telephone before booking. Unless otherwise indicated, rates are per person sharing and do not include meals or service.*

County Offaly

▶ **Dooly's Hotel.** Emmet Square, **Birr**, County Offaly. Tel: (0509) 200-32, Fax: (0509) 213-32 £25, breakfast included. Special weekend rates.

▶ **The Old Forge.** West End, **Banagher**, County Offaly. Tel: (0509) 515-04. £14.50, breakfast included.

County Westmeath

▶ **The Greville Arms Hotel. Mullingar**, County Westmeath. Tel: (044) 485-63, Fax: (044) 480-52. £25, breakfast included.

▶ **Kilcleagh Park Hotel. Castledaly**, Moate, County Westmeath. Tel and Fax: (0902) 812-21. £30, breakfast included.

▶ **Prince of Wales Hotel. Athlone**, County Westmeath. Tel: (0902) 726-26, Fax: (0902) 756-58. £30–£35, breakfast and service included.

▶ **The Village Hotel. Tyrrellspass**, County Westmeath. Tel: (044) 231-71, Fax: (044) 234-91. £25–£30, breakfast and service included.

County Roscommon

▶ **Abbey House. Boyle**, County Roscommon. Tel: (079) 623-85. £150 per week per apartment, £15 for bed and breakfast.

County Leitrim

▶ **Riverdale. Ballinamore**, County Leitrim. Tel: (078)

441-22. Self-catering bungalows £115–£135 per week; bed and breakfast in farmhouse £15.

▶ **Sliabh an Iarainn. Ballinamore**, County Leitrim. Tel: (078) 440-03. £14, breakfast included.

▶ **Stanford's Village Inn. Dromahair**, County Leitrim. Tel and Fax: (071) 641-40. £14, breakfast and service included.

County Longford

▶ **"Chez Nous."** Arua Road, **Manaduff**, Drumlish, County Longford. Tel: (043) 243-68. £75 per week per apartment. Weekends by arrangement.

THE SOUTHEAST

WEXFORD, KILKENNY, TIPPERARY, WATERFORD

By Lorcan Roche

Lorcan Roche, formerly associate editor of Travel-Holiday *magazine in the United States, is a freelance writer as well as a drama critic for the* Irish Independent, *Ireland's largest-selling daily newspaper. He is a direct descendant of a Norman family that first arrived in Wexford in 1167.*

There is a certain irony inherent in this chapter being written by a "Jackeen," a born-and-bred Dubliner. Tradition in this part of the world would have it that a Jackeen is utterly incapable of assessing Life Beyond The Pale, because for him it simply does not exist. It is rather like asking that quintessential Manhattanite Woody Allen to discourse on the probability of a new form of Renaissance thinking emerging in Peoria, Illinois. To most Jackeens Dublin is the center of the universe, and it is highly improbable, if not altogether impossible, that anything interesting in terms of accommodations, cuisine, and amenities might be stirring beyond the confines of the capital.

A journey into the Southeast of only a few days or, ideally, a week, will scotch such foolish misconceptions and introduce you to some of the finest food (particularly seafood) and friendliest people this island can muster. The area also has a plentiful supply of excellent country manors, inns, and farmhouse holiday homes, most of which offer bed-and-breakfast accommodation. Such establishments are not only less expensive than hotels, but they offer an opportunity to meet local families in an intimate and enjoyable setting.

The Southeast has several distinct natural advantages: The Wexford/Waterford coastline is warmed by the Gulf Stream, and its waters are an immensely rich source of seafood. Its rivers are clean and provide excellent fishing; its beaches are unsurpassed on the island. And finally, the entire region—Wexford county in particular—records more hours of sunshine than any other in Ireland. Because of this climatic asset the county is Ireland's chief producer of soft fruits.

Situated as it is, so close to Britain and the Continent, the Southeast was one of the first parts of Ireland to experience invasion. The clement weather, fertile soil, and bountiful seas saw to it that the "visitors" invariably chose to stay, and they have left a lasting impression on their point of entry. The Southeast can, in fact, be regarded as the beachhead of Ireland where, in terms of history and the development of culture, some of the first tentative and not so tentative steps were taken.

MAJOR INTEREST

Wexford
Selskar Abbey
Wexford Festival of Opera
National Heritage Park
Enniscorthy Castle
Johnstown, 19th-century Gothic castle
Beaches in Wexford
Saltee Islands bird sanctuary

Kilkenny
Kilkenny Castle
The Black Abbey
St. Canice's Cathedral
Kilkenny Arts Week
Arts and crafts
Jerpoint Abbey, 12th-century Cistercian ruin

Tipperary
Cahir Castle
Rock of Cashel
GPA-Bolton Library

Holy Cross Abbey
Ormonde House, Anne Boleyn's birthplace

Waterford
Reginald's Tower
The French Church medieval ruins
Waterford Glass Factory
Deep-sea fishing at Dungarvan
Celtworld

COUNTY WEXFORD

The so-called "Model County" lies at the southern tip of the east coast, below Dublin and Wicklow. It has been for generations a popular holiday destination for Dubliners, who take advantage of the country's curiously clement weather, its bewildering choice of safe, sandy beaches, and, lately, its accessibility from the capital. (EC-funded roads through Wicklow into Wexford, in particular the Bray By-Pass, are among the finest in this pot-holed country.)

To be honest, though, in many respects Wexford fails to live up to the scenic standards set by the majestic, rolling countryside of, say, Tipperary. And its mostly ruined, scattered castles (nearly 140 were built here between the 12th and 16th centuries, as Norman knights were rewarded with tracts of land) cannot hope to instill in the visitor the same instant respect as medieval Kilkenny. In Wexford, more than anywhere else in the Southeast, it is the people who matter most.

A stoic breed with an appealing sardonic wit, they are fiercely proud of their well-ordered county and of its noble history. Their collective folk memory of the 1798 Rising, which was spurred more by outrage at English injustice than by any French-inspired desire for liberty, equality, and fraternity, remains strong.

Those superb seamen, the Vikings (a.k.a. Norsemen), first made their presence felt in Wexford in A.D. 819, when they raided a monastic settlement on the island of Begerin in today's Wexford Harbour. Like the Belgic Celts who had sailed into Wexford around 500 B.C. in search of the Wicklow gold mines, the Vikings, with their austere Scandinavian background, probably felt they had tumbled across Valhalla on earth. The Irish monks, whose sacred objects of gold and silver were snatched by the marauding sea rovers, described the Vikings as being "vomited up" by the waves.

The Vikings formed a settlement at the mouth of the River Slaney, on a bay (Wexford Harbour) right at the southeast corner of Ireland, and called their new home Weissfjord, after the mate of their one-eyed warrior god, Odin. Weissfjord developed into one of their most lucrative strongholds, and like its nearby Viking twin, Waterford (Vadrefjord), it retains a dominant Viking influence in its haphazard design and in the profusion of steep lanes and slips leading from the harbor to the town center.

The first Norman incursions at Bannow and Wexford in 1169 and at Baginbun in 1170 were largely freelance family affairs provoked by the banished king of Leinster, Dermot MacMurrough, who promised the Welsh-Norman mercenaries land, easy living, and the hand of his handsome daughter, Aoife, in return for a secure throne. Whereas the Vikings left only a strong seafaring tradition, a few surnames (Doyle, Larkin, Cosgrave), and a few placenames (Selskar, Tuskar, Saltees), the Normans bequeathed a new way of life. And there were positive attributes: Organized farming replaced the wandering herds of the Irish, and Wexford was swept into a new agricultural era from which it derives its current "Model County" standards.

Wexford Town

Wexford Town, a delightful introduction to the Southeast, is essentially a series of narrow lanes and alleyways crisscrossing the snaking Main Street. Although there is no public transportation, none is really necessary to see Wexford's attractions. The very active **Wexford Historical Society**, beyond ensuring that the town's monuments are well documented, organizes excellent walking tours of the town from its location at 12 Ard Carman; Tel: (053) 222-11, ext. 355.

On Crescent Quay at the harbor you will find a statue of Commodore John Barry, born in nearby Ballysampson in 1745, who was the first commissioned officer to capture a ship under the authority of the U.S. Navy during the American War of Independence, and who is in fact credited with the founding of that navy. The mudflats, or slobs, of Wexford Harbour are now home to the impressive

Wildfowl Reserve, where 50 percent of the world's white-fronted geese winter.

In the **Bull Ring**, the ancient marketplace where the horrible practice of bullbaiting was introduced in Norman times, stands the statue of a pikeman, a tribute to the people who took part in the 1798 Rising. This small historic square, near the north end of Main Street, was also the site of a Cromwellian massacre in 1649, when many of the townspeople were butchered. The house on the northeast corner of the Bull Ring was where Jane Francesca Elgee, a.k.a. Speranza, the writer and mother of Oscar Wilde, was born. And across the road above the cozy **Thomas Moore Pub**, Anastasia Codd (mother of Thomas Moore of *Irish Melodies* fame, as well-known a man as Byron in his time) first saw the light of day.

Near **Westgate Tower**, the only one of the five fortified gateways in the town's walls that still stands, are the ruins of **Selskar Abbey**. It is commonly held that Henry II of England did penance here in 1172 for the murder of Thomas à Becket. The abbey is also believed to have been the site, in 1169, of the signing of the first treaty between the invading Anglo-Normans and the Viking-Irish inhabitants of the town. A notice on the main gate will tell you how and where to procure the entrance key.

Initiated in 1951, the **Wexford Festival of Opera** has earned an international reputation by staging rarely performed operas. During the festival—the last 11 days of October—the town adopts a Mardi Gras atmosphere, and accommodations are always heavily booked. You could not, however, hope to arrive at a better time for a visit.

Wexford is well served by hotels, restaurants, and bed and breakfasts. Both the **Talbot** and **White's** are reputable and moderately priced hotels and dining spots. The **Pike Grill Room** of the Talbot and **Captain White's** seafood restaurant in White's Hotel are long-standing, traditional eateries for locals on special occasions. The **Guillemot** restaurant in the Talbot serves excellent seafood—try the lobster or pink trout—and has a very good wine list. In all, the Talbot, being the more modern of the two, probably has the edge in terms of cuisine, and without argument in terms of leisure facilities; it has a swimming pool, gym, squash courts, saunas, and a solarium. If you're looking for bed-and-breakfast accommodation in town, check out the spacious, comfortable, and reasonably priced **Faythe House**, at the top of the town, once the site of an old fishing suburb.

At the **Bohemian Girl,** on North Main Street, Kay and Seamus McMenamin serve excellent bar food during the day, and after 8:00 P.M. they open a small but distinguished restaurant above. Their attractive establishment has won several noteworthy National Bar and Catering awards. **Tim's Tavern**, at the south end of Main Street, is another reliable house of cheer, serving decent food in a homey atmosphere. **The Granary Restaurant**, at Westgate, offers good food in an informal atmosphere at reasonable prices. Another favorite is the **Crown Bar**, down little Monck Street. A late-19th-century coach inn, the Crown may on first impression appear to be a museum—it has an unusual collection of weaponry, including Michael Collins's revolver and pikes from the Vinegar Hill battle of 1798— but it is in fact a pleasurable drinking spot. Con Macken runs another unusual establishment, **Cape of Good Hope**, a grocer's-cum-pub-cum-undertaker's on North Main Street. And the **Centenary Stores** on Charlotte Street is another worthy watering hole, serving delicious sandwiches in a relaxed atmosphere.

Around Wexford Town

In 1987 the very important **National Heritage Park** opened in Ferrycarrig, just 5 km (3 miles) north of Wexford Town on the main road. Intelligently designed, wonderfully executed, and ideally situated on the Slaney estuary, the Heritage Park brings the major eras of Irish history to life through an audio-visual presentation that is followed (several times a day) by a lively, informative guided tour through the park. On the tour you will see detailed, highly effective re-creations of Neolithic and New Stone Age dwellings, exact replicas of ancient burial tombs, Celtic settlements, and historical landmarks ranging from an early Christian monastery to a Norman mott and bailey style castle, as well as an original Norman watchtower built in 1167 by the Roches. The tour also provides a nice opportunity to take in panoramic views of the Slaney.

The excellent **Ferrycarrig Hotel** at Ferrycarrig Bridge is only a stone's throw from the park. All of the guest rooms have views of the Slaney, and the hotel's **Conservatory** restaurant is a gourmet's delight. The wine list is excellent—the specialty of the house is a very interesting Cahors wine from France—and one of the best dinners in Ireland can be relished here for just £20 per person.

No trip to Wexford is complete without a visit to the Ferrycarrig Hotel. If, on the other hand, you feel the need for a light meal or snack, a good choice in this area would be the recently refurbished—and now more popular than ever—**Oak Tavern**, a seafood restaurant at Ferrycarrig Bridge on the lovely Slaney. Grilled salmon steak and Dover sole are recommended; Tel: (053) 249-22.

If you head northwest from Wexford Town on the N 11, after about 25 km (16 miles) you'll reach Enniscorthy and **Enniscorthy Castle**. The castle's well-preserved square-towered keep, built in 1568, houses a folk museum. A good place to stay in the area is **Marlfield House**, a fine Regency-period home standing in its own woodland at Gorey, about another 25 km on the N 11. A 1990 Relais & Château Worldwide Breakfast Award winner, the hotel is owned and managed by Ray and Mary Bowe, who are discreet, attentive hosts. The food at Marlfield is mouth-wateringly good, and the atmosphere perfect for unwinding.

Horetown House in Foulksmills, west of Wexford Town, is officially a bed-and-breakfast establishment, but in reality this grand 18th-century manor is a home away from home where the proprietors, the Young family, have made an art out of making people feel relaxed and comfortable. Horetown House boasts one of the finest equestrian centers in the Southeast, and Mrs. Young's son David is happy to arrange outings for novice, intermediate, and experienced riders. The adjoining **Cellar Restaurant**, also run by the family, offers exceptional value and delicious country cuisine. If you want something out of the ordinary at unbelievably low prices visit Horetown House; you won't want to leave. To get there take N 25 west from Wexford Town and turn left after 10½ km (6½ miles) at Taghmon Village. Continue south on L 160 for 6½ km (4 miles) to Foulksmills.

If you continue west on N 25, 24 km (15 miles) west of Wexford Town you will see the clearly marked exit for the **John F. Kennedy Arboretum** on Slieve Coillte, a hill near the birthplace of the late president's great-grandfather. The arboretum contains 3,000 varieties of trees and shrubs. Still farther west, at **New Ross**, 35 km (22 miles) west of Wexford Town, you can take one of the **New Ross Galley Cruises** on the River Barrow and enjoy lunch, afternoon tea, or dinner while plying the calm waters of the winding tidal river, which is banked by wooded slopes and pretty vistas. The boats leave from the quay below New Ross bridge and reservations are required;

Tel: (051) 217-23. South of New Ross, on the estuary, is the little ferry port of **Ballyhack**, where you'll find an excellent example of a Norman keep built in the 13th century by the Knights Templars.

For those on a restricted budget, **Whitford House**, just southwest of Wexford Town off the N 25, is one of the finest modern guest houses in the area, being more of a small hotel than a bed and breakfast. Its swimming pool is open in the summer. Also off the N 25 southwest of Wexford Town is **Johnstown Castle**, a 19th-century Gothic Revival structure with magnificent gardens and an agricultural museum of farming implements and the like.

Rosslare Harbour, with its busy ferry terminal, pubs, and restaurants and, just a couple of kilometers (a little more than a mile) away, the resort of **Rosslare Strand**, with its fine sandy beaches, are 18 km (11 miles) south along the coast from Wexford Town via the N 25. Both are bustling places, and well served by restaurants and hotels. In particular, the traditional **Kelly's Strand Hotel** and the modern **Hotel Rosslare** are good choices, if somewhat expensive. Kelly's has a swimming pool, tennis, and golf; the Rosslare has a squash court, a sauna, and a perenially popular bar where sailors, tourists, singers, and fishermen stand three deep. The crowd is always lively, and impromptu music sessions are frequent. **Le Gourmet**, a small, local restaurant, serves consistently superior cuisine at affordable prices during June, July, and August; Tel: (053) 321-57. **The Cedars Hotel** is another Rosslare establishment with a growing reputation for fine food at reasonable prices. It's a relaxing place; other hotels in the area can be noisy, but The Cedars is a little bit off the beaten track and very enjoyable for overnight stays.

An 8-km (5-mile) drive south of Rosslare Harbour through bumpy territory will bring you to **Carne** (Carnsore Point on most road maps) and **The Lobster Pot Bar and Restaurant** (Tel: 053/311-10), where you can enjoy delicious homemade soups, salads, and sandwiches in a maritime setting. In the evening, sing-alongs are commonplace. The Lobster Pot is worth making the effort to reach, particularly now that a new dining room serving the freshest and finest of seafood is open from 6:30 P.M. The Lobster Pot was awarded a National Catering Award in 1990.

Similarly, the fishing village of **Kilmore Quay**, on the south coast about 30 km (19 miles) southwest of Wexford Town, merits a visit. You can enjoy the freshest of prawns in the transformed deckhouse of a wrecked sailing ship at the attractive **Wooden House** here; Tel: (053) 298-04. Kilmore, mentioned in ballad-writer P. J. McCall's "Wexford Fishing Song" (which you should request if you happen on a late-night sing-along), is also the stepping-off point for the **Saltee Islands**. Local raconteurs and fishermen Willie Bates, Jack Devereux, and Devereux's son John will take you out to the islands for a small fee. Jack is a veritable Old Man of the Sea, and is possibly the only fisherman in these isles who is also the proud possessor of an honorary master's degree in arts, bestowed upon him by the National University of Ireland in Maynooth for his sterling work in assisting historians and scholars in their research and in preserving ancient dialects and ballads. (Contact him through the Wooden House and, if you can, give him your ear for half an hour over a pint.)

The Saltees, a 45-minute boat trip from the mainland, are Ireland's largest bird sanctuary; during spring and summer the Great Saltee and Little Saltee are home to more than three million birds. The islands are also a source of rich lore, having been the haunt of Neolithic man, medieval monks, and 17th-century pirates and smugglers.

Pottery, leatherwork, weaving, woodworking, and silversmithing are the major crafts in County Wexford. Sources are **Wexford Pottery** in Duncormick; **Albert Kendrick Leather and Suede Work** and **Carley's Bridge Pottery**, both in Enniscorthy; and **Pat Dolan Silversmith**, in Glenmore, New Ross. The **Kiltrea Bridge Pottery** in Enniscorthy is notable for its beautiful plant pots and terracotta kitchen accessories. The shop is located in a tranquil setting overlooking the River Urrin, near the Blackstairs Mountains.

COUNTY KILKENNY
Kilkenny Town

Kilkenny Town, about 75 km (46½ miles) northwest of Wexford Town and 50 km (31 miles) north of Waterford, is Ireland's finest medieval city (there are 28 in all), and stands as an eloquent monument to aesthetic value and architectural grace long since departed. The breadth of vision with which its original Norman planners were gifted has not been lost on the latter-day citizens, who have maintained and developed the city as an unrivaled, atmospherically rich attraction. The Keep Kilkenny Beautiful (KKB) campaign, initiated in the early 1980s, has ensured that streets are spic and span and that shop fronts are suitably Old World. The campaign has paid large dividends: **Kilkenny Castle** is now the single most visited historic building in Ireland, although few visitors will disagree that it is the city itself that has the real drawing power.

After the death of Dermot MacMurrough, king of Leinster, at Ferns in 1171, his son-in-law, Richard, earl of Pembroke, better known as Strongbow, laid claim to his vast territories, which included Ossory (County Kilkenny). William le Mareschal, Strongbow's son-in-law, constructed the first stone castle here between 1207 and 1213. Numerous prosperous Norman families were attracted to the area, and a vital, affluent city literally sprang up. During the 13th and 14th centuries Kilkenny was second in importance only to Dublin.

Parliament convened regularly in Kilkenny Castle. It was here, in 1366, that rigorous apartheid laws were enacted. These Statutes of Kilkenny prohibited, among other things, intermarriage between Anglo-Norman and Gaelic families, as well as the adoption of Irish surnames, dress, language, music, and legal code by the colonists, who were rapidly becoming more Irish than the Irish themselves. These laws led to bitter acrimony in Kilkenny, as elsewhere, and set the stage here for the turbulent rise to power of the Butler family (earls of Ormonde). Their role in the history of Kilkenny, and indeed Tipperary, cannot be overemphasized. The Butlers' wealth and political stability ensured that the city remained a focal point of power and prestige. In 1641, when the Great Rebellion of Ulster broke out, a roughly hewn but ambitious parliament, the Confederation of Kilkenny, convened in the city in an attempt to restore the civil and religious rights of the old Irish families and the "old [English] foreigners."

The Confederation brought unprecedented glamour and excitement to the city for eight years, but the English Civil War disrupted the fragile arrangement, and when the wretched Cromwell arrived in 1650 he found Kilkenny disillusioned and unwilling to put up even token resistance. There followed the ritual statue-breaking and window-smashing in the still-glorious St. Canice's Cathedral (where Cromwell stabled his horses), but the city (which derives its name from the Irish Cill Chainnigh, "Canice's Church") escaped relatively unmolested. Its citizenry, however, was offered that infamous Hobson's Choice: "To Hell or Connacht," Connacht being a province in the west. In reality many of the dispossessed became victims of Cromwell's lesser-known policy of "Barbadosing"—sending Irish to work sugar mills and plantations in the West Indies.

Around in Kilkenny Town

Kilkenny City is sited on an "S" bend in the River Nore. The castle, high on a northern slope, is redolent of the magnificent robber-baron castles along the Rhine, with the graceful Nore acting as a natural moat. Streets in the city are broad and elegantly laid out and at times make Kilkenny appear larger than it is.

Start your tour of Kilkenny with the *City Scope,* a 20-minute computerized sound and light show at the Tudor **Shee's Alms House**, on Rose Inn Street, where the tourist office is located. The film, which can be seen any day but Sunday, is based on a meticulously crafted model of the city at its zenith in 1641 and will provide you with excellent information on the city's interesting sights, such as Kilkenny Castle, the Black Abbey, and St. Canice's Cathedral.

Tynan Walking Tours provide an intelligent, relaxing way to explore Kilkenny. Tours depart Monday through Saturday from outside Shee's Alms House (9:15 A.M., 10:30 A.M., 12:15 P.M., 1:30 P.M., 3:00 P.M., and 4:30 P.M.) and on Sundays at the same times from outside the gates of the magnificently restored **Kilkenny Castle**, at the southeastern end of the city (while there be sure to see the tapestries and great hall). **Rothe House**, an archaeological museum on Parliament Street, has a nice collection of medieval costumes and musical instruments. **Smithwicks Brewery**, just across from Rothe House, offers tours at 3:00 P.M., Monday through Friday. This is where the popular local ale is brewed and dispatched across the country; if you find Guiness too heavy, give Smithwicks a try.

The **Black Abbey**, on Abbey Street, was built in 1225 by William le Mareschal, earl of Pembroke, for the Dominicans, or Black Friars, as they were known, and survives today as an active Dominican priory. In 1543 the property was confiscated by Henry VIII, and the church became a courthouse, leaving the friars homeless. The friars returned during the Confederation, but Cromwell's troops defaced and vandalized the abbey. It was partially restored in the 19th century and more recently in the late 1970s. Among the items of interest are a 1264 figure of the Blessed Trinity and the 500-square-foot east window, which depicts the 15 mysteries of the Holy Rosary.

Built in the 13th century on the site of an early Irish monastery, **St. Canice's Cathedral** is the second-largest medieval cathedral in Ireland. It is noted for its stained-glass windows and 16th- and 17th-century tomb sculptures. St. Canice's Library, to the northwest of the cathedral, holds 3,000 volumes from the 16th and 17th centuries. The cathedral is reached via St. Canice's Steps (1614), which are linked to St. Canice Place by Velvet Lane.

The **Marble City Bar** is an excellent wateringhole, but **Edward Langton's Pub**, an Edwardian-style establishment, is even harder to pass by once you've viewed the inside. Langton's is continuously garnering National Catering Awards, and with its recently expanded French-style tearoom, it's definitely not to be missed. The genial proprietor, Eamonn Langton, provides a discreet but attentive personal touch, and the food is excellent. Tell him the man from Berlitz sent you. Or, if you prefer the genuine article in terms of Old World decor, visit **Tynan's**, established 1861, where the young barman Michael is a fund of local information and gossip.

If you like to mix history with your drink, visit **Kyteler's Inn** on Kieran Street, which has recently been refurbished with great care and attention. In the early 14th century this building was the home of Dame Alice Kyteler, a beautiful and powerful woman accused of witchcraft and condemned to death by the lord justice of Ireland (four of her husbands had died mysteriously, leaving her considerable wealth on each occasion). Dame Alice's friends managed to smuggle her out of the country, but her handmaiden, Petronella, was burnt at the stake in her place. Kyteler's Inn serves bar snacks and is a congenial meeting place for locals and visitors alike. Directly opposite Kyteler's is another popular spot, **The Pantry**, an affordable, extremely well run coffee and cake shop. (Readers with a sweet tooth should visit **White's**, the oldest sweet shop in town, boasting a magnificent shop front.)

The **Kilkenny Arts Week**, now in its second decade, is without question the most important and best-attended arts festival in the Republic. During the third week of

August, Kilkenny's many fine buildings become venues for classical music by orchestras, chamber music ensembles, instrumentalists, and singers, and for readings by poets, novelists, and filmmakers. Jazz and traditional music are also on the agenda, and the city fairly hops for these nine days.

Kilkenny is sometimes called the Marble City because of a highly attractive black marble produced in its quarries. Many local artists work in this medium. The **Kilkenny Design Workshops**, located opposite Kilkenny Castle in its beautifully restored stables and coach houses, are renowned for their locally crafted silver jewelry, ceramics, fashionable clothes and knitwear, leather, and even pots and pans. However, some of the items made here seem to be unnecessarily expensive, and many locals will tell you the center is, of late, a "tourist trap." Elsewhere in County Kilkenny, **C. and E. Chesneau Leather Goods** in Bennettsbridge, south of Kilkenny Town on the Wexford road, is a very worthwhile shop, and **Callan Crystal** sells beautiful hand-cut lead crystal at its works in Callan, 16 km (10 miles) south of Kilkenny Town on the N 76. In Graiguenamanagh, 35 km (22 miles) southeast of Kilkenny Town on the L 32, **Duiske Glass** presents an excellent range of hand-cut, decorated giftware, and **Cushendale Woollen Mills** has an interesting range of rugs and shawls in mohair and wool.

Outside Kilkenny Town

Dunmore Cave, 11 km (7 miles) north of Kilkenny on the Castlecomer road, is an outstanding example of a natural limestone cavern. Now a national monument, the cave features a massive 20-foot stalagmite called Market Cross, and is open June to October every day except Monday; guides are available.

If you are a racing fan you will be pleased to know that 14½ km (9 miles) east of Kilkenny on N 10 is the recently refurbished **Gowran Park**, one of the finest racetracks in the Southeast. Kilkenny folk like to have a flutter on the horses, and there is always good fun to be had here.

Jerpoint Abbey, south of Kilkenny via the N 10 and the N 9, was founded in 1158 by Donal MacGiollapatrick, king of Ossory, and has had a colorful, though troubled, history. In 1387 the abbot of Jerpoint was fined heavily for accepting Irish monks into his community, a direct transgression of the infamous Statutes of Kilkenny. The abbey was tremendously important to the Cistercians; its surviving architecture testifies to this. Here in this peaceful riverside setting you can see a Hiberno-Romanesque chancel and transepts, 15th-century cloisters and monuments, and effigies from several centuries. The powerful Butler and Walsh families are entombed here, and a fascinating array of carvings adorn the main cloister. There is also a pleasant, tidy café opposite the abbey where you can enjoy a snack or refreshment. Jerpoint Abbey is open during June, July, and August.

Staying and Dining in the Kilkenny Area

Most hotels in the Kilkenny city center lack parking facilities and are not on a par with the modern, comfortable, and expensive **Newpark Hotel**, just north of the city on Castlecomer Road. It is situated in 50 acres of parkland and has tennis courts, a swimming pool, children's playground, sauna, and gym. The hotel's Damask Dining Room provides satisfying fare, and its recently added suites are attractive. The **Hotel Kilkenny**, in a restored 19th-century mansion off the city's Ring Road, is comfortable but not as luxurious as the Newpark, and is more of a local drinking and dancing spot, so it can get noisy at night. It does have a swimming pool and a gym, however.

The **Lord Bagenal Inn**, in Leighlinbridge, is more than worth the short drive over the Carlow border, just 25 km (16 miles) northeast of Kilkenny on the way to Carlow Town. Chef Derek Hughes provides exciting food; his beef Wellington stuffed with chicken liver pâté is especially impressive. The Lord Bagenal's fixed-price dinner menu from Wednesday through Sunday is an excellent value; Tel: (0503) 216-68.

In Kilkenny, Eugene McSweeney runs **Lacken House**, a restaurant adjoining inexpensive rooms to let. McSweeney serves superb though expensive cuisine, and like many of the other establishments mentioned here makes the most of local game and fish. McSweeney is in a class of his own, however: He is 13 times a national Gold Medal champion chef who has demonstrated his considerable skills on TV in the United States. Breda McSweeney was recently elected to the prestigious Guild of Sommeliers and provides valuable assistance with their extensive wine list.

The Maltings, owned and run by the O'Neill family, is a beautifully situated restaurant along the banks of the Nore in the gentle village of **Inistioge**, 16 km (10 miles) southeast of Kilkenny. The Nore salmon served here is mouth-watering, and the minted lamb is also highly recommended; prices are moderate; Tel: (056) 584-84. Inistioge itself is reminiscent of a sleepy Bavarian or Rhineland hamlet, situated in a deep valley surrounded by wooded slopes and ringed by the undulating waters of the River Nore. It is a peaceful place where very little of consequence happens, and you get the distinct impression that the locals intend to keep it that way. If you fall in love with Inistioge, as is highly probable, stay here a day or two with Patricia Cantlon, proprietress of **Cullentrae House**. A colorful character even by Irish standards, Patricia is a superb cook, and her "bring your own wine" idea is very popular with her many diners. The more energetic may explore Cullentrae House's 17 acres, while the less active can sit in its peaceful conservatory and enjoy the view. Dinner is served by candlelight, and all guests dine together.

COUNTY TIPPERARY

Tipperary, west of Kilkenny, is Ireland's largest inland county (although Lough Derg in the county's northwest can create the illusion of vast coastline). It offers unmatched scenery, with rolling green flatlands (The Golden Vale) and the gently rising Galtee Mountains, which afford lovely views of the county from Mitchelstown to Cahir. "Tipp" is a prosperous county with a distinguished sporting tradition; its stud farms and greyhound-breeding skills have won it international acclaim.

Inland Tipperary, north of County Waterford, was spared most of the ravages of the Viking era, and its Early Christian (eighth- and ninth-century) illuminated manuscripts and sacred vessels reside in abundance in Dublin's National Museum. In the late 12th century King John arrived to grant lands to, among others, the illustrious Butler family (mentioned in the Kilkenny section). The Butlers are so called because they held the exclusive right to pass the first goblet of wine to the newly crowned king of England—a right that they continued to exercise down to the coronation of George IV. Until 1811 the Butler family was also entitled to one-tenth of the cargo of any wine-laden vessel landing in Ireland. As was the case in Kilkenny, the stability of the Butlers played a dramatic role in the preservation of County Tipperary, which escaped many colonization attempts, except those of Cromwell. (As an acknowledgment of their influence, the Butler family crest was incorporated into the county coat of arms.)

Tipperary is famed also for its role in the birth of the "Whiteboy" movement. In the late 18th century, bands of tenant farmers wearing white smocks over their clothing exacted cruel reprisals on landlords and their livestock. At a later period Tipperary was disparagingly referred to as "Turbulent Tipp" because of the Market Day fights that occurred regularly between rival clans. Tipperary suffered terribly in the famine of the 1840s, principally because the dispossessed had moved neither to Hell nor to Connacht, but to marginal upland areas where the potato had become their staple diet. From 1841 to 1861 the population withered from 435,000 to 239,000 as a result of emigration and starvation. In fact, the county's population was in steady decline until the late 1960s, when its newfound pride and its now-thriving dairy farming began to attract people back to the land.

Cashel

Most visitors to Cashel come to see the **Rock of Cashel**, often referred to as "the Acropolis of Ireland," which rises dramatically from the flat surrounding terrain just north of town, but it is also a good place to base yourself in Tipperary. The Rock is crowned by a jumble of structures from several periods of history, including a 12th-century round tower, the 13th-century Cormac's Chapel, and the 15th-century Hall of the Vicars Choral, but this detracts nothing from its imposing power. Floodlit at night, it looks like a still from a Gothic horror movie. The Rock was the seat of the kings of Munster for 700 years, and it was here that Saint Patrick said one of his first masses in Ireland. The great saint is reported to have explained the concept of a three-in-one divinity with the aid of a shamrock, thereby unwittingly giving Ireland its emblem.

In Cashel you should also visit the restored 17th-century artisan's cottage **Bothan Scoir** (Tel: 062/613-60) and the impressive **GPA-Bolton Library** (Tel: 062/619-44), which displays manuscripts from the 12th century and books and bindings from the earliest years of printing, as well as early editions of Machiavelli, Erasmus, Luther, Calvin, Dante, Cervantes, and others.

The structure now housing the **Cashel Palace Hotel,** built in 1730 by Bishop Bolton, served as a bishop's palace for 230 years, and is perhaps the only building in town that manages to stand up to the domineering Rock; in fact, the hotel has its own walkway up to the Rock. The walkway, however, is the least important attraction of this opulent, very expensive hotel. The food at its **Bishop's Buttery** is expertly prepared and served; the Irish stew of the young chef, Brendan Sheridan, is renowned. The bedrooms, all recently refurbished, will also delight, in particular the sumptuous Bishop's Suite. Formal and informal dining is available. Cashel Palace is a treat, if you can afford it.

The recently opened **Bru Boru Cultural Center,** which sits under the Rock, is attracting many visitors and very favorable comment. Named after King Brian Boru, who was crowned King of Munster in the tenth century, the center offers a well-stocked, competitively priced shop full of Irish goods, such as Cashel pottery and Beleek and Waterford crystal. Every evening Bru Boru also offers a banquet accompanied by excellent traditional Irish music and entertainment. The menu is extensive and the food of a very high standard (prices range from £20 to £25).

Also near the Rock in Cashel is **Chez Hans,** an expensive restaurant where the German chef/proprietor makes excellent use of fresh local game, organically grown vegetables, and freshly caught brill, salmon, sole, trout, and plaice. His desserts are delicious, and traditional music accompanies the meal.

Cashel has several decent pubs along Main Street, among them **Daveren's, Reilly's,** and **Paky Leahy's.**

Cahir

Cahir is a peaceful, prosperous market town on the River Suir at the east end of the Galtee Mountains, 18 km (11 miles) south of Cashel. It has a beautiful wooded park and a lovely church (St. Paul's, designed by Nash in 1820), and is the starting point for the spectacular scenic drive known as the Vee, which takes in views of the Galtee, Comeragh, and Monavullagh mountains.

James the Foreigner, ancestor of the Butlers, had constructed for himself in the early 15th century the largest castle of its time at Cahir (*cathair,* meaning "stone fort").

The highly defensible **Cahir Castle** managed to escape Cromwell intact, and it has recently been skillfully restored. The castle has been used as a set piece for various period movies, including *Barry Lyndon* and *Excalibur*. A 20-minute audiovisual presentation shown in a cottage on the castle grounds will orient you before you go to see the county's sights and monuments.

If you follow the signs from Cahir Castle's parking lot, a one-mile forest walk will bring you to the **Swiss Cottage**, a 19th-century cottage designed for the Earl of Glengall in the style of Le Petit Trianon at Versailles. It has recently been restored and is a worthwhile detour.

Southwest of Cahir, off the N 8, are the **Mitchelstown Caves**, where the staggering limestone formations have been christened House of Commons, House of Lords, the Cathedral, and the Organ. A kilometer or two (about a mile) southeast of the caves on R 665 is an eyeblink of a village called Ballyporeen, which achieved some small fame when it was learned that Michael Regan, great-grandfather of Ronald Reagan, was baptized in the church here in 1829. (Reagan shed a tear at the family burial place in Templetenny Cemetery during a much-ballyhooed visit several years back.)

Kilcoran Lodge Hotel, a former hunting lodge 10 km (6 miles) south of Cahir on the sheltered slope of the Galtee Mountains, is a delightful place to stay in the area. Fishing (for salmon and trout), shooting, horseback riding, and golf can be arranged. Both the restaurant and lounge bar open onto spectacular views of the Galtees, and food and service are excellent.

Elsewhere in Tipperary

The fully restored **Holy Cross Abbey**, 20 km (12 miles) north of Cashel on the N 62, on the west bank of the Suir, is an architectural masterpiece. Of particular interest are the stone-mullioned windows in the nave and chancel. The groined ceiling and the abbey's elaborate stonework are of beautiful carved black marble. Founded in 1168 for the Benedictines, it was transferred to the Cistercians in 1182 and is now a parish church, where two relics of the Holy Cross are enshrined. Its gardens, identical to those of the Vatican, are a perfect picnic spot.

Dundrum House Hotel, built in the same year as Cashel Palace, is a splendid country manor home in Dundrum, about 12 km (7½ miles) northwest of Cashel via the R 505.

Austin and Mary Crowe are the hosts, and the tranquillity here is beyond description. Good food and good trout fishing (from a series of islands linked by catwalks on a nearby lake) are among the many plusses of Dundrum House. **Rectory House Hotel** is another reliable establishment in Dundrum. Intimate, charming, and family-run, it serves good food at reasonable prices. Farmhouse holidays are popular in Tipperary, and **Rahard Lodge** is a fine choice in this category.

In the busy market town of **Tipperary**, 12 km (7½ miles) southwest of Dundrum via R 661 or 20 km (12½ miles) west of Cashel, the hearty helpings at the inexpensive **Brown Trout Restaurant** on Abbey Street will satisfy even the largest of appetites. The **Glen of Aherlow**, between Cahir and Tipperary Town, is the site for, quite simply, one of the most stunning views of the Galtee Mountains in Ireland. Your itinerary should also include **Carrick-on-Suir**, east of Cahir and just northwest of Waterford City; it was the birthplace of Anne Boleyn (at **Ormonde House**, which has been reopened after a major refurbishment and is well worth a visit between June and September), the Clancy Brothers, and cyclist Sean Kelly.

If you find yourself in **Clonmel**, about 15 km (9 miles) east of Cahir—and you should—lunch at **La Scala** on Market Street, where Tom Cryan serves very good food, from beef fondue to crêpes de mer, at reasonable prices in a nice atmosphere. The **Clonmel Arms Hotel** in Clonmel is a moderately expensive hotel with 34 rooms and a pleasant atmosphere. It's been refurbished recently under the watchful eye of owner/manager Brendan Pettit, whose family has run the hotel for three generations. The food is fair and the bar is lively; live music is played frequently.

COUNTY WATERFORD

Waterford City on Ireland's south coast is similar in layout to the smaller Wexford Town, with narrow streets and lanes leading to the town center from the long quayside. Waterford Harbour, with its 700-foot-long bridge, is a beautiful sight; at the harbor mouth three peaceful rivers—the Nore, Barrow, and Suir—merge as they meet the sea.

Reginald's Tower, built in 1013, takes its name from the Viking warrior Ragnvald, son of Sitric, founder of the city. Located at the west end of the quay (next to the Tower

Hotel), it provides the key to unlocking the history of Waterford and should be your first destination. Strongbow and Aoife MacMurrough held their wedding reception here in 1170; the marriage consolidated Strongbow's legal title to the lordship of Leinster, thus setting the seal on the future of the nation. The tower played host to a succession of invited and uninvited guests throughout the centuries. Robert Fitzstephen, one of the first Normans to land in Ireland, was imprisoned here by Henry II for failing to ask leave of his majesty to lead the Irish expedition.

Henry's son, the 18-year-old spoiled brat Prince John, cavorted here for eight months in 1185, much to the disgust of the Norman knights, who saw in him an obstacle to their dream of a country of their own, and of the Irish chieftains, who held him in contempt; Perkin Warbeck, pretender to the throne of Henry VII, attempted to stay here in the 15th century; and in 1650 Oliver Cromwell tried unsuccessfully to take the tower.

The oldest parts of Waterford are to be found around Reginald's Tower; only Derry Town in Northern Ireland has more of its original walls and wall towers intact. Several of the Norman towers are extant and in perfect condition, the most important located at Railway Square, Castle Street, Patrick Street, and Jenkins Lane.

The **French Church** of Greyfriars, in Barley's New Street, was founded by Sir Hugh Purcell for the Franciscans in 1240 and was splendidly endowed by Henry III. It became a place of worship for a colony of Huguenots, who fled religious persecution in France during the 17th century. You can visit the ruins by obtaining the entrance key from the house across the road.

For shopping, try **Michael Street**. At number 28 you will find the **Waterford Craft Center**; at number 9, the **Book Center**, which has a decent stock of Irish works; at number 16, **Handcrafts**, specializing in made-to-order Aran knitwear; at number 30, **Joann's**, with a good line in brass, silver, china, and crystal; and at number 11, **Woolcraft**, which has been selling lambswool sweaters since 1887. **Joseph Knox**, at 3 and 4 Barronstrand Street, has been one of Waterford's most-respected merchants for many years and stocks porcelain, fine bone china, and, naturally, Waterford crystal. (There aren't any savings in buying Waterford crystal near the source, however, and you might be better off waiting until you get to the airport duty-free shops.)

The **Waterford Crystal Factory** in Kilbarry, 3 km (2

miles) southwest of the city on the Cork road (N 25), sells crystal in its Gallery Shop and draws large numbers of visitors. During the summer its very worthwhile half-hour tours are heavily booked, so call ahead (Tel: 051/733-11); the factory is closed weekends and during the first three weeks in August. Beyond what is mentioned here there is little else of major interest in Waterford City.

Strongbows is a pleasant coffee shop on the quays, and the **Reginald Lounge**, on The Mall next to the tower, is a fine place to slake your thirst and enjoy good pub food. Waterford has two very fine, if somewhat expensive, hotels: the Granville, on the quay, and Jury's. The family-run **Granville Hotel** possesses a relaxed, dignified charm; its recently added suites are tasteful and comfortable. The hotel bar is popular with locals and is a good spot for a chat. Meals at the Granville are hearty, enjoyable affairs, whether they be in the formal dining room or the informal grill room. **Jury's Hotel**, on a wooded hill overlooking the city on the northern bank of the Suir estuary, caters to business travellers and coach tours, and thus is not as luxurious as the Granville. Even so, the accommodations are quite pleasant. The hotel's leisure center contains a heated pool, a gym, and tennis courts.

For those who are not operating on a budget, or for those who want to treat themselves to a once-in-a-lifetime experience, **Waterford Castle** is a deluxe affair about 2 km (1¼ miles) below Waterford City on the Island at Ballinakill. The carved Elizabethan oak dining rooms, Portland stone walls, ornate fireplaces, and the superior cuisine combine to create the splendor of a bygone age—at very high prices. There is no bridge to the island; the castle's private launch brings guests across. There is also a ferry for cars.

However, if your budget is limited your best base for touring the area is the village of Dunmore East, 15 km (9 miles) southeast of Waterford City.

Dunmore East

A 19th-century chronicler described this fishing village southeast of Waterford City at the head of Waterford Harbour thus: "It is a fashionable, aristocratic neighborhood which verily looks down on all watering places along the southern coasts. All other places of resort bow their heads. . . . "

Despite the hyperbole, Dunmore East, with its neat thatched cottages and its friendly, unassuming residents, *is* irresistible. There are no deluxe accommodations here, but at the small, family-run **Candlelight Inn** you will find enticing local specialties at very reasonable prices. Antoinette and Charlie Boland and their family will ensure that your every need is met. Accommodation here is simple, but the 11 rooms, which all have TVs, telephones, and showers or baths *en suite,* are clean and cozy. The nearby **Haven Hotel** is a stylishly converted former mansion in six and a half acres of tiered lawns and woods overlooking the sea. Hosts John and Jean Kelly together with their large family are attentive and considerate people; the hotel is inexpensive. The **Ocean Hotel**, nearer the harbor, is a popular gathering spot for locals. Run by Brendan and Noleen Gallagher and family, it has 14 rooms, mostly *en suite,* all with color TV and telephone. A pleasant, informal atmosphere pervades.

Mrs. Klemm, a transplanted German and a gifted cook, runs a praiseworthy guest house, **Corballymore House**, another good base for forays into the countryside. (From Dunmore East, head for Waterford Airport; the house is clearly signposted from the easy-to-spot Murphy's Pub.)

Day Trips from Dunmore

From Dunmore you can journey west around Tramore Bay to the town of **Tramore**. For years wise travellers have avoided Tramore, knowing that it was little more than a sprawling, unattractive amusement-park haphazardly tagged onto a beach. However, since the opening of **Celtworld** in May 1992, Tramore should be included on all itineraries, if only for an afternoon.

Celtworld, located in downtown Tramore on the Strand Road directly opposite the Majestic Hotel, is the culmination of almost a decade's planning and development. Using three-dimensional computer animation and state-of-the-art graphics, it brings to life the world of the Celts, a powerful, mystic, and mysterious race who inhabited Ireland until the advent of Christianity in the fifth century. There are those who feel that Ireland would have been much better off, thank you, if Saint Patrick and his Bible belting, crozier-stomping colleagues had never interrupted the flow of Celtic culture; this illuminating hour-long journey through time certainly does nothing to change that view.

The exhibit's principal artist is Jim Fitzpatrick; it is worth visiting Celtworld merely to see his beautiful and painstakingly detailed work.

Celtworld is open from 10:00 A.M. to 10:15 P.M. daily, and good lunches are served in a relaxed, old-world atmosphere at the Majestic Hotel across the street.

From Tramore continue southwest to the Gaeltacht (Irish-speaking) area around **Dungarvan**. Some of Europe's most rewarding deep-sea angling for blue shark, haddock, and cod takes place from Dungarvan Harbour, where boats are available for day trips. Around the south arm of the harbor at Ring (on the L 177), Laurann Casey and her brother Michael have restored and converted an old farm building into a thatch-roofed pub and restaurant worth investigating. It's called **The Seanachie**, Irish for "storyteller," and the food is first rate. **Cheekpoint**, a town to the east of Waterford City on the river, provides a lovely view of the area, and the **Suir Inn** and the **Jolly Sailor**, two friendly pubs here, are always worth a visit.

Situated almost midway on the Clonmel–Dungarvan road is the scenic **Nire Valley**, which snuggles in the foothills of the Comeragh Mountains; excellent trout fishing can be had along the River Nire. Pony-trekking along forest trails is a pleasant way to view this unspoiled area. **Paddy Melody's Pony-Trekking Centre** (Tel: 052/361-47), off the Clonmel road, has horses for both the novice and the experienced rider, as well as jaunting cars (horse buggies) for nonriders.

Larry and Eileen Ryan run a very reputable, modern dairy farmhouse in the middle of the valley at Ballymacarbry, north of Dungarvan (Tel: 052/361-41). The Ryan Farm, or **Clonanav Farmhouse**, is just 300 yards off the Clonmel–Dungarvan road and is set in landscaped gardens with panoramic views of the Comeragh and Knockmealdown mountains. Fishing and walking are available, and good food is served (the vegetables and herbs are picked from the Ryans' own kitchen garden).

GETTING AROUND

There is regular rail service from Dublin to Waterford, Wexford, Kilkenny, and Tipperary. Renting a car in Dublin or Shannon and driving to the Southeast is strongly suggested, however, as the towns in this part of the Republic are not well connected to one another and hiring a car in the country is more expensive. Each of the towns is walkable, but for travel beyond the city walls a car is necessary. Dooley Kenning Car Hire, with offices in Limerick, Dublin, and the Dublin Airport, provides good service—and automatic-shift cars. Tel: in Dublin, (01) 77-27-23; at Dublin airport, (01) 37-11-56; in Limerick, (062) 531-03; in U.S., (800) 331-9301 or (908) 381-8948.

ACCOMMODATIONS REFERENCE

The telephone country code for the Southeast is 353. When dialing telephone numbers in the Republic from outside the country, drop the 0 in the area code. The rate ranges given below are projections *for the low and high seasons in 1993; for up-to-the-minute rate information it is always wise to telephone before booking. Unless otherwise indicated, rates are per person sharing and do not include meals or service.*

County Wexford

▶ **The Cedars Hotel**. Strand Road, **Rosslare**, County Wexford. Tel: (053) 321-24; Fax: (053) 322-43. £32–£40, breakfast and service included.

▶ **Faythe House Bed-and-Breakfast**. Swan View, **Wexford**, County Wexford. Tel: (053) 222-49. £14–£15, breakfast and service included.

▶ **Ferrycarrig Hotel**. Ferrycarrig Bridge, **Wexford**, County Wexford. Tel: (053) 229-99; Fax: (053) 419-82. £49, breakfast and service included.

▶ **Horetown House**. **Foulksmills**, County Wexford. Tel: (051) 637-71; Fax: (051) 636-33. Closed January and February. £15–£19, breakfast and service included.

▶ **Hotel Rosslare**. **Rosslare Harbour**, County Wexford. Tel: (053) 331-10; Fax: (053) 333-86; in U.S., Tel: (800) 223-9832; in Canada, Tel: (800) 531-6767. £27–£35, breakfast and service included.

▶ **Kelly's Strand Hotel**. Strand Road, **Rosslare**, County Wexford. Tel: (053) 321-14; Fax: (053) 322-22. Closed mid-December through February. £42–£46, breakfast included.

▶ **Marlfield House**. Courtown Road, **Gorey**, County Wexford. Tel: (055) 211-24; Fax: (055) 215-72; in U.S., Tel: (800) 372-1323, (800) 223-6510, or (212) 696-1323. Closed early December through January. £60–£200, breakfast included.

▶ **Talbot Hotel**. Trinity Street, **Wexford**, County Wexford. Tel: (053) 225-66; Fax: (053) 233-77; in U.S., Tel: (800) 223-6764. £40–£46, breakfast included.

▶ **Whitford House**. New Line Road, **Wexford**, County

Wexford. Tel: (053) 438-45 or 434-44. Closed mid-December to mid-January. £24–£34, breakfast and service included.

▶ **White's Hotel.** George's Street, **Wexford**, County Wexford. Tel: (053) 223-11; Fax: (053) 450-00; in U.S., Tel: (800) 528-1234 or (602) 957-4200. £27–£33, breakfast and service included.

County Kilkenny

▶ **Cullentrae House (Patricia Cantlon).** The Rower, **Inistioge**, County Kilkenny. Tel: (051) 236-14. £17, breakfast and service included.

▶ **Hotel Kilkenny.** College Road, **Kilkenny**, County Kilkenny. Tel: (056) 620-00; Fax: (056) 659-84. £37–£42.50, breakfast and service included.

▶ **Lacken House.** Dublin Road, **Kilkenny**, County Kilkenny. Tel: (056) 610-85; Fax: (056) 624-35. £22–£25, breakfast included.

▶ **Newpark Hotel.** Castlecomer Road, **Kilkenny**, County Kilkenny. Tel: (056) 221-22; Fax: (056) 611-11. £32–£37.

County Tipperary

▶ **Cashel Palace Hotel.** Main Street, **Cashel**, County Tipperary. Tel: (062) 614-11; Fax: (062) 615-21; in U.S., Tel: (800) 223-6510 or (212) 832-2277. £68–£134.

▶ **Clonmel Arms Hotel.** Sarsfield Street, **Clonmel**, County Tipperary. Tel: (052) 212-33; Fax: (052) 215-26. £35–£45.

▶ **Dundrum House Hotel.** Cashel, County Tipperary. Tel: (062) 711-16; Fax: (062) 713-66. £41–£45, breakfast included.

▶ **Kilcoran Lodge Hotel.** Cahir, County Tipperary. Tel: (052) 412-88; Fax: (052) 419-94; in U.S., Tel: (800) 521-0643 or (305) 566-7111. £30–£35, breakfast included.

▶ **Rahard Lodge (Mrs. M. Foley).** Kilkenny Road, **Cashel**, County Tipperary. Tel: (062) 610-52. Closed December through February. £14–£15, breakfast and service included.

▶ **Rectory House Hotel.** Dundrum, **Cashel**, County Tipperary. Tel: (062) 712-66; Fax: (062) 711-15. Closed December through February. £25–£31.50, breakfast and service included.

County Waterford

▶ **Candlelight Inn.** **Dunmore East**, County Waterford.

Tel: (051) 832-15 or 39; Fax: (051) 832-89. Closed January. £25–£32, breakfast and service included.

▶ **Clonanav Farmhouse. Ballymacarbry,** County Waterford. Tel: (052) 361-41. Closed mid-November through January. £20, breakfast and service included.

▶ **Corballymore House. Dunmore East,** County Waterford. Tel: (051) 831-43. £15, breakfast and service included.

▶ **Granville Hotel.** Meagher Quay, **Waterford,** County Waterford. Tel: (051) 551-11; Fax: (051) 703-07; in U.S., Tel: (800) 528-1234 or (602) 957-4200. £55–£97, breakfast and service included.

▶ **Haven Hotel. Dunmore East,** County Waterford. Tel: (051) 831-50. Closed November through February. £25–£35, breakfast and service included.

▶ **Jury's Hotel. Waterford,** County Waterford. Tel: (051) 321-11; Fax: (051) 328-63; in U.S., Tel: (800) 843-6664; in Canada, Tel: (800) 268-1133; in London, Tel: (81) 569-5555 or (71) 937-8033; in U.K., Tel: (345) 01-01-01. £39.

▶ **Ocean Hotel. Dunmore East,** County Waterford. Tel: (051) 831-36; Fax: (051) 835-76. £20–£28, breakfast included.

▶ **Waterford Castle.** The Island, **Ballinakill,** County Waterford. Tel: (051) 782-03; Fax: (051) 793-16. £77–£97, breakfast included.

THE SOUTHWEST
CORK AND KERRY

By John O'Donoghue

John O'Donoghue has been a freelance journalist for many years, working mainly for the Irish Times. *He is also a senior staff reporter at the Irish National Broadcasting System covering a wide range of topics and events in Ireland, and has written and presented documentaries for the BBC.*

The counties of Cork and Kerry, which together make up the southwest of Ireland, are like the palm of a hand, its fingers stretching into the Atlantic Ocean. The conflux of the land and sea provide this region with singular qualities.

The warm waters of the Gulf Stream first reach Ireland along this coast. Subtropical trees and plants spread inland from the shores of the many fiordlike bays and inlets, where frost and snow are extremely rare. In many parts of Cork and Kerry the red and purple bells of fuschia form natural wild hedgerows.

Cork's sobriquet is the Rebel County, for reasons that are obvious enough in its many monuments and its place in the struggle for Irish independence. Kerry—no less mentioned for its part in that history—is also known as the Kingdom. This honorary title signifies the county's excellences, in the nonboastful opinion of its own people and also of the rest of Ireland and beyond.

Most travellers visit these two counties for majestic scenery of mountain and sea, usually discovered unexpectedly around an unpromising bend in the road; for a gourmet tour; for golf acknowledged by experts as some of the best in the world; for fishing (inquire at your hotel or the local angling club for a license); for mountaineering; for the cadences of both the English and Irish languages; and for the music, wild as the waves on the rocky shores. The waters and beaches of the Southwest, while very welcoming to swimmers from the temperate zones of the globe, are possibly too cold for others except during long, warm summers. Visitors also come for the history, which goes back to the earliest settlers from the Iberian Peninsula, but above all for the shrewd but friendly and curious people, whose sense of humor has made the turn of phrase a sport among themselves and a pleasurable (though not self-conscious) performance for the stranger—who will never feel like one in these parts.

MAJOR INTEREST IN CORK

Literary traditions
Irish music
Sea and river fishing

Cork City
English Market
Christ Church
Sullivan's Quay
South Chapel
Cork Public Museum
Crawford Municipal Art Gallery

Blarney Castle
Fota Island
Bantry Bay
Music in Ballyvourney and Coolea

MAJOR INTEREST IN KERRY

Kenmare
Sneem
Lakes of Killarney
Inisfallen
The Ring of Kerry
Dingle Peninsula

COUNTY CORK

CORK CITY

Cork City, after Dublin, is the largest city in the Republic of Ireland. Though its population of under 150,000 is not as busy as it used to be because of plant closings— including that of the local Ford assembly plant, a particularly poignant blow because Henry Ford's family originally came from County Cork—it is still an active commercial center. It is also a lively university town with a charm and openness that makes you feel comfortable chatting with anybody.

If the city of Cork—the center for touring the south and southwest of Ireland—was never called the Venice of Ireland, then it probably should have been; a walking tour of Cork City crosses innumerable bridges over the branches of the River Lee flowing into Cork Harbour. In the sixth century, when Cork (which means "marsh" in the Irish language) was founded by Saint Finbarr, these various courses of the Lee divided up areas of marshland and some dry land, on which the original city was founded.

As late as the 18th and early 19th centuries, many of the waterways were primary thoroughfares, bringing wine, butter, meat, wool, and leather to and from the houses of the city. Some of the waterways were later roofed over and then filled in to form some of the beautiful streets of the city today: the South Mall, for example, and Grand Parade and St. Patrick's Street, the main street of the city. A bollard on Grand Parade is a maritime reminder. Other signs of the early waterborne trade can be seen particularly along the **South Mall**, where one building's old main entrance door is today at the top of a flight of outside stairs; the huge doors at what is now street level once led to the boathouses of one of Cork's leading families, who called themselves the "Merchant Princes"—an example of Venetian pretensions. The dart (preserved in the Fitzgerald Museum) that the lord mayor of Cork threw into the waters annually to define the limits of his jurisdiction recalls the ring thrown into the waters to confirm Venice as its bride.

Cork City is surprisingly short of hotels. However, the

Fitzpatrick Silver Springs in Tivoli on the approach road from Dublin is a large, modern hotel looking down over the River Lee. It has a leisure center, with all of the usual amenities. **Moore's Hotel**, off the South Mall on Morrison's Island between one of the Lee's many channels, is near the center of the city but quiet, homey, and friendly.

The center of Cork City is **St. Patrick's Street**, at the bottom of which is the statue of Father Mathew, the apostle of temperance. The central city area is very compact, and it is easier to walk than to use public or even private transportation. To the east is the main channel of the River Lee, leading out into Cork Harbour. To the northeast is the suburb of Montenotte, once regarded as an exclusive residential area and still retaining some of that character; to the north are the areas of Blackpool and Fairhill, home to sizable numbers of blue-collar workers; to the southeast are Douglas and Donnybrook, largely middle-class residential areas; and to the southwest, in Togher, other densely populated areas. To the west along the Western Road are fine old Georgian houses and residences.

Dr. Sean Pettit of the Department of Education, University College, Cork (Tel: 021/27-68-71), will take you on a highly selective and colorful tour of the city, or you can easily explore on your own. Start with a part of old Cork, the **Paul Street** shopping area, which is currently enjoying a renaissance.

Begin your tour at the side entrance of the **Clouds Bar and Restaurant** in the modern, comfortable **Imperial Hotel** on the South Mall (where the fashionable of Cork assemble). The long-established hotel has a quiet and friendly atmosphere, and offers easy access to the many neighborhoods of Cork City. Not all rooms at the Imperial are of the same standard of comfort or quietness, so be precise about your needs. The tearoom to the right of the foyer is a great place for morning and afternoon gossip, as is the Captain's bar to the left.

Turn left from the hotel onto Pembroke Street and head for Paul Street, where the **House of James** has renovated an old building with huge vertical windows that draw your eyes to his arts and crafts, pottery, wooden bowls, and glass. Beside the shop, and equally attractive in its restoration, is the **House of Donegal**, where you can pick up a length of tweed or arrange to have it sent to you. **Lady May**'s stylish clothing store is in nearby French Church Street.

Cork's explosion of artistic activity—in the visual arts, crafts, fashion, and design—would have gladdened the hearts of the Huguenots who fled here at the end of the 17th century following the revocation of the Edict of Nantes. Though their church in French Church Street no longer exists, the **Huguenot** restaurant is here, as are many other bistros, coffeehouses, and bookshops in which to savor an atmosphere that combines the best of contemporary Continental taste with the spirit of Cork. Try the **Gingerbread Man**, also on French Church Street, for homemade bread, cakes, tea, coffee, and take-out.

Two other main shopping centers, not very far from this central maze of streets, are in the **Queen's Old Castle** on Grand Parade, and in the **Savoy Centre** on St. Patrick's Street. A new shopping area on Merchant's Quay is worth a visit as well. What's appealing about the young designers exhibiting and selling here is that they are not specifically "ethnic Irish" designers.

Though what might be called "updated" Irish fashion is available—and very good it is—designs here tend to belong to a new wave in Ireland, quite distinctive, not ironed-out cosmopolitan. Prominent young designers in Cork decidedly do not inhabit Hicksville—people such as Michael Mortell, with an international reputation for, particularly, suits and coats; Lainey Keogh, with her innovative Irish knitwear; and Mariad Whisker, who designs for those under 25. The clothes of many of these up-and-coming designers can be found at **Rachel C.**, a shop in the Savoy Centre (mainly for women between 30 and 40). All of the Cork designers bear comparison with the best on the Continent.

Eating and Drinking in the Paul Street Area

To combine high fashion with quintessential Cork, walk down among the bistros and cafés in the pedestrian-only Paul Street area. You might want to cross into Oliver Plunkett Street to get stamps at the General Post Office or visit **Egan's Store**, right opposite, which has a fine display of china and Waterford glass. Almost next door is the **Hi-Bi**, a small upstairs bar with real personality. Hi-Bi is sometimes overrun by the restless young but by and large draws an intellectual crowd. Generally it is even quiet enough to bring in a book. The barman may ask for help with his upscale crossword, from which the background music—not Muzak, but classical—will not distract him or you; or he may be organizing an operatic quiz for the regulars. However, this is not at all a cliquish place.

An appetite for more than coffee can be satisfied at **The Vineyard**, a marble-topped-tables pub in Market Lane, or in Marlborough Street at the **Long Valley**, which serves homemade soup and prepares sandwiches with fresh meat cut off the joint as you watch. In St. Patrick's Street, affectionately known to Corkonians as Pana, you'll find **Le Château** (recently renovated), where pizzas, lasagne, and perhaps a word with the chatelaine, Maura Reidy, may be enjoyed. Nearby in Emmet Place is **Glasseyallies Restaurant**, distinguishable by its clock under the gable—good airy ambience, but fairly pricey. Off St. Patrick's Street is the **Mutton Lane Inn**, a small, intimate pub popular with the locals that specializes in pints of Murphy's black stout and serves scampi and salads. Many other eateries and drinkeries in this small area are worth sampling. As you wander look for the life-size bronze statue of the Echo Boy paper seller, commemorating 100 years of the afternoon newspaper *Cork Echo*.

Historical Cork

Along Grand Parade is the National Monument—a statue of the Maid of Erin, honoring the Royal Munster Fusiliers who died in the First World War—and the restored **English Market**, which, with its wonderful fountain decorated with traditional Cork ironwork, has justly won the European NOSTRA award for architectural restoration. On Grand Parade a fine new public park features not only the sculpted figure of an onion seller of the market but also part of the old city walls. Developed on a site donated to the city by the Church of Ireland (Protestant), the park, with true Irish (and Cork) irony, is named the Bishop Lucey Park, after a famous Cork Roman Catholic bishop well known for zealously maintaining his church's pre-ecumenical views.

That is not to say, though, that harmony has not existed between the two major religious denominations in the city, and indeed among all denominations. A few years after the granting of Catholic Emancipation in 1829, the opening and dedication of Cork's first really major Roman Catholic church—that of the Dominican order, on

Pope's Quay—was attended by a huge crowd of both Catholics and Protestants.

A common cause for both traditions arose when the Capuchin friar Father Mathew (whose statue—"the Statcha"—in St. Patrick's Street is the traditional meeting place for Corkonians) launched his crusade for temperance in the 19th century. The need for this campaign and the social value of the friar's work was noted by Thackeray—no lover of the Irish majority religion—on his visit to the city in the middle of the last century. But he also had some better things to say of Cork and Corkonians. "The Market is but two minutes' walk out of St. Patrick's Street where you come across a Grand French emporium of dolls, walking sticks, carpetbags, and perfumery. The markets hard by have a cheerful look. . . . I think in walking the streets and looking at the ragged urchins crowded there, every Englishman must remark the superiority of intelligence is here and not with us. I never saw such a collection of bright-eyed, wild, clever, eager faces." He spoke as well of "the flash French and plated-goods shops." Little has changed in Cork since 1842 except the rags. For the flavor of times past, visit the open-air market at Coal Quay on weekends.

Traces of other history, especially of medieval Cork, are nearby. **Christ Church**, an 18th-century Protestant parish church between Grand Parade and South Main Street, houses many of the surviving archives of old Cork, which could be of interest to those who would like to look up their ancestors. There is also a considerable likelihood that the English poet Edmund Spenser of *Epithalamion* and *The Faerie Queene,* who had estates from Elizabeth I in North Cork, was married in this very building. Next to Christ Church is the Queen's Old Castle (already suggested for shopping), more or less on the former site of a castle that guarded the old walled city's Watergate, through which ships entered up the various watercourses of the Lee.

For a good view of downtown Cork, continue south from Christ Church and pause just before you cross the bridge to **Sullivan's Quay**. Painters and photographers favor this spot near the South Gate Bridge; upriver, you can see St. Fin Barre's Cathedral set against an evening sky, and downriver you look toward the magnificent white limestone confection of Holy Trinity Church.

Tucked away in Dunbar Street, typical of the kind of

out-of-the-way site chosen for Catholic churches as the penal laws relaxed, is the **South Chapel**, a fine building in contrast to the classical façade of the previously mentioned Dominican church. Nearby, as if ordained specifically for our friends of the easel and the camera, is the **Quay Co-Op**. Established in a converted pawnshop, it comprises a vegetarian restaurant, a bookshop with unusual selections, including travel and antiquarian books you may not find in more ordinary stores, and meeting rooms for self-help groups. The Quay is a fresh, clean, and inexpensive place to have a meal or a glass of wine, browse, or meet friends, and serves as redemption for the neighboring new government buildings, which many people consider obtrusive monstrosities. Before leaving Sullivan's Quay, step down the very old **Keyser's Lane** to the river and the original Viking area of Cork. (The same name crops up in many other places in Ireland and Europe, also indicating a Viking presence.)

Head west now past Barrack Street (known affectionately as "Barracka"), dropping in on the way at the **Gateway** pub (one of Ireland's oldest), where the duke of Wellington may have told stories from Waterloo. At the end of Bishop Street, **St. Fin Barre's Church of Ireland Cathedral**, designed by William Burges and completed in 1870, has many interesting and even amusing Gothic-style decorations on its exterior. The cathedral occupies the site of the original round tower of Saint Finbarr's monastic settlement of the seventh century, and it is not difficult to imagine the monks looking down on the lights of the first Viking encampment on the South Channel of the Lee, looking down, as it were, on their impending doom.

Down now to Lancaster Quay, on the banks of yet another of the channels of the Lee. By this time a new pub, across from Jury's Hotel, might be a welcome sight: **Reidy's** (of St. Patrick's Street's Le Château family) spirit and wine store. The building, renovated to an extremely high standard, makes good use of timber and prints to give it character; perhaps the fact that altar wines were blended here at one time will give a particular spark to your Port or Sherry, which you can have in the pub or purchase to take away. The aforementioned **Jury's Hotel**, on Western Road, offers a high standard of luxury and service. In addition to the usual amenities—outdoor and indoor swimming pools, sauna, and exercise gym—it has a very interesting pub that achieves an authentic Corkonian ambience, with murals featuring, in amusing juxtaposition, many of the city's personalities, past and present. Posters, old bottles, and documents from Cork's breweries complete the picture.

Michael and Deirdre Clifford, formerly of Dublin's exclusive White's on The Green, have moved their restaurant to 18 Dyke Parade on Cork City's Mardyke, famous in song and local folklore, parallel to the Western Road to the north. **Cliffords'** serves a table d'hôte of fine French food in what used to be the old Cork County Library—a Georgian house in which the Cliffords have preserved the beautiful old arches, stairways, and pillars, and restored the cornices. Open for lunch and dinner Tuesday through Friday and for dinner only Mondays and Saturdays (closed Sundays). Reservations are advised; Tel: (021) 27-53-33.

Two local breweries produce stout: Murphy's Brewery, and Beamish and Crawford. Their ownership has changed hands over the years, but the distinctive flavor of each of these brews is still appreciated in Cork, as is the whiskey known as Paddy, which is made by Irish Distillers. Launched in 1924, the liquor was so assiduously promoted by a salesman of the time named Paddy Flaherty that retailers simply reordered "Paddy's" whiskey, hence the name.

The Western Approaches

Out a little farther west along the Western Road is the **Western Star** pub. Because of its proximity to University College, Cork (UCC), it has a student element, but, as always in Cork and Kerry, the clientele come from many walks of life. On Monday, Wednesday, and Saturday evenings you will find a junction of city and country here. These are the nights for dog racing in the stadium on the Western Road, and the bookies, farmers, and city gents come to the Western Star before and after they have had a flutter on the dogs. The bar displays old mementos— jerseys and so on—of battles fought long ago in the rugby code of football; rock-music lovers are represented as well, but only in the back room. Add to this the staff from the UCC philosophy department, who might drop in for a meal or drink before an evening lecture. What amount to informal seminars sometimes take place between staff and students; why bother moving into a formal lecture room when you can be edified in more relaxed surroundings?

Wherever you look in Cork or Kerry, you'll see stone and bronze monuments. Sculptor Seamus Murphy (1907–1975) was part of an important tradition in Irish stone carving, making statues and busts of historical figures, memorial headstones, and plaques. One amusing piece, a dog trough, can be found on St. Patrick's Street with the Irish inscription *madraí*—dogs. (Even the dogs in Cork are presumed to be literate.) Murphy's work is omnipresent in Cork and Kerry. Of particular note is the beautiful and unique Gaelic style of lettering on his monuments.

At **University College, Cork,** two Murphy sculptures not to be missed are life-size bronze figures of the Cork writers Sean O'Faolain and Frank O'Connor. A five-minute walk away, in Glasheen, an old Cork City locality, is St. Finbarr's Cemetery, where in Musicians' Corner you will find Murphy's headstones with carvings of musical instruments for Sir Arnold Bax and others. Between Mardyke Walk and the river in the gardens of Fitzgerald Park is the **Cork Public Museum**; exhibits include Murphy's heroic-size bronze of Corkman General Michael Collins, first commander-in-chief of the Irish Free State, killed in the Civil War after independence. Another Murphy piece in the park, described as the most important carving made in Ireland in this century, is a full-size polished limestone carving, *The Virgin of the Twilight.* Murphy also designed the Church of the Annunciation at Blackpool.

Shandon Street

Take a short walk from UCC north across the river to the **North Mall**, which is a continuation of Pope's Quay and leads on to Sunday's Well. Looking northeast from the North Mall, with its fine 18th-century doorways, you can see St. Ann's Tower of Shandon and its clock. **St. Ann's Church**, built in 1722, is the subject of Sylvester O'Mahony's "The Bells of Shandon"—a call back to Cork for every Corkonian. By arrangement it is possible to climb to the top of Shandon Tower and play a tune on the carillon; see the verger between 10:00 A.M. and 5:00 P.M. Monday through Saturday, or call Tel: (021) 50-16-72 to set up a time. This is one of the oldest parts of Cork, where the original Viking settlement at Sullivan's Quay eventually moved. It was known until the Middle Ages as the Cantred of the Ostmen.

Near Shandon is the **Old Butter Market** and its circular building known as the **Firkin Crane**, restored with a new roof and windows, which exported Cork and Kerry butter through the 18th and 19th centuries, and where a great many cattle were once slaughtered and salted for export. This area was a great center for the collection of produce for victualing ships of the British navy, which came into Cobh (on the outer edge of Cork Harbour) and also into Bantry Bay before setting off on their worldwide voyages. It is now an arts center with crafts, a theater, and conference rooms.

Very near Shandon are two fine pubs: **The Chimes**, in Church Street, owned by the Quirke family and home of the Fair Hill Harriers (see Sports and Recreation in the Cork City Area, below) and St. Mary's Football Club, with darts, rings, and card games. The clientele is a mixture of visitors to the city, old-age pensioners, university students, and office workers. A hundred yards farther along, in the area known as St. Luke's, at the junction of Dillon's Cross and Wellington Road, is **Henchys**, one of the oldest pubs in Cork, dating from 1837. Home of a literary society, Henchys is where young poets recite their latest works; one of Ireland's best-known poets, John Montague, first tested the literary waters here. Mind you, you may have to wait for your pint as a price for this culture.

Thirty yards or so farther, in Montenotte, is the **Arbutus Lodge Hotel**, which has one of the very best tables in Ireland and which serves a Cork culinary specialty— *drisheen,* a relative of black pudding and the Scottish *haggis.* The Arbutus Lodge does not boast about the standard of its accommodations. Eat here but stay elsewhere, unless the table has been so lavish that early retirement is desirable. The **Montenotte District** has been said by Corkonians to be the epitome of upper-class self-consciousness, but this is no longer so. If some of Montenotte's glory may be faded, it still has its fine buildings with their magnificent views over the city.

Step into any of the very well-appointed bars in the **Metropole Hotel**, at Lower Glanmire Road and Mac Curtain Street, near the Kent Railway Station. The back bar and restaurant have a view over the River Lee and can be reached either from Mac Curtain Street or from the river—a great place for discreet encounters, or evasions! The Metropole is one of the principal venues of the **Cork Jazz Festival**, to which venerable and new practitioners of that art flock every year; in 1993 it will be at the end of October. (For information contact the Cork Tourist Office.) The street was named after Thomas Mac Curtain, one of the two lord mayors of Cork who died in the War of Independence; his successor, Terence McSwiney, died on a hunger strike in Brixton Jail in London.

The Arts in Cork City

Our next stop brings us almost full circle from our start at the Paul Street shopping area. Cross the bridge south from St. Luke's past the Father Mathew statue into St. Patrick's Street and turn right down Emmet Place. You'll then come to the **Opera House**, a fine enough building that unfortunately turns an immense blank wall to the river. Most of the year a program of variety shows, as well as some straight drama, is offered, though from time to time a season of opera or individual performances by visiting operatic artists is scheduled. Inquire at the theater or the tourist office whether the Cork Theatre Company, which produces plays by noted Irish dramatists, such as John Millington Synge, Brian Friel, Brian McMahon, and Samuel Beckett, is performing at the Opera House. The Everyman Theatre, like the Cork Theatre Company, also lacks a permanent home. It may be found most often now in Mac Curtain Street in the **Everyman Palace**, formerly the Palace Cinema, which retains an elaborate, old-style interior reminiscent of a music hall. Performances are usually scheduled only during the winter months. Despite the fact that Cork drama does not have a permanent base, it is alive and well most of the year. The **Triskel Arts Centre**, in an old back alley off Grand Parade near Singer's Corner (as in sewing machine), is a center for all the arts: painting, classical music, film, puppetry, and mime. It houses a small, relatively inexpensive restaurant as well, where food is available all day.

University College's Aula Maxima and the City Hall Auditorium host symphony orchestras and larger events. The large Gaelic Games venue sometimes hosts open-air rock- and Irish-music concerts.

The **Cork Film Festival** takes place at the beginning of October each year, and the Cork Jazz Festival is at the end of October. The famed **Cork International Choral and Folk Dance Festival** occurs in May.

On Emmet Place the **Crawford Municipal Art Gallery** is a must-see. Its work by sculptor/stonemason Seamus Murphy includes a plaster death mask of the wayward but brilliant composer Sean O'Riada and a bronze bust of Daniel Corkery, author of a book called *The Hidden*

Ireland and rightly credited with identifying some of the movements in Irish culture not always fashionably noticed.

But what might be called the glory of the gallery is the Harry Clarke room. Enjoy his stained-glass, pencil, watercolor, and pen-and-ink work, with such marvelous titles as *Ages Long Ago These Lovers Fled Away into the Storm* and *Far o'er the Southern Moors I Have a Home for Thee.* An excellent restaurant at the gallery serves lunch and dinner among the pictures, more intimate and more direct in their impact than those in the National Gallery in Dublin, Corkonians claim. The executive chef here is Myrtle Allen, whose internationally known cuisine (see Cobh, below) is absolutely the best. It's a little expensive, but worth it. Try the mushroom and spinach pancake.

Not far away, the Cork Art Society's gallery at Lavitt's Quay houses exhibitions by Irish artists.

James Scanlon, a modern stained-glass artist, has contributed six windows to the new apartments for the elderly (corner of Grattan and Sheares streets)—probably the best-known charitable cause in Cork City. The building is worth a visit for both the prize-winning architecture of Neil Hegarty and one ultramarine blue window in particular. The building and windows are floodlit at night, and during the day the interior may be seen courtesy of the caretaker.

James Scanlon's private studios may be visited by appointment; Tel: (021) 50-27-70. His public sculpture is on display in Sneem village (see below, in the County Kerry section).

Sports and Recreation in the Cork City Area

There are two particular sporting activities for which Cork and its suburbs are famous. One is **bowl-playing**, or "bowlin," a far cry from the gentle French *boules* or the English bowling green. You'll find bowlers on Saturday afternoons, Sunday mornings, and midday on weekdays on quiet country roads on any side of the city. The game (its rules are a bit complicated) consists of bowling an iron ball at high speed along country roads, on a three-mile course and back again. There is considerable betting and great good humor. Bowl-playing is best enjoyed as a spectator sport and for the camaraderie when the players and supporters return to the starting pub afterward. The crowds assemble at the **Black Man** pub out beyond Blackpool on the Dublin Pike, at **Healy's** of Cloghroe northwest of the city, or at **Blair's Inn** near Cloghroe.

Another great sport of the working man is **drag-hunting**. A piece of horse meat is drawn across a predetermined course in the countryside to lay down a scent, and the foot beagles (not foxhounds) assemble with their owners and supporters at various points around the area known as the Lough or up on Fair Hill. Groups called the North Harriers and the South Hunt have partisans every bit as fierce as the Blues and Greens of Byzantium. Drag-hunting tests the endurance of the various champion dogs. One of the greatest of them all, "The Armoured Car," is celebrated in a song of the same name by local folklore singer Jimmy Crowley. (History is never far away in Cork; this dog got his nickname from the armored car used extensively by the British forces in the War of Independence.) You can follow the hunt from stage to stage by car, but properly clad and on foot it's a great way to burn up calories.

Set dancing adds a flavor to Cork that is well worth seeking out. A form of country dancing with overtones of the hoedown, it's a very precise art, and some of its best proponents from the past are still remembered with awe. The doyen of dancing masters of the present generation is Timmy the Brit, a butcher in the city. Apart from his legendary prowess in Irish dancing, he issues his instructions with a distinct English accent (more Cork irony). Look for exhibitions of Irish dancing at the South Parish Community Centre and various other venues and hotels all around Cork; any of the experts will be glad to teach you some basic steps. The most likely location in Cork City to try set dancing yourself is at one of the "spit and sawdust" pubs, meccas for young and old for evening or weekend sessions. The current favorite of the folk pubs is probably **An Spailpin Fanach** in South Main Street.

Gaelic hurling and football in Cork engender enormous rivalry between the north and south sides of the city. Cork is accepted by the majority of Irish people as the home of the best and most consistent practitioners of **hurling**, a fast and furious game that looks as if it must bring serious injury, if not death, to the participants (its best players rarely do any harm to themselves or one another). The game, related to Scotland's shinty, is played mostly from the hand with a small, hard leather ball struck by sticks similar to those used in hockey but with broad, flat heads. The ball is hit in the air, not along the ground. Check local papers or posters in shop windows, or just keep an ear open for the word in the streets about upcoming games. Matches are played in various sites around the city throughout the year. If your visit happens to coincide with a county final or, better still, the Munster Final in Thurles or Limerick, it is worth getting a train ticket to see this spectacle. The main venue for **Gaelic football** is Pairc Ui Caoimh to the west of the city. (Gaelic football is explained at the end of the section Around Killarney, below.)

AROUND CORK CITY

From Cork City, a round-trip journey of about 40 to 50 km (25 to 31 miles) will take you to a number of interesting places. An important foray from the city is a drive out to Blarney to the northwest and to Blarney House, a beautiful residence of the Colthurst family (not open to visitors) on the grounds of **Blarney Castle**, famous of course for its Blarney Stone, the kissing of which is supposed to impart eloquence. The story goes that the resident MacCarthy chief of the time, on a visit to Elizabeth I, so pleased her with his flattery that she praised him for his eloquence, a virtue that then became attached to his castle—an early piece of Cork public relations. While here, take in the display at the well-signposted Blarney Woollen Mills.

If too much of the good life has made you dyspeptic, a round of golf may be the answer. Courses are numerous in the area. Try the **Frankfield House** nine-hole golf course and golf range in Kinsale Road. Clubs may be hired at some courses, including **Bandon** and **Muskerry**; some of the courses, **Mahon Municipal Golf Course**, for example, cater especially to visitors. Mahon is busy, though. Make inquiries at **Maher's Sports Shop**, 6 King Terrace, Lower Glanmire Road, for equipment rental and friendly pointers. On Model Farm Road, off Deneheys Cross in the Wilton area of the city in the western suburbs, there is a new **tennis complex**, including a shop, bar, showers, and other facilities.

Out on the road to Dublin (N 8), in a wooded area in the attractive village of Glanmire, is **Riverstown House**, open to the public and containing some of the best plasterwork of the Italian *stuccodores* the Francini brothers. Back several kilometers (a couple of miles) at the roundabout the road to Midleton leads (five hundred yards beyond, on the left-hand side) to **Dunkathel House,** an original country house, not fancified, open from May to September, noted for its collection of Irish furniture and for a permanent exhibition of the watercolors of Beatrice Gubbins. Gubbins was one of the best of the many women watercolorists working in the late 19th and early 20th centuries at a hobby considered appropriate to ladies of the upper class. The subjects of her work, now valued more highly than that of many of her professional contemporaries, include views of the heavily wooded slopes of the River Lee near Dunkathel House.

Fota Island

Signposts point the way to Fota Island, a wildlife park with an arboretum and a wonderful house containing a collection of Irish landscape paintings from the mid-18th to the late 19th century, including some art masterpieces of national importance. The house is not open to the public, however the arboretum, built up by the Smith-Barry family, brings together in this magnificent setting trees and shrubs from all over the world. You can also reach Fota by train from the main station in Cork; in the days when the island was a private estate, the train stopped here on its way to Cobh and Youghal for the members of the family, but nobody else was allowed to get off or board, perhaps the only example of a private station on a public transport system in the world. In the near future part of Fota's grounds will be developed into an exclusive housing and country-club facility, despite the objections of environmentalists. Proceeds from the development will go to maintaining Fota's house and grounds.

Cobh

Southeast of Cork City at the transatlantic port of Cobh is a memorial by the Irish sculptor Jerome O'Connor to the victims of the sinking of the *Lusitania* during the First World War (the wreck is off Kinsale). For countless thousands of Irish people, the view of Cobh was the last they saw of their native land as they emigrated to the New World. Chained in hulks offshore waiting to sail would be many other thousands, sentenced to the penal colonies in Australia and Tasmania. Tragically, it was also the final view of any land for those drowned in the *Titanic,* for which Cobh was the final port of call before the ship's fateful voyage. On a happier note, the *Sirius* sailed from here, the first steamship to cross the Atlantic.

Not far away is the townland (an ancient land division) of Shanagarry, headquarters of the Allen family and their many talents, the most famous of which is manifested in the food in the **Yeats Room** at **Ballymaloe House**, run by Myrtle Allen and her husband. In the Ballymaloe's dining room you'll enjoy a feast, not of Lucullan proportions but of the most delicate fresh and choice dishes, before you return to Cork City; or stay overnight in comfortable, though not sumptuous, surroundings.

You can share in the secrets of these culinary delights by reading the *Irish Times* weekend supplement (Myrtle Allen's offerings), or by taking a cooking course with Myrtle's daughter-in-law, Darina, at Ballymaloe (the imaginative courses vary in length, beginning with two days), using produce from the farm and the nearby Atlantic and the River Blackwater. Darina can also be seen on her popular TV cooking series, which has been transcribed and is now available in a number of best-selling books.

North Cork

Many delights await farther east in the town of Youghal and up and along the Blackwater Valley on into North Cork. In the tiny village of Curraglass you can buy a side of smoked salmon at Raymond Carr's smokehouse. The **Blackwater Valley**, with its specially signposted scenic drive is a beautiful pastoral area and home to one of the better-known fishing rivers in Ireland. The local post office (An Post) or police station (Garda) can tell you where to get the necessary permits and advise you regarding rates and size of catch. Casual permits for one- to two-day salmon fishing are not available. Near the Blackwater's source between Mallow and Kanturk is **Longueville House**, an 18th-century period house and hotel looking across the river to the ruins of **Dromaneen Castle** (16th century), a well-preserved national monument. The owners of Longueville House are the O'Callaghans of the clan who once owned Dromaneen Castle. Longueville House is one of the best hotels in Ireland, with all the charm and elegance of a small, stately home combined with the informal hospitality of the family that runs it. Longueville's restaurant serves fresh salmon in various delicate disguises with a warm, personal touch.

North Cork has been home to many authors, including Elizabeth Bowen, who was born and lived in Bowen Court (which no longer exists), near the village of Kildorrery off the Fermoy-to-Mitchelstown road. One of the bridges in the pretty village of Kanturk bears lines about the poet Edmund Spenser, who had estates (Kilcolman Castle) hereabouts granted to him by Elizabeth I. Northwest Cork also hosts the Millstreet Horse Show, in the village of Millstreet at the end of July. But time constraints will probably make it more sensible to head west from Cobh to the rest of County Cork and into Kerry than to further explore North Cork.

Kinsale

A half-hour's drive to the southwest of Cork City is the seaside town of Kinsale, scene of the ultimately decisive defeat for the forces of Gaelic Ireland and their Spanish allies at the hands of the English at the beginning of the 17th century. (On the way to Kinsale, try **Pew's Bistro** in Carrigaline and perhaps take a detour off the R 611 to Tracton village and the unusual **Overdraft** pub, which takes its monetary theme from the same place it got its brass and mahogany fittings: the old Munster and Leinster bank.)

A walled town with a narrow entrance, Kinsale is guarded by two magnificent forts, James Fort and Charles Fort, both dating to the 17th century. You can take a tour of **Charles Fort** or guide yourself through with a leaflet. The 16th-century **Desmond Castle** is also known as the French Prison because it was used to house prisoners during the Napoleonic Wars. Tours of Desmond Castle are possible; Tel: (021) 77-22-34 or follow the signposted tourist trail. Just north of the town is the site of the battle of Kinsale, where the O'Neills and O'Donnells from the north tried to relieve a force of Spaniards who had come to assist them; in a confused situation they lost the battle to the Elizabethan forces under Mountjoy. The attempted linkup with Spanish forces was only one of many examples over the centuries of Catholic Gaelic Ireland trying to elicit assistance from Catholic Europe, particularly Spain and France.

Kinsale is a lovely little town reminiscent of an elegant New England fishing port, and is small enough to cover on foot. The town clusters around its harbor, where a large yacht marina entices boats from France, Germany,

Britain, and much farther afield, creating a cosmopolitan atmosphere. Many of Kinsale's buildings have been beautifully restored, and the town has won European and Irish architectural awards. Every summer the residents make a special effort to earn the reputation of a French-style *ville fleurie*, with flowers in municipal and private display.

On a fine evening join the locals in an Irish *paseo*, where people stroll and greet each other. Or sample some of Kinsale's many wine-bars. Because the town is a trendy, upwardly mobile place the restaurants are quite good. **Wendy Tisdall's** on Main Street is featured in the TV series "A Taste of Ireland." Try the garlic mussels. **Man Friday** is rather plush, with a bar where you can have drinks before your meal; Tel: (021) 77-22-60. The **Vintage Restaurant** and **Max's Wine Bar** are also worth a visit.

Places to stay around here are with the Griffin family at **Hillside House**, in Camphill, with a sea view on a campsite of the battle of Kinsale, or at the fashionable **Acton's Hotel** in town (it's a bit like Jury's), where you will find the Continental flavor of Kinsale and indoor swimming as well. The **Blue Haven Hotel**, on the site of the old fish market, is restful, its cuisine, as in so many cases, dependent on the skill of the current resident chef. There are three distinctive dining rooms; try the Garden Room, overlooking a floodlit garden, and pick your own shellfish from the restaurant's tank. The wood-paneled Haven Bar has a conservatory, a patio, and a nautical theme. Blue Haven residents have access to the pool at Acton's Hotel.

The Old Bank House hotel is housed in a fine Georgian building, and preserves much of its 18th-century ambience. Rooms are comfortable and old fashioned. The owners, Michael and Marie Riese, also run the **Vintage** restaurant, with open fires in dining rooms assembled with 200-year-old beams and masts from vintage sailing ships. Booking is advisable; Tel: (021) 77-25-02. Or you could stay at the **Trident Hotel**, a large concrete building on the old pier, attractive for the comfort it offers as well as the harbor views. Kinsale is the venue for a number of theme festivals throughout the year.

West to Kerry and Killarney

As you travel west out of Cork City, you are, in the local parlance, "making for" Killarney, the main tourist center of County Kerry, via Glengarriff and Kenmare (each at the head of a bay in the farthest southwest), a journey of

about 130 km (80 miles)—or a little longer if you take
certain routes and make small detours. On the assump-
tion that your time has some limitation, only the more
important stops will be mentioned (though there is
plenty to be seen and noted) before getting to Killarney.
Of the two basic ways to get to Killarney, the southern
route is longer and runs closer to the sea. The other is
more direct and more inland; we call it the alternate
route.

THE SOUTHERN ROUTE TO KERRY

Douglas Street in Cork city center becomes Douglas Road
and then Carrigaline Road as you head south out of the city
(in Carrigaline visit the source of Carrigdhoun pottery).
You might prefer to stay in Kinsale, discussed above, before starting westward, rather than beginning the journey
right from Cork City. From Kinsale you can join the main
Cork–Bandon road at Innishannon, or go straight to
Innishannon from Cork City if you have already made the
Kinsale visit. Innishannon and this stretch of the River
Bandon are quite beautiful, especially in the autumn. The
road runs along the banks of the river with wooded hills
on either side displaying the full range of Shelley's "yellow,
pale, and hectic red" colors on their broadleafed trees.

Bandon

All around Bandon are the signs—parklands, symmetri-
cally planted trees, old, carefully sited houses—of the ordering influence of the English settlers who came here,
particularly in the 16th and 17th centuries. But other people have lived here for thousands of years, and the skeletal
remains of the past jut out from the landscape: stone alignments, hilltop forts, and, later in history, the tower houses
and castle strongholds of the native Irish chiefs, the
O'Mahonys, MacCarthys, and O'Driscolls. This area, once
the center of Gaelic culture, politics, and the Brehon legal
system (much more given to compensation than custodial
resolution of crime), settled into decline after the battle of
Kinsale. Here too are the splendid ruins of pre-
Reformation monastic foundations, such as the **Franciscan
Friary** at Timoleague, due south of Bandon, so beautifully
commemorated in an 18th-century Gaelic poem:

Ivy sprouting in your arches
Nettles on your cold, flagged floor.

See it on a summer's evening when the sounds of the day have died down and the ruins are framed against the light coming from the sea to the west. When the noise of the jackdaws (which, according to the above poem, have replaced the solemn Gregorian chant) has trailed away, listen for echoes of the past. Tours of the friary are also available; call Con Harrington at Tel: (023) 461-60.

Drive through the village from Kinsale, take the first right up the hill, and at the first left turn into **Lettercollum House**, a hostel with fairly Spartan accommodation but good organic country cooking in a former country mansion-turned-convent. Unusual.

The struggle between the old and the new—the planter and the old clan system, the old religion and the new—was long and bitter. Bandon Town was founded in 1608 by the great earl of Cork Richard Boyle (father of scientist Robert Boyle, of Boyle's Law). It was one of the first walled Protestant towns in Ireland, notable for its almost isolated resistance in Munster province to the Jacobite forces in the wars that extended to Ireland and finally established, after William of Orange, the Hanoverian succession. An amusing, though probably apocryphal, story told is that when the gates of Bandon were closed against the expected Jacobite forces somebody had written on the outside of the walls, "No papist may enter here," to which the reply was daubed, "Whoever wrote this wrote it well for the same is written on the gates of Hell"—all great rabble-rousing stuff that would probably land the protagonists in court today under the Prevention of Racism acts. As you drive through Bandon, and if you know your history and can distinguish a name of Gaelic origin from an English name, you can still distinguish papist from Protestant here.

Bandon to some has an air of puritan propriety about it yet. Down the canal that runs into the River Brandon, an old, vacant schoolhouse, once a landmark of Protestant education, retains remnants of the old walls and displays a plaque commemorating its history.

The term "Horse Protestant" has an interesting provenance. Under 18th-century penal laws a Protestant could insist that a Catholic sell him his horse for £5—thus the centaurlike description. Today the Horse Protestants ride to hounds or compete in the many excellent horse shows in the area—Millstreet being the biggest—with their Catholic neighbors.

For highly regarded bittersweet evocations of Anglo-Irish culture, sample authors William Trevor (*Fools of Fortune*) and Molly Keane (*Good Behaviour*), both of whom have connections with this area.

Nowadays all the traditions, past and present, old and new, have been subsumed into one recognizable Irish, and even Cork, distinctiveness. Perhaps just in time, some of the English settlers' influence is being preserved. For example, the Kilbrogan Church (Church of Ireland) in Bandon has now been restored to house the West Cork Heritage Centre, which includes a collection of genealogical and other historical records for the area.

Around Clonakilty

The Presbyterian church in **Clonakilty** (southwest of Bandon on N 71) has been converted to a post office, overlooked by a statue of a pikeman from the other tradition. **Carbery Knitwear Ltd.**, in the town's former railway station, produces garments made only from natural fibers: wool, silk, cotton, and linen—56 shades in wool alone. A plain knit sweater costs between £50 and £80, and the top of the range is £100 to £130. The exclusivity of the designs alone are worth the prices. Closed Saturdays.

The Irish country house is typified by **Drishane House** in the village of **Castletownshend**, farther west along the coast from Clonakilty, where Edith Somerville and Violet Martin lived. (The authors of *Some Experiences of an Irish R.M.* describe in a wonderful and unselfconscious manner the hierarchy of class and privilege that marked the end of the Anglo-Irish era.) The house is now a private residence and can only be viewed from the outside. Inquire at the Vickerys of Bow Hall (see below).

Castletownshend is a remarkable spot, described by Peter Somerville-Large in *The Coast of West Cork* as a "mini Valley of the Kings." It's an oasis of Anglo-Irish history and people, with a Townshend still living in the castle and a genealogical tree of the family in St. Barrahane's Church. If you'd like to pause overnight here, you might try 17th-century **Bow Hall** in the village, run by Dick and Barbara Vickery. They serve up buttermilk pancakes with syrup and applesauce for breakfast, and freshly baked chocolate-chip cookies to send you on your way. Welcoming scones are offered by owner Noreen O'Neill at **Woodland**, a very comfortable modern bungalow in a pleasant country setting five minutes' walk from the village.

The improving efforts of people like Sir William Cox, lord chancellor of England under William III, who planted a colony of weavers and established the linen industry in this part of Cork, mainly around **Dunmanway**, has come to be acknowledged by the newer Ireland. Dunmanway itself, northwest of Clonakilty on R 599, has two triangular "squares"—a shape typical of an Irish planned town of the 17th century, the houses around the triangle forming a defense. The town won the national Tidy Towns competition in 1982, a sign of a change of the times very much for the better.

The New Invasion

Over the past 20 or 30 years many Continental Europeans and English, fleeing from the pressures of industrialized, competitive society, have settled in West Cork. Sabine and Phillipe de Mey, for example. **Blair's Cove House**, the Georgian manor restaurant overlooking Dunmanus Bay, sits on a lane that connects to the Durrus–Goleen road about 2 km (1¼ miles) outside of Durrus village. Look for the blue entrance gate. With their command of four languages, the couple makes their guests feel at home no matter where they hail from. Booking is essential; Tel: (027/610-41). There's even a Japanese restaurant, the **Shiro Japanese Dinner House**, at Ahakista on the Durrus Peninsula, southwest of Bantry (Tel: 027/670-30). It's run by cosmopolitan German businessman Werner Pilz and his wife, Kei, whose beautifully dressed dolls and exquisite calligraphy decorate their tiny restaurant.

With their artistic skills the new invaders have created a veritable series of colonies of gifted people who blend in wonderfully with their Irish neighbors, and in fact have given rise to the development of many new local skills and industries—not to speak of employment. Some of their work is in the **West Cork Arts Centre** on North Street, **Skibbereen**, west along the coast from Clonakilty. Many of these very welcome newcomers have exhibited another characteristic of all invaders of Ireland: They have become more Irish than the Irish themselves.

The older, native tradition in these parts is very well represented by the **Ceim Hill Museum**, 3 km (2 miles) southwest of Union Hall, east of Skibbereen (signposted).

Ceim Hill is the ancestral home of Therese O'Mahony, of a historically dominant clan in this area. (Like other clans such as the O'Callaghans and the O'Keefes, they still hold their annual gathering, attended by members of the clan from all over the world, at the ruins of a former family castle nearby.) The museum displays prehistoric objects, instruments, and weapons as well as lace, farm implements, and, perhaps most interesting, examples of the West Cork cloak, so common until a few years ago and now gone altogether from daily use. Therese is an herbalist who believes in picking her herbs from the wild and in sharing her many recipes and prescriptions. She will quote to you from her mother's 1911 handwritten notebook formulas for making starch, and methods for bleaching and washing linen, washing lace and satin, and treating different fabrics using plants to keep the colors fast—a genuine piece of local continuity.

At **Baltimore**, southwest of Skibbereen, you can contact Dermot Kennedy (Tel: 028/201-41) about sailing charters or rentals. He can also provide you with names of boatmen to contact at the hundreds of small piers and harbors along this coast who make runs to many of the islands, including the "1000 Islands of Carberry" in the safe and sheltered (and misnamed) Roaring Water Bay. Afterward you can visit the pub with a Moor on its sign—there is a tradition here that Baltimore was sacked by Barbary pirates. Sherkin and Hare Islands as well as Gaelic-speaking Clear Island are worth a visit if time permits.

The Bantry Bay Area

The former oil terminal on Whiddy Island, just offshore of **Bantry Town**, on the coast northwest of Skibbereen, may not be one of the most picturesque sights in the world, but the successful camouflage of the storage tanks is an interesting attempt to reconcile industrial development with a scene of striking natural beauty. **Bantry House** and gardens, a well-sited home of local gentry for many generations and a museum as well, is open to the public from Easter to the end of October. The present owner is slowly restoring the magnificent interior of the house and the gardens, which present views to the west and south. Otherwise, Bantry itself is no more than an average market town on the way to more attractive places. Bantry Bay is best appreciated from the Bantry–

Glengarriff road, with a full unimpeded view that is at its best at sunset.

This tranquillity is not at all the scene that greeted a French naval expedition at the end of the 18th century, when, during an attempt to export the French Revolution by assisting the Irish patriot Wolfe Tone and his United Irishmen, it was scattered by a storm—echoes of the fate of the Spanish Armada. (The ancestors of Bantry House's current owner were instrumental in warning of the invasion.)

Glengarriff village, on the other side of the bay head from Bantry, has now recovered somewhat from its former tawdry reputation, and offers some excellent crafts shops and good accommodations. The old-fashioned **Blue Pool Hotel** in the middle of the village is highly regarded; there are no rooms *en suite,* but it's filled with antique furniture and is a marvelous value. You will find excellent cuisine and good value at **Casey's Hotel** next door, renowned among trenchermen. The rooms are comfortable (lots of chintz), and a middle-class, middle-aged atmosphere pervades. Impromptu sing-alongs have been known to break out. Another good choice is the **Bayview House**, nestled in the hillside here and run by Margaret Heffernan.

On a fine evening, walk back up the Bantry road from Glengarriff; about a mile up on the right-hand side is the site of the former Ma Roche's Hotel. On the grounds down toward the sea are the original monkey-puzzle trees (so named because their spiky leaves supposedly make them too difficult for even a monkey to climb). Imagine the sound of racquets on balls, midshipmen and local young ladies playing tennis in the 1920s and 1930s, when the hotel was one of the great social centers for the British navy, based at Berehaven at the mouth of the bay. This was one of the ports left in British government control at the time of independence, and it was not reclaimed until the agreement between Neville Chamberlain and Eamon de Valera in 1938—just in time to preserve full Irish neutrality in the Second World War.

In this area the historic O'Sullivan Bere family granted leases to Spanish fishermen to fish in Bantry Bay for pilchards (if the Spanish could elude O'Driscoll pirates). After the defeats of Kinsale (the early 1600s) and later, the O'Sullivan Beres migrated northward hundreds of miles, an exodus comparable in its hardship to Mao Tse-tung's Long March in China, or the movements of the Voortrekkers in South Africa.

However, the romanticism associated with the ancient Irish chieftainships must be set against a background of brutality and primitive treatment within the clan system. The O'Sullivan chiefs, for instance, frequently maltreated their subordinate peoples; the hounds of the clan chiefs were fed better than the lowly members of the clan. If the dogs were not found in good condition when the chief came to hunt, the heads of his followers rolled.

The R 574 road, north from the middle of Bantry Bay's north shore a bit west of Glengarriff, crosses over the Caha Mountains through Tim Healy Pass—named for a former governor-general of Ireland—a journey that offers truly magnificent views over Bantry Bay and Kenmare Bay on the north (Kerry) side of this rugged spine of mountains.

Orienteering, mountaineering, or just rock climbing is excellent around here but can be dangerous because of the capriciousness of the Atlantic weather. This is wild, beautiful, rugged, but unyielding country, as indicated by the name of one of its bare peaks: Hungry Hill.

THE ALTERNATE ROUTE FROM CORK CITY TO KERRY

The main road out of Cork City west to **Macroom** (N 22) goes past the County Hall, a tall building beyond the Western Road with an amusing statue of two workmen looking up at it. The men seem to be not so much impressed as mockingly bewildered at the building's pretensions to grandeur, a good reminder of the essential personality of your average Corkonian. William Penn of Pennsylvania visited Macroom many times, and by all accounts was not very enamored of the people or their culture; but then the good William was an upright and somewhat straitlaced person, not a type very conspicuous in these parts.

Another route to Macroom, route 618, runs north of and parallel to the main road, along the valley of the River Lee through the pretty villages of **Dripsey** and **Coachford**. Additionally, if you haven't already visited **Blarney** on a foray out of Cork City, you can detour north to it and return again to the N 22.

As you approach Macroom on the main road you will have to decide which of two routes to Killarney in Kerry to follow. One, N 22, leads straight through Macroom, to its tiny, main-street museum with many reminders of a local writing tradition founded in a strong pride of place, and on to the Irish-speaking area of **Ballyvourney** and **Coolea**. These two Cork villages (together, population 300) boast an enormously rich and productive tradition of Irish music and literature—a quarter of this tiny population writes poetry in the Irish language. With the opening of radio and TV studios in the area, it is more likely that this material will be preserved, developed, and used as a treasure house, instead of being turned into pseudo-cultural productions. But above all the area was home to the composer and music teacher Sean O'Riada, who commuted regularly to University College, Cork, to teach his art and craft. He wrote Irish traditional music themes in the shapes and forms of classical music, and experimented with marrying those themes with Continental and other styles. His son Peadar and others of his family have maintained and developed the standards and inspiration of their father and mother. The choir from the area, which has won many plaudits, is based on an old Irish tradition of the exclusively male choir, which goes back to an established monastic practice that excluded women because they were considered a distraction—an insult and a compliment combined.

If you wish to spend the night nearby, you might try the **Dineen family** bed and breakfast, beyond Coolea toward Kilgarvan. It may suit your taste, as it has that of author Richard Condon. Set in what Condon calls the "beautiful, wild, gorgeous red sandstone mountains of County Kerry," it has "Irish linen, Irish china, Irish silverware, Gaelic spoken, and Irish bacon and cabbage, country style," plus a welcome drink and whiskey cake on arrival. After this stop return to N 22 and continue through wild mountain country into Kerry and Killarney.

To follow a second, more southerly, route to Kerry, make a left just past Macroom and, going over the Shehy Mountains, join the R 584. A short detour via R 587 off R 584 will take you to the site of the 1920 IRA ambush of the British at **Kilmichael**, famed in song. This particular episode was followed shortly after by the burning of a considerable part of Cork City by the British, whose responsibility for this obvious reprisal was indicated in following days by Crown forces wearing burnt corks in their hats on the streets of Dublin.

Rejoining the R 584 you'll soon come to the peaceful **Lough Gougane Barra**, where, the poem says, the Lough

"Allua of swans flies forth as an arrow," and indeed the little oratory that commemorates where Saint Finbarr of Cork City began his monastic life still has swans on the nearby waters. On through the Pass of Keimaneigh, through the Shehy Mountains, the road comes out at Ballylickey, an oasis amid the wilder scenery. Accommodations in the area include **Ballylickey Manor House**, nestled among well-planted gardens and offering good but not outstanding cuisine. The road continues on to Glengarriff and north to Kenmare and Killarney.

COUNTY KERRY

One of the clichés of travelling—"so much to see and so little time to see it"—is particularly true of Kerry. The long indentations and peninsulas of the county and the richness of its archaeological remains make it difficult to cover in a short time. It isn't really possible to do justice to the area of Killarney and also make a detailed tour of the Ring of Kerry (discussed in detail below), which takes in Cahirciveen, Waterville, Sneem, Kenmare, and back to Killarney—about four hours—*and,* without a very long stay, visit the Dingle Peninsula, too. Yet the latter is the richest source of archaeological sites, and at its tip are ancient Irish cultural artifacts with remarkable literary connotations. With limited time, then, see the Dingle Peninsula, and if you have a half day to spare take a bus tour (Dero's or another from Killarney, booked with the tourist office in the Town Hall) of the Ring. In bad weather doing the Ring in your own car can be tricky. We begin our tour of Kerry in Kenmare—its name in Irish means "little nest"—which comes as an orderly surprise after the wild countryside leading to it.

Kenmare

Expansive views meet the approach to Kenmare through the tunnels of the Glengarriff road and across the old bridge at the head of the bay. The seaside town, not at all a resort, invites walks along the rocky river and in the neatly laid-out town itself. Kenmare, designed by the marquess of Lansdowne in 1775, was a model of a land-lord's town: Two principal streets form an X, with a park at the bottom of the base. County Kerry in general is an impressive area of prehistoric monuments, and one of them is right here in the town: **Druid's Circle**, a ring of 15 stones with one boulder in the middle, an arrangement probably associated with human sacrifice. Set among trees overlooking the river, Druid's Circle is especially beautiful and eerie in the evening light. Follow signposts that lead off the square, down a narrow lane, and through a swinging gate.

The town was the scene of a different kind of human sacrifice in the middle of the last century, with the terrible suffering of the Great Hunger, followed by succeeding famines. With the terrible irony of changing times, the workhouse (now the district hospital), the scene of so much suffering during the famines, is only a short distance away from four of Kenmare's many excellent eating spots: **The Lime Tree**, which serves dinner in charming natural-wood and stone surroundings from 6:00 to 10:00 P.M. every day, with prices ranging from £10 to £18 (Tel: 064/412-25); **The Purple Heather**, a daytime bistro; **An Leath Phingin**, on Main Street (Tel: 064/415-59), another bistro; and, the most renowned of them all, the **Park Hotel**, which won the Egon Ronay award for the best hotel in Ireland and the United Kingdom in 1988. The food at the Park is truly superb, at prices ranging from a bit higher than average to a good deal higher. But there is always a fire in the lounge, and the atmosphere is almost like that of an opulent but extremely friendly home. The dining-room window overlooks the River Kenmare, and the service here is of the kind that meets your needs before you have actually realized them. For lodging in the same price bracket you might choose the recently opened **Sheen Falls Lodge**, built around the former residence of the earls of Kerry and surrounded by 300 secluded acres of forest and lawns. Tall windows frame exquisite views of woodland, sea, and mountains.

For those with less demanding tastes there are **Mylestone House** (a spacious guest house next to Kenmare Golf Course, a three-minutes' walk from town center), **Kenmare Bay Hotel**, or, just back across the bridge, the very reasonable **Riversdale House Hotel**, which has a good dinner menu and is also beautifully situated by the river among ancient pines. Here you will be warmly received by Peter and Peggy O'Sullivan. As for shopping in Kenmare stop in at the branch of the **Quill's** chain, a large emporium with a helpful staff. Near the Purple Heather, **Nostalgia** features Irish lace and linens and is ideal for browsing.

Around Kenmare

If you must skip the Ring of Kerry, then before leaving Kenmare it's worth going out a little to see the beautiful and striking village of **Sneem** (the Irish word for "Knot"), in this case a figure eight. (Sneem is west of Kenmare on N 70, part of the Ring of Kerry.) For a wealth of local lore and tradition, consult T. E. Stoukeley's *The Knot on the Ring* or, if you're very lucky, Sneem's schoolmaster Batt O'Shea.

This garden village boasts the biggest collection of outdoor sculpture in Ireland, including a remarkable series of international tributes to former president of Ireland Cearbhall O'Dalaigh, a distinguished Gaelic scholar and former chief justice of the Supreme Court. The national memorial to the former president is the work of young Irish sculptor Vivien Roche. The flat stone—*leacht* in the Irish language—over the president's grave is by Seamus Murphy and takes the Irish traditional form of a simple cross and the name.

Here also stand James Scanlon's stone and glass constructions inspired by **Staigue Fort**, one of the best-preserved examples of the ancient forts that surrounded dwelling places. Staigue Fort is at Castlecove, about 11 km (7 miles) to the west of Sneem.

Tamara Rikman, a prominent Israeli sculptor, has contributed a steel tree that combines some of the attributes of a cedar of Lebanon with Irish overtones. This was unveiled by the Israeli president Chaim Herzog, who was born and partly educated in Ireland, when his father was chief rabbi here.

In Sneem stay at quiet **Woodvale Guesthouse** overlooking Kenmare Bay, or at **Derryeast Farmhouse**; both are bed-and-breakfast accommodations. One of the **Quill's** shops is here, too. A little farther on is the **Parknasilla Great Southern Hotel**, a very well appointed 19th-century mansion on extensive grounds with full facilities for indoor and outdoor sports and recreation: indoor heated saltwater pool, horseback riding, tennis, angling, sailing, water skiing, and free golf for guests (nine holes). The

Parknasilla shares with Dromoland and Ashford castles the distinction of having been the venue for meetings of the European Community ministers and heads of state during Ireland's E.C. presidency in 1990.

From Kenmare the N 71 takes you north to Killarney via Moll's Gap (visit **Cremin's** shop in Moll's Gap for woollens, rugs, and the like) and offers magnificent views of the Killarney lakes. Or you can go by the more eventful and equally rewarding Kilgarvan–Coolea–Ballyvourney route (for Coolea and Ballyvourney see The Alternate Route from Cork City to Kerry, above). In early August, **Kilgarvan** has a Rhymer's Festival, which carries on an oral-history tradition involving local and not-so-local events. In the past some of the recitations and their authors, now honored in the festival, were distinctly not in favor with the area's clergy because of their irreverence—another example of local thumbing the nose, even at the religious establishment.

This area around the Cork/Kerry border seems to breed an atmosphere of individualism and revolt against the accepted wisdom. *In a Quiet Land,* by John O'Donoghue (no relation to this author), describes how at one level there was great piety, such as attendance at "patterns," religious exercises conducted around wells dedicated to ancient saints, and yet at the same time there was latent anticlericalism, in the not-surprising form of objections to paying cash dues at appointed times of the year.

Because the people of Cork and Kerry were involved probably more than residents of other counties in both the War of Independence and the Civil War, many fell foul of the leaders of their majority church. Often they incurred excommunication and therefore exclusion from the comforts of their religion, a great deprivation considering the prospect of sudden death that awaited them. But they followed the advice of the 19th-century political leader Kerryman Daniel O'Connell that they should take their religion from Rome and keep their politics at home. They also received the consolations of their religion from monks who functioned outside the monolithic official structure of the Catholic Church, which was later grateful for the allegiance of former rebels who became national and international figures, such as Eamon de Valera.

THE KILLARNEY AREA

In the second half of the 19th century the lakes of Killarney were as famous as Sir Walter Scott's Gothic Highlands and Wordsworth's Lake District. On a more popular level, the town of Killarney, nestled in the mountains, and its surrounding lakes figured in the operetta "The Lily of Killarney" and Bing Crosby's "How Can You Buy Killarney." In any event, Killarney's beauty spots were either given to, or bought by, the state, and now constitute an extensive and beautiful national park.

Around Killarney the vegetation is especially lush. Wild rhododendrons make a great wash of pale purple along the lake shores in May and early June, and the waters, accessible everywhere to the public but dangerous for swimming and sailing, reflect the colors of heather and furze, and the clouds above.

Killarney used to be very commercialized but is no longer so pushy, and if you don't want souvenirs you don't have to buy them. The scenery fortunately has not been tampered with, though some who want only to row boats on the famous lakes don't like the idea of being crowded by the new covered water buses. But if it is raining... *chacun à son goût*. All the obvious tourist attractions are well advertised and signposted. The following suggestions concentrate on what doesn't always get deserved prominence.

Killarney Town

Killarney in the Irish language is Cill Airne, the "Church of the Sloe" in one interpretation. Famous for the arbutus, a wild fruiting bush that grows nowhere else in Ireland, the town is an excellent base for visiting the surrounding woods, the waterfalls at Torc Mountain, and the Gap of Dunloe. In Killarney are the jaunting cars and the Great Southern Hotel, which evoke the atmosphere of the 19th-century Grand Tour. A full viewing of the town takes two hours, but the following features can be seen in less time.

Behind the Town Hall is an ancient holy well where people "do the rounds," that is, walk around the well reciting certain prayers before drinking the well water (not polluted). Just across the street is St. Mary's (Church of

Ireland), which is notable only as a landmark. Worthy of a visit is the Roman Catholic St. Mary's Cathedral (by Pugin), a fine example of Gothic Revival architecture.

The **Lewis Gallery** in Bridewell Lane includes the work of some 30 contemporary Kerry-based artists, the best known of whom is probably Pauline Bewick, whose delicate, languorous paintings have received wide acclaim. Also ask to see the weird and wonderfully fanciful paintings of an O'Donoghue chieftain's saga by a returned exile from America of the same clan (the legend is described in the discussion of Ross Castle, below). Director Frank Lewis is generous with his honest recommendations and insights.

Around the corner from St. Mary's Church is the starting point for journeys by horse-drawn jaunting car, a rather daunting mode of transport, but one which most tourists feel is worth taking. Be sure to pick a sturdy equipage: Hiring vintage horses, jarveys (drivers), and jaunting cars is ill-advised. Travellers in the past have paid the dubious compliment to the Killarney jarveys of including them in a triumvirate of people of whom international travellers must beware: the taxi drivers of Marrakech, the gondoliers of Venice, and these local tellers of tall tales—but the jaunting car can be good value if you negotiate the price.

There are a number of interesting pubs in Killarney. At **Jimmy O'Brien's**, near the friary, you will meet country people and hear traditional music; **The Laurels** on Main Street specializes in ballads beloved of Irish-Americans; and in **Tattler Jack's** in Plunkett Street you will hear gossip and—among many other matters of great import—the latest state of play in Gaelic football.

Killarney offers an embarrassing proliferation of souvenir shops, almost all open from 9:00 A.M. to 6:00 P.M., many of them until 10:00 P.M. **Quill's**, with two shops in the main street, specializes in woollen goods, sweaters, tweeds, and jackets of good value. Also in the main street is **Maybury's**, known for its Waterford glass, woollens, and tweeds, and now owned by Blarney Woollen Mills. For crafts shopping, there's Muckross House (see below). In general, be cautious of prices in areas of high tourism.

In the Black Valley (follow the signpost to Sneem and the Youth Hostel at Moll's Gap), Flemish-born designer Lily Van Oost designs way-out wool knitwear with a look rather like craters on the moon. Though she doesn't have

a shop as such, her work is on sale in the area, and she can be located by inquiring at the Black Valley Youth Hostel.

Just as Cork would be recommended by many people as a place to see the glories of the Irish sporting game of hurling, Kerry would certainly be equally advised as a place to see **Gaelic football** at its best. During the summer months matches are held at Fitzgerald Stadium on Anne's Road, beyond the junction of Anne's Road and Lewis Road. Gaelic football and hurling are becoming minor cult viewing on TV as far away as Japan, and are spectacles not to be missed when played by skilled opponents on a fine day. Gaelic football, which involves both handling and kicking the ball, is more physical than soccer and less so than rugby. The team scores when the ball passes between goalposts set on a pitch (longer than that used for soccer). The nearest comparison is to Australian Rules football, and competitions are played in Ireland and Australia according to an amalgam of the two codes. Information about the games is enthusiastically available from just about everyone.

The first fixture on Killarney's well-sited **horse-racing course** is in early May each year; the second is toward the middle of July. The track is on the road to Ross Castle, 2 km (1¼ miles) out of town.

Staying and Dining in the Killarney Area

The 168-room 19th-century **Great Southern Hotel**, set in spacious gardens right in Killarney, offers gracious comfort as well as easy access to all the major attractions. Once one of the great hotels on the upper-class tourist routes of Europe, the Great Southern is equipped with an indoor swimming pool, a gym with a Jacuzzi, tennis courts, and more. Also in town, beside the Town Hall (where the jarveys leave for their trips), is the reasonably priced **Three Lakes Hotel**. It has three types of rooms—standard, superior, and deluxe—all with private bath and shower and TV. Choose your room carefully; most have views over the town but some at the back of the hotel look out over the national park (see below, in the Around Killarney section). The food is good but nothing special.

Also near the starting point for the jaunting trips is the

newly built **Killarney Park Hotel**, next to the old cinema. Modern, of course, and fully air-conditioned, it isn't architecturally attractive and offers no views, but it has a leisure center and a swimming pool.

The **Lake Hotel**, about 2 km (1¼ miles) from Killarney Town out on the Muckross road, sits on lovely grounds overlooking Lough Leane. Originally a private mansion, it was converted to a hotel in the 19th century. A new sun lounge looks out over the lake as do some newer bedrooms (request one of the 70 recently refurbished rooms when booking) and the spacious dining room; the food, unfortunately, is rather ordinary. Try the **Cahernane Hotel**, also on the Muckross road, for drinks on the lawn and reasonably priced snacks.

On the Muckross road about 1 km (½ mile) from town, the old rectory has been converted into the **Muckross Court Hotel**, with mahogany, cherry, and ash woodwork, antiques, and a splendid blend of the old and the new. About 3 km (2 miles) farther along the road is the **Muckross Park Hotel**, universally known as "Molly D'Arcy's." Its thatched bar is a great place to exchange gossip with the locals.

The 65-room **Castlerosse Hotel**, 2 km (1¼ miles) out on the Killorglin road—the Ring of Kerry road—has its own 36-hole golf course a half mile away on its extensive grounds, plus a restaurant that overlooks the lake. A pianist plays some nights, a guitarist on others; the music represents various periods and styles. The bedrooms are separate from the hotel, chalet/motel style, and their views are spectacular.

The **Gleneagle Hotel**, on the road to Kenmare, is a very large sports/entertainment complex with indoor and outdoor tennis and other indoor sports. Water buses for lake tours can be booked from here. Though the place is rather rambling, busy with wedding parties and such, it's a good base for an active stay in Killarney.

At the village of Fossa on the shores of Lough Leane is the large (176 rooms) **Hotel Europe**, which, along with its excellent cuisine, offers what has been described as a James Bond–type gymnasium and exercise/relaxation facility: indoor swimming pool and tennis, horseback riding, and special rates on greens fees for certain golf courses.

Offering a stunning view of the lakes from north of town is the large, modern **Aghadoe Heights Hotel**, situated just opposite the ruins of a seventh-century church with the remains of a round tower; the restaurant provides a panoramic vista of Killarney as well as good food.

On the road northwest from town to Killorglin, past the Hotel Europe, is a modern church in a new Irish non-imitative tradition. Its shape, in black slate, suggests the mountains in which it is set; the startling interior, almost all in white, carries the eye up to the plate-glass window behind the altar, which frames the lakes and the mountains beyond in one massive, living landscape—reinforced by a line from Psalms engraved on the wooden altar: "Praise the Lord all ye hills and mountains." Five hundred yards from the church is **Loch Lein House**, Kathleen Coffey's inexpensive and very welcoming bed and breakfast, which offers a lovely view of the lakes from a different perspective.

Carriglea Farmhouse, south of Killarney on the road to Muckross, provides the comforts of an old but well-restored farmhouse at similarly low rates (dinner is not available). The residence is beautifully maintained, as are the gardens that flourish between two imposing driveways leading to the house. The owner of **Linden House**, in a quiet location on New Road in Killarney Town, is longtime resident Peter Knoblauch, who also serves as the chef. The rooms here are peaceful, and the restaurant (open to non-guests) offers a set menu, an à la carte menu, table d'hote, and a tourist menu. Also on New Road is **Gleanntan House**, a good value for bed and breakfast. The **Mystical Rose** on Woodlawn Road recently won an award for comfort and welcome offered.

For more alternatives to staying in Killarney Town, consider one of the guest houses located about halfway between Killarney and Tralee near Kerry County Airport at Farranfore in the valley of the River Maine. (The nearby village of Castlemaine is the birthplace of "The Wild Colonial Boy," one of Ireland's best-known ballads.) Among the best are the **Hilltop Farmhouse** and the **Oakhill Farmhouse** (both are 1½ km/1 mile from Kerry Airport), the **Grange Grove Farm**, the **Murphy Farmhouse**, and **Tom and Eileen's Farmhouse**, not far from the beach. All can be highly recommended. Also north of Killarney and near the airport is the **Walhalla Visitor Farm**, for viewing or participating in small-farm activities (visitors are welcome to join the family for morning or afternoon tea). The site, run by Irish-Australian Jane O'Sullivan, has several prehistoric archaeological remains worth seeing (Tel: 066/643-82 for information).

The best places for eating in Killarney are: **Foley's**

(Denis and Carole Hartnett), serving dinner from 5:00
P.M. and providing excellent service and fresh orange
juice (unusual in Ireland); **Gaby's** (at a new location on
Hight Street), set amid eye-catching stonework and oak
beams reclaimed from an old orphanage and offering
meals accompanied by wine from one of the best cellars
in Ireland; the good but not so upmarket **Flesk Bar and
Restaurant**, where the food is excellent value but you
may have to wait for it (the Flesk is run by the "Klondyke"
O'Learys, whose fine physiques obviously come from an
ancestral gold rush survivor); the **Strawberry Tree**, a new
trendy restaurant with Laura Ashley decor, in Plunkett
Street; and the **Malton Room** of the Great Southern Hotel,
which retains much of the elegance and plushness of its
19th-century origins.

Around Killarney

Killarney is surrounded by the large **Killarney National
Park**, which was originally individual estates. The park,
which has a herd of indigenous red deer, takes in all the
lakes of Killarney. The estates of the earls of Kenmare—
title and family now extinct—passed first into American
and then state ownership. The estates form part of the
national park and are open to the public, as is **Knockreer
House**, with permanent exhibitions on the Browne family
(earls of Kenmare) and the flora and fauna of the park.
The entrance to Knockreer House is opposite St. Mary's
Cathedral.

The Browne family, given in the 17th century the estates that formerly belonged to the O'Donoghues, was
one of the very few among the newer settlers to maintain
the practice of the Roman Catholic faith. Under the penal
laws of the 18th century, every Catholic had to divide his
property among his male heirs, which ensured a progres-
sive reduction in the size and value of that property, as
most Catholic families had quite a number of children.
The interesting exception of the Brownes was that during
that entire century each generation had only one male
heir, and so this family managed to maintain both its
religion and its estates intact. Their status lived on into
the 1940s, when the local cinema still had specially uphol-
stered and gilded seats for the lord and his lady.

In Muckross, south of Killarney on the east side of
Lough Leane, is **Muckross House**, formerly owned by the
Herbert family. Muckross House retains its period furnish-

ings, and downstairs is a working folk museum, where a weaver, a potter, a bookbinder, and a blacksmith actually make their goods. A crafts shop sells their products here.

In the **arboretum** close to Muckross House, plants that can't grow anywhere else in Ireland except in green-houses flourish in the open. The so-called Kerry straw-berry tree, the *Arbutus unido,* is remarkable in that its northern limit is otherwise the south of France. Two of the three most important natural oak woods in Ireland are in the area, one at Derrycunnihy Cascade and one at O'Sullivan's Cascade on the far side of **Lough Leane** (also known as the Lower Lake). You can hire a boat or have yourself rowed over from the Muckross Boat House; or you can drive your car through the park, despite what the horse jarveys say, to Muckross House and you'll find the boats a few yards away, through the gardens. Incidentally, the yew woods on Muckross Peninsula have been shown by pollen analysis to go back 10,000 years, to the Ice Age.

In modern contrast to the ancient religious history with which Kerry is so well endowed are the **Stations of the Cross** in the Catholic church near Muckross. These are by Imogen Stuart, daughter of the legendary Republican fig-ure Maud Gonne MacBride and half-sister of the late Sean MacBride, international statesman and winner of the No-bel Peace Prize, the Lenin Peace Prize, and the highest U.S. decoration for efforts to further peace.

Mountain climbers and geologists will find the rock formation at the back of the **Lough Guitane** area, east of Muckross, remarkable; it was formed by volcanic activity and is quite similar to the formations at the Giant's Cause-way in County Antrim in Northern Ireland. And for those who are seriously interested in strenuous activities, there are various orienteering courses at the resort of **Cappanalea**, 28 km (17 miles) west of Killarney on **Lough Caragh**, with canoeing and mountain climbing in the majestic **MacGillicuddy's Reeks**, home to eight peaks over 3,000 feet; heed local advice about survival gear and weather. You can stay at Cappanalea in rather Spartan surroundings, but it's not recommended. Try the 1913 red-sandstone **Ard na Sidhe**, a comfortable Victorian-style mansion complete with antique furniture, on Lough Caragh, or stay in Killorglin, 11 km (7 miles) away (see below).

Ross Castle, about 3 km (2 miles) from Killarney (as you head out of town turn toward Kenmare, then turn right at Bowler's Garage), was once the fortification of an

O'Donoghue chieftain whose spirit, according to legend, rises from the Lower Lake on a white horse every May 1. Ross was one of the last Gaelic strongholds to fall to the forces of Cromwell. There was a prophecy that the castle would remain impregnable unless attacked by water, and indeed the attackers did make their assault from the lake.

The island of **Inisfallen** across from Ross Castle in Lough Leane has the remains of the ancient monastery where Brian Boru, the first really effective high king of Ireland, is said to have received his early education, and where one of the most carefully compiled histories of ancient Ireland, the *Annals of Inisfallen,* was produced toward the end of the first millennium. An earl of Kenmare in the 19th century, seeing the possibility of tourist development, had part of the old ruins roofed in and held an international banquet here, attended by Leopold I, king of Belgium, Thomas Moore, the melody writer, and many other notables. Killarney has never looked back. There is no longer any visitor activity on the island, but you can land here if you row a boat over or hire one from Ross Castle, and you can see the island, though you won't be given a chance to land on it, on the water-bus tour.

A trip through the **Gap of Dunloe**, a defile in the Kerry Mountains, west of Killarney on the other side of Lough Leane, is a must. One of Killarney's clichés, it is nonetheless beautiful. Visitors go by pony, or by pony and trap, through the gap (about seven miles) and down to the lake. They boat across, passing rapids, and join up again on the other side to return to Killarney. The combination of mountain, woodland, and lake vistas, and the simple array of scenery and perspectives—as well as the chat of the boatmen (not quite as mendacious as that of the jarveymen)—is worth a full day.

You can book the Gap of Dunloe tour through the Killarney Tourist Office. The bus leaves by 10:30 A.M. from the Town Hall and returns there at 5:15 P.M. (it's a good idea to get there 20 to 30 minutes early). All of the coach tour services are the same price, £21 for a full day, and in every other way similar. The pony ride begins 11 km (7 miles) from Killarney at Kate Kearney's Cottage, a historical cottage housing the Gap of Dunloe shop (no Kate Kearney still lives here). It is advisable to go by pony and trap—pony and spring cart—because some of the animals are temperamental (the pony guides walk alongside pony riders). Either way, you get to Gearameen and Lord Brandon's Cottage (Lord Brandon is also long gone). You may bring your own lunch or you can buy tea, coffee, and snacks here. After lunch you walk a few yards to the shore of the Upper Lake and take a large rowboat down to the Meeting of the Waters at Dinis Cottage and into the Lower Lake, where you cross over to Ross Castle on its promontory.

The distinct advantage of booking a coach tour for this trip is that when you finish at Ross Castle you'll be returned to your car, seven miles away in Killarney. Of course you can drive up to Kate Kearney's Cottage and walk through the gap and simply take the views, but it's not quite the same thing as going on a pony trek.

THE REST OF KERRY
The Ring of Kerry

Even to use such a description as "the rest of Kerry" is an unfair remaindering of the rest of "the Kingdom." There is a choice of seeing the Ring of Kerry either by coach tour or by car. Any tour should take in the town of **Killorglin**, northwest of Killarney, which in August is the scene of Puck Fair, a traditional occasion for a gathering of Ireland's travelling people, presided over by a large billy goat, or Puck goat, ensconced on a monument in the center of the town. Long believed to be a symbol of fertility, the Puck quietly munching carrots is only one of many animals randomly chosen as a symbol for fairs around Ireland. But the idea of a pagan satyr symbol for an ancient fair lasting into present times—three days of madness—should not be lightly thrown over. **The Fishery**, at the bridge in Killorglin, serves smoked-salmon sandwiches for eating on the spot, and sells sides of smoked salmon, sealed in plastic, to take away. Stay at **Ashling House**, a family-run bed and breakfast here, or at the Ard na Sidhe nearby on Lough Caragh (discussed above).

The Ring of Kerry will take you near **Valentia Island** to the west, near Cahirciveen, and a quarry that provided slate for 14 miles of library shelving in the House of Commons at Westminster, as well as countless tops of snooker and billiard tables.

From this point (though not feasible at some times of the year) take a trip to the Skellig island named after Saint

Michael: **Skellig Mhichil**. Here, in a most austere and isolated atmosphere, lived the hermits of the fifth and sixth centuries, followers of Saint Fionan. As Kenneth Clark said in his famous "Civilisation" TV series, " . . . for quite a long time—almost a hundred years—Western Christianity survived by clinging onto places like Skellig Michael, a pinnacle of rock eighteen miles off the Irish coast, rising seven hundred feet out of the sea." Here also is the second-largest gannetry in the world. To arrange a trip to Skellig Mhichil, also known as the Skellig Rock, ask for Brendan Keefe in Portmagee (Tel: 066/771-03), or ask around in Cahirciveen or Derrynane. A round trip takes all day and will cost about £15 per person. Bring lunch, a flask, and a guidebook, as there are no facilities at all on the island. Offshore, these waters provide the northernmost limit of tropical fish as well as the southernmost limit of Arctic fish. More ordinary fish may be caught from shore at **Culloo Rock**, 6 km (3½ miles) west of Knightstown. Beware of the weather and the tides; the Atlantic Ocean can be treacherous.

Waterville, a small, simple town—just one long street—situated between Lough Currane and a rather nice beach, is a center for golf and fishing, with some good accommodations. The 27-room **Butler Arms Hotel** on the main street is an old family hotel (run by Peter and Mary Huggard); they will arrange for golf, fishing, or a boat trip to Skellig Mhichil from the new interpretative center on Valentia Island.

The **Club Med Waterville** is a hotel owned and run by Club Méditerranée. Ideal for those who appreciate activity, the leisure center offers tennis, archery, an indoor pool, a sauna, fishing in the lake (you can rent a rod), and, of course, golf (a shuttle to the course is provided). Those who prefer an even slower pace can take advantage of the guided walking tours and musical entertainment (Irish music night on Thursdays interrupts the regular classical music schedule). Other lodging choices include the **Strand** and the **Villa Maria**, both pretty average. For food head for the **Sheilin Seafood Restaurant**.

Sights of interest and accommodations in Sneem, to the east of Waterville on the Ring of Kerry, have been discussed earlier, at the beginning of the section on County Kerry (see Around Kenmare, above).

The Dingle Peninsula

Whether or not you "do" the Ring of Kerry, be sure to make a tour of the Dingle Peninsula, northwest of Killarney and west of Tralee. It features at its extreme tip, around Dingle and Ballyferriter, a most extraordinary survival of an ancient culture. Here is the main center for the Kerry Gaeltacht, where the Irish language is still spoken in an unbroken heritage going back thousands of years, where every refinement and subtlety of meaning has evolved over time.

An archaeological survey on this peninsula has identified more than 2,000 prehistoric sites, an even heavier prehistoric presence than in southeast England. On top of Mount Brandon are the remains of an oratory where legend has it Saint Brendan prayed before his seven-year voyage, in the sixth century, which is believed to have included the discovery of America before Leif Ericsson or Columbus. There are 1,100 versions of Brendan's *Navagatio,* a copy of which can be consulted in Kerry County Library in Tralee (discussed below). Brendan was born outside the town of Tralee, and his influence spread through various parts of the ancient province of Munster. His voyage was said to have been undertaken with 12 other monks, reminiscent of the image of Christ and his Twelve Apostles. A similar voyage was made by Tim Severin in 1976 and 1977 in a boat similar to that which would have been used by Brendan, made from animal skins, in an attempt to prove the possibility of Brendan's trip. It is also wholly credible that the monks who lived in the isolation of the Skellig Rock and in other hermitages would have been hardy enough of body and mind to undertake a voyage of such length and hardship.

The contemporary mind boggles at the preoccupations of the person who prayed in **Gallarus Oratory**, a tiny stone structure built in the first millennium, near **Ballydavid** in the northwestern part of the peninsula. The oratory, constructed of dry stone blocks gradually sloping in to form a ridged roof, hardly allowing room for an individual to stand upright, is an example of the rigorous isolation that early Irish monks endured. And that ancient holy person's mind would equally boggle at the **Round House**, the holiday home of a legal luminary, down the road in Ballydavid (tourist buses also stop here, though the interior is not open to the public). The shape of the house was inspired by the ring and by the round forts that abound on this peninsula. Both sites are unique in Europe. If you would like to stay hereabouts, **Vincent and Sheila O'Gorman** at Café na Mara provide pleasant bed-and-breakfast accommodations about 2 km (1¼ miles) west of Ballydavid, on the path of the Dingle Way. There is easy access to the archaeological sites, and bicycles are available for rental.

For accommodations at the western end of the peninsula (12 km/7½ miles from Dingle) look for the **Slea Head House** guest house overlooking Blasket Islands. It is fully modern and boasts a large collection of dolls and teddy bears. In **Dingle Town**, on Conor Pass Road, Pat and Anne Neligan will welcome you to a distinctive bed and breakfast, the **Duinan House. Benner's Hotel**, a charming 250-year-old establishment on the main street, has been comfortably refurbished, with a TV and telephone in every room. If you'd like one of their two rooms with four-poster beds (a slightly higher rate), be sure to request it.

Doyle's Seafood Bar, on John Street in Dingle Town, run by Stella and John Doyle, has an old kitchen range, *sugán* (plaited straw) chairs, and an appealing stone-and-wood decor. Pick your own lobster from the tank in the bar (Tel: 066/511-74). On the same street is the **Half Door**, also excellent for local fish. Ask about the Gregory Peck connection at **Ashe's** pub in town. If you want to meet seafood socially, go down to Dingle Harbour; you may see the somewhat renowned dolphin named Fungie. While you're near the water stop in at the **Pier Head** pub, run by a husband-and-wife team who left the glamour of Dublin for the greater atmosphere of their native town. Snacks are available all day; for lunch or dinner try their mutton pies—a specialty off-season. Traditional music is the entertainment every evening from 9:30 P.M. Dingle also has a couple of good crafts shops: **McKenna's** and **Louis Mulcahy's**, especially fine for rugs and pottery. The Mulcahy's have an international reputation, and will honor requests (within reason) to glaze an extra piece for a dinner service or set of pottery. **Café Liteartha** has a wide range of books both in English and in Irish. The **Singing Salmon** is open for lunch seven days.

On the way to or from Dingle and Ballyferriter, along the south shore of the peninsula, drop in at Annascul to **The South Pole Inn**, a pub started by one Tom Crean, who went to Antarctica with Scott and Shackleton. (There are more Crean memorabilia in the Dingle Library, and his

relatives—the O'Brien sisters—can be contacted through
Benner's Hotel in Tralee.) On the return journey to Tralee
you will most certainly find somebody in the vicinity of
either Castlegregory or the Dooks on the north shore to
point out to you the habitat of the Natterjack toad, unique
to this part of Ireland. You could also join an outing in
search of the Kerry slug, likewise unique. Both animals
either retreated here for the congenial climate or landed
with the first inhabitants.

Tralee and the End of Kerry

Tralee, a prosperous and busy market town, is famous for
its **Rose of Tralee International Festival** of not only beautiful but talented girls whose ancestors emigrated from
Ireland in less than glamorous fashion; it is usually held
in August or the first week of September.

The **Siamsa Tire Folklore Theatre**, based in a modern
and attractive theater in Tralee and in a thatched building
in Finuge, a small village to the north of town and just
southwest of Listowel, has toured the world with great
success and acclaim, representing the traditional crafts
and agricultural life of the area. The group has attracted
the admiration of the Pope and an invitation from Australian Prime Minister Bob Hawke with its professional mani-
festation of a way of life that either has disappeared or is
disappearing (performances here run from early June to
late September; information may be obtained at the
theater in Tralee). Tralee is also known for good horse
racing (toward the end of August each year).

For dining in town, try **Duffins** (Tel: 066/21-30), a converted coach house on Prince Street with an award-
winning chef, oak paneling, and a gallery; bar food is
served from 5:30 to 9:30 P.M. Or try the eponymous **Chez
Jean-Marc**, which serves, as you might expect, mainly
French cuisine. Recommendable hotel restaurants include the **Mount Brandon** (as a hotel it's big, modern, a
little impersonal—but the easiest to book in high season), and **Benner's Hotel**, with a fire in the lobby and
legal eagles at table during court sittings, which provides
plain food at almost any time of the day and into the
night. Accommodation at Benner's is Spartan, though
adequate, with toilets and showers in most rooms.

Another good place for dining in the area is a few miles
from Tralee on the Killarney road, in **Ballyseede Castle**,
attractive mostly for the atmosphere here amid period

furniture; the **Ballygarry House**, on the same side of Tralee, is also recommended. On your way to or from **Barrow Golf Course**, which is 11 km (7 miles) from Tralee on the Fenit road, enjoy fresh seafood or splendid steaks in the **Oyster Tavern** at the site of the old spa, one of the best-known eating places in Munster and beyond. Owner Jim McGrath provides wines that visiting French yachters can no longer find at home. Up the road is more good food in Jerry and Mary O'Sullivan's **The Tankard**.

There are plenty of good pubs in the Tralee vicinity. In town are the **Greyhound Bar**, for Gaelic football chat and local lore; **Bailey's Corner**, for the upwardly mobile of the area; the **Old Brogue Inn**, for the same, and an offhand atmosphere; and **Jess McCarthy's** on Castle Street, with a good fire, local bachelors and bankers, and others of the middle-aged upscale crowd. About 16 km (10 miles) west of Tralee, at Camp, is **Ashe's**, a cottage-style pub; check the menu before making reservations; Tel: (066) 301-33.

On the way to Camp is **Fitzgerald's** pub on the right, with a bar footrail consisting of old rails from the long defunct narrow-gauge railway to Dingle (now re-opened from Tralee to Blennerville with one of the original steam locomotives, retrieved from a U.S. museum). Also for railway buffs, there are old photos here and plenty of stories from Joe Dunne, if you coincide with his daily visit. From Ashe's inquire about a road passing under the magical Caherconree promontory fort and winding down to Dingle Bay. On the way to or from Camp visit the beautifully restored windmill, with its exhibitions, at Blennerville.

Another route from Tralee passes through Fenit and then heads north to four-mile-long **Banna Strand** before continuing through another of the areas associated with Saint Brendan—**Ardfert** (stop at **Flaherty's** pub, which has pleasing wood furniture and good company). The road proceeds to **Listowel** (National Festival of Irish Music in August and Race Week in September), which is a staging point for entry into Limerick to the east and Clare/Shannon to the north (via the car ferry at Tarbert, north of Listowel). This drive (via N 558 and then N 557 from Ardfert) also takes you through **Finuge**, one of the venues of the splendid entertainment group Siamsa Tire, mentioned above. It is an excellent, although narrow and winding, alternative to the direct and dull N 69.

Ballybunion, on the coast to the northwest, has two world-rated golf courses right by the sea (Jack Nicklaus frequently flies in to play them) and the very comfortable

Marine Hotel, run by Con and Bridget McCarthy. The hotel's restaurant has a reasonable menu and a view of the Atlantic—a view shared by *all* the well-appointed rooms. Try the hot seaweed baths nearby, and on a warm day run into the sea just yards away—bracing stuff!

GETTING AROUND

The principal access to this area is by air either to Cork City or Shannon Airport. Flying directly to Cork gives access to the routes and destinations mentioned in our text. Flight to Shannon and car rental at Shannon Airport brings you to the Killimer (County Clare) terminal for the car ferry across the River Shannon to Tarbert, County Kerry. (The approach to the car ferry is narrow and dangerous, but travel time in taking the ferry is one hour shorter than driving through Limerick.) The suggested tour in this chapter would be reversed for those entering from Shannon. Aer Lingus has flights twice daily from Dublin into the expanding Kerry County Airport at Farranfore, midway between Killarney Town and Tralee. (For accommodations near the airport, see the Killarney section, above.)

There are also rail links to Cork City from Dublin and from Dublin to Killarney Town. The junction at Mallow is the one that goes to Killarney, but most trains go directly to Killarney and Tralee.

Alternative access routes include ferrying from Brittany to Cork and also from Britain and France to Rosslare, from which you can make a car trip to Cork.

ACCOMMODATIONS REFERENCE

The telephone country code for the Southwest is 353. When dialing telephone numbers in the Republic from outside the country, drop the 0 in the area code. The rate ranges given below are projections *for the low and high seasons in 1993; for up-to-the-minute rate information it is always wise to telephone before booking. Unless otherwise indicated, rates are per person sharing and do not include meals or service.*

County Cork

▶ **Acton's Hotel.** Pier Road, **Kinsale**, County Cork. Tel: (021) 77-21-35; Fax: (021) 77-22-31. £35–£47, breakfast and service included.

▶ **Ballylickey Manor House. Bantry**, County Cork. Tel:

(027) 500-71; Fax: (027) 501-24. £42–£60, breakfast included.

▶ **Ballymaloe House. Shanagarry**, County Cork. Tel: (021) 65-25-31; Fax: (021) 65-20-21; in U.S., Tel: (800) 223-6510. £49–£54, breakfast included.

▶ **Bayview House. Glengarriff**, County Cork. Tel: (027) 630-20. £12, breakfast and service included.

▶ **Blair's Cove Apartments. Durrus**, County Cork. Tel: (027) 610-41. £20.

▶ **Blue Haven Hotel. Kinsale**, County Cork. Tel: (021) 77-22-09; Fax: (021) 77-42-68. £30–£40, breakfast and service included.

▶ **Blue Pool Hotel. Glengarriff Village**, County Cork. Tel: (027) 630-54. Closed November through February. £15–£22, breakfast and service included.

▶ **Bow Hall. Castletownshend**, County Cork. Tel: (028) 361-14. £26, breakfast and service included.

▶ **Casey's Hotel. Glengarriff Village**, County Cork. Tel: (027) 630-10. Open Easter through October. £20, breakfast and service included.

▶ **Dineen family.** Kilgarvan Road, near **Coolea**, County Cork. Tel: (064) 853-26. Closed October through March. £13, breakfast and service included.

▶ **Fitzpatrick Silver Springs.** Tivoli Road, **Cork City**, County Cork. Tel: (021) 50-75-33; Fax: (021) 50-76-41. £75–£92.

▶ **Hillside House.** Camphill, **Kinsale**, County Cork. Tel: (021) 77-23-15. £13–£15.50, breakfast and service included.

▶ **Imperial Hotel.** South Mall, **Cork City**, County Cork. Tel and Fax: (021) 27-40-40; in U.S., Tel: (800) 223-6510. £55–£60, breakfast and service included.

▶ **Jury's Hotel.** Western Road, **Cork City**, County Cork. Tel: (021) 27-66-22; Fax: (021) 27-44-77; in U.S., Tel: (800) 843-6664; in Canada, Tel: (800) 268-1133; in London, Tel: (81) 569-5555 or (71) 937-8033; in U.K., Tel: (345) 01-01-01. £49.

▶ **Lettercollum House. Timoleague**, County Cork. Tel: (023) 462-51. £8.

▶ **Longueville House. Mallow**, County Cork. Tel: (022) 471-56. £50–£75 (the highest rate gets you a deluxe room with views of the Blackwater River), breakfast included.

▶ **Moore's Hotel. Morrison's Island**, Cork City, County Cork. Tel: (021) 27-12-91. £26–£34.

▶ **The Old Bank House. Kinsale**, County Cork. Tel: (021) 77-40-75 or 77-29-68. £25–£35.

▶ **Trident Hotel. Kinsale**, County Cork. Tel: (021) 77-23-01; Fax: (021) 77-41-73. £28.

▶ **Woodland.** Coast Road, Castletownsherd, **Skibbereen**, County Cork. Tel: (028) 361-25. £13.50.

County Kerry

▶ **Aghadoe Heights Hotel. Killarney**, County Kerry. Tel: (064) 317-66; Fax: (064) 313-45; in U.S., (800) 44-UTELL. £48–£65, breakfast and service included.

▶ **Ard na Sidhe.** Caragh Lake, near **Killorglin**, County Kerry. Tel: (066) 691-05; Fax: (066) 692-82. Closed October through April. £45–£57.50, breakfast and service included.

▶ **Ashling House.** Sunhill, **Killorglin**, County Kerry. Tel: (066) 612-26. Closed October through April. £10, breakfast and service included.

▶ **Benner's Hotel.** Main Street, **Dingle**, County Kerry. Tel: (066) 516-38; Fax: (066) 514-12. £30–£39, breakfast included.

▶ **Benner's Hotel.** Castle Street, **Tralee**, County Kerry. Tel: (066) 214-22; Fax: (066) 212-07. £21–£23, breakfast and service included.

▶ **Butler Arms Hotel. Waterville**, County Kerry. Tel: (066) 741-44; Fax: (066) 745-20. Closed mid-October through mid-April. £35–£45, breakfast and service included.

▶ **Carriglea Farmhouse.** Muckross Road, **Killarney**, County Kerry. Tel: (064) 311-16. Open Easter through October. £13.50 (shared bathroom)–£15 (en suite), breakfast and service included.

▶ **Castlerosse Hotel.** Beaufort Road, near **Killarney**, County Kerry. Tel: (064) 311-44; Fax: (064) 310-31; in U.S., (800) 528-1234 or (602) 957-4200. Closed November through March. £41–£45, breakfast included.

▶ **Club Med Waterville. Waterville**, County Kerry. Tel: (066) 741-33. Open April through October. £80, all meals and use of facilities included.

▶ **Derryeast Farmhouse. Sneem**, County Kerry. Tel: (064) 451-93. Closed mid-November through February. £13.50, breakfast and service included.

▶ **Duinan House.** Duinan House, Conor Pass Road, **Dingle Town**, County Kerry. Tel: (066) 513-35. Closed November through February. £14, breakfast and service included.

▶ **Gleanntan House.** New Road, **Killarney**, County

Kerry. Tel: (064) 329-13. Closed December through February. £14, breakfast and service included.

▶ **Gleneagle Hotel.** Muckross Road, **Killarney**, County Kerry. Tel: (064) 318-70; Fax: (064) 326-46. £24–£39, breakfast and service included.

▶ **Grange Grove Farm.** Firies, **Killarney**, County Kerry. Tel: (066) 643-72. Closed October through March. £13, breakfast and service included.

▶ **Great Southern Hotel. Killarney**, County Kerry. Tel: (064) 312-62; Fax: (064) 316-42; in U.S., Tel: (800) 44-UTELL. Closed January through mid-March. £47–£53.

▶ **Hilltop Farmhouse. Farranfore**, County Kerry. Tel: (066) 641-93. Open Easter through October. £12, breakfast and service included.

▶ **Hotel Europe.** On T 67 at Fossa near **Killarney**, County Kerry. Tel: (064) 319-00; Fax: (064) 321-18; in U.S., (800) 221-1074 or (212) 684-1820. Open April through October. £39–£57.50, breakfast and service included.

▶ **Kenmare Bay Hotel. Kenmare**, County Kerry. Tel: (064) 413-00; Fax: (064) 415-41; in U.S., Tel: (800) 528-1234 or (602) 957-4200. £24.00–£26.50, breakfast and service included.

▶ **Killarney Park Hotel. Killarney**, County Kerry. Tel: (064) 355-55. £45.

▶ **Lake Hotel.** Muckross Road, **Killarney**, County Kerry. Tel: (064) 310-35; Fax: (064) 319-02. Closed December through February. £35, breakfast and service included.

▶ **Linden House.** New Road, **Killarney**, County Kerry. Tel: (064) 313-79. Closed December and January. £16–£22, breakfast and service included.

▶ **Loch Lein House.** Golf Course Road, near **Killarney**, County Kerry. Tel: (064) 312-60. Closed mid-October through mid-March. £13.50–£15.50, breakfast and service included.

▶ **Marine Hotel.** Sandhill Road, **Ballybunion**, County Kerry. Tel: (068) 275-22 or 271-39; Fax: (068) 276-66. Closed November through mid-March. £24.50, breakfast included.

▶ **Muckross Court Hotel.** Muckross Road, **Killarney**, County Kerry. Tel: (064) 353-33; Fax: (064) 352-06. £51–£62.

▶ **Muckross Park Hotel. Killarney**, County Kerry. Tel: (064) 319-38; Fax: (064) 319-65. £55.

▶ **Murphy Farmhouse. Castlemaine**, County Kerry. Tel: (066) 673-37. £13, breakfast and service included.

▶ **Mylestone House. Kenmare**, County Kerry. Tel: (064) 417-53. £15.

▶ **Mystical Rose**. Woodlawn Road, **Killarney**, County Kerry. Tel: (064) 314-53. £14.

▶ **Oakhill Farmhouse. Farranfore**, County Kerry. Tel: (066) 642-76. Closed October through April. £12, breakfast and service included.

▶ **Vincent and Sheila O'Gorman** (Cafe Na Mara). Glaise Bheag, Baile Na nGall, **Ballydavid**, County Kerry. Tel: (066) 551-62. £13, breakfast and service included.

▶ **Park Hotel. Kenmare**, County Kerry. Tel: (064) 412-00; Fax: (064) 414-02; in U.S., Tel: (800) 223-6764. Closed mid-November through mid-March. £88–£190, breakfast and service included.

▶ **Parknasilla Great Southern Hotel. Parknasilla**, County Kerry. Tel: (064) 451-22; Fax: (064) 453-23; in U.S., Tel: (800) 44-UTELL. Closed January through mid-March. £48–£59.

▶ **Riversdale House Hotel**. Muxnaw, **Kenmare**, County Kerry. Tel: (064) 412-99; Fax: (064) 410-75. Open Easter through December. £23–£30.

▶ **Sheen Falls Lodge. Kenmare**, County Kerry. Tel: (064) 416-00; Fax: (064) 413-86. Closed mid-January through mid-March. £95–£100, breakfast and service included.

▶ **Slea Head House**. Coumeenole, **Ventry**, Tralee, County Kerry. Tel: (066) 562-34. £11, breakfast and service included.

▶ **Strand Hotel. Waterville**, County Kerry. Tel: (066) 744-36. Open June through September. £16, breakfast and service included.

▶ **Three Lakes Hotel**. Kenmare Place, **Killarney**, County Kerry. Tel: (064) 314-79; Fax: (064) 332-17. £32–£40, breakfast and service included.

▶ **Tom and Eileen's Farmhouse. Castlemaine**, County Kerry. Tel: (066) 673-73. Open Easter through October. £13, breakfast and service included.

▶ **Villa Maria**. Main Street, **Waterville**, County Kerry. Tel: (066) 742-48. £16, breakfast and service included.

▶ **Woodvale Guesthouse. Sneem**, County Kerry. Tel: (064) 451-81. £13, breakfast and service included.

THE WEST
CLARE AND CONNEMARA

By William Maxwell

William Maxwell, a resident of Dublin and a literary critic for the Irish Independent, *was for 30 years the press-division manager at Aer Lingus, Ireland's national airline. A longtime journalist, he contributes articles to many travel magazines.*

Clare and Connemara are two of the most popular tourist regions of Ireland. Geographically they comprise a stretch of spectacular rugged scenery, a combination of gray limestone and blue heather and a range of mountains that descends to fjords leading to the Atlantic Ocean. The area is bounded by the River Shannon in the south and the Twelve Pins to the north of Clifden, and includes two of the oldest Norman cities in Ireland, Limerick and Galway. The modern metropolis of Limerick straddles the River Shannon and has a majestic old Norman castle and church, excellent hotels, and lively pubs. Galway, the gateway to Connemara, feels the influence of its thriving university, and supports a vibrant artistic community. It too has good pubs (known for fine singing), and is a perfect base for activities that include golf, fishing, and horse racing.

MAJOR INTEREST

Rugged scenery
Irish culture
Luxury castle hotels
Fishing

Clare
The Cliffs of Moher
The Burren's lunar landscapes

Limerick City
Excellent hotels and lively pubs

Galway City Area
Shopping
Singing pubs
Aran Islands day trips
Tower at Thoor Ballylee (Yeats home and
   museum)

Connemara
Wild beauty of mountains and the sea
Celtic cultural revival
Shopping for Irish craft goods
Clifden's setting above the sea
Medieval Cong Abbey

For the purposes of planning a trip, Country Clare should
be divided into three areas: first, cultural orientation in
the River Shannon region, near the airport; then the drive
to the Cliffs of Moher on the sea; and lastly the Burren,
before driving up the shores of Galway Bay to Galway
City, capital of the West, and on to Connemara.

THE SHANNON REGION
OF COUNTY CLARE

Whereas most of Ireland is a plush green, Clare is predominantly gray. In places such as the Burren, a plateau
of limestone rock covering more than 100 square miles
in northern Clare, the land has a lunar quality. Between
May and October—but especially early spring—is the
best time to visit the Burren, when the rocks come alive
with a beautiful carpet of wild flowers and heather. To the
botanist the Burren is one of nature's wonders. To the
casual visitor the wonder is how man has survived in
these small rocky fields. As Cromwell said when he banished the Irish "to Hell or Connacht," there wasn't
enough in this most westerly of Ireland's provinces to
feed a snipe. But the people did survive, and today they

retain an individuality from those in other parts of the country. When the Dublin businessman says he is getting away from it all, he is most likely heading for Clare. A 30-minute flight to Shannon International Airport and a short drive, and he is in a different world.

Air travellers arriving in this part of Ireland from across the Atlantic or via Britain generally come through Shannon Airport, on the north side of the River Shannon west of Limerick City. Shannon Airport has a modern bustling terminal famous for its duty-free shops, the oldest in Europe (but only visitors leaving the country can make purchases). Irish coffee is no longer mandatory, but it still has wonderfully insulating qualities on a chilly morning, just as it once warmed the cockles of flying-boat passengers in the pioneering days of transatlantic aviation in the 1930s.

For those wishing to make hotel reservations, hire a car, or plan an itinerary, the arrivals terminal at Shannon has a wide selection of major car-rental firms and a very good tourist information center. There are many bus tours available here, but the most leisurely way to see Clare is by car. Don't leave the airport area without shopping at the **Ballycasey Craft Centre** at Hurler's Cross, about 1½ km (1 mile) from the airport, which offers an unusually wide range of Irish handcrafted products, including embroidery, gold and silver jewelry, leather and suede garments, pictures, prints and frames, pottery, quilting, and wood turning; open Monday through Friday.

Carrygerry House, a 200-year-old manor house elegantly restored to its former glory, is a good base in the Shannon area; it's about 5 km (3 miles) north of the airport in surrounding woodlands overlooking the estuaries of the Shannon and Fergus rivers. Run by Gerry Hughes and his family, the hotel offers warm and personal service; rooms are *en suite,* and the chef features locally produced food prepared in the traditional Irish manner. Dinner is available to non-guests; reservations required. Tel: (061) 623-39.

Another possible base from which to explore the Shannon region is the modern **Shannon Shamrock Inn**, just 10 km (6 miles) east of the airport in Bunratty. It has an excellent kitchen, great ambience for cocktails and dinner, and is very popular with international businesspeople flying from Shannon. In the shadow of the inn is **Bunratty Castle**, the first of many castles you will see dotted all over Clare. Like most of them it was owned at different times by the two great families that ruled this county, the O'Briens and the McNamaras. It is said that the boy William Penn was lowered in a basket from one of the turrets of Bunratty and so escaped the wrath of Cromwell. He went to America, where he would later found the state that bears his name.

The present castle has been tastefully restored, and medieval-style banquets featuring minstrels and their ladies who sing and dance are held in the Main Hall every evening throughout the tourist season. **Bunratty Folk Park**, built around the castle, has re-created farmhouses, village shops and streets of a century ago. Be advised that these two attractions are favorite tour-bus stops and can be overrun with tourists, especially on the weekend.

A more literary version is held at two other castles— **Dunguaire** and **Knappogue**—where the script draws less on ballads and more on the writings of Yeats, Shaw, Wilde, and O'Casey to convey in pageant the story of Ireland. Knappogue is near Quin, off route N 18 from Limerick, and Dunguaire is in Kinvara, on the south shore of Galway Bay. Reservations for any of these banquets must be made in advance, through your hotel or Shannon Castle Tours; Tel: (061) 617-88.

For more private dining there is **MacCloskey's**, situated in an old converted cellar of Bunratty House, one of the old manor homes in the area. The decor is Old World discreet; Gerry and his wife, Marie, do all of the cooking, and they have won a deserved reputation for excellent cuisine among the many visiting businesspeople who fly in and out of the Shannon industrial zone nearby. Reservations are required; Tel: (061) 36-40-82. Closed Sundays and Mondays.

Those who prefer less formal dining at lower prices should make a reservation (Tel: 061/617-88) for the **Shannon Ceili**, a dinner held in the Bunratty Barn, part of the Folk Park. The furnishings are original, and local women prepare food and bake griddle bread just as in the days of their grandmothers. The meal itself is a delicious Irish stew served with wine and tea, with dessert of hot apple pie and cream. The entertainment is traditional music and dance, guaranteed to send you off with happy memories. Then you are ready for **Durty Nellys**, a very convivial local pub that seems never to be empty (largely due to the tour-bus crowd) and serves an excellent pint. Durty Nellys is also near Bunratty Castle.

THE LIMERICK CITY AREA

Limerick City, 16 km (10 miles) east of Bunratty, is the gateway to the east and south, the place to cross the River Shannon, and a great base for those interested in fishing, boating, water sports, and hunting. The surrounding lush, green countryside is one of the best for breeding great hunters, and many a Derby winner has come from this area as well. The city is the third oldest in the Republic: It was fought over by the Norse, who built a fort here in the ninth century, then by the Normans and the English. Today's battles are more likely to be about rugby, as there are five clubs in the city, all rivals who have supplied some top players to Ireland's Triple Crowns. The city is also the hometown of film star Richard Harris and the BBC's Terry Wogan.

The visitor will find Limerick an easy city for walking. The tourist office is located in the **Granary**, a beautifully restored 18th-century warehouse in Michael Street. After browsing or picking up literature about the goings on here, including lists of the best entertainment, drop into the charming **Viking Coffee Shop**. A short walk north, across Thomond Bridge, are **King John's Castle** (circa 1200)—imaginatively restored and incorporating a new visitor building—and **St. Mary's Cathedral** (1172). This is the old city. The cathedral has some of the best medieval carvings in Ireland and some fine antiquities; there is a sound-and-light show on Sunday nights.

Today's city, on the south side of the river, includes the wide expanse of O'Connell Street, with side streets that feature some great old Georgian town houses and squares. **O'Mahoneys** in O'Connell Street is a good bookstore for browsing. The staff is very helpful, and the historical material on the Limerick area here is hard to beat.

Top-quality accommodations include **Jury's Hotel**, the **Limerick Ryan Hotel**, and the **Limerick Inn**. All are on the Ennis road and are modern, if slightly impersonal, establishments. They offer private rooms with bath and in-house entertainment throughout the season, and their staffs will gladly arrange special parties for golfing, fishing, or hunting. The first two are within a short distance of the city center; the Limerick Inn, 10 km (6 miles) out on the Ennis road, has excellent dining, swimming, and sauna facilities. All three can be recommended to those in search of good cuisine.

For pubs and entertainment, students from the city's university, one of the best third-level institutes in Ireland, tend to gravitate toward **Willie Sexton's** in Henry Street or the **Shannon Arms**, next door. Good traditional music is available nightly at **Nancy Blake's** (Denmark Street); **Larry Murphy's** (Wolfe Tone Street); **Malibu Bar** (Cecil Street); and **Glen Tavern** (Mallow Street). Cabaret is provided nightly at the **Two-Mile Inn** (Ennis road) and at the **Brazen Head** in O'Connell Street. For the disco set there is the **Speakeasy** in O'Connell Street, and dancing at the Glentworth hotel. Literary types doing what they refer to as the "Stations of the Cross" (pub crawl) tend to forgather in the **White House** in Glentworth Street or at **Tom Collins** or **Foley's** pubs in Cecil Street. All of Limerick's pubs offer limited menus featuring soup, sandwiches, and pub grub.

Theatergoers should check in with the **Belltable Arts Centre**, for a wide range of play performances throughout the year (Tel: 061/31-98-66). **St. John's Square Museum** houses art exhibitions from Dublin and London; closed Sundays and Mondays.

Adare, 16 km (10 miles) southwest of Limerick on the N 21, is the social center for most of the hunting season. The village is maintained to picture-postcard perfection with thatched cottages just as they were when they were built by the lords of Dunraven many centuries ago. The lords' ancestral home, **Adare Manor**, is now a luxury hotel similar in style to Dromoland Castle or Ashford Castle (see below). The manor's 840 acres of woods and parkland offer great fishing, hunting, and shooting. All rooms are luxuriously furnished, and rates are reasonable considering that you are staying in a historic castle. Should you wish to hunt with the famous Scarteen Black and Tans, the man to contact is Chris Ryan, master of the hunt, who lives at Scarteen, Knocklong; Tel: (062) 531-95. Or you can make contact in Adare through Brian Murphy, manager of the Dunraven Arms Hotel, himself no mean horseman. The Arms is the meeting place for the hunts, but be warned: If you are not an experienced horseman or woman, stay put and enjoy the hot toddies—following the "Tans" is not for amateurs.

The towns of **Killaloe**, north of Limerick City on the L 12, and **Dromineer**, in County Tipperary just outside Nenagh on the L 152 via the N 7, are excellent centers for yachting, fishing, cruising, or water-skiing.

COUNTY CLARE
OUTSIDE SHANNON

From Limerick there are two routes into Clare. You can travel along the southern shore of the River Shannon through the little town of **Foynes**, formerly the base for flying boats before Shannon Airport was developed. (There is an aviation museum in the former terminal building that is open from March to October.) From there head on to **Tarbert** and a ferry crossing of the river to Killimer, will bring you into the southern part of County Clare, with access to seaside beach resorts such as **Kilrush** and **Kilkee** on the N 67. These are of interest primarily for family-style vacations, with golf, sailing, and fishing.

The other route goes more directly from Limerick: the N 18 north to Ennis, the capital of Clare. En route is the little village of **Newmarket-on-Fergus**, and close by is **Dromoland Castle**, one of Ireland's leading luxury hotels. It belonged to the O'Briens, but was sold in the 1960s to an Irish-American entrepreneur, Bernard McDonough, who lavishly restored it. The view from the Long Gallery is worth the price of morning coffee, but if you have the time and can afford the high price for a suite in peak season, then this is one of the great baronial experiences of Ireland. Dromoland Castle is now run by an American syndicate, as is Ashford Castle at Cong, County Mayo (discussed in the Connemara section, below). The castle-hotel has its own 18-hole golf course, year-round tennis courts, croquet, and bicycling. Nearby there is horseback riding and snipe and duck shooting in season, as well as access to deep-sea fishing and sailing, all of which will be arranged for you.

For those on a smaller budget there is the motel-style, upmarket, 121-room **Clare Inn**, situated in the seclusion of the trees near Dromoland and within easy access of Shannon Airport. From Clare Inn or Dromoland you can make a series of day trips to Killarney and Dingle in Kerry, the Burren in County Clare, and even Blarney Castle in Cork (see also the Southwest chapter).

After Newmarket-on-Fergus the road continues through Clarecastle to **Ennis**, a genuine Irish medieval town of narrow streets and ancient abbeys. The old religion survived the Reformation here into the 19th century; the

Ennis Friary, a Franciscan abbey, was by turns church and courthouse. Today it is back in the hands of the friars and worth seeing as a fine example of medieval architecture. Ennis's **Old Ground Hotel**, part of which dates from the early 18th century, has big log-burning fires, a good restaurant, and a cabaret every evening in the tourist season.

Eamon de Valera was first elected to Dáil Eireann (the Republic's parliament) by the people of Ennis, and the Nationalist tradition is still alive here. So is the good tradition of *fleadh,* the folk-music festivals that are held in many parts of the county in summer. (The precise dates vary; details can be provided by the local tourist office.)

Around Ennis there are a number of venues for what can be classified as specialty interests that you may wish to pursue. Anglers can sample more than a hundred lakes in the county. Indeed, they are to be found almost everywhere, even in the Burren (see below). The best golf is at **Lahinch**, about 30 km (19 miles) northwest of Ennis via N 85. The course here—laid out against the seacoast—is considered one of the most testing in Ireland. Lahinch is also a beach resort, ideal for swimming and sailing and with facilities for children. **Milltown Malbay**, south of Lahinch via N 67, is a similar beach resort.

Quin, a small village about 10 km (6 miles) southeast of Ennis via R 469, was a monastic site in the old days, and as such had a famous school. The restored **Quin Abbey** is a good example of what has been done in the area to re-create the everyday life of medieval monks. The effect is heightened by taped music and readings that allow you to get an insight into the monks' daily lives. Everything is tastefully and realistically done.

Craggaunowen, east of Quin, is a re-creation of a Bronze Age lake dwelling, called a crannog. On the grounds of the dwelling is a ring fort, a reconstruction of a farmer's house as it stood some 1,600 years ago. A more modern relic here is the *Brendan,* the hide boat that author Tim Severin sailed from Ireland to North America to prove that Saint Brendan the Navigator could have made the discovery of the New World long before Columbus.

From Ennis take the N 85 northwest to the sleepy town of Ennistymon and from there on to Lahinch and Liscannor on the coast. This route will bring you up the coast to the **Cliffs of Moher**, one of the most breathtaking and most visited sights in Western Europe. The cliffs rise like a great natural cathedral almost 700 feet from the

Atlantic Ocean and stretch for miles along the coast. The best view is from O'Brien's Tower, on the headland above the cliffs. To get a glimpse of the great variety of wild birds that nest on the ledges, visitors can use a number of walks that have been provided along the top. Care must be taken, however, especially in bad weather. Try going early to avoid the tour buses and souvenir stands that line the route to the viewing area.

From the cliffs continue north on the coast road to **Doolin**, where there is ferry service from April to October out to **Inisheer, Inishmore**, and **Inishmaan**, the three Aran Islands. If the crossing intimidates you (the seas are seldom mirror-calm), save yourself for the daily 20-minute flight from Galway City to Inishmore or Inishmaan (see Aran Islands in the Galway section). The sea crossing to Inisheer from Doolin takes about 40 minutes.

There are some great singing pubs in Doolin. **Gus O'Connors** is especially worth a visit. The blond woman in the corner is most likely Swedish and her friend Dutch or Swiss; the reputation of Doolin for folk music has spread well beyond Ireland.

A few miles inland is **Lisdoonvarna**, famous for its spa waters and singing pubs, and a center for one of Ireland's leading summer schools: the Merriman Festival. This festival combines, as only the Irish could, learned papers given by distinguished academics with seemingly interminable pub talk. It is not for the weak of liver and should be taken in slow draughts. Just outside Lisdoonvarna (look for the signs as you go through town) is **Burren Fish Products Ltd.**, a small factory where fresh Clare salmon, mackerel, and trout are smoked, packaged, and shipped all over the world. The friendly staff will give you a free tour and explanation of the cold-smoking process; products are available for sampling and for purchase.

Leaving Lisdoonvarna, take the scenic coast road to Ballyvaughan via Black Head or head inland directly toward Ballyvaughan via N 67. The latter road goes through **the Burren**, a landscape of gray rocks and a reminder of what the last Ice Age inflicted on Ireland. In springtime it becomes a sea of splendid colors, covered with wild flowers and heather. Botanists come here to study the unique mixture of Arctic, Alpine, and Mediterranean plants. The whole area is rich in antiquities, pre-Christian burial mounds, and the ruins of ancient abbeys. For an explanation of the development of the geology and botany of the

Burren as well as illustrations of prehistoric life in Clare the **Burren Display Centre** at Kilfenora, about 8 km (5 miles) southeast of Lisdoonvarna by R 476, provides good background information using film and music.

Ailwee Cave, well signposted off the Ballyvaughan road as well as along the route from the Cliffs of Moher, is one of the few stalactite caves in Ireland (it was only discovered in 1944). There's an excellent luncheon restaurant at the site, as well as a bookstore and crafts shop that sells beautiful pottery in addition to good quality knits and paintings by local artists. Tours are conducted regularly for a small fee.

The most luxurious accommodation in the area is at **Gregan's Castle Hotel**, 5 km (3 miles) from Ballyvaughan on the site of an ancient castle; some of the ruins are still visible. The hotel is recommended for its lovely ambience, exceptional menu and food prepared by the owner/chef Peter Hayden, and for the splendid views of the Burren Hills standing out against the green lowland valley where the hotel is located. After a night's hospitality with the Haydens you will be ready to drive up the shores of Galway Bay to the capital of the West.

Those on a more limited budget might try family-run **Hyland's Hotel** in the charming village of Ballyvaughan. Dating back to the 18th century, Hyland's offers good, fresh home cooking with excellent seafood, and has in-house entertainment during the tourist season.

The itinerary suggested here is but one of many that can be taken, and if you wish to spend more time in the area and want more scientific information on the Burren we suggest *Burren Journey,* by George Cunningham, a guide available at any of the tourist offices. It comes with detailed maps and illustrations.

GALWAY CITY

Galway City, north of Ballyvaughan across Galway Bay, is the political and commercial capital of the West of Ireland. It was once the major trading port on this coast, when Ireland had strong links with Spain. Today most of its industrial wealth comes from overseas subsidiaries of multinational companies who have been attracted to Ireland in recent decades because of tax incentives and have set up in industrial zones or estates, of which Galway is one.

As a university town Galway has a permanent floating population; when the students move out in the summer, the tourists take over. There is, therefore, a wide range of accommodations, from five-star hotels to guest houses and bed-and-breakfast inns. Particularly recommended are the **Galway Great Southern Hotel**, a luxurious accommodation in a 19th-century edifice on Eyre Square in the middle of town, with the excellent **Oyster Room**, famous, as you may guess, for its seafood, and extensive facilities and amenities (such as an indoor swimming pool and health complex); the modern, 96-room **Galway Ryan Hotel**, on the Dublin road, not as close to the city center but comfortable and with all modern conveniences; and a local favorite, the **Ardilaun House** at Taylor's Hill, a charming hotel housed in a former mansion and set on lovely grounds, reasonably priced and situated close to Salthill and its beautiful oceanfront west of the city.

Recommended bed-and-breakfasts in Galway include **Mandala** (Mrs. Georgina Darby) in Salthill, **Roncalli House** (Tim and Carmel O'Halloran) also in Salthill, **De Sota** (Margaret and Demot Walshe) on Newcastle Road in Galway, and **Ardawn House** (Breda Guilfoyle) on College Road, in the city.

Ireland West Tourism, the body responsible for promoting travel to the West, is located in Aras Fáilte, just off Eyre Square. Their office is worth a visit: In the same building you can rent a car, make hotel reservations, or book for the medieval banquets at **Kinvara Castle** on Galway Bay. A very useful little book, *Tourist Trail of Old Galway,* lays out a series of short walking trips around the old quarters of the city.

Most of these areas are not readily obvious because of the modern buildings, but they are worthy of your attention. For example, on Market Street you'll find **St. Nicholas's Church**, where it is claimed Columbus stopped off on his voyage of discovery, and on the riverbank south of the church is the **Spanish Arch**, a relic of the days when galleons tied up at the pier. The old **Claddagh District**, a short walk west from Eyre Square, was a state within a state up until the last century; Claddagh residents still see themselves as somehow separate. The place gave its name to the famous Claddagh ring, designed for lovers, though in terms of jewelry Galway offers a lot more than the Claddagh ring.

Galway City has one of the greatest ranges of stores and shopping malls outside of Dublin. Because of the tourist influx there is an abundant display of tweeds, linens, lace, crystal, and china. The leading shopping centers in the city area, all centrally located and mostly on William Street close to Eyre Square, are: **Stephen Fallers**, for jewelry and china, Williamsgate Street; **Dillons Jewellers**, William Street; **Treasure Chest**, for the widest range of china, crystal, and the like, William Street; **Moons**, William Street; **O'Mailles**, for tweeds, Dominick Street; **Anthony Ryans**, for drapery and such, Shop Street; **Stephen Pearce**, Church Street, and **Judy Greene**, Cross Street, for pottery and ceramics. **Galway Irish Crystal** has a shop on the Dublin road open seven days a week; another shop offering crystal and other high-quality goods, **Royal Tara** at Mervue, offers daily tours for visitors.

Kenny's Bookshop and Art Gallery on High Street is one of those places that's hard to leave. The artworks are, for the most part, by contemporary Irish artists. The bookstore is divided between rare books for collectors, with a strong emphasis on Irish works, and a general selection of hardcover and paperback titles. The place is peppered with busts of some of the greats in Irish writing, and if you accidentally hit on a wine party, it is just one more Irish writer being launched. The brothers Kenny who run the business will be happy to take the time to find a rare book or advise you on Irish writers, and if you want a purchase shipped home they can arrange for that as well. As with any great bookstore, if Kenny's doesn't have it they'll get it.

Just across the street from Kenny's is an upmarket bookshop, **Sile na Gig** (The Galway Bookshop); the two women who run the store will remind you that "there is no cheap junk sold here." They stock the best in university publishing. Close by is another good general bookstore, **Hawkins House**, and when you are done here you can walk across to Bowling Green and see the house where **Nora Barnacle**, the wife of James Joyce, was born. The house is maintained by Sheila Gallager as a museum; for £1 you can go in and read some of the letters Nora wrote Joyce and see the bed she slept in as a young woman before heading off for Finn's Hotel in Dublin, where she met the Dubliner himself. The museum is open daily from May through September (except at lunch) and is worth a visit.

Good eateries abound in Galway, such as **The Park House** and **Eyre House** on Foster Street (reservations recommended; Tel: 091/625-96) and the **Great Southern**

Hotel on Eyre Square. **The Fountain, The Bentley,** and **Paddy's,** all on Eyre Square as well, serve excellent lunches. For great grub with atmosphere try **The Old Malt** off High Street, **The Quay's Pub** and **McDonaghs** on Quay Street, **McSwiggans** on Wood Quay, and **Naughtons** on Cross Street. McDonaghs also has a fish-and-chips-only take-out area reputed to offer one of the finest plates of fried fish in Ireland. Galway is compact, and all of these pubs are within walking distance of the city center; anyone will give you directions.

Evening entertainment in Galway City is mostly in singing pubs or good discos. Singing pubs include the **King's Head,** on High Street; the **Crane and the Clogs,** on Dominick Street; and the **Pucan,** in Eyre Square. The **Lion's Tower** in Eglington Street is a good disco. A wide variety of nightly entertainment, dances, discos, restaurants and pubs can be found in **Salthill,** a holiday resort on the bay on the western outskirts of the city that comes alive during the summer season. For the over-35 set choices include **The Salthill Hotel** at the end of the Promenade (for dinner and dancing), **Twiggs,** and **The Holiday Hotel.** The younger crowd tends to gather at **The Oasis, The Castle, The Promenade,** and **Rumours.** All feature a bar and dancing with a small cover charge. The resort is within a short drive or bus journey from the city center.

Theater in Galway is limited to the **Druid** (in Druid Lane), which puts on the classic Anglo-Irish playwrights (Tel: 091/686-17), and **An Taibhdhearc** in Middle Street, which has produced such greats as the actress Siobhan McKenna (Tel: 091/620-24). They put on musical theater with special emphasis on traditional music and folk presentations. Reservations—essential for both theaters—can be made through your hotel or directly.

University College, Galway, is a sprawling campus west of Eyre Square with a central Neo-Gothic quad. Summer courses for overseas students are held here annually in July and August, and the university is a base for the study of Celtic languages worldwide, under the sponsorship of UNESCO.

The annual races at **Ballybrit,** a kind of local Mardi Gras, should be taken in if you are anywhere in the proximity of the city at the end of July. (Ballybrit is on the eastern outskirts of Galway, about 1 km/½ mile from the city center.) Accommodations in Galway must be reserved in advance, as demand is high then. The races form the fringe of a week's singing and entertainment that are special to the Irish racing calendar. Another noteworthy event is the **Oyster Festival**, held in Galway and at **Clarinbridge** (southeast of the city) toward the end of September. The festival marks the opening of the oyster season with two days of feasting. The center of activities is generally at the Great Southern Hotel. For horse lovers two great traditional Irish fairs in the general area are the **October Horse Fair** in **Ballinasloe** in east Galway and the **Pony Show** in **Clifden**, at the western end of Connemara, in August.

The Aran Islands

No visitor to Galway should miss out on the Aran Islands. There are modern links by air and sea to the mainland, but once you arrive you will see that few other concessions to modernity have been made here. Life on this most westerly of outposts is much as it was when Oliver Cromwell's soldiers landed here in the 17th century. The largest of the islands, **Inishmore**, contains one of the greatest prehistoric stone forts in western Europe, **Dun Aengus**. The fort, thousands of years old, reaches out of the Atlantic at the very edge of an immense cliff, the last landmark before Boston.

Indeed, it is to America rather than to Ireland itself that the Aran people have always turned. There is a long tradition of emigration from the islands to America; today many islanders spend most of the year in the United States and return home for the summer. They are a warm people who still speak the native Irish as well as English, and they have a repose and resourcefulness that fascinates the artists, writers, and ordinary visitors who come here.

There are not many cars on the islands, thus most visitors rent bicycles, take organized tours, or walk to the ecclesiastic ruins and prehistoric forts and tombs that dot the landscape. Biking is the most rewarding way to see the area, and although the roads are bumpy, narrow, and steep, the bikes available for rent are exceptionally sturdy.

The landscape, which can seem lunar, is a maze of small fields divided up by stone walls. In many places the soil was formed from layers of seaweed and cow manure and carried inland from along the shore on the backs of donkeys or men in order to have enough in which to grow potatoes. This is a place to walk near-empty roads, where if you run across someone you will be greeted with the traditional "God be with you."

Culturally, the Aran Islands are a mixture of ancient pagan and Christian traditions. The people live by fishing, mostly in trawlers, although they still use the long beetle-shaped curraghs made of timber laths and canvas. The islands are very popular with artists, who are drawn to the seclusion and peace. John Millington Synge lived on **Inishmaan** for some time and thereby was inspired to write two of the classics of the Irish theater: *The Playboy of the Western World* and *Riders to the Sea*. The latter play captures the hardships of the islanders' lives, especially before they acquired some modern amenities. The famous Aran sweater originated here; according to tradition every family had its own special weave to facilitate identification if one of its members was lost at sea.

Accommodations on the islands are pretty much in guest houses, and the entertainment is in pubs, where tourists gather to meet the local people and join in an evening's dance and sing-along. Island life is not without its complexities and frustrations, however, as portrayed in the contemporary novel *The Rock Garden,* by Leo Daly, who lived on the islands for many years. His insights contrast with the outer appearances seen by casual visitors. Clean, comfortable guest-house accommodation on the islands is available at **Gilbert's Cottage** on Inishmore, **Mrs. Faherty's** on Inishmaan, and the **Hotel Inisheer** on Inisheer.

There are daily flights from Galway City's airfield out to Inishmore, Inisheer, and Inishmaan; there is also boat service from Doolin (in County Clare) to the islands. A more leisurely transport, if the seas are calm, is to take a ferry from Galway or Rossaveal, 23 miles (37 km) from Galway City on the Connemara shore; bus service from Galway City to Rossaveal is included in the ticket price. Details are available from Aer Aran (091) 930-54, from the ferry companies themselves (both are located on Eyre Square), or from the Galway tourist information office. Note that air and ferry passage is far less frequent during the winter due to weather conditions and demand.

Around Galway City

Before leaving Galway and moving on to Connemara, visitors with a literary interest might like to visit Coole Park and Thoor Ballylee in the small town of **Gort**, about

40 km (25 miles) southeast of Galway on the N 18. Both places are associated with Lady Gregory and the poet William Butler Yeats.

Only ruined walls and stables remain of the Lady Gregory home in **Coole Park**, but the woods and gardens where she entertained the literary giants of the day are still here. If you take the time you can pick out the initials of the following on the autograph tree: George Bernard Shaw, Sean O'Casey, John Masefield, Augustus John, Oliver St. John Gogarty, and Douglas Hyde, who became the first president of Ireland. Close by are the lakes with the swans that inspired some of Yeats's best lyric poetry.

The **Tower at Thoor Ballylee** dates back to the 16th century; Yeats had it restored in 1917 and lived here for about ten years. It is now a Yeats museum (open to the public daily from May to October), where you can see some of the first editions of the poet's works. There is also an audiovisual presentation about Yeats and his place in Ireland's literary and political history.

On your way back to Galway you might drive northeast through **Craughwell**, a little village on the Dublin road (N 6) where film director John Huston lived for many years and where he led the famous Galway Blazers Hunt. While you're in Craughwell stop in at **The Blazers Bar**, an excellent pub run by Donal Rafferty.

CONNEMARA

West of Galway City lies the region known as Connemara. A glance at the map shows that it is bounded on the east by Lough Corrib and, farther north, Lough Mask. On the west is the Atlantic Ocean. Galway Bay and Galway City link the Atlantic with Lough Corrib.

People who have never been to Ireland think of Connemara as that beautiful, wild, mountainous country that was depicted by Paul Henry in his popular paintings: the mist on the mountain, the stack of peat against the thatched cottage, and the lonesome little donkey somewhere in the foreground. Well, the thatched cottage is gone and replaced for the most part by modern, well-designed, one-story bungalows. The peat, the mist, and the mountains remain, but the air of loneliness is well dispelled. Connemara today is a community that has developed a genuine folk culture in the best possible sense.

It has become a place where the Irish go to find themselves, to renew their own roots, to rediscover their identity.

At the turn of the century the search for identity was largely tied in with language. Yeats sought the Irish soul in the Celtic myths. The revolutionaries of 1916, founders of the modern-day nationalist movement, traced that soul to the Irish language. Padraig Pearse, the leader of the 1916 Easter Rising, had a cottage in Connemara. He believed that the essence of the Irish psyche lay in the simplicity of the Connemara lifestyle. The Irish language is still spoken in Connemara today; young schoolchildren and some adults, too, spend summers here to gain a facility in Irish. The area has its own Gaelic radio station.

But more than the language matters these days. Connemara has seen a great revival of local community centers, which in turn has brought a new outpouring of the visual arts, music, and sculpture. The products are to be seen in places like the **Crafts Centre** in Spiddal, where highly skilled artisans produce fine Irish handmade goods such as knits, linens, tweeds, and ceramics. Other fine shops for Irish goods are **Miller's** in Clifden, **Joyce's** in Letterfrack, **Michael Keogh** in Maam Cross, and **Pollycraft** in Kilraines near Spiddal. During Clifden Arts Week at the end of September, poets, writers, scholars, and artists—some Irish, most of them from overseas—come together to celebrate what Ireland means to them.

In addition to giving rise to its culture, Connemara is like a great Irish national park, comprising such outdoor activities as mountain trekking, boating and cruising on Lough Corrib, deep-sea angling off Galway Bay, golfing, shooting, and fishing.

The lasting pleasures of Connemara are only absorbed in silence. However, the silence of Connemara is not that of the vast, wide-open plains of the American West or of the Australian Centre, but the silence of awe at the beauty of the natural landscape and the genuine, caring friendliness of the people. In Connemara you will never be disturbed if you don't wish to be.

Around in Connemara

Many bus tours of Connemara are available, some booked in advance as part of an Irish tour, others departing from Galway. You can find out details from the West Tourism Office in Galway. The *Galway Guide,* available from the local tourist office, suggests tour options other than the ones we suggest here. Tel: (091) 630-81; Fax: (091) 652-01.

One possible itinerary includes a drive out to Clifden and the surrounding area. Take the N 59 out of Galway through Moycullen to Oughterard and stop for coffee in the **Connemara Gateway Hotel**. From Oughterard go on to Maam Cross (don't forget to visit Michael Keogh's shop here) and then on to **Ballynahinch**, the birthplace of Richard Martin, the duelist known as "Hairtrigger Dick" but rechristened "Humanity Dick" because he founded the Royal Society for the Prevention of Cruelty to Animals. The salmon and sea-trout fishing in the lake here is world renowned. Note, however, that salmon fishing requires a license from the local police (Garda) station; no license is needed for trout fishing. Continue from Ballynahinch through the scenic Inagh Valley and the Twelve Pins mountains to Clifden for the night.

Clifden, perched in an Alpine-like setting above an inlet of Ardbear Bay, is a lovely spot for families and an excellent base for touring the surrounding countryside. The little town really comes alive in the summer months, so be sure you have booked ahead for rooms. (Clifden hosts the Pony Show each August.) There is an abundance of hotels, guest houses, and restaurants here; to sample the local color, try the Alcock & Brown Hotel, the Clifden Bay Hotel, or the Abbeyglen Castle. The modern **Alcock & Brown Hotel**, named for the first fliers to cross the Atlantic from west to east, is located in the center of Clifden and offers all amenities, though it is somewhat lacking in charm. (Sir William Alcock and Sir Arthur Whitten Brown made their famous soft landing in a bog just outside Clifden after flying across the Atlantic non-stop from Newfoundland in 1919. A memorial marks the spot close to the ruins of the Marconi radio station.) More appealing is the **Clifden Bay Hotel**; equally well situated (on Clifden's square), it has been in operation for over a century. Perched on a hillside just outside of Clifden, **Abbeyglen Castle** offers the area's most luxurious accommodation in a turreted castle. All have good dining facilities, but if you will only be in Clifden for one night you should go instead to **O'Grady's Seafood**, a lovely restaurant that serves local lobster and steamed clams. O'Grady's is very popular; call in advance at Tel: (095) 214-50. You might also want to drop into **Mannion's Bar**, where there are nightly sessions of traditional music and singing all summer.

Several good side trips can be made from Clifden. From the center of town you can go northeast on N 59 through an area dominated by the mountain range known as the **Twelve Pins**, to Killary Harbour and the Partry Mountains and on to the South Mayo border. There is good fishing in myriad small lakes in the region, notably at Ballynahinch, discussed above.

The Benedictine convent, **Kylemore Abbey**, also northeast of Clifden via N 59, was formerly the home of a British member of Parliament. In the Great Hall is a flag captured by the famed Irish Brigade at the battle of Fontenoy. Visitors are welcome at the restaurant/pottery showrooms within walking distance of Kylemore; they have a very good selection of tweeds, linen, and china. **Connemara National Park** at **Letterfrack** near Kylemore Abbey has an audiovisual center that gives a good introduction to the geology and botany of the area. The park features several suggested walks for backpackers and mountain climbers.

The village of **Renvyle**, out on a peninsula north of Clifden and west Kylemore, is home to **Renvyle House Hotel**, once the summer residence of Oliver St. John Gogarty, Joyce's model for Buck Mulligan in *Ulysses*. Yeats and Gogarty used to hold séances here; manager Vincent Flannery will be happy to show you the Ghost Room. The hotel has great facilities for children, good tennis courts, and sailing in the sheltered bay just out front.

From Clifden you might take the coast road southwest through **Ballyconneely**, where there is an excellent golf course at which visitors are always welcome, then on to Roundstone and back along the northern shore of Galway Bay on the R 336 to **Spiddal**. Spiddal, just 12 km (7½ miles) west of Galway, is in the heart of the Irish-speaking area. Its **Crafts Centre**, just outside of the village toward Galway, offers weaving, pottery, stone carving, screen painting, and jewelry; the setting, however, is unpleasantly tourist-oriented, with a parking lot for buses and a café for hungry shoppers. **Staunton's** is a high-quality store here with great buys in knits and sweaters. The village also boasts one of the area's best fresh seafood pub-restaurants—**Boluisce's**, a place where the fishermen cook their catch. Reservations advisable; Tel: (091) 832-86.

If you have the time, there are several other attractions in this area. **Inishbofin**, a large inhabited island off Cleggan, northwest of Clifden, can be reached by a trawler that leaves daily from Cleggan; call Paddy Halloran for bookings at Tel: (095) 458-06. (Most of the many small islands off the coastline have no residents.) On Inishbofin you will find peace, tranquillity, and beaches for walking rather than swimming; should you wish to stay overnight, there are two good hotels: **Day's Hotel** and **Doonmore**. Both are clean and comfortable, but not luxurious.

Cong, on the northern shores of Lough Corrib and actually in County Mayo, is one of the oldest monastic sites in Ireland. The famous Cross of Cong, now in the National Museum in Dublin, was originally at **Cong Abbey**, now in ruins, which was built about 1123 by Turlough Mor O'Conor, king of Connacht. Roderick O'Conor, the last high king of Ireland, spent the last 12 years of his life here following his failure to defeat the Normans; he died in Cong Abbey in 1198.

The natural beauty of the countryside in the Cong area was the setting for John Ford's film *The Quiet Man*. Perhaps Cong's greatest claim to fame today is **Ashford Castle**, originally built by the Norman family De Burgo (Burke) in 1228. Later it was owned by the Guinness family. Now refurbished, it operates as a luxury hotel resort like its sister hotel, Dromoland Castle in Clare. The rooms look out on Lough Cong and Lough Corrib, two of the most scenic lakes in the West of Ireland. There are tennis courts and a golf course on the grounds and cruising and fishing on the lakes. It is now a major center for conferences, and when Ronald Reagan visited Ireland he stayed here. The dining room is truly baronial and has a menu to match; before you leave Ireland, you really ought to try it.

GETTING AROUND

Passengers arriving at Shannon Airport who have not already booked a tour package with their travel agent should consult the Shannon Castle Tours counter at the airport. A wide variety of tours, ranging from one to five days and more, is offered by coach with guide.

There is air commuter service, up to three flights daily, by Aer Lingus from Dublin Airport to Galway City. The trip is about 40 minutes, and the aircraft returns to Dublin after a 35-minute ground turnaround at Galway.

Irish Rail makes the trip between Dublin's Heuston

Station and Galway City four times a day (three times on Sundays); there is usually a buffet car. The trip takes about 3 hours.

ACCOMMODATIONS REFERENCE

The telephone country code for the West is 353. When dialing telephone numbers in the Republic from outside the country, drop the 0 in the area code. The rate ranges given below are projections *for the low and high seasons in 1993; for up-to-the-minute rate information it is always wise to telephone before booking. Unless otherwise indicated, rates are per person sharing and do not include meals or service.*

County Clare

▶ **Carrygerry House Hotel. Shannon Airport,** County Clare. Tel: (061) 623-39 or 621-37; Fax: (061) 621-23. £30, breakfast included.

▶ **Clare Inn. Newmarket-on-Fergus,** County Clare. Tel: (061) 36-81-61; Fax: (061) 36-86-22. £33–£49.

▶ **Dromoland Castle. Newmarket-on-Fergus,** County Clare. Tel: (061) 36-81-44; Fax: (061) 36-33-55; in U.S., Tel: (800) 346-7007. Double room, £52.50–£77.50; suite, £92.50–£137.50.

▶ **Gregan's Castle Hotel. Ballyvaughan,** County Clare. Tel: (065) 770-05; Fax: (065) 771-11; in U.S., Tel: (800) 223-6510. Open Easter through October. £44–£75, breakfast included.

▶ **Hyland's Hotel. Ballyvaughan,** County Clare. Tel: (065) 770-37; Fax: (065) 771-31; in U.S. and Canada, Tel: (800) 223-1588. Open Easter through October. £19.50–£23.50, breakfast included.

▶ **Old Ground Hotel.** O'Connell Street, **Ennis,** County Clare. Tel: (065) 281-27; Fax: (065) 281-12; in U.S., Tel: (800) CALL-THF. £35–£50.

▶ **Shannon Shamrock Inn (Fitzpatricks). Bunratty,** County Clare. Tel: (061) 36-11-77; Fax: (061) 612-52; in U.S., Tel: (800) 221-1074. £46.50.

County Limerick

▶ **Adare Manor. Adare,** County Limerick. Tel: (061) 39-65-66; Fax: (061) 39-61-24; in U.S., Tel: (201) 379-6286. £47.50–£230.

▶ **Jury's Hotel.** Ennis Road, **Limerick City, County Limerick.** Tel: (061) 32-77-77; Fax: (061) 32-64-00; in U.S., Tel: (800) 843-6664; in Canada, Tel: (800) 268-1133; in London, Tel: (81) 569-5555 or (71) 937-8033; in U.K., Tel: (0345) 01-01-01. £40.

▶ **Limerick Inn**. Ennis Road, **Limerick City, County Limerick**. Tel: (061) 32-66-66; Fax: (061) 32-62-81; in U.S., Tel: (800) 223-0888. £44–£49.50.

▶ **Limerick Ryan Hotel**. Ennis Road, **Limerick City, County Limerick**. Tel: (061) 539-22; Fax: (061) 32-63-33; in U.S., Tel: (800) 44-UTELL. £35–£45.

County Galway

▶ **Abbeyglen Castle**. Sky Road, **Clifden**, County Galway. Tel: (095) 212-01; Fax: (095) 217-97. Closed January. £33.50–£45, breakfast and service included.

▶ **Alcock & Brown Hotel**. The Square, **Clifden**, County Galway. Tel: (095) 210-86 or 06; Fax: (095) 218-42. £18.50–£26, breakfast included.

▶ **Ardawn House**. 31 College Road, **Galway**. Tel: (091) 688-33. £18.

▶ **Ardilaun House**. Taylor's Hill, **Galway City**, County Galway. Tel: (091) 214-33; Fax: (091) 215-46. £35–£50, breakfast included.

▶ **Clifden Bay Hotel**. **Clifden**, County Galway. Tel: (095) 218-01; Fax: (095) 214-58. £32, breakfast included.

▶ **Day's Hotel**. **Inishbofin Island**, County Galway. Tel: (095) 458-29. £15–£17, breakfast included. Open May through September.

▶ **De Sota**. 54 Newcastle Road, **Galway**. Tel: (091) 650-64. £16.50.

▶ **Doonmore**. **Inishbofin Island**, County Galway. Tel: (095) 458-04. Open Easter through September. £14–£18, breakfast included.

▶ **Galway Great Southern Hotel**. Eyre Square, **Galway City**, County Galway. Tel: (091) 640-41; Fax: (091) 667-04; in U.S., Tel: (800) 44-UTELL. £47–£53.

▶ **Galway Ryan Hotel**. Dublin Road, **Galway City**, County Galway. Tel: (091) 531-81; Fax: (091) 531-87; in U.S., Tel: (800) 44-UTELL. £35–£45.

▶ **Gilbert's Cottage (Mr. S. Dirrane)**. Oatquarter, Kilronan, **Inishmore**, County Galway. Tel: (099) 611-46. £10–£15, breakfast and service included.

▶ **Hotel Inisheer**. Lurgan Village, **Inisheer**, County Galway. Tel: (099) 750-20. Open Easter through September. £12–£17, breakfast and service included.

▶ **Mandala**. 10 Gentian Hill, **Salthill**. Tel: (091) 241-77. £14.50.

▶ **Mrs. Faherty's**. Creigmore, **Inishmaan**, County Galway. Tel: (099) 730-12. £12, breakfast and service included.

▶ **Renvyle House Hotel. Renvyle**, Connemara, County Galway. Tel: (095) 435-11; Fax: (095) 435-15. Open March through November, Christmas, and New Year's. £31–£45, breakfast included.

▶ **Roncalli House.** 24 White Strand Avenue, **Salthill.** Tel: (091) 641-59. £14.50.

County Mayo

▶ **Ashford Castle. Cong**, County Mayo. Tel: (092) 460-03; Fax: (092) 462-60; in U.S., Tel: (800) 346-7007. £69–£110.

THE NORTHWEST

MAYO, SLIGO, AND DONEGAL

By Mary Dowey

Mary Dowey is editor of the Aer Lingus in-flight magazine Cara, *for which she undertakes regular travel assignments. She also contributes articles to newspapers and magazines in Britain and Ireland, including the* Sunday Times, Country Living, *and the* Irish Times. *She has north Donegal roots—and a cottage there to go with them.*

The Northwest is Ireland's Wild West. Nowhere else in the country is there such an overwhelming sense of nature unleashing her forces—in pounding seas, windswept mountains, and a pattern of weather that can fluctuate within minutes between torrential rain and sun, sometimes creating brilliant rainbows in between. The landscape is as theatrical as the climate that has helped to form it. Rocky plateaus, sheer cliffs, and mile upon mile of golden beach make up a coast so battered by the Atlantic that it is in a constant process of disintegration into islands. The Northwest has a breathtaking, stark beauty, compared to which Connemara, with its orderly stone walls and small lakes, looks almost tame.

The emptiness of this region is remarkable. Nowhere else in Ireland are the wide open spaces so extensive, or human beings so seriously outnumbered by sheep. Crumbling cottages in these counties point to a sad history of

Mayo, Donegal and Sligo

| 0 | miles | 15 |
| 0 | km | 20 |

ATLANTIC OCEAN

N

Glencolmcille
Ki
*Slieve
League*

Donega

Inishmur

*Lisadel
Fores*

Downpatrick Head
Killala
*Killala
Bay*
Ballycastle
Bederrig
Inniscrone
Coney Islan
Knocknare
Dromore
N59
Belmullet
**Belmullet
Peninsula**
Bangor Erris
Bellacorick
R314
R314
Iniskea Islands
Crossmolina
Ballina
S L
Blacksod Bay
N59
Mt. Nephin
Lough Conn
R313
Dooagh
Doogort
R321
Foxford
Keem Strand
Cashel
Keel
Mulrany
R312
R317
N17
Croaghaun
Achill Island
R319
Clew Bay
Newport
Westport
Castlebar
Knock
Clare Island
Louisburgh
Lecanvy
N84
Ballintubber Abbey
Roonah Point
R335
Caher Island
Croagh Patrick
Doo Lough
M A Y O
Claremorris
R330
Partry
Killary Harbour
Lough Mask
Ballinrobe
Leenane
N59
Cong
Lough Corrib
N84
TO SHANNON
G A L
Connemara

depopulation, beginning with the potato famine in the 1840s and continuing today. Young people are still emigrating to England, the United States, or Australia to carve out a more comfortable living than their parents or grandparents did from small farms on rocky hillsides.

The extraordinary thing is that, in an area of such spectacular scenery, the disappearing natives have not yet been replaced by a huge influx of tourists. Visitors come, of course, but in small numbers—mainly French, Germans, and Italians drawn by outdoor pursuits such as fishing, hiking, and shooting. Irish vacationers tend to migrate south, like birds, to Cork and Kerry, so that even at the height of summer the Northwest remains relatively empty. In travel terms it is Ireland's best-kept secret.

Maybe the weather has something to do with it. Maybe people are put off by the prospect of raincoats and Wellingtons—there is no getting away from the fact that this is, in every sense, a watery landscape. But there are subtle benefits. The soft rain (which rarely lasts for very long) drenches the countryside with gentle melancholy blues and grays; and the winds that bring in the clouds from the Atlantic create, at the same time, magnificent, shifting skies. Even the mountains seem to move back and forth in the western light.

History and geography have conspired to keep this corner of Ireland much the same for centuries. Because farms are still small and intensive farming methods foreign, plenty of unruly hedges grow between fields—a mass of whitethorn, blackthorn, and blackberries—sheltering birds whose numbers are declining elsewhere. Wild flowers flourish, too; not just the heather, which gives the mountains their purple carpet, but butterworts and bladderworts and orchids on peat bogs that have lain undisturbed for 6,000 years. The unpolluted lakes of Mayo and Sligo offer some of the best fishing in western Europe and here, too, it is still possible to shoot wild pheasant and woodcock in quiet thickets. You may even savor your success at dinner the same evening in some of the old country houses that offer splendid accommodation.

Besides outdoor pursuits in an unforgettable landscape, the Northwest holds plenty of other fascinations, from the last fragments of an Irish-speaking culture in west Donegal to an Anglo-Irish tradition in Sligo that underpins the poetry of William Butler Yeats.

Wherever you go in the Northwest, you will be made

especially welcome—partly, perhaps, because the people here haven't yet had the chance to become complacent about tourists.

MAJOR INTEREST

Beautiful, wild scenery, with relatively few tourists
Mix of Irish and Anglo-Irish culture

Mayo
Doo Lough Valley
Clare Island
Croagh Patrick, Ireland's holy mountain
Georgian Westport Town
Achill Island
Fishing: Doo Lough Valley, Lough Mask, Lough
   Conn

Sligo
Sligo Town
Yeats Country
Lough Gill Scenic Drive
Carrowmore megalithic remains
Carrowkeel passage graves
Shooting: woodcock and snipe

Donegal
Slieve League sea cliffs
Bloody Foreland and Tory Island
Glenveagh National Park
Fanad Peninsula
Handweaving and knitting
Golf: Bundoran and Rosapenna

COUNTY MAYO

Of the three Northwest counties, Mayo is the most thinly populated—so much so that it's important to check your car's fuel gauge before setting off across its wild acres. Lose yourself in Mayo for a few days and you will understand why its remoteness and untouched panoramas have attracted writers such as J. M. Synge and the Northern poet Michael Longley, and distinguished painters like Tony O'Malley and Camille Souter.

While the beauty of the north of the county lies in vast open expanses of bog, the south has spectacular mountains down whose slopes trickle streams that feed rich fishing rivers and lakes. No wonder the recent discovery of gold deep in some of these south Mayo mountains has provoked such bitter controversy. Despite the promise of jobs, most local people feel strongly that mining, no matter how carefully it might be controlled, would surely damage Mayo's beauty, put its fishing at risk, and harm a burgeoning tourist industry at the same time.

South Mayo

Assuming that you are driving north from Connemara there are two quite different approaches to Westport, Mayo's gateway: one from the west via Louisburgh, through vistas of untamed mountain and moor, and the other a gentler approach from the southeast via Cong. Whichever way you choose, you may start in the sleepy village of **Leenane** on Killary Harbour, not so much a harbor as a curved fjord separating the coasts of Galway and Mayo. You could do worse than stop here and contemplate your map in **Gaynor's**, a pub that moved quietly through five generations of the same family before the filming of *The Field* (1990) made it famous. It still has plenty of men in flat caps, like characters from the movie, at the long bar.

The more awe-inspiring route snakes around the end of Killary, past the waters of the Aasleagh Falls on R 335 and up through the majestic **Doo Lough Valley** with its linked chain of lakes. This is prime fishing territory for salmon and sea trout—but bear in mind that game fishing in Ireland isn't something that can be indulged in casually: You must have a rod license (obtainable from post offices) and pay the owner of the fishing rights on a particular stretch of water for your day's sport. One of the advantages of staying at a fishermens' hotel is that all these arrangements will be made for you. In the southernmost stretch of Mayo, on the shores of Finn Lough, the loveliest is **Delphi Lodge**, with its own extensive private fishery. It was built by the second marquess of Sligo in the 1840s as a fishing lodge. Grandly, he named both house and valley after Delphi in Greece, reminded of that ancient site's scenic splendor by this breathtaking sweep of Mayo.

In latter years Delphi lay empty and neglected until 1986, when Peter Mantle, a young Englishman and a fanatical fisherman, passed by on vacation and fell in love with the place. He and his wife, Jane, have now magnificently restored every inch of the lodge, including all the (en suite) Victorian bathtubs. They also have four well-equipped cottages on the grounds for fisherfolk who prefer simple self-catering accommodation. (Guests here may dine at the lodge if they wish, which is all to the good, as Jane Mantle is a Cordon Bleu cook who works particular wonders with seafood.)

You don't have to fish, however, to enjoy the tranquility of this underdeveloped valley. The mountains rear up on both sides of the road like slumbering dinosaurs, with nothing except your own transient presence to disturb them.

The R 335 climbs up toward the town of **Louisburgh**, which has two places of pilgrimage virtually on its doorstep. The first—a quiet sanctuary in the nonreligious sense—is **Clare Island**, five miles off the coast. Clare Island is a place to enjoy bracing walks with spectacular sea views, and to see some of the most intriguing wildlife in the West: dolphins, seals, otters, and the rare red-billed crow. If you are feeling energetic you may even wish to arrange a spot of shark fishing or scuba diving.

The island is also the first of many places in Mayo where you will marvel at the bravado of Grace O'Malley (or Granuaile, as she is known in Irish), Ireland's 16th-century pirate queen who had three husbands and established herself as the terror of the western seas by the time she arrived at the court of England's Queen Elizabeth I, demanding to be left alone. (She was.) When she died of old age in 1603 she was buried on the island in the small **Monastery of St. Bridget**. There is something careless about the old ruins: The wall paintings, or what remains of them, are left exposed to the wind and salt, eroding more from year to year. Somewhere on the wall is the O'Malley coat of arms and motto: "Invincible on land and sea." Two ferries run daily between the island and Roonah Quay to the west of Louisburgh. (Check the times with Clare Island Ferry Service: Tel: 098/263-07.)

The area's other place of pilgrimage, this time in the true sense, is **Croagh Patrick**, Ireland's holy mountain, whose distinctive quartzite cone rises up to the right a few miles out of Louisburgh on the Westport road. Saint Patrick is said to have prayed and fasted here for 40 days in the year 441; on the south side of the summit is the precipice where he is said to have rung his bell, apparently attracting all the snakes in Ireland, who obligingly hurled themselves into oblivion.

The annual Croagh Patrick pilgrimage takes place on the

last Sunday in July, as it has for centuries. As an added penance, many of those who participate climb the mountain in their bare feet as their ancestors did; but whereas in days gone by the ascent was made in the dark in order to observe dawn breaking from the peak, the night vigil has been banned by the church authorities to deter those who entered into the spirit of the thing too enthusiastically— with the help of alcohol. The mountain may of course be climbed at any time, weather permitting (pay attention to local advice, as sudden mists can be treacherous). It takes about one and a half hours from the village of Murrisk; the last third of the climb is difficult, with loose stones all the way, but worth it on a clear day for the view of Clew Bay, studded with tiny islands.

The road from the base of Croagh Patrick leads to Westport, 8 km (5 miles) to the northeast. If you decided earlier to approach the town by the alternative route from Leenane, your choice will take you through the heart of hilly Joyce Country (once the territory of the Joyce clan), via the R 336 southeast to Maam, then continuing on the R 345 along the northern shores of Lough Corrib to **Cong**.

This small town in a lovely sylvan setting is famous for two things. The ruined **Cong Abbey**, built in 1123 by Turlough Mor O'Conor, king of Connacht, was the original home of the superb **Cross of Cong**, now one of the greatest treasures of Ireland's National Museum. Cong also has a reputation for famous visitors ever since John Wayne and Maureen O'Hara filmed *The Quiet Man* here in 1952. Most of them stay in **Ashford Castle**, a baronial pile built for a member of the Guinness family in magnificent grounds, where the view over velvety lawns is marred only slightly by a helicopter pad. This is not the place to come without a well-stuffed wallet.

From Cong it is a pleasant drive north to the N 84 and to **Partry**, a small town that has given its name to the mountains sheltering the northern shores of **Lough Mask**, one of Mayo's famous trout lakes. Here the choice lies between scenery and history. You may decide to take the Lough Mask Drive, or continue straight on the N 84 to view the Norman legacy of another king of Connacht: **Ballintubber Abbey**. Unlike so many others of its period, this church, founded in 1216 by Cathal O'Conor, is still in use today; mass has been said here continuously for seven centuries. Whichever sightseeing detour you choose, be sure to take the necessary turn onto the R 330, which leads northwest to Westport.

Westport

The town of Westport is attractive both architecturally and in atmosphere. Unlike most Irish towns that developed piecemeal, it was carefully planned in the late 18th century as an adjunct to Westport House, seat of the marquesses of Sligo. It still has its rather grand tree-lined mall, many of its Georgian houses, interesting shop fronts (**M. Mulloy, Ironmonger & Grocer**, dates from 1762), and, down by the quay, some fine old warehouses from a linen- and cotton-trading past. (**Quay Cottage** on The Quay is a good place for a snack.)

The writer W. M. Thackeray pronounced **The Olde Railway Hotel** on The Mall "one of the prettiest, comfortablist Inns in Ireland" when he stayed here in 1842. He stretched spelling a little, perhaps, but not credulity. It is still a cozy place, moderately priced and family run, and close enough to town for a pleasant stroll through the friendly bustle of Westport. If you happen to be there on a Thursday morning don't miss the country market held in the Town Hall on the Octagon (as Westport's central square is known, for geometrical reasons). You can buy lovely, locally made farmhouse cheeses such as Carrowholly, and sweaters hand-knitted from locally spun wool.

Westport's other mandatory attraction is **Matt Molloy's**, a great traditional pub on Bridge Street. If you can see them for the crowd, you'll notice cream wooden walls hung with Victorian mirrors, old advertisements, and some not-so-old posters of The Chieftains, the well-known Irish folk group whose flautist owns this establishment. There are often terrific spontaneous Irish music sessions in the back room.

You should also allow time to see **Westport House**, developed for tourists by the tenth marquess of Sligo in an effort to stave off mounting debts. Go to see the house itself, dating to about 1730, which is quite magnificent and has a worthwhile collection of furniture and silver; don't bother with the somewhat honky-tonk zoo, miniature railway, and other "attractions" in the grounds. Open daily; hours vary according to season.

From Westport continue north 12 km (7½ miles) on N 59 to Newport. **Newport House**, overlooking the River Newport, is a delightful retreat—a Late Georgian country house that is more like an old-fashioned gentlemen's club than a hotel. Many (but by no means all) of the guests are fishermen who come back year after year to enjoy the unchanging charms of the place. The owner, Kieran Thompson, was himself a fishing guest; he bought Newport House a decade ago with the notion that it would enable him to indulge in his favorite pastime all the time. Some of the staff have been here almost as long as the prize-winning stuffed pike in the hall—not least among them Owen Mullins, the fishery manager, whose secret recipe gives Newport smoked salmon its special flavor. All the food served under the glittering old chandelier in the dining room is excellent, and the claret section of the wine list positively biblical. (The dining room is open to non-guests provided reservations are made in advance; Tel: 098/41-222.)

Before you leave town climb up the steep hill to **St. Patrick's Church**. The rich jewel colors of the east windows, made in 1922 by Harry Clarke, Ireland's best-known stained-glass artist, glow even when the weather is dull.

From Newport it's an easy drive west along N 59 to Mulrany and the final leg west to Achill Island.

Achill Island

Achill is Mayo's tourist magnet, and has been since early this century when the Belfast-born artist Paul Henry began to paint its purple-blue mountains and turfstacks. Linked to the mainland by a bridge and a good road, Ireland's biggest island is so accessible that for years it has attracted a curious mixture of visitors. In the sixties it appealed to Heinrich Böll (who included it in his *Irisches Tagebuch*) and to Dublin students intent on a wild weekend in pubs that never closed. These days, with campers, RVers, Wind-surfers, canoeists, shark-fishers, Scuba divers, hang-gliders, and—in August especially—a sizable platoon of day-trippers, its clientele is even more varied than before. One regrettable result is a rash of ugly bungalows, guest houses, and fast-food joints in small towns like Keel, which deserves better, given its dreamlike location on a crescent of white sand.

In spite of that, Achill is definitely worth seeing. No photograph can capture the scale of its **Atlantic Drive**: So immense is the sweep of mountains to the sea that the white houses at their foot look like lightly scattered breadcrumbs. This is Mayo at its most dramatic. Sometimes the clouds sweep down so low that they mingle with the turf smoke; then suddenly they lift to reveal a great arc of sand or tracts of fox-colored bog.

Each of Achill's little towns holds something of interest. At **Doogort** in the north are the remains of what is known as "the Colony," an extraordinary missionary scheme to convert local children to Protestantism, launched in 1830 and successful for a time partly because no converts went hungry through the years of the Great Famine.

Keel, southwest of Doogort, is the main center for water sports and boat rentals (both fishing and sightseeing). It also has two good crafts shops—a relative rarity for travellers through Mayo: **Keel Craft Shop** and **The Beehive** both have things you might actually want to buy. A short distance out of Keel on the Slievemore Road you'll come to one of the island's most appealing restaurants: **The Boley House**, a stone cottage with plain wood tables where you can enjoy a five-course dinner (try some fresh Achill fish) for about £15. Open every evening for dinner; reservations are advised. Tel: (098) 431-47.

On the slopes of Slievemore (accessible from Keel or Dooagh) is the haunting **Deserted Village**, a once-thriving settlement that was mysteriously abandoned. Two kilometers (1¼ miles) to the west of Dooagh is **Corrymore House**, home of the hated landlord Captain Boycott, who gave a new word to the English language (the house may only be seen from the outside).

Although Achill has no really outstanding accommodation, it is possible to stay in comfort for a reasonable price. The **Atlantic Hotel** at Dooagh and **Gray's Guest House** at Doogort, for example, are popular with regular visitors. There is also no shortage of bed and breakfasts.

North Mayo

If, after Achill, you crave still more seascapes, this time with flat land melting into pale water, drive farther north along the N 59, then northwest on R 313 to Belmullet and down the hooked finger of the Mullet Peninsula itself. From **Blacksod Point** Vincent Sweeney runs boat trips out to the **Inishkea Islands**, inhabited until the 1930s by resilient fishermen; now the only residents are colonies of seabirds. The boat goes every day May through September if demand is great enough; the journey takes only an hour, and these utterly deserted and partially overgrown islands are pleasant places to stroll or have a picnic; Tel: (097) 857-74.

As you drive east on the R 314 between Belmullet and Ballina (77 km/48 miles), there are three worthwhile stopping points. The first, on the upper side of the road between Belderg and Ballycastle, is the **Céide Fields**, an extensive Stone Age settlement currently being excavated. It makes you wonder what this outpost of Europe was like 5,000 years ago, and how much more fertile the land must have been to support a community of some 10,000 people.

At Ballycastle, 50 km (31 miles) west of Belmullet, take the coast road to **Downpatrick Head**, where the sea races underneath the cliffs in subterranean channels before shooting up through blow holes in the top of the rocks. So powerful is the lashing sea that it has broken part of the land right off; triangular Doonbristie now stands out from the coast like an abandoned slice of cake.

Some 15 km (9 miles) farther south is the little town of **Killala**, where an ill-fated French expedition led by General Humbert landed in 1798. The significance of that event in Irish history is finely evoked by the American writer Thomas Flanagan in his historical novel *The Year of the French*.

Ballina, Mayo's largest town, 15 km (9 miles) south of Killala, provides a pleasant change after hours or days spent out in the wilds. Its location on the estuary of the River Moy, Mayo's great salmon river, makes it a very good place indeed to buy smoked salmon—especially at **J. Clarke and Sons**, known far beyond the boundaries of Mayo for the quality of their smoked fish. On either side of this shop on O'Rahilly Street are two other establishments that may intrigue you.

Clarkes (yes, a relation) looks like an ordinary newsagent shop until you explore the recesses farther back of this Aladdin's cave—everything from Meissen porcelain figures to Crabtree & Evelyn toilet water, with bizarre novelties like pig pencil sharpeners in between. "It's wildly eccentric—I am aware of that," says Loretta Clarke, whose Chicago-born mother ran the place in the 1930s as an American ice-cream parlor. A few doors farther down the street, **Gaughan's** pub, straight out of the thirties, specializes not only in what the owner calls "natural" Guinness (flavor enhanced by storage at a steady 60 degrees), but snuff, pipes, and tobacco. This last Edward

Gaughan blends himself and weighs out at the bar counter, while his wife works at producing good pub food and superlative brown bread.

As in so many other towns of medium size in Ireland, there are a few hotels of medium size, but what they offer is rather bland and unremarkable. If you prefer character to a cocktail bar and fine old furniture to a fitness center, you might find one of the country houses in the neighborhood more rewarding.

Enniscoe House on Lough Conn (fishing on the estate can be arranged) is run by Susan Kellett, a direct descendant of the family that built the place in the 1750s. It has just six rooms and a slight air of faded elegance, but guests are enthusiastic about the fine plasterwork, canopy beds, and blazing fires. The food is in the best country-house tradition, fresh and unfussy. Enniscoe acts as the headquarters for the **North Mayo Heritage Centre**, both a museum of rural life and a family-history research center, which runs a service for people interested in tracing their ancestry.

The other memorable place to stay in north Mayo is **Mount Falcon Castle**, halfway between Ballina and Foxford 16 km (10 miles) farther south. This granite mansion, built in the late 19th century in Scottish baronial style, appears austere on the outside, but life within is the nearest you are likely to come in Ireland to an old-fashioned country-house party. Guests help themselves to drinks in the butler's pantry and dine together at an immense table presided over by Mrs. Constance Aldridge, the wittiest octogenarian in the West. As Mount Falcon has its own salmon fishing on the River Moy, a few fishermen usually find their way to the table in season; in winter they tend to be replaced by those who come to shoot (Mount Falcon will make the arrangements).

If you venture this far into the heartland of the county you may find it worth your while to drive 35 km (22 miles) farther south from Foxford on the R 321 to **Knock**, a small town transformed into a major Marian shrine. The apparition of the Virgin Mary, Saint Joseph, and Saint John to a gathering of local people in 1879 produced a steady stream of pilgrims, culminating in the building in this barren spot of both an immense basilica and an international airport (which could be your access point to Mayo and the Northwest). The town can be unpleasantly crowded in the pilgrimage season (April to October), especially on weekends and during special vigils or novenas.

COUNTY SLIGO

Wedged in between the two much bigger, wilder counties of Mayo and Donegal, Sligo looks and feels quite different. Its contours are softer, its climate less austere, its ancient history remarkably intact, and its culture influenced by 300 years of Anglo-Irish tradition.

The two mountain landmarks that are so compelling as you travel through Sligo help to summarize its significance. On one side is the wide, gently rounded mountain of **Knocknarea**, crowned with Queen Maeve's tomb—the legendary Queen of Connacht and one of several thousand Stone Age burial sites in this county. On the other side is the flat-topped escarpment of **Ben Bulben**, under whose "bare head" the poet W. B. Yeats asked to be buried.

In the mid-17th century Oliver Cromwell, the scourge of Ireland, allotted huge tracts of Sligo land to his officers and soldiers in lieu of wages. Within a few years the old Sligo families with Gaelic roots—the O'Connors, O'Dowds, O'Garas, and McDonaghs—had been replaced by Coopers, Wynnes, Ormsbys, and Gores. Gradually Sligo Town became a prosperous commercial center of Protestant, English-speaking traders. Among them were the Pollexfen family of Yeats's mother, and the poet grew to love Sligo during summer visits to his grandparents.

Sligo Town

There is a feeling of solidity about the town of Sligo—a no-nonsense air about its narrow, shop-lined streets and important-looking banks. It is a merchants' town—one which, interestingly, developed close trading links with Scotland toward the end of the 19th century, adding a new layer to the Gaelic/Anglo-Irish cultural mix. Sligo is still a busy place, as its constant traffic jams testify, but these days one of its main industries surrounds the work of William Butler Yeats.

Nobody should pass through Sligo without having read at least some of his poetry; anthologies of his work and, for background, *The Yeats Country* by Sheelah Kirby, are easily obtainable in Sligo bookshops. You can then begin your own exploration of the poet at the **Sligo County Library and Museum** on Stephen Street, which has a worthwhile collection of Yeatsiana. Later, as you cross the bridge over the River Garavogue, think of Mr. Yeats in soft hat and flamboyant cravat, leaning over the parapet and dreaming of swans, lakes, or the heavens' embroidered cloths. Some of his plays are usually mounted in August at the **Hawk's Well Theatre**, in the same building as the tourist office on Temple Street.

Among Sligo's many long-established shops, **Mullaney's** in O'Connell Street is one of the most interesting. Not only does it have a good selection of Irish knitwear and tweed (suits made to measure), but it also has an operational travel agency counter where you can inspect old ledgers listing the names of local people who sailed to New York a hundred years ago or more. For American visitors who are trying to trace Sligo ancestors, these registers can provide valuable clues.

John Mullaney, the present owner, is a charming and erudite authority on Sligo history. Among other things, he will tell you that although the town was founded by Normans and eventually peopled by Cromwellians, the native Irish culture that flourished in between still lives on in Irish music. **McLynns** on Old Market Street is probably the best pub in which to hear it; try to grab the seats beside the open fire.

Sligo's other masterly pub is **Hargadon's** on O'Connell Street, where sagging old wooden drawers and uneven floors create a premature illusion of intoxication. No music here: The "snugs" into which the place is subdivided are designed for serious conversation.

If you don't feel like a Sligo pub lunch, **The Cottage**, a coffee shop in Grattan Street is good; or you might buy the makings of a deluxe picnic at **The Gourmet Parlour** on John Street. For evening sustenance the California-style "New Age" pizzas in **Truffles** on The Mall are so outstanding that this unassuming eatery has found its way into *The Bridgestone 100 Best Restaurants in Ireland 1993*.

Yeats Country

I will arise and go now, and go to Innisfree
And a small cabin build there, of clay and
     wattles made
Nine bean rows will I have there, a hive for
     the honey bee
And live alone in the bee-loud glade.

Yeats's **Lake Isle of Innisfree** is still a peaceful prospect, even though the poet would surely smile sardonically at the intrusive sight, on the mainland opposite it, of public lavatories for sightseers. To reach the viewing point drive south out of Sligo for 2 km (1¼ miles), then turn left for the **Lough Gill Scenic Drive**. Lake Isle, signposted in brown, is at the end of a long, winding cul-de-sac between Ballintogher and Dromahair. From where the road peters out a splendid view opens across the fir-fringed lough to the mountain known as the Sleeping Warrior—inspiration enough to continue on the scenic drive. On a fine day it can be like a scaled-down version of the Lakes of Killarney.

The north side of the loop brings you back into Sligo. Leaving again, this time by the Bundoran road (N 15), it is only a short drive north to **Drumcliff** and the churchyard where Yeats lies buried. (His great-grandfather was rector here.) To stand in the shadow of Ben Bulben and read the oft-quoted lines, "Cast a cold eye on life, on death,/ Horseman pass by" etched in the modest stone above his grave, is deeply moving.

Beyond the village a left turn leads to **Lissadell**, home of the Gore-Booth sisters with whom Yeats was friendly ("The light of evening, Lissadell/Great windows open to the south . . ."). The house, built in the 1830s in Greek Revival style, is open to the public from May to September and full of curiosities. Some of them relate to Sir Henry Gore-Booth, who went off with his butler to explore the Antarctic in the 1880s. The grizzly bear the butler shot to save his master is on display here. The missing explorer the two men discovered on an island in the South Pole is not. The house is open from May to September; closed at lunch and on Sundays.

Beyond Sligo Town

Even without the Yeats connection, Sligo is an attractive county offering many interesting activities. If you feel the need for a restorative of a rather unusual sort, it's worth taking the N 59 and then the coast road (R 297) west of Sligo Town to **Inniscrone**. **Kilcullen's Hot Seawater Baths** on the waterfront (open 11:30 A.M.–10:00 P.M. May to October; Tel: 096/362-38) is an Edwardian bathhouse that has attracted people to this sleepy Sligo seaside town for generations. It recently has been restored by Edward Kilcullen, grandson of the founder and, conveniently, a hydrologist at Galway University. An hour's immersion in an immense porcelain tub afloat with steamed *Fucus serratus* (brown algae) freshly gathered from the rocks can work wonders for aches, pains, stress—and even dry skin! (The cost is £6.) To complete the wholesome picture, good homemade food is served in the adjoining tearoom. Although the coastal scenery here is less spectacular than in Mayo or Donegal, there is excellent surfing at **Strandhill**, **Easky**, and **Inniscrone**. Besides, Sligo has no fewer than three magnificent beaches—at **Inniscrone**, **Rosses Point**, and **Mullaghmore**, where Classiebawn Castle, former holiday home of Lord Mountbatten, stands like a clenched fist against the sky.

If you are an experienced rider, one of the best ways to enjoy some of the beaches is on horseback. The **Sligo Riding Centre** (book a day in advance; Tel: 071/613-53) at Carrowmore organizes trail rides that include galloping across the sands at Strandhill and clambering up Queen Maeve's Knocknarea—an easy climb even on foot. Return on the inland side past **Carrowmore's megalithic tombs**; there are so many of them that this is said to be the biggest ancient cemetery in Europe. Some of the 60 tombs, dolmens, stone circles, and passage graves that dot this Bronze Age cemetery can also be explored on foot, but you must enter the site at the Visitor Centre. To reach the center take the Strandhill road out of Sligo town and turn left toward Carrowmore, which is signposted after 5 km (3 miles).

Farther inland, more ancient remains await inspection. At **Carrowkeel**, high above Lough Arrow (south of Sligo), it is possible to peer inside some of the 14 stone **passage graves** that have dotted the hillside since 2500 B.C. Little seems to be known about who was buried in these graves; it is supposed that they were the more revered members of the community. Cremation was popular then, and the ashes went inside the graves. You may even be lucky enough to spot a peregrine falcon while you're there, and there's a superb view over Lough Arrow (famous for its mayfly fishing). To reach the access point to the climb, drive south on the main Sligo–Boyle road (N 4) for 25 km (15 miles) and take the right turn for Ballymote. The passage graves are 6 km (3½ miles) farther on.

It is here, in the soft countryside of south Sligo, that some of the best accommodation in the county is to be found—and the region is small enough for you to tour all of it from any base you choose. **Coopershill House** near Riverstown, a magnificent Georgian mansion that has been the home of the O'Hara family for seven generations, is a civilized place to stay, with good period furniture and silver. It also has homey touches such as the key (large as a dessert spoon) that hangs by the front door so that you can always let yourself in.

Temple House, near Ballymote, home of the Percevals (cousins of the O'Haras) since the 17th century, has a slightly more worn air (you are politely requested not to pull the ancient curtains for fear of further disintegration); but it is a fascinating place, stuffed with treasures brought back from the Orient by a great-great-grandfather. The largest inhabited house in Ireland, it has just five rooms for guests. Both of these houses have the best sort of fresh, simple Irish country-house food. At Temple House guests sit at table together, and if you are lucky Sandy Perceval will appear at the end of dinner to whisk everybody off to dance at a *ceili*. (One of the best is in **Killoran's** in Tubbercurry on Thursday evenings throughout the summer: set-dancing for anybody aged nine to ninety, partnered by copious drink, *crubeens*—pig's feet—and other traditional morsels.)

By way of complete contrast: **Cromleach Lodge** near Castlebaldwin is a brand-new country house, purpose-built for luxurious living. Its large, plush rooms look right out across Lough Arrow, and the food (served on their best Rosenthal china) is ambitious and sophisticated. You can dine here even if you don't stay the night (book in advance; Tel: 071/651-55), but bear in mind that breakfast is a gourmet feast as well, with freshly baked scones and pan-fried *boxty* (Northern Irish potato bread). As all of these country retreats are relatively small it is wise to book in advance.

If you prefer the ambience and amenities of a larger place, **Ballincar House Hotel** halfway between Sligo and Rosses Point, to the north, is comfortable and friendly. Also in this area and recommended for old world charm and excellent value is **Urlar House** in Carney, beyond Drumcliff, where Mrs. Healy provides traditional bed and board in her 300-year-old farmhouse. (She also offers facilities for pets.)

Both Ballincar House and Urlar House are particularly well positioned for golf enthusiasts who want to test their skills at **Rosses Point**, one of the best courses in the

Northwest. A second golfing treat awaits them at **Bundoran**, on the main road from Sligo into Donegal.

COUNTY DONEGAL

If you climb Slieve League some sunny afternoon—the highest sea cliffs in Europe, located on the western tip of Donegal above Donegal Bay—and are brave enough to scale the final, narrow ridge that plunges straight to the sea on one side and down to the valley floor on the other, nature may reward you with a trick that is typical of Donegal: your own enormous shadow moving across the mountains behind you like some primeval giant. For one fleeting moment you might feel in scale with the scenery.

Ireland's second-largest county is a place of breathtaking extremes. Returning recently to the Donegal of his childhood summers, the Belfast-born writer Brian Moore wrote of "this wild, bare, brutal, enchanted landscape," his judgment unmuted by half a lifetime close to the Canadian wilderness. Travelling through Donegal you sometimes feel that the roads that rollercoaster up over rocky headlands and down to spectacular golden beaches twist more than any others on earth, and that the misty lines of mountains, ranged one behind the other in pleats, go on forever. It all has the effect of making human beings feel insignificant and tiny—but Donegal has an answer for that, too. The people are wildly generous and the helpings of food enormous, as if to fatten you up for an experience that often seems larger than life.

There is, of course, more to Donegal than awe-inspiring scenery. Although English in this area often sounds distinctly Scottish (from Malin Head, the most northerly point, you can see the Scottish isles on a clear day), there are more native Irish speakers here than in any other county in Ireland; and the independent spirit that has helped the language to survive has also guarded old traditions such as weaving, knitting, and storytelling. Even casual conversation is a string of metaphors, with wit as dry as the weather is wet.

The county is neatly sliced in two, the north and the south, by a line running from just north of Ardara through Letterkenny and on to the eastern shore of Inishowen. As both halves are equally rewarding and the uneven topography makes travel slow, it is a good idea to base yourself in each for a day or two.

South Donegal

Tour buses, the worst sort of taped Irish music wafting onto the streets, and a rash of rather rubbishy gift shops have conspired to downgrade **Donegal Town** and its once-handsome Diamond (market square), but it still has sights worth seeing and is a good touring base.

Right beside the Diamond is **Donegal Castle**, built in the 1470s and the stronghold of the O'Donnells for almost 150 years. (It is temporarily closed for renovation.) Dating from the same period, and with the same O'Donnell parentage, are the ruins of **Donegal Abbey** on the banks of the River Eske, a five-minute walk south of town center. It was here in the early 16th century that a group of Franciscans began work on *The Annals of the Four Masters,* a monumental history of Gaelic Ireland; a memorial to the Four Masters stands in the Diamond. The **Four Masters Bookshop**, opposite the memorial, is an excellent place to stock up on Donegal reading material. (Look for *Tales from the Blue Stacks* by Robert Bernen, beautifully observed cameos of life in the hills by an American who came to visit and stayed on to farm.) Almost next door is the retail outlet of **Magees**, famous for tweeds since 1866. These days the company sells fabric to Ralph Lauren, Austin Reed, and Aquascutum, and is known as much for quality menswear with a modern look as for traditional Donegal tweed jackets. The shop also carries a good range of women's wear.

Magees employs a wonderfully jocular weaver to demonstrate his craft in the store, and at the **Donegal Craft Village** just south of town it is possible to see other craftspeople at work, producing jewelry, pottery, ceramics, and batik, which you can buy. (Open May through September; there is also a pleasant coffee shop here.)

Continuing on this road out of town you come to three very good options for accommodation. Loveliest of all, on what was once a tiny island in Donegal Bay, is St. **Ernan's House Hotel**. John Hamilton, a nephew of the duke of Wellington, built the house in 1826 on a grand romantic impulse to cheer his ailing wife. So respected was he as a landlord who cared for his tenants through the harsh years of the potato famine that they later repaid him by building a causeway to the island. From almost all the rooms in what is now a splendid hotel there are marvelous views across a mirror of water. Dinner here is a treat, with candlelight and moonlight adding to the magic.

A much less expensive alternative, sharing some of the same scenic appeal, is **Island View House**, a pristine new bed and breakfast with spacious rooms, less than 1 km (½ mile) on the Donegal Town side of St. Ernan's. The third possibility, a few miles farther south at **Rossnowlagh**— the best surfing beach in Ireland—is the **Sand House Hotel**, a sizable but still cozy establishment that has been run by the Britton family for as long as anybody can remember.

From the Donegal Town area it's only a short drive to **Lough Derg**, which attracts many people between June 1 and August 15 for a rigorous three-day pilgrimage. On Station Island, where Saint Patrick is said to have spent 40 days in prayer and fasting hoping to expel the last evil spirits from Ireland, pilgrims walk barefoot around the "penitential beds" (the remains of monastic cells), deprive themselves of sleep for 24 hours, and are allowed only one "meal" a day (bread and black tea). Only pilgrims are allowed on the island at this time; no prior booking is necessary, but if you are interested in joining the 30,000 people who seek spiritual renewal here every year, you must reach the lakeshore by 3:00 P.M., having fasted from the night before. At Laghy, 5 km (3 miles) south of Donegal Town, take the R 232 southeast to Pettigoe, then the R 233 north, following the Lough Derg signposts. Further information can be obtained from The Prior, St. Patrick's Purgatory, Lough Derg, Pettigoe, County Donegal; Tel: (072) 615-50 in season; (072) 615-18 out of season.

For a memorable challenge of a different sort, follow the main road west out of Donegal Town, praying for fine weather as you go. The drive through the pretty 18th-century village of **Mountcharles** to Killybegs is delightful, with the murky ridge of the Bluestack Mountains to your right and a view to the left of headland upon headland, stretching all the way back to Ben Bulben in County Sligo. Killybegs itself isn't worth stopping in (unless you want to see fish-processing factories and a huge international collection of trawlers); instead, follow the coast-hugging scenic route on to **Kilcar**, where **Studio Donegal** hand-weaves exquisite tweeds for its well-designed hats, jackets, and wall hangings.

Then, if the Donegal mist has kept its distance, go on to

climb **Slieve League**. Stout shoes and stamina are essential, but if you have them both this ascent through landscape that looks as if it was carved out by the Ice Age yesterday may be the nearest you come to heaven on Donegal earth. From the top of the precipice—1,972 feet of worn-away cliff face—there is an unforgettable view. As far as the eye can see, currents sweep the sea in silver arcs, and behind you, far below, two glacial lakes lie like ink blots on the scooped-out valley floor.

The best approach is through Carrick and Teelin, following the signposts up a rough mountain track until you can drive no farther. From here the climb takes about an hour and a half. The last few feet are not for the faint-hearted, or indeed anybody with a tendency to swoon. Should you choose to forego the final ascent you'll still be rewarded: Even the sea views from a slightly lower vantage point will take your breath away.

From Carrick it is only 9 km (5½ miles) west to **Glencolmcille**, an attractive little town nestling in the glen where Donegal's patron saint, Colmcille (Columba), is said to have lived in retreat during the sixth century. On his feast day, June 9, there is a three-and-a-half-hour penitential tour of 15 holy sites in the area. Also of interest is the **Folk Village**, with cottages typical of three different centuries, a tea house, a crafts shop, and a homemade-produce shop selling, among other things, seaweed wine (open Easter to mid-October).

To round off a perfect day on this peninsula, drive back via Killybegs and dine in fine French style in **Castlemurray House** at St. John's Point. It is hard to know which is more delectable, the seafood or the sea views as the sun sets. Thierry Delacros has a few rooms with old Irish furniture above his restaurant for guests who can't bear to tear themselves away.

Ardara, the next town up the coast, established its reputation more than 100 years ago as the weaving capital of Ireland. The poor land of southwest Donegal, better suited to sheep than crops, forced small farmers to supplement their meager income by weaving, while the womenfolk involved themselves in spinning and knitting. Every market day weavers from all over the county would bring their cloth to sell in the streets of Ardara. Now there are only 28 handweavers still at work in the area and the market system is no more, but the town, conscious of its heritage, is opening a new **Weaving Interpretative Centre** this summer in the restored courthouse.

Hand-knitting is still widely practiced all over Donegal, as you will see from Ardara's shop windows, and although the traditional Aran sweaters, which take two weeks to work, are still popular, the range of patterns has broadened to include brighter, more unusual designs. **Kennedys of Ardara** at the top of the town has an excellent selection.

Anyone who is more interested in Guinness than a *geansai* (sweater) should pop into **Nancy's**, a minuscule pub little changed for 200 years, or **The Central Bar**, where the proprietor, Peter Oliver McNelis, plays traditional music every night through the summer. If you decide to stay in the area, **Woodhill House**, once owned by the Nesbitt family, who were landlords around here from the time of Charles I until the 1900s, can be recommended. Its restaurant, serving good, fresh local produce, is open for dinner to non-guests as well; Tel: (075) 411-12.

Central Donegal

From Ardara drive north toward **Dunglow**, taking the scenic loop via **Crohy Head**, where the crashing Atlantic has sculpted the rocks into extraordinary shapes. You are now back in the Gaeltacht (Irish-speaking area); note, on signposts, that Dunglow suddenly becomes An Clochán Liath, "The Gray Stone." In the summer, for the good of their Irish, hordes of young people come from other parts of Ireland to The Rosses and Gweedore (the next peninsular bulges in the coastline to the north). Sometimes they crowd the small ferry that plies between Burtonport and **Arranmore Island** (Arainn Mhór), where they swell the population by 200 during July and August. Even so, the island is perfect for a day-trip. The three-mile crossing takes just 20 minutes, and when you arrive you have a choice of walks with magnificent views back to the mainland, where the white crown of Mount Errigal rises in the distance. The tramp to the lighthouse brings you up over the hills where 300 French soldiers died in battle with the British in 1798.

From Burtonport drive north through the home territory of Donegal's singing heart-throb Daniel O'Donnell. Bunbeg and the small towns that come after it have a dismal, neglected look, and indeed the countryside around them suffers from a severe case of bungalow blight; but it is worth continuing to see the **Bloody Foreland**, so named because this stark headland glows red in the setting sun. As the road ascends you look down on a fringe of rocky coast, and small fields whose stone walls are made of boulders so enormous it is difficult to believe that they were built by hand.

From the Bloody Foreland it is a pleasant 32-km (20-mile) drive on to **Dunfanaghy**, where **Arnolds Hotel**, overlooking Sheephaven Bay, is a good stopping point. A family hotel for generations, Arnolds always has been popular with vacationers in search of simple, moderately priced accommodation; it also offers a wide range of special-interest package vacations, focusing on painting, photography, wildlife, and so on.

If you use Dunfanaghy as a base you will be within easy reach of some of the most splendid scenery in this part of north Donegal. In the center of town you will see a sign for **Horn Head**, a spectacular vantage point from which, looking east, you can see layer upon layer of mountains dipping into the sea. Walking is not necessary, now that a circular road skirts the entire headland. More energetic visitors should consider climbing **Errigal** and/or **Muckish**, the two peaks that dominate so many views of north Donegal—the first a quartzite cone not unlike Croagh Patrick and the second a long, sloping mountain (Muckish means "pig's back" in Irish). The easiest ascent of Errigal is from the R 251 east of **Dunlewy**. Muckish may be climbed from **Falcarragh**, west of Dunfanaghy on the N 56.

Falcarragh is also one of the access points to Tory Island, which you may have glimpsed from the Bloody Foreland, its outline like a paper knife with a curved handle lying in the sea.

Tory Island

For the most adventurous, a trip to Tory could be the high point of everything seen or experienced in Ireland. It must be stressed, however, that this is not a place to go on a day trip, nor is it a suitable destination for those who like their comforts. The island lies 8 miles out to sea, and the crossing is often slow and rough (there is also a risk of being marooned on the island when the weather turns treacherous). To make matters worse, there is no Irish Tourist Board–approved accommodation on the island; intrepid visitors, most of them young and prepared to rough it, bring a sleeping bag and find themselves a floor on which to sleep. Alternatively, islanders can sometimes be talked into providing simple bed and breakfast. Those who do make the trip, however, usually feel it is worthwhile.

Bound up with the legend of Balor of the One Eye, god-chief of a race of pirates, the island is primitive, pagan, and terribly beautiful. In spite of its isolation it has been populated (however sparsely) for 4,000 years. In the sixth century Saint Colmcille founded a monastery here, whose round tower survives. More recently Tory has become associated with naïve art: Island fishermen with a talent for painting have been encouraged over the last 30 years by the British artist Derek Hill, who visits Tory every summer. For ferry details see Getting Around at the end of this chapter.

North Donegal

After Dunfanaghy on N 56 south, the next town to look out for is Kilmacrennan. **Lurgy Vale Cottage** here is a restored thatched dwelling with interesting old farm implements on show, and *ceili* music on Thursday evenings throughout the summer. From Kilmacrennan follow signposts for two of north Donegal's loveliest inland attractions.

The first, southeast of Kilmacrennan near the village of Church Hill, is the **Glebe House and Gallery**, donated to the nation, along with the adjacent house, by the painter Derek Hill. The gallery, in a converted stableyard, exhibits works from Hill's own collection of major Irish and European artists (Picasso included). The gallery is open daily from May–September; closed Fridays. In St. Columb's, his old home opposite, you can see fascinating objets d'art collected over a lifetime and arranged with flair. Don't miss the kitchen with its traditional Donegal spongewear bowls and Tory Island paintings. (Open Easter and the end of May through September.)

From Church Hill it is a short drive west to **Glenveagh National Park**, 25,000 acres of mountain, lake, and woodland with wild deer at large and the turrets of a fairytale castle poking above the tree line. It brings to mind a 19th-century romantic landscape painting—and is quite unlike anything else in Donegal. Leave your car in the parking lot, get your bearings in the Visitor Centre, and from here catch one of the frequent shuttle buses down to the castle, tea rooms, gardens, and the starting points of various delightful walks.

The castle (open to the public) was built in 1870 by John Adair, notorious for his savage practices as a landlord. His wife, remembered more graciously, was the wealthy daughter of General James Wadsworth, eminent in the American Civil War. She survived her husband by some 30 years, and the American connection she brought continued after her. The Philadelphia millionaire Henry McIlhenny restored the entire property between 1940 and 1970, creating some of the most exotic gardens in Ireland—one Italian, one Belgian, one terraced with statues, one walled with a Gothic orangery, and the last aptly named "Pleasure Ground." Sheltered here beside the house, exotic trees and flowers flourish, in striking contrast with the wildness of the glen. Glenveagh is open daily, April through October; Tel: (074) 370-88. En route to or from Glenveagh, look out for the **Glenveagh Inn**, an attractive pub with good bar food in an old stone farmhouse.

Letterkenny, north Donegal's main commercial center, is a sprawling town with no particular appeal, but you should consider staying a night or two in the vicinity in order to explore the unspoiled **Fanad Peninsula**. One possible lodging choice is **Castlegrove House**, 5 km (3 miles) out on the Ramelton road, a fine Georgian guest house on the shores of Lough Swilly. An impressive dinner menu is served in the room where young Daniel O'Connell practiced rhetoric long before he embraced politics. Shooting (coarse, driven pheasant, and duck) can be arranged for small groups.

Ramelton, also on Lough Swilly, is a handsome town that has retained its Georgian character, with fine warehouses left over from prosperous trading days. For information on a suggested walking tour check the map posted outside the 18th-century Fish House–turned-museum on the quay.

Pretty **Rathmullan**, 11 km (7 miles) northeast along the shore, sits at one end of a glorious mile of golden sand. It was from here, in 1607, that the earls of Tyrconnell and Tyrone embarked for France—an event known as the Flight of the Earls—which marked the virtual end of the Gaelic order in Ireland and made way for the plantation of Ulster with English and Scottish colonists. **The Flight of the Earls Heritage Centre** beside the pier recounts the story.

Rathmullan House, above the beach, was built by the Batt banking family of Belfast in the 1830s. At the time of the First World War there were five girls in the family, and the Batts went bankrupt holding expensive parties in an attempt to marry them off to officers of the British navy, which was then using Lough Swilly as a base. Since 1963 Rathmullan House has been a country-house hotel, which grows ever more luxurious. The grandiosely named "Egyptian baths" (sauna, steam room, and salt-water swimming pool with pillars and mosaic) are the latest addition.

If you prefer less expensive accommodation, head over the garden wall (literally) for the grounds of **The Old Rectory**, an exceptionally comfortable and friendly place adjoining the property of Rathmullan House.

One kilometer (½ mile) north of Rathmullan on the **Portsalon** road, look for a yellow house perched on a hill to your left, with an elephant sign at the end of its long drive. Here, **Garrett Carton** turns beautiful bowls, lamp bases, breadboards, and other useful items from the many kinds of wood found in Donegal, while his wife, Margaret, creates exquisite cards and pictures from pressed flowers. Browsers are welcome.

Stay on this road for the magnificent **Fanad Drive**. It hugs the cliffs, then climbs right up over the end of Knockalla Mountain, revealing the wide yellow ribbon of **Ballymacstocker**, one of the loveliest beaches in Donegal, directly below. After Portsalon (where **Rita's** old-fashioned bar-cum-shop has an intriguing assortment of wares dangling from the ceiling), the road twists and climbs all the way up to Fanad Head, where the **Lighthouse Tavern** is the last refuge before Reykjavik. For a change of scene on the way back, follow the road that skirts Mulroy Bay. Its quiet waters are dotted with tiny islands, one, it is claimed, for every day of the year.

Try, before you leave Donegal, to visit the **Inishowen Peninsula**, easily reached via Letterkenny up the east side of Lough Swilly. Even if you don't have time to do the 160-km (100-mile) scenic tour loop (clearly signposted "Inis Eoghain 100"), there are two high points that shouldn't be missed. On a hilltop 11 km (7 miles) south of Fahan off the N 13 stands the **Grianan of Aileach**, a spectacular circular fort, terraced inside in the style of a Roman arena. It is thought to date to 1700 B.C. and was later the royal headquarters of the O'Neills, kings of Ulster. About 30 km (19 miles) farther north, an uncharacteristically straight stretch of road leads skyward into the **Mamore Gap**, from the top of which there is yet another wonderful view of the sea. Far below on the coastal plain the long narrow fields are stitched together in one long row—a brilliantly designed green patchwork.

GETTING AROUND

Regular air service links Sligo and Knock to the international airport at Dublin. For Donegal, the nearest airport is in Derry, a short distance across the border in Northern Ireland; flights are available from Glasgow and Manchester. Rental cars are available at all these airports, but it is advisable to reserve in advance. In Sligo, Tel: (071) 682-80; Knock, Tel: (094) 672-22; Derry, Tel: (08504) 81-07-84.

ACCOMMODATIONS REFERENCE

The telephone country code for the Northwest is 353. When dialing telephone numbers in the Republic from outside the country, drop the 0 in the area code. The rate ranges given below are projections *for the low and high seasons in 1993; for up-to-the-minute rate information it is always wise to telephone before booking. Unless otherwise indicated, rates are per person sharing and include breakfast but not service.*

County Mayo

▶ **Ashford Castle. Cong**, County Mayo. Tel: (092) 460-03; Fax: (092) 462-60. £69–£110.

▶ **Atlantic Hotel. Dooagh**, Achill Island, County Mayo. Tel: (098) 432-39. Closed October through Easter. £14–£16 plus 10 percent service.

▶ **Delphi Lodge. Delphi.** (Note: postal address is Leenane, County Galway). Tel: (095) 422-11; Fax: (095) 422-96. Closed November through December. £30–£42.50.

▶ **Enniscoe House.** Castlehill near Crossmolina, **Ballina**, County Mayo. Tel: (096) 311-12; Fax: (096) 317-73. Closed mid-October through March. £40–£45.

▶ **Gray's Guest House. Doogort**, Achill Island, County Mayo. Tel: (098) 432-44. £16–£20.

▶ **Mount Falcon Castle. Ballina**, County Mayo. Tel and Fax: (096) 211-72. £32.50–£40.

▶ **Newport House. Newport**, County Mayo. Tel: (098) 412-22; Fax: (098) 416-13. Closed October through mid-March. £45–£58.

▶ **The Olde Railway Hotel. Westport**, County Mayo. Tel: (098) 251-66; Fax: (098) 250-90. £25–£42.

County Sligo

▶ **Ballincar House Hotel.** Rosses Point Road, **Sligo**, County Sligo. Tel: (071) 453-61; Fax: (071) 441-98. £40–£45.

▶ **Coopershill House. Riverstown**, County Sligo. Tel:

(071) 651-08; Fax: (071) 654-66. Closed November through mid-March. £38–£40.

► **Cromleach Lodge. Ballindoon,** Castlebaldwin, County Sligo. Tel: (071) 651-55; Fax: (071) 654-55. £40–£68.

► **Temple House. Ballymote,** County Sligo. Tel: (071) 833-29; Fax: (071) 838-08. Closed December until Easter. £30.

► **Urlar House. Carney,** Drumcliff, County Sligo. Tel: (071) 631-10. Facilities for pets. Closed November through February. £14–£16.

County Donegal

► **Arnolds Hotel. Dunfanaghy,** County Donegal. Tel: (074) 362-08 or 361-42; Fax: (074) 363-52. Closed November through mid-March. £21–£25.

► **Castlegrove House.** Ramelton Road, **Letterkenny,** County Donegal. Tel: (074) 511-18; Fax: (074) 513-84. £20–£25.

► **Castlemurray House.** Saint John's Point, **Bruckless,** County Donegal. Tel: (073) 370-22. Closed mid-September through mid-June. £18–£22.

► **Island View House.** Ballyshannon Road. **Donegal Town,** County Donegal. Tel: (073) 224-11. £13–£15.

► **The Old Rectory. Rathmullan,** County Donegal. Tel: (074) 582-26. Closed November through Easter. No smoking. £14–£15.

► **Rathmullan House. Rathmullan,** County Donegal. Tel: (074) 581-88; Fax: (074) 582-00; In U.S., (800) 223-6510. Closed mid-November through mid-March. £36–£58, 10 percent service included.

► **Sand House Hotel. Rossnowlagh,** County Donegal. Tel: (072) 517-77; Fax: (072) 521-00. Closed October through Easter. £35–£45.

► **St. Ernan's House Hotel. Donegal Town,** County Donegal. Tel: (073) 210-65; Fax: (073) 220-98. Closed mid-November through Easter. £38–£60.

► **Woodhill House. Ardara,** County Donegal. Tel: (075) 411-12. £22.

THE BORDER COUNTIES

FERMANAGH, TYRONE, AND DERRY—WITH A DIP INTO CAVAN AND MONAGHAN

By Colm Tóibín

Colm Tóibín was born near Dublin and works there as a journalist and broadcaster. He has edited both of Ireland's current affairs magazines and is the author of a novel, The South, *and a travel book,* Walking Along the Border.

The border counties in Northern Ireland are dominated by water—rivers and lakes that offer some of the best and the widest range of fish and fishing facilities in the country. The political divide itself is full of anomalies: A boat can cross the border on Lough Erne without the slightest interference from the security forces, for example, and yet some of the official road crossings have fortress-like checkpoints.

Huge differences exist as well in the quality of the land in these counties. Large estates of good pasture stand side by side with 30-acre holdings of poorly drained land, just as hauntingly desolate scenery, narrow roads, bogland, and lakeland can be found only a few miles away from major motorways.

MAJOR INTEREST

Ardhowen Theatre
Blake's of the Hollow public house in Enniskillen
Lough Erne cruising
The Marble Arch Caves
Monaghan County Museum
Ulster Fleadh Ceoil
Ulster American Folk Park
Ardboe High Cross
Walls of Derry Town

Many of the smaller border roads are now sealed, although it is still possible in certain areas for a car to cross and recross the line that divides the North of Ireland from the Republic without drawing the attention of the security forces. At most border crossings, however, British Army checkpoints bring cars to a stop until a soldier can check the license number of the car on a computer. Normally he asks for identification, and he may also ask where you are going. The soldiers are usually polite, and in general crossing the border is not a problem.

In this landscape of low hills and constantly changing light, the villages are general sleepy and old-fashioned, the atmosphere quiet, modest, and low-key. The recent filming of *The Playboys* here, starring Albert Finney, captured this beauty. Most people in the border areas genuinely welcome tourists, although the clientele in certain bars in some towns and villages may be less than forthcoming (the local economy on both sides of the border depends on smuggling, and some people are wary of strangers). However, most locals will be extremely helpful when asked for directions—which is fortunate, because the signposting in this part of Ireland is truly appalling; even when signs exist, they may point the wrong way.

The hotels in the border area offer some of the only restaurant facilities. Lunch is generally available for less than five pounds in hotels, and soup and sandwiches can be had in the bigger and more modern public houses and lounge bars. There is no particular style of cooking or type of fare available in these towns to make them different from anywhere else in Ireland. Most menus include roast beef, chicken, and some common type of fish both for lunch and for dinner; some offer fresh vegetables, although most of the food comes from the freezer. For this reason Franco's restaurant in Enniskillen,

the Sheelin in Bellanaleck, and Brown's in Derry (see below) stand out as the only three restaurants in this whole area that can be wholeheartedly recommended.

This section details the three counties that make up the western half of Northern Ireland. First we explore Fermanagh, the northern county whose border touches four counties in the Republic—Monaghan, Cavan, Leitrim, and Donegal; then we move north through County Tyrone, bordered on the west by Donegal, and the most sparsely populated of the six Northern Ireland counties, up into Derry, which forms the northwest corner of Northern Ireland.

COUNTY FERMANAGH

Fermanagh is the most developed and the most interesting of the border counties. The center of Fermanagh is Enniskillen, which has all the signs of a garrison town rather than a border town. The difference is important: A border town depends on trade and the economy of its hinterland. Thus, most border towns in recent years have become synonymous with depression, particularly in the South. Irish towns such as Dundalk, Clones, and Lifford have been badly affected by border tensions, by the loss of their natural hinterland, and more so in recent years since many products have become cheaper across the border in the North.

Enniskillen

Oddly enough, however, the border towns on the North side, such as Newry, Castlederg, and Strabane, have the same air of depression. Architecturally these towns all have a ramshackle appearance. Although each has individual buildings of distinction, there is no harmonious streetscape, no legacy of planning, no sense of money—things that distinguish Enniskillen and make it a sort of capital for the border counties.

Although there are a few 19th-century terraces in Enniskillen, most of the business quarter in the town center was built piecemeal. Some of the buildings are from the last century, but most date from the early years of the 20th century (as do most buildings in Irish market towns). Despite Enniskillen's lakeside location it is possible to

walk along the main street without being aware of Lough
Erne, as hardly any buildings in town front the water.

The best place to stay is the **Killyhevlin Hotel**, about 2
km (1¼ miles) south of town near the River Erne, which
connects Upper and Lower Lough Erne. In addition to the
usual rooms, the hotel has more than a dozen comfortably furnished small wooden chalets right on the bank of
the river, which, unlike many rivers in the border region,
is full and strong-flowing, even in the summer. These
accommodations are meant for fishermen but are available to other guests as well. The chalets have been carefully designed to blend in with the landscape and, because they can be heated in winter, are open year-round.
All have cooking facilities, but guests can also avail themselves of the hotel's dining room. Rates for rooms in the
hotel and those for the chalets (which each sleep up to
six people) are reasonable.

Of special architectural interest in the area, between
the Killyhevlin Hotel and Enniskillen, is the recently built
Ardhowen Theatre, a simple construction of steel and
glass that reflects the vast expanse of water in front of it—
a bend in the River Erne—and the sky above. The
theater's program is eclectic, ranging from local bands
specializing in American country-and-western music
(which is extremely popular here) to touring drama
groups. The complex also includes a café.

The program for the Ardhowen and other information
on local events and accommodations are available at the
excellent visitors' center opposite the bus station in Enniskillen. The center also has information on local fishing
facilities and stocks any fishing permits and licenses that
may be necessary.

Beyond the bus station on the banks of the river is the
public leisure center, which contains a heated swimming
pool and other sports facilities including squash and
racquetball courts. Nearby is the dock from which the
Kestrel leaves every day between July and September for
cruises around the islands in Lough Erne. In May and
June this trip is available only on Sunday afternoons.

Enniskillen has one of the best public houses in Ireland and one of the best restaurants in the border area.
The bar, **Blake's of the Hollow**, stands in the town's main
shopping street almost exactly opposite the Church of
Ireland. It is, first of all, an extremely friendly bar and a
good place to find out about local events and sights. More
than a hundred years old, it has a beautifully carved

wooden ceiling. Most Irish public houses are smoky and dark; Blake's, on the other hand, is opulent and bright. If most Irish pubs are churches or chapels, then Blake's is a cathedral. In cold weather a fire blazes in the downstairs snug (a small closed-off area of a bar offering a certain amount of privacy); up a few steps you'll find more tables and chairs, another snug, and a pool table in the back room.

If you go down the lane across the street from Blake's and then turn right, you'll find **Franco's Italian Restaurant**, which serves particularly fine fresh seafood as well as excellent pizzas and Italian dishes. Should pheasant be on the menu, you've come on a good day and are in a for a particular treat. The wine list is also good.

Enniskillen is full of small pleasures like Blake's and Franco's, and also boasts a good bookstore, **Hall's**. For crafts in Enniskillen visit **Fermanagh Cottage Industries** at 14 East Bridge Street, where handmade crochet work and local linen are sold. Enniskillen is a solid town, prosperous during business hours and quiet, almost empty, after six in the evening. There is no strong British Army presence here; instead, the town is patrolled by the local police. It is the perfect place to spend a few days before getting to know the lakes.

The Lough Erne Area

The best way to enjoy the lakes is by power boat; a car journey around the shores of Lough Erne can give you only a vague sense of what is hidden away on its small islands. The cruisers, comfortable and easy to manage, range in size from two to eight berths. They are available for rental virtually year-round, and can navigate the lakes from Belleek near the border with the Republic's County Donegal in the northwest down to Belturbet across the border in County Cavan at the south.

Even in high summer there is a great stillness on the lakes, and it is always possible to tie up at one of the numerous islands without meeting another boatload of sailors. The jetties are well maintained without being too obtrusive. Even when the weather is bad a steely gray splendor about the lakes and the islands makes this trip a unique experience.

You can get a sense of Lough Erne on a two- to three-day trip. Numerous places on the lake rent boats, the most popular probably being at **Kesh**, north of Enniskillen, but the tourist office in Enniskillen can sort this out for you. Also at Kesh is the **Ardress Craft Centre**, run by Dorothy Pendry, who spins her own wool from her own sheep and runs a crafts shop where work by local people is shown and sold. She also runs courses in various crafts.

The islands are clearly marked on the detailed map provided with each boat. Three of the islands in the Lower Lough should definitely be visited, as they contain fascinating monuments from the 10th, 11th, and 12th centuries; all three—White, Inishmacsaint, and Devinish—have jetties for cruisers. The seven stone figures on **White Island** date from the 10th century and have been placed under a shelter within the ruined 12th-century church. The first one on the left is a *sile-na-gig,* a traditional female fertility figure; the other six are clerical figures holding religious objects. It could be said that some of them look distinctly glum in the presence of the fertility figure.

To come across these strange figures suddenly in the middle of an old ruin on a lonely island is a good reminder that Lough Erne was once inhabited by monks, and that Early Christian sites have been found on most of the islands. If you keep the cruiser away from the main mooring places and tie up instead on one of the smaller islands, you will be able to sit up on deck and watch the sky darken over the dim outline of the islands all around and know that almost nothing has changed in this landscape since the time of the monks.

The second island in Lower Lough Erne is **Inishmacsaint**, which has a very stark and beautiful 14-foot-high 10th-century cross, as well as the ruins of a 12th-century church. The third island, **Devinish**, is included on the daily *Kestrel* boat tour from Enniskillen, and is by far the most popular in Lough Erne. Its most prominent feature is a 12th-century round tower more than 80 feet high, which can be ascended by a series of wooden ladders. There are also a number of interesting Early Christian ruins on the island, which is just north of Enniskillen. From the cruiser you can see Portora Royal School in Enniskillen (on the hill to the left as you approach the town)—the alma mater of both Oscar Wilde and Samuel Beckett.

Upper Lough Erne, on the south side of town, is narrower than the Lower Lough and more desolate. ("Upper" means farther from the outflow, so in this case it means the southern part of the lake.) The **Sheelin Restaurant**, in a thatched cottage just beside the jetty at **Bellanaleck**, south-west across the lake from Enniskillen on the A 509, is open for lunch and dinner six days a week in the summer (it's closed for dinner on Mondays), but it is important to book in advance (Tel: 0365/822-32). This popular old-fashioned restaurant draws locals, tourists, and visitors alike to enjoy the fresh local produce, meats, and fish served in a comfortable, intimate atmosphere. Saturday night is gourmet night, when the duck and salmon are particularly good. The Sheelin can also be reached by road; stop off first at **Cathcart's Supermarket** across the way and buy some of its excellent brown bread. (If you're on a boat with children, the Sheelin will find you a baby-sitter while you have dinner.)

The Upper Lough is navigable as far south as **Belturbet** in County Cavan in the Republic. During this stretch the cruiser will cross the border several times, although there will be no line, mark, notification, or, indeed, customs control. If you're going as far as Belturbet, however, it's important to have Irish currency. The **Diamond Bar** in Belturbet's main square is a friendly, well-kept, popular meeting place. Fishing in the waters around Belturbet is excellent, and draws visitors back to the town year after year. There are a number of adequate bed-and-breakfast houses in town, but nothing exceptional.

Several other sights in the Enniskillen area should not be missed. The first of these is the Janus-faced red-sandstone **Boa Island Figure** on an island in Lower Lough Erne that can be reached more easily by car than by boat. It's a short drive north from Enniskillen to Kesh and then to Boa Island, which can be reached by a bridge. The trip can also be made by taxi, readily available in Enniskillen and quite cheap—50p per mile, as opposed to a pound per mile in the Republic. A list of taxi drivers can be found in the local telephone book.

Once on Boa Island, be aware that the signposting is not clear. Look for a wooden sign on the left that says "Caldragh Cemetery." The figure, which dates from the pre-Christian period, squats in the graveyard, almost hidden by gravestones and tall grass. One side has been slightly damaged, but both faces still manage to look somewhat menacingly at the unwary and wary alike. Most such statues are kept in museums, so it is extraordinary and refreshing to come across this image from pagan times on a plinth in the middle of a cemetery in a remote part of the country. There is a replica of the figure and other ancient artifacts in the museum at Enniskillen Castle.

On the way back to Enniskillen, but still on Boa Island, there is a sign on the right for **Lusty Beg**, a small island on Lough Erne. In the summer you can telephone from the mainland for a ferryboat to pick you up and take you over to the **Lusty Beg Chalets and Restaurant**. The island is small enough so that guests in the chalets are always aware of the lake all around. In addition to providing the novelty of sleeping on a small island, the accommodation offered is comfortable, clean, and useful as a base for fishing on Lough Erne.

There are also ten log cabins known as the **Ely Island Chalets** on Ely Island, which can be reached by taking the A 46 from Enniskillen toward Belleek and turning right 8 km (5 miles) outside of Enniskillen. The cabins, which have recently been completed, are very comfortable and tastefully decorated, and sleep five or six people. The owners rent boats and equipment for water-skiing and fishing. The island is extremely popular, so it's advisable to book well in advance.

Around Enniskillen

Southwest of Enniskillen there are two interesting sights. One is **Florence Court**, an 18th-century mansion that was once the home of the earls of Enniskillen; it's famous today for the sumptuous Rococo plasterwork on the ceilings. The house is open to the public each afternoon except Tuesdays. To get there take the A 4 and then the A 32 for roughly 6 km (3½ miles) south of Enniskillen, then turn right. Florence Court is clearly marked on the road that leads to Blacklion in County Cavan in the Republic.

Farther west toward Blacklion, on the same road as Florence Court, are the **Marble Arch Caves**, open from April to September. It is important to telephone in advance (Tel: 0365/82-88-55) to reserve a place on the guided tours of this complex and elaborate underground system, which has only recently been opened to the public. (If there's been a lot of rain, the caves are closed.) The tour consists of a boat journey along an underground river and a trip along a "Moses Walk" cut through an underground lake, as well as a tour of caverns. (A Moses Walk is a passage cut through a pool or lake; cement is placed on the bed of the pool and walls are constructed to the same height as the water, thus creating a path through the water that seems to defy logic. As you pass through, your feet are at the same level as the bottom of the pool; you are protected from the water by the walls, but your face, say, is at the same level as the water.)

Tullyhona House, a bed and breakfast close by the Marble Arch Caves, can be recommended for its hospitality and general air of warmth as well as its excellent breakfasts. It's located on the right-hand side of the road as you drive toward Belcoo from Florence Court, and is marked by a sign at the entrance to the long avenue that leads to the new two-story farmhouse. An evening meal is also served here (there is an à la carte menu); the prices are extremely reasonable.

In addition to Lough Erne three other lakes close to Enniskillen are worth exploring. The first is **Lough Melvin**, which straddles the border between Leitrim and Fermanagh southwest of Belleek. The landscape around this lake is rugged and remote, resembling the rough terrain of the West of Ireland more than the softer landscape of Fermanagh. The fishing in Lough Melvin is very good, and it is easy to hire a boat with a boatman who knows the lake. There are no hotels in the lakeside village of Garrison, but there is a hostel, the **Lough Melvin Holiday Centre**, with none of the discomforts usually associated with such facilities; there is no curfew, there are carpets on the floors and duvets on the beds, and the building is adequately heated. The hostel has a family room as well as a number of dormitories, a room for drying out wet clothes, and a dining room. The Holiday Centre also organizes a great number of water-based sports activities, such as wind-surfing, sailing, and canoeing, and its restaurant, open all day until 8:00 P.M., serves dishes prepared with fresh fish from the lake, among other selections. A serviced campsite and caravan (RV or trailer) park attached to the hostel is open between April and September.

An even more felicitous option is to stay at **Roskit**, a house on a small island in Lough Melvin, run by Mrs. Moody. A causeway to the island leads from the road that goes west from Garrison to the border. Take the Beleek Road from Garrison and turn at the sign for the east side of Lough Melvin; continue for 7 km (4 miles) to the sign for Roskit. The land around Lough Melvin is poor, the roads are narrow, and most of the houses are modest. Roskit is different. Though medium in size, it is beautiful—carefully decorated and surrounded by superbly kept gardens. There is a boat on hand for fishing for guests staying at the house, and full board is available. The rates are very reasonable indeed, considering the amount of comfort and care given. The lake beyond the garden is famous for two rare types of trout, the gillaroo and the sonaghan. For anyone needing a rest in comfortable, tasteful surroundings with good food, this island haven in one of Ireland's best fishing lakes is perfect. Understandably, Roskit is often booked, so Mrs. Moody requires at least two days' notice. Usually guests stay for several days; it is hardly worth trying Roskit for one night.

Another lake, **Lough Macnean**, is close to the Marble Arch Caves and Florence Court. Between the upper and lower lakes of Lough Macnean are the towns of **Belcoo** in the North and **Blacklion** in the Republic; a short bridge links the two. Both towns are close to the **Ulster Way** and the **Cavan Way**, trails that have been built and cleared for intrepid walkers and hikers. The area around Blacklion—where the two Ways in fact converge—is of great interest because of the sheer concentration of ancient monuments. With a good map (an Ordnance Survey map can be purchased from most large newsagents) it should be easy to explore the chamber tombs and gallery graves (dating from the early Iron Age to the late Middle Ages) in nearby **Burren**, the cairns in **Legalough**, and the ringforts in **Moneygashel**—all within 6 km (3½ miles) of Blacklion and along the 17-km (11-mile) Cavan Way.

While the Cavan Way runs south from Blacklion in the Republic, the Ulster Way runs exclusively through the North. It is 500 miles long and is clearly signposted all of the way. You can start, for example, near Blacklion and continue across South Fermanagh to Lough Erne. Or, take up the Way just below Fivemiletown, near the border between Fermanagh and Tyrone, and continue into Antrim and Down. The landscape, so varied in these regions, is reflected along the Ulster Way. Most of the time the trail keeps away from main roads, leading through a wild rural landscape of small hills and forests interspersed by the tributaries of Lough Erne.

Walking anywhere in the border area is richly rewarding, not only because most local people will stop and talk, but also because of the views proffered from the many hills and ridges. This is particularly true along the route through counties Fermanagh and Tyrone. The tourist office in Enniskillen has brochures on each stage of the

Ulster Way, and the route is marked on the Michelin map of Ireland. Full details on the Ulster Way are also provided in a series of well-illustrated pamphlets from the Northern Ireland Tourist Board in Belfast (Tel: 0232/23-12-21).

Upper and Lower Lough Macnean are famous for their heavyweight pike; boats can be hired on either side of the border by those who want to do battle with these monster fish. Another excellent fishing lake is **Lough Oughter**, in County Cavan in the Republic, south of Belturbet and west of Cavan Town. The lake is surrounded by **Killykeen Forest Park**, where 20 self-catering chalets—the **Killykeen Forest Park Chalets**—have been built. There's a tennis court on the site, a golf course nearby, and a beach beside the lake; chalet guests can also take boats out to the lake islands. The chalets themselves, which sleep up to six people, are beautifully designed, though they resemble Scandinavian houses more than any native Irish model. Weekly rates are quite reasonable, even in the high summer season, and the chalets can be rented year-round, for a weekend or a few midweek days, as they have central heating and double glazing as well as solaria and balconies.

The latest addition to visitor facilities in the Cavan area is the 150-room **Slieve Russell Hotel**, which can be reached by taking the N 3 from Cavan to Belturbet and then continuing toward Ballyconnell. Although the hotel itself is somewhat overdesigned, its excellent indoor sports facilities include a large swimming pool, a gym, squash courts, and two tennis courts. The **Conall Cearnach** restaurant, which serves good (if not too adventurous) Irish food, is generally very heavily booked, so visitors would be well advised to telephone in advance; Tel: (049) 264-44.

COUNTY MONAGHAN

Northeast of Cavan is the Republic county of Monaghan, with its principal town of the same name. The **Monaghan County Museum** in the town's main square is one of the best of its size in Ireland, having among its exhibits examples of local traditional arts and crafts, archaeological finds, and the 12th- to 13th-century Cross of Clogher. There are also displays of clerical vestments and an assortment of prehistoric artifacts.

Also on the square is the **Market House**, which dates

from 1792 and is noted for its fine stonework and woodwork. Recently restored, it now houses the tourist office and an exhibition space and is one of the venues for the **Monaghan Jazz Festival**, which is held every September in Monaghan Town. For information, Tel: (047) 811-22.

In November at **Carrickmacross** Kavanagh's Yearly festival celebrates the life and work of the poet Patrick Kavanagh, who died in 1967. He was born at Iniskeen in the eastern part of County Monaghan, where his birthplace is open to the public. For more information contact Bernard Loughlin (Tel: 047/540-03).

In the month of July there are two events in the border area that are worth attending. The first is known as the **Ulster Fleadh Ceoil** (Gaelic for "Festival of Music"). Normally, the Ulster Fleadh Ceoil is held at the end of July in one of the towns on the Republic's side of the border, but several years ago it was held in Warrenpoint in the North. Musicians and traditional singers come from all parts of Ireland for the events, but most of the participants are from the North.

The best music can be heard at informal sessions that begin casually when two or three musicians who know one another go into a pub and start playing. During the Ulster Fleadh (there are also *fleadhanna* in other provinces, as well as the All-Ireland Fleadh) there are sessions going on in most bars and, if the weather is good, in the streets as well. The public houses stay open until the early hours of the morning, and a sense of wild abandon fills the main streets and squares before dawn arrives. The phone number, in Dublin, for information on dates and venues is (01) 280-0295.

The other major event of the month occurs on July 12, the anniversary of the battle of the Boyne (1690), in which the Protestant king William defeated the Catholic king James. Twelfth of July marches take place all over the North. In certain regions the celebration has very serious sectarian overtones, and in other places it is just a pleasant outing for the family.

Of all the places to stay in the border area, one house stands out for its luxury, hospitality, and good food. This is **Hilton Park**, beside the village of Scotshouse just south of the border on L 44, 6 km (3½ miles) southwest of Clones. Home of the Madden family since the 18th century, Hilton Park is a huge house, having been added to and refurbished repeatedly during the past two centuries. The shutters on the ground-floor windows are made of steel

and have small apertures for rifles should the need arise
to defend the house. Most of the guest bedrooms have
enormous four-poster beds and overlook beautifully landscaped gardens, which include oak trees grown from the
acorns brought here more than a hundred years ago as
wedding presents by ancestors of one of today's incum-
bents. In the evening before dinner there is usually a
roaring fire in the drawing room. The owner and host,
Johnny Madden, is a great source of information on local
events and the history of the area. His wife, Lucy, is a
marvelous cook; most of the food, including the cheeses,
comes from the estate. The house is close enough to the
principal towns— less than 24 km (15 miles) from Monaghan Town or Enniskillen—to be used as a base for
touring.

The North is full of big houses, small cottages, and
hardly anything in between. One of the largest of the
estates belonged to the Leslie family, who still live at
Castle Leslie at **Glaslough** (on R 185) north of Monaghan
Town. However, their lands, once 80,000 acres, are now
much reduced. The Leslies run an equestrian center on
the estate, and horses are available for trekking. One of
the gate lodges to Castle Leslie was designed by Nash; the
house itself was built in 1878.

The **Pillar House** is a good, small, inexpensive hotel at
one of the entrances to the Leslie estate. The houses in
the village of Glaslough, a town built and maintained by
the Leslies, are stone-built, and the village is unusual for
its picturesque uniformity. About 1 km (½ mile) to the
southwest is an ancient site at **St. Donagh's Church**, which
has a medieval High Cross that was found in a bog in 1911
and erected in the graveyard.

COUNTY TYRONE

A quarter of a million Northerners emigrated to the
United States in the 18th century. By the time of the
signing of the Declaration of Independence, one-sixth of
the population of the 13 colonies was of Ulster origin.
Dotted throughout the North are the ancestral homes of a
number of American presidents, including that of Ulysses
S. Grant in Aughnacloy, on the border between Tyrone
and Monaghan, and the home of Woodrow Wilson's
grandfather in Dergalt, near Strabane.

The **Ulster American Folk Park** at Camphill, 8 km (5

miles) north of Omagh off the main Omagh-to-Derry road (A 5), is dedicated to the preservation of the memory of the Ulster-American heritage. This open-air museum consists of various preserved or reconstructed buildings, as well as a visitors' center with an exhibition space and theater. An audio-visual presentation tells the story of Ulster's emigrants to America, such as the Mellons, forebears of the financier Andrew Mellon. There is also a gift shop and a café.

Typical Early American houses, including a log cabin and an elaborately furnished Pennsylvania long farmhouse, have been set well apart from each other on the 26-acre wooded site. Also on the grounds are a forge, a Presbyterian meeting house, a schoolhouse, a weaver's cottage, and a covered wagon. Blacksmiths, weavers, spinners, and candlemakers in traditional costumes demonstrate their ancient crafts for visitors. Though the performances are interesting, if slightly corny, of real interest are the houses themselves and the furniture, which have been so well reconstructed that you get a genuine sense of being in another world. A new section recently added to the folk park includes a Belfast waterfront scene with an emigrant ship and original quayside buildings that were dismantled in Belfast and reconstructed here. Taped sounds of seagulls, babies crying, and a bustling port accent the presentation. A typical Irish village street, complete with a pub and a traditional chemist shop, has also been added.

Fermanagh, Tyrone, and Derry have a wealth of ancient historic and prehistoric sites, and more are being uncovered constantly in the bogland that abounds in these counties. These include passage graves, dolmens, and stone circles. Some of the most spectacular of the last are the **Bronze Age stone circles** at Beaghmore, northwest of Cookstown near Dunnamore, which were discovered in the peat-covered upland in the 1930s. Most of the stones here are small, less than a foot high; the highest is four feet. They have been cleared of peat, and seven circles are distinct. The site itself, with a spectacular view of the Sperrin Mountains to the north, prompts imaginings of a time when these stones were first put in place. The alignments within this particular system are intriguing and mysterious. Each stone circle would have been aligned with the other monuments in the immediate area, yet they also appear to correspond to the stone circles at Moymore, near Pomeroy, a couple of miles away.

East of Cookstown is **Lough Neagh**, the largest lake in the British Isles and Ireland. Although the lake is navigable, it has not been developed for leisure pursuits in the same way as Lough Erne. The rivers that flow in and out of the lake are very good for fishing, however. **Lough Beg**, north of Lough Neagh on the lower River Bann, has giant pike. There are several swimming and bathing spots on the western side of Lough Neagh, including Traad Point off B 18 near Ballyronan, which also has a marina.

The most interesting ancient monument in the area is the **High Cross** at **Ardboe**, on the lake 14 km (8½ miles) east of Cookstown off B 73. Dating from the tenth century, it is more than 18 feet tall and has 22 carved panels. Although badly worn, they depict stories that can still be identified as Adam and Eve, the Sacrifice of Isaac, the Crucifixion, and other scenes from the Old and New Testaments. The High Cross at Ardboe was once a special place of worship, where the devout prayed and washed in the lake. In the corner of the churchyard is an old tree to which supplicants would hammer coins or other pieces of metal in the hope of having their wishes granted.

The bogland area of North Tyrone and South Derry, between Ardboe and the village of Bellaghy, north of Magherafelt (where many of Seamus Heaney's evocative poems are set), is full of hidden reminders of history and prehistory, and the past seems to hover over everything like a ghost.

West of Omagh, toward the border with County Donegal, the land is barren and lonely, the roads narrow. The small holdings, in general, are Catholic-owned. The British Army and the Royal Ulster Constabulary tend not to use these roads. Instead, they come in and out by helicopter.

There is a strong British Army presence in **Strabane**, which has one of the best and most comfortable hotels in the area, the **Fir Trees Hotel**. Outside town on the Sion Mills road, it offers good food and good service, but more important, perhaps, it is the *only* hotel in the area. Bed-and-breakfast houses are plentiful in the South but scarce in the North; there is nothing in a 15-km (9-mile) radius of Strabane on the northern side of the border other than the Fir Trees Hotel. Reservations should be made in advance to ensure accommodations.

Strabane, a predominantly Catholic town with the highest unemployment rate in western Europe, has been severely damaged by bombs during the past 15 years. One of the buildings that has survived from the 18th century is **Gray's Printing Shop**, on Main Street facing the bridge as you come into town from the Fir Trees Hotel. The shop, which has a Georgian front, is now in the hands of the National Trust. Among the many who served their apprenticeship here was John Dunlap, who would later print the first copies of the American Declaration of Independence, and James Wilson, grandfather of Woodrow Wilson, whose house at Dergalt, 3 km (2 miles) southeast of town, is open to the public.

Strabane and the town of **Lifford**, across the River Foyle, are joined by a short bridge. Lifford, however, is in County Donegal in the Republic. There is a British Army checkpoint on the bridge and a customs post on the Lifford side. The atmosphere in Lifford is strangely similar to that of Strabane—sleepy, untidy, and economically deprived. Its only hotel is now closed, but there are a number of houses in the center of town that offer bed and breakfast. One of the best examples of stone circles in Ireland is the **Beltany Stone Circle**, 64 Bronze Age stones close to Raphoe, not far from Lifford.

COUNTY DERRY

On many maps and some signposts, this county and its principal city are referred to as Londonderry, which is the name the Unionist population would give to Northern Ireland's northwest corner. But no one, Catholic or Protestant, calls the place Londonderry in everyday conversation. The word Derry, by the way, derives from the Gaelic *doire,* which means "place of the oak trees." The Sperrin Mountains, which also spill into County Tyrone, are the most imposing topographical feature in the southern part of County Derry, and its most northerly reaches form part of the Antrim coast. But it is the city of Derry, astride the River Foyle, that dominates the county.

Derry Town

Derry, Northern Ireland's second city, is deeply divided, and it is important to understand the divisions before setting out to explore it. The eastern bank of the Foyle is called the **Waterside** (the railway station—there is a rail link to Belfast—is on this side, as is the A 5, the main road to Strabane) and is inhabited mainly by Protestants. The western side of the river, with the exception of the small area in the center called the Fountain, is inhabited primarily by Catholics in a district called the **Bogside**. The two sides are connected by the Craigavon Bridge. Until the early 1970s the Protestant minority ran the city through an elaborate system of gerrymandering, but the civil rights movement changed that, and there is now a Catholic majority on the city council.

Derry Town, like Strabane, has suffered heavily from bombs, but its 17th-century walls still stand proudly and are one of the most interesting features of the city. Finished in 1618, they withstood three sieges, including the famous (or notorious, depending on which side you're on) siege of 1688, which began when 13 apprentice boys seized the keys of the town and locked the gates against the approaching forces of the deposed Catholic king James II. (This event is celebrated by Protestants each August 12; because of the sectarian tensions it engenders, this is a poor time to visit Derry.) The **walls of Derry** are a mile in length, the old cannon still peer over the ramparts—one a gift in 1590 from Elizabeth I—and, inside, four streets radiate from a center called the Diamond.

It is still possible to make a complete circuit of the walls, except for a short stretch close to St. Columb's that has been taken over by the British Army as a lookout post. Within the walls of Derry, the most interesting building is **St. Columb's Cathedral**, the city's Protestant cathedral, which dates from the early 17th century and was originally built for the early settlers by the City of London. It is full of plaques and memorials to three centuries of the city's rulers. In the chapter house of the cathedral there are relics of the siege, as well as old guns and paintings.

The **Creggan graveyard**, situated on a hill above the Catholic Bogside area, is a stark and powerful monument to the city's recent past. This is by and large a Catholic graveyard, but it is also used by the paramilitaries of the Nationalist side. The gravestones and monuments have elaborate inscriptions; the attendants are very friendly and usually will point visitors to the most interesting graves. There is a superb view of the city below and of the River Foyle as it curls out toward the sea.

As in Strabane, Derry's main hotel is outside the city, on the east side of the Foyle. The modern, well-run **Everglades Hotel** is on the right-hand side of the road as you drive toward the city from Strabane, past the oddly named village of New Buildings. The Everglades has a good restaurant, but the best in Derry and perhaps in all the border counties is **Brown's**, at 1 Victoria Road on the Waterside. The restaurant is in an old converted railway building just before the bridge as you approach the city from the Everglades Hotel. The decor is bright and imaginative, the service friendly and efficient. The extensive menu consists of a mixture of French and Italian cuisine using fresh seafood and fresh local produce. The restaurant is open Tuesday through Friday from 12:30 to 2:30 and 5:30 to 11:00 P.M.; Saturdays from 5:30 to 11:00 P.M., and Sundays from 12:30 to 2:30 and 5:30 to 9:30 P.M. Tel: (0504) 451-80.

During the past few years there has been a considerable amount of development in Derry, including the building of a **castle** on an old site at the entrance to Shipquay Street. It is the focal point for the gatherings of the O'Doherty clan, descendants of the Irish chieftain who led an attack on Derry in 1608. There is a new **railway museum** beside the main bridge that spans the Foyle; displays include many of the old engines and coaches that formerly were used on the lines from Derry to Donegal and from Strabane to Derry. An engine and coach in working order take visitors on a short trip down to the river and back. The museum is open from 10:00 A.M. to 5:00 P.M. Tuesday through Saturday and Sundays from 2:00 to 6:00 P.M., May through September.

Over the past few years Derry has celebrated the festival of Halloween, the last night of October, with fancy-dress parades and much drinking and carousing, followed by a week-long arts festival. The impressive red-sandstone **Guildhall** on Shipquay Place, just outside the walls and close to the river, is the venue for the annual **Field Day** theater production at the end of August. Field Day is a theater touring group whose directors include the poet Seamus Heaney and the playwright Brian Friel, whose great play *Translations* was given its first production here. Each year the company puts on a production of a new Irish play at the Guildhall and then tours it throughout the country. Call the theater company's office in Derry for more information about Field Day; Tel: (0504) 36-01-96.

The **Orchard Gallery**, also in the center of the city, is one of the most energetic and exciting modern art galleries in Ireland (closed Sundays and Mondays). Similarly, the **Bookworm Bookshop**, just off the Diamond, is excellent; it's particularly good on local history, archaeology, and books of Irish interest, but also carries a fine general selection. The Bookworm and Hall's in Enniskillen are the best bookshops in the border area.

Outside Derry Town

Derry Town is a mixture of the dreary and the dynamic. Like other towns in the North, it tends to close down after six, and the streets are often deserted in the evening. The area northeast of the city can be lively, however, particularly the seaside towns of **Portrush** (which is actually in County Antrim and is further discussed in that section, below) and **Portstewart**. Full of old-fashioned summer hotels and boarding houses, these places are a great escape from the troubled history that seems to hang over Derry. **Maddybenny Farm** is a traditional farmhouse run by Mrs. Rosemary White on the Loguestown road. The farm is still in use (they have recently added a riding school), and the house is close to the beach as well as to the town of Portrush. There's a new "Grade A" hotel in Portrush called the **Magherabuoy House Hotel**, built around an old house. The hotel's restaurant is quite good, the average dinner costing about £15. (East along the coast from Portrush are Dunluce Castle and the Giant's Causeway, for which see the Antrim section in the following chapter.)

In Portstewart the family-run **Edgewater Hotel**, at 88 Strand Road, is beautifully situated overlooking the strand. Also in Portstewart, Mrs. Vi Anderson runs a good guest house called **Oregon** in one of the terraced houses so common in Irish towns.

The six-mile-long Atlantic beach northeast of Derry Town begins at Magilligan Point near the mouth of Lough Foyle. This west end of the beach has a **Martello tower** (built in the early 19th century as a look-out and a fortification) like the one in Sandycove in Dublin, where the opening scene of *Ulysses* is set; the other end has the picturesque **Mussenden Temple**, also circular but rather more ornate. This Corinthian-columned temple was once the summer library of Downhill Palace, now in ruins; it was completed in 1785 and is kept in perfect condition by the National Trust.

The sea here is good for fishing, especially for bass, and there are several good golf courses, including the outstanding **Royal Portrush Golf Club** (there are two 18-hole courses at the club), which is open to visitors. Greens fees range from £8 to £15, depending on the season. The telephone number is (0265) 82-23-11. The sport in Derry Town is rather less sedate. The Derry soccer team has its own pitch in the Brandywell area of the city. The club's supporters are without doubt the most loyal and devoted in Ireland; thousands of fans travel with the team to away games. The sense of local pride is enormous. Another good venue for sampling the peculiar flavor of Derry is the **greyhound track** in the Brandywell, where racing is a popular and reasonably nonsectarian sport.

GETTING AROUND

The best roads from Dublin are the N 2 to Monaghan, which crosses the border at Aughnacloy, and the N 3 to Cavan followed by the N 54 from Cavan to Clones; after the border crossing, the A 34 from Clones connects with the A 4 to Enniskillen. The best road from Sligo is the N 16, which crosses the border at Blacklion and Belcoo, and then becomes the A 4 in the North between the border and Enniskillen. There are two ways in from Donegal: The N 15 from the south of the county and the N 14 from the north of the county meet at Lifford, where there is a border crossing into Strabane; the other crossing is at the end of the N 13, which crosses the border close to Derry. All these are official crossings, manned by either Irish or British security forces, and are the routes to and from these counties used by most people, locals included.

Derry is the only town in the border counties that can be reached by rail. The journey from Belfast is very picturesque for the first hour, as the train travels along the coast.

ACCOMMODATIONS REFERENCE

The telephone country codes for these accommodations vary, so they are listed individually. When dialing telephone numbers from outside the country, drop the 0 in the area code. The rates given below are projections for 1993; for up-to-the-minute rate information it is always wise to telephone before booking. Unless otherwise indicated, rates are per person sharing and do not include meals or service.

County Fermanagh

► **Ely Island Chalets.** Ely Lodge, **Enniskillen**, County Fermanagh. Tel: (44) 0365/897-77; Fax: (44) 0365/893-28. £250–£350 sterling per week for six people.

▶ **Killyhevlin Hotel.** Dublin Road, **Enniskillen**, County Fermanagh BT74 4AU. Tel: (44) 0365/32-34-81; Fax: (44) 0365/32-47-26. £35 sterling, breakfast included.

▶ **Lough Melvin Holiday Centre. Garrison**, County Fermanagh. Tel: (44) 0365/65-81-42. £7 sterling for a bed in the dormitory.

▶ **Lusty Beg Chalets and Restaurant.** Lusty Beg Island, **Kesh**, County Fermanagh. Tel: (44) 0365/63-13-42. £350–£450 sterling per week for six people.

▶ **Roskit (Mrs. Moody). Garrison**, County Fermanagh. Tel: (44) 0365/652-31. £40 sterling, breakfast, dinner, and service included.

▶ **Tullyhona House (Mrs. Rosemary Armstrong). Florence Court**, County Fermanagh. Tel: (44) 0365/824-52 or 82-81-70. £13 sterling, breakfast and service included.

County Cavan

▶ **Killykeen Forest Park Chalets (Jim O'Reilly).** Killykeen Forest Park, **Cavan**, County Cavan. Tel: (353) 049/325-41; Telex: 46809 KFP. A six-berth chalet costs IR£230 per week in June, £290 per week in July and August.

▶ **Slieve Russell Hotel. Ballyconnell**, County Cavan. Tel: (353) 049/264-44; Fax: (353) 049/264-74. IR£37.50, breakfast and service included. Weekend rates are IR£125 for two nights' bed and breakfast and two dinners.

County Monaghan

▶ **Hilton Park (Johnny and Lucy Madden). Clones**, County Monaghan. Tel: (353) 047/560-07. Open April to September. IR£42, breakfast and service included.

▶ **Pillar House Hotel. Glaslough**, County Monaghan. Tel: (353) 047/881-25. IR£14, breakfast and service included.

County Tyrone

▶ **Fir Trees Hotel.** Melmount Road, **Strabane**, County Tyrone BT82 9JT. Tel: (44) 0504/38-23-82; Fax: (44) 0504/88-59-32. £30 sterling, breakfast and service included.

County Derry

▶ **Edgewater Hotel.** 88 Strand Road, **Portstewart**, County Derry BT55 7LZ. Tel: (44) 0265/83-22-24; Fax: (44) 0265/83-33-14. £27.50–£33 sterling, breakfast and service included.

▶ **Everglades Hotel.** Prehen Road, **Derry City**, County

Derry BT47 2PA. Tel: (44) 0504/467-22; Fax: (44) 0504/
492-00. £38 sterling, breakfast and service included.

▶ **Oregon (Mrs. Vi Anderson)**. 168 Station Road,
Portstewart, County Derry BT55 7PU. Tel: (44) 0265/83-
28-26. £15–£18 sterling, breakfast and service included.

County Antrim

▶ **Maddybenny Farm (Mrs. Rosemary White)**. 18
Maddybenny Park, Loguestown Road, **Portrush**, County
Antrim BT52 2PT. Tel: (44) 0265/82-33-94. £16–£17.50
sterling, breakfast and service included (there is a discount for children).

▶ **Magherabuoy House Hotel**. 41 Magherabuoy Road,
Portrush, County Antrim BT56 8NX. Tel: (44) 0265/82-35-
07; Fax: (44) 0265/82-46-87. £35 sterling, breakfast and
service included.

THE NORTHEAST

ANTRIM, BELFAST, DOWN, AND ARMAGH

By Sam McAughtry

Sam McAughtry, a native of Belfast and the author of six books, including three collections of short stories, is a former award-winning columnist for the Irish Times *and well known as a radio and television scriptwriter and broadcaster both north and south of the border.*

The Northern Ireland counties of Armagh and Down run northward from the border with the Irish Republic and are adjacent to the South's counties Monaghan and Louth. Armagh is bordered on the west by the North's County Tyrone and on the east by County Down, which runs north on the channel coast as far as Belfast, where it meets County Antrim. Antrim, which has one of Ireland's most beautiful coasts, lies on the eastern side of Northern Ireland all the way up to the northern tip of the island. The largest lake in Ireland, Lough Neagh, is located in the very center of Northern Ireland, its shores formed by parts of five counties: Antrim, Down, Armagh, Tyrone, and Derry.

Like the people in Northern Ireland generally, the residents of counties Antrim, Armagh, and Down are direct and plain in their speech and use fewer words through the day than the people of the rest of Ireland. If they do you a favor and you thank them, they simply will say "You're welcome." It was New World immigrants from Northern

Ireland who put this nice phrase into everyday speech in the United States. To visitors the local people are shyly polite; they usually will not speak to strangers unless they are addressed first. Once the ice is broken, however, the visitor will be surprised at the friendliness of the people, who will go to great lengths to make strangers feel welcome.

Northern Ireland has 300 miles of unpolluted coastline, virtually all of it in County Antrim and County Down, offering some of the best sea fishing in Europe. Sea trout, skate, dogfish, halibut, bass, and mackerel abound. The coast around the Giant's Causeway, near Portrush in north Antrim, is an especially popular fishing ground with visitors, but the County Down coast, including Strangford Lough, offers equally exciting sport to the sea fisherman.

For freshwater fishing there are more than 60 rivers and lakes available, where it is not uncommon to have a long stretch of good trout water to yourself. In the Glens of Antrim there are rivers where both salmon and trout can be caught; the lakes of County Armagh are stocked with rainbow trout and managed by the Department of Agriculture, but good fishing waters in Northern Ireland are, quite literally, too numerous to mention.

MAJOR INTEREST

Fishing

Antrim
Giant's Causeway
Dunluce Castle
Rathlin Island
The nine Glens of Antrim
Carrickfergus Castle

Belfast
Dining and shopping

Down
Saint Patrick's burial place
Mountains of Mourne
Ards Peninsula

Armagh
Armagh City
Navan Fort, ancient Celtic stronghold

Antrim, Down, and Armagh

0 |———————————————| 15
    miles

0 |———————————————| 20
    kilometers

Portballintrae

Portrush **Dunluce Castle**

Portstewart Bushmills

Coleraine

Inishowen Peninsula

A37

River Bann

A29

Derry

D E R R Y

A5

Lifford

Strabane

SPERRIN MOUNTAINS

Lough

Cookstown

T Y R O N E

Omagh

M1

Armagh

Navan Fort

TO KESH

Enniskillen

Gosford Forest

ARMAG

F E R M A N A G H

Monaghan

Upper Lough Erne

M O N A G H A N

Belturbet

C A V A N

Cavan

To explore the three counties that make up the eastern half of Northern Ireland, we begin on the extreme north-west near County Antrim's border with County Derry and then follow the Antrim coast east and south to Belfast, the capital of Northern Ireland. From there, we take in the highlights of County Down, south and east of Antrim, and then move west to County Armagh.

COUNTY ANTRIM

There is a strong affinity for Scotland in the Northeast; only 13 miles separate them at one point. Because of this proximity, the people of Scotland have, for thousands of years, regarded the Antrim Coast as their own back yard. Hence there is a particularly strong Scottish influence in the speech and the way of life of the County Antrim folk. County Down shares this influence too, but to a lesser extent.

Antrim is the only one of Northern Ireland's six counties that is not contiguous with some part of the Republic. It is bordered on the west by County Derry, on the south by County Down, and on the east and north by the North Channel. Most people who explore Antrim beyond Belfast, its principal city, are drawn to the north coast, where the chief attractions are the Giant's Causeway and the Glens of Antrim.

Ancestral sites associated with two U.S. presidents are to be seen at **Cullybackey**, 7 km (4 miles) northwest of Ballymena, a home traditionally linked with Chester Alan Arthur, 21st president; and at **Boneybefore**, half a kilometer east of Carrickfergus, where there is a period cottage on the site of a similar one from which the parents of Andrew Jackson, seventh president, emigrated.

The North Antrim Coast

The **Giant's Causeway**, a vast promontory of more than 40,000 hexagonal basaltic columns formed by volcanic action during the Cenozoic period 70 million years ago, is easily the most popular and most interesting geological sight in Northern Ireland and one of Europe's major tourist attractions. Many ancient myths are connected with this site on the west side of Benbane Head, including one that Finn McCool, Ireland's fabled giant, used one of the formations as a Giant's Chair. An exhibit and audiovisual presentation are shown at the Tourist Center and a tea room is available. Entry to the Causeway, maintained by the National Trust, is free; however, parking can be difficult and expensive in high season (July and August). Perhaps the cheapest and best view of the Causeway, which disappears into the sea to re-emerge in Scotland, is from the cliff-top walk above, a position largely free of crowds that cover the area during peak tourist times.

The Giant's Causeway is located 13 km (8 miles) east of Portrush, near the Derry border. **Portrush** itself is a bright, breezy seaside resort and is particularly well known for its championship **Royal Portrush Golf Club** (Tel: 0265/82-23-11). For those who find themselves over-nighting in the Portrush area, the **Ramore Restaurant and Wine Bar**, a pub with great atmosphere right on the harbor edge of town, serves very good meals, fish dishes being a specialty. Note that the Ramore does not offer accommodation, and is closed Sunday and Monday. The **Royal Court Hotel** at Whiterocks, just outside Portrush, is highly recommended, with 18 bedrooms, each with private bath. The hotel is the largest in the area, and its restaurant, popular with locals for dining on special occasions, has an ornate and luxurious decor and friendly staff. The **Ballymagarry Country House** at 46 Leeke Road in Portrush is a beautifully converted 400-year-old farm building, once the property of the earls of Antrim, in a secluded rural setting with attractive gardens and all the services you would expect in a larger hotel. A friendly welcome is assured here as is excellent food. However, book in advance to avoid disappointment; there are only two rooms with twin beds and two suites. (See also County Derry in the Border Counties chapter, above.)

While you're in the Portrush area, visit **Dunluce Castle**, a substantial ruin on the edge of a cliff 5 km (3 miles) or so east of Portrush on the coast road. The castle was occupied first by Normans in the 13th century, then by Irish and Scottish chieftains until the 17th century. The Scots were everywhere in this part of Ireland for thousands of years; they were so proprietary that one of them, Sorley Boye MacDonnell, after a run-in with Queen Elizabeth's men, sent a note to the local garrison commander saying that the English had no right to be in Ireland. There are guided tours of the Dunluce Castle area, and in good weather a sea cave that was part of its defense can also be visited.

Rathlin Island, a small, boomerang-shaped bit of land

off the north coast of Antrim, is a 50-minute trip by motorboat from **Ballycastle**, 25 km (16 miles) east of Portrush (see Getting Around). While Sir Francis Drake was an ordinary sea captain in 1575, he helped massacre the MacDonnell population on the island while Sorley Boye MacDonnell, chief warrior of the clan, looked on helplessly from Fair Head across Rathlin Sound. The most famous feature of the island is **Bruce's Cave**, where Robert the Bruce stayed when he was outlawed from Scotland in 1306. It was here that he was reputed to have been so inspired by a spider's will to win that it lifted his sagging morale, and he returned to Scotland and licked the English at the battle of Bannockburn in 1314. Daily excursions to the island leave from Ballycastle from April through September. Torr Head, less than 16 km (10 miles) due east of Ballycastle, is the point in Northern Ireland closest to Scotland—from here it's only 13 miles across the Channel to the Scottish coast.

It's a glorious drive from Ballycastle around to the west through Ballintoy, past the Giant's Causeway to **Portballintrae**. This road leads along clifftops where sheep seem to defy gravity and where the traveller is rewarded with sudden dramatic glimpses of the many coves and beaches below. The route continues southeastward to **Bushmills**—the world's oldest legal whiskey distillery—on the River Bush, famed for its salmon and trout. In olden times travellers restored themselves with a glass of whiskey here, for it has been distilled at Bushmills since 1608. The spirit can be sampled within reason in the course of a tour of the distillery and malt house; closed Sundays.

For an overnight stay here, the medium-priced **Bayview Hotel** in Portballintrae is recommended. Accommodation is comfortable, and this small, family-run hotel specializes in home-cooked food and personal service. The **Auberge de Seneirl**, on the Ballyclough road in Bushmills, provides excellent accommodation and French cuisine. Just about any hotel in this area, though not luxurious, will be comfortable and friendly for an overnight stop.

The Glens of Antrim

If the Giant's Causeway is Northern Ireland's most intriguing scenic attraction, its most beautiful is without doubt the Glens of Antrim, nine lovely valleys—created by retreating glaciers—that stretch inland from the Antrim coast road between Cushendall and Cushendun, two

pretty little villages 20 km (12 miles) southeast of Ballycastle, and Larne, 34 km (21 miles) north of Belfast. If you
want to see the glens properly, you'll need to set aside the
best part of a day. With names like Glendun and Glenaan,
Glenarm and Glenariff, and with their murmuring waterfalls and wind-rustled ferns, the Glens of Antrim could be
dangerous for poets, the mixture is so rich.

Glenariff Forest Park, just off the coast road at
Cushendall, is the best center for walkers of any kind.
Well-marked scenic pathways for walkers of various ability cut through a glen with a high-sided gorge and past
three waterfalls to mountain viewpoints. The dense forest
also harbors an Early American–style log cabin built for a
local TV film on Ulster-American pioneers. A visitors'
center with a restaurant and shop caters to the less energetic.

If you have time for a meal while you're in the area,
look for the **Londonderry Arms** on Harbour Road in
Carnlough, about 20 km (12 miles) north of Larne, at the
mouth of Glencoy, one of the smaller Antrim glens. The
homemade wheaten bread, locally caught salmon, and
trout (in season) are excellent. The Londonderry Arms is
also a small, charming, family-operated hotel. The building itself is of some historic interest; it was once owned
by Winston Churchill.

For those intending to spend some time exploring the
Antrim coastal area, the **Ballygalley Castle**, right on the
coast road about 5 km (3 miles) north of Larne, is both a
comfortable and an interesting place to stop over. The
castle was built in 1625 by James Shaw, according to an
armorial escutcheon and a date carved above the door.
Rooms and food here meet all good expectations, and the
manager will talk history for half the night if encouraged.

Another point of interest in Antrim is **Carrickfergus
Castle**, a very well preserved 13th-century Norman castle
overlooking the harbor. Carrickfergus, northeast of Belfast
on the north side of Belfast Lough, is where King William
III landed to do battle with King James in 1690, at the River
Boyne, just south of the border. The castle houses an
interesting museum relating to the general history of the
area.

Also worth a visit is the **Lisburn Museum** in Lisburn, 11
km (7 miles) southwest of Belfast. John Wesley preached
here in 1756; exhibits are mainly concerned with local
involvement in the 1798 Rising in Ireland, in which Presbyterian insurgents in this area were active. French Hu-

guenots found sanctuary in the vicinity during the 17th century, and introduced new techniques for weaving damask and cambric. A weaver in the museum demonstrates the craft on a handloom of the period. Five kilometers (3 miles) east of Lisburn on the main Belfast road is the modern **Forte Crest Hotel**, which specializes in Irish salmon dishes and offers lodging as well. The accommodations here are up to international standards, and a squash court and gymnasium are available.

BELFAST

A once-pushy Victorian city that grew more quickly than any other in Europe during the 19th century, Belfast is attractively situated at the mouth of the River Lagan where it enters Belfast Lough, with blue hills—particularly the peak of Ben Madigan to the north—providing a lovely, atmospheric backdrop in the distance. Once Belfast had the biggest shipyard in the world, and the largest ropeworks; recently, like so many European cities, the capital of Northern Ireland has had to come to terms with its reduced importance in the scheme of things. Today's Belfast is modest and the pushiness is gone, the only visible evidence left being the proud City Hall and some lovely, gracious buildings arranged in a high-sided square around it. About a third of Northern Ireland's 1.5 million people live in the capital. Belfast folk are very friendly: If you look as if you're having a problem, passersby will stop to offer help.

The atmosphere in Belfast and the provincial towns is usually easy and without occurrence. There are barrier gates, but traffic flows freely through these. Security measures are greatly relaxed since the days when terrorists regularly attacked town centers; however, recent tactics (including occasional city-center bombings with advance warning) have led to a reassessment of security practices. A more overt security presence may result.

Parades on both sides of the city are held from early July through August. These cause some tension, but are routed through well-marked areas where visitors would not normally go even in happier times because, as a rule, they are away from shopping areas. Downtown stores now seldom search customers' purses, etc., upon entering. For years there have been no cases of visitors being injured. The police are armed but are invariably polite.

Army vehicles and soldiers are evident but the activities that interest them mostly occur in small side streets where tourists never go.

The Lagan river, which separates County Down from County Antrim, also bisects Belfast, so parts of the capital lie in both counties. There are three main bridges across the river in the heart of the city, over which traffic flows smoothly; though there may be some congestion at peak times, it clears quickly. Belfast's downtown district is the most modern in Ireland, with new shopping malls and excellent pedestrian facilities. The street layout is not complicated, and most places in the shopping area can be reached in the space of half an hour's walk.

The downtown area's most striking feature is the **City Hall**, which holds a prominent position in Donegall Square. Completed in 1906, this rectangular classical Renaissance building has four towers, one at each corner, and a magnificent copper-covered dome. The City Hall staff conducts tours of the building, which houses many mementos of turn-of-the-century Belfast; for times, Tel: (0232) 32-02-02, extension 2227. The **Linen Hall Library**, on Donegall Square North near the City Hall, established in 1788, is still maintained by public donation and subscription. The library contains some very fine Irish collections and other rare books. Its first librarian, Thomas Russell, was executed in 1798 for rebellion, but the current librarian conspires only about ways and means to keep the Linen Hall's excellent reputation. Closed Sundays year-round and Thursdays in July and August.

The **Grand Opera House**, on Great Victoria Street, is another of Belfast's best-known buildings. Pavlova danced here, Sarah Bernhardt trod its boards, and Orson Welles did his thing here in *Chimes at Midnight*. The Grand Opera House was allowed to fall into decay in the mid-1970s, but it was restored with help from the Northern Ireland Arts Council and reopened in 1980. Today it is considered to be one of the most stylish and evocative theaters in the British Isles and Ireland, its Victorian reds and golds, tassels and velvets as bright and warm as they were when it first opened in 1895. Leading British and European performers appear here regularly in modern and classical drama productions and in musicals.

Just across the road from the theater is the **Crown Liquor Saloon**, another building rescued from dereliction by the Arts Council. This is the sort of pub that was commonplace before the Second World War: all brass and mahogany, with intimate "snugs" where small parties may drink together in privacy. It has been shown on TV so many times that the regulars who drink here now stand at the bar as if they are acting in a classic Victor McLaglen or John Wayne film about Ireland. Both the Opera House and the Crown Liquor Saloon were badly damaged by a bomb in 1991, as were both major city-center hotels. It is a sign of Belfast's resilience that all were quickly back in full operation.

Where the performing arts are concerned, Belfast is not nearly as well provided for as Dublin, but the **Lyric Theatre** on Ridgeway Street, near Stranmillis Embankment, and the smaller **Arts Theatre** in Botanic Avenue receive strong support from the Belfast public. The Queen's University English Society holds poetry and prose readings most Thursday evenings in a house adjacent to the university building or in the English lecture theater.

About 8 km (5 miles) east of Belfast on the Upper Newtownards road is the **Stormont Parliament Building**, erected in 1928 in beautiful parkland and woods to house a Northern Ireland parliament that no longer exists. The **Ulster Folk and Transport Museum**, off the Bangor road at Cultra, northeast of Stormont, is a 136-acre complex where cottages and other buildings and artifacts of Ulster social history are displayed.

On the wooded slopes of Cave Hill, 7 km (4 miles) north of the city, sits **Belfast Castle**. Built in 1870, it is now a restaurant, with a delightful panoramic view over the city and Belfast Lough to the east. This restaurant has a reputation for its wide choice of cuisine and for the peace of its surroundings.

Elsewhere, the 38-acre **Botanic Gardens**, on the Stranmillis road in the southern suburbs, is a fine example of Victoriana. An outstanding feature is the Palm House, one of the finest early examples of curvilinear glass and cast ironwork in Europe. It was built in the 1840s and was restored to splendid condition in the mid-1970s. The large variety of exotic plants in the Tropical Ravine nearby made it a setting much loved by the folk who lived here a hundred years ago—all Oriental, jungly gloom, and rustling mystery. It still works. The **Ulster Museum**, also on the grounds of the Botanic Gardens, is a major museum and art gallery. Among its displays is some of the Spanish treasure found in the sunken wreck of the Armada galleon *Girona,* which went down in a storm off the Giant's

Causeway in 1588. There are also exhibits on the making of linen, once one of Northern Ireland's specialties.

Staying and Dining in Belfast

Half a dozen leading hotels are located at or near the center of Belfast. The biggest and most expensive of these is the **Europa** on Great Victoria Street, only yards from the place where the airport bus deposits passengers. The Europa is favored by visiting press and TV news crews, and as such has gained a reputation for staying in operation no matter what is happening around it. The atmosphere is businesslike and impersonal, but the facilities are excellent. The **Plaza Hotel** on Brunswick Street near the City Hall is one of the newest in the city. It has 83 bedrooms and was designed to attract Belfast's increasing number of business visitors, making it the chief competitor to the nearby Europa. The **Wellington Park Hotel** on the Malone Road near the university area is a smaller alternative, not quite so central but still close to the main restaurants and within walking distance of the museum and art gallery at the Botanic Gardens.

A number of good hotels are scattered around the edges of Belfast as well. The most expensive of these is the **Culloden Hotel**, off the Bangor road at Craigavad. Graded "A" by the Northern Ireland Tourist Board, the Culloden Hotel has everything from sports facilities to a beauty salon, in an attractive older building set on well-maintained grounds. All rooms have private baths, and suites are also available. The slightly lower priced **Stormont Hotel**, east of Belfast on the Upper Newtownards road, is another top-graded hotel with an excellent view of the historic parliament buildings opposite. The **Dunadry Inn** at Templepatrick is a large hotel and country club just 6 km (3½ miles) from Belfast International Airport. Situated in a quiet, rural area, it's frequented by flight crews for its proximity to the airport as well as for the quality of its food and facilities.

Belfast has a number of very good restaurants. Most of these are intimate and fairly new as well, and are fighting for clientele in a competitive market, so prices tend to be reasonable. Hotels provide good food in pleasant surroundings, but the little bistros and restaurants have more inviting atmospheres. The area near Queen's University is particularly well served, with **Branigan's**, which has a good vegetarian menu, and **The Strand**, mentioned in all the good food guides, both on the Stranmillis road. Nearby are **Saints and Scholars**, on University Street, with a reasonably priced and varied bistro menu, and the more specialized **Roscoff**, at Shaftesbury Square, which features nouvelle cuisine. In central Belfast, near City Hall, **Restaurant Forty-Four** at 44 Bedford Street includes both vegetarian and meat dishes on its menu. Also in the city center, Great Victoria Street claims a wide range of restaurants and is close to the entertainment area of Belfast. The best of these restaurants is **La Belle Epoch**, with an excellent but expensive French menu. Nearby, **Salvo's** offers Italian food, and is very popular with locals; bring your own wine if you wish.

These choices are not far from random, Belfast having so many good places. New restaurants are opening all the time; the old Dockside area, which is being extensively redeveloped, promises to become a new center for entertainment in Belfast, and is worthy of further investigation. As yet, though, it is incomplete and lacks an established atmosphere. Talk to the locals and they will be only too happy to recommend the latest popular restaurant.

Shopping in Belfast

Because prices for many goods are lower in Northern Ireland than in the Republic, Belfast is used to seeing visitors from the South looking for bargains in the city center. For many years it was the other way around, and the people of Belfast are now enjoying the city's shopping appeal and are always ready to help direct visitors to the best stores. Getting around the city is easy; cabs are plentiful and cheap—and the drivers are as talkative as New York cabbies. For those who come from the South by rail, Central Station is only minutes from the main shopping areas of Belfast, and there is bus service from the station.

It is impossible to go wrong as far as shopping in Belfast is concerned. The heart of the city has contracted and is now located north of the City Hall. The high dome of this building towers over the city. Stand with your back to the City Hall entrance and the shopping lies before you. **Parson's and Parson's**, 29 Wellington Place, stocks high-quality menswear, as does **Anderson and McAuley** at 1 Donegall Place. **Rene Meneely**, at 5 Donegall Square

West, sells fine gowns; **Jaeger's**, on nearby Royal Avenue, has both men's and ladies' casual wear.

For jewelry, **Fred J. Malcolm** at 18 Chichester Street is recommended. **Hogg's**, 10 Donegall Square West, is the top place to go for fine bone china, Irish crystal, and good-quality gift items, and **Smyth's Irish Linen**, at 14 Callender Street, sells fine embroidery and laces. Several of the main British department stores have large branches in the center of Belfast, one of the biggest being **Debenham's**, a prestigious clothing store for both men and women, in the new, impressive Castle Court shopping center in Royal Avenue. Belfast is now equal to any city in Britain or Ireland for its range of shops, and most of the major chains are represented. There may be security checks on entry to some stores, but these are quick and painless.

COUNTY DOWN

All across Northern Ireland there is a neat and tidy appearance to the countryside; the hedges are trim, the fields well managed—and in County Down this is especially so. Probably the best-kept town is **Hillsborough**, about a 45-minute drive southwest of Belfast. Hillsborough is something of a showpiece, very Southern English in appearance.

Between the famed Mountains of Mourne, which sweep down to the sea near Newcastle some 40 miles south of Belfast, and the Ards Peninsula, which curves southeast from the capital around Strangford Lough, County Down is a place of gentle hills and valleys very attractive to the eye. Its coast can be covered in two hours by car, but the numerous pleasant resort towns tempt travellers to tarry. And throughout the county traces of three outside cultures—Norse, French, and Scottish—are still strongly evident.

In the town of **Downpatrick**, some 40 km (25 miles) southeast of Belfast, a granite boulder marks the spot beside the **Church of Ireland Cathedral** where Saint Patrick himself is said to be buried. On Saint Patrick's Day pilgrims strew his gravesite with daffodils. Not many people outside Downpatrick know why; it's because the saint wasn't Irish at all, but Welsh—and the Welsh think highly of the daffodil. In Downpatrick, too, is a **museum** housed in the Old County Jail, built in 1796; the museum has a section devoted to Saint Patrick. A model of its kind in Ireland, it is well worth a visit if only to find out the truth behind the myth of the saint; closed Sunday and Monday.

The **Abbey Lodge**, a reasonably priced 21-bedroom hotel on Belfast Road in Downpatrick, is a good but not luxurious lodging in a modern, recently refurbished building. A high tea menu starts at £6 and an à la carte menu from £8. For shopping in Downpatrick, **The House of De Courcy**, on Church Street, is highly recommended for quality ladies wear; the **De Courcy Arms** next door is the perfect place to enjoy a light meal and a drink during a break. Both establishments are owned and run by the Dunseith family. **H.W. Kelly** on Market Street is the main outlet for fine china and glassware, and **McGorrian's**, also on Market Street, is a quality jeweler. Downpatrick is a small town with a rich history, and like Belfast is undergoing large-scale redevelopment in an effort to attract more visitors.

The **Butterfly House** is an unusual attraction at Seaforde, 10 km (6 miles) southwest of Downpatrick, where visitors walk among more than 30 species of tropical butterflies; a nursery garden and tea room are also at the site; open from Easter–September. Take the A 25 from Downpatrick, which joins the A 24 at Clough.

In the southern part of County Down are the **Mountains of Mourne**, immortalized by the songs of Percy French. A drive through these mountains is an experience not to be missed. Take any side road and discover an Early Christian farmstead or ancient earthwork and explore it undisturbed. If you get lost the local farmers will be happy to direct you back to the main roads. Slieve Donard (2,796 feet), their highest peak, provides an imposing backdrop for **Newcastle**, a small and hospitable seaside resort with an extensive sandy beach and one of the world's finest golf courses, the **Royal County Down**. Visitors are welcome, but advance bookings are recommended; Tel: (0396) 72-33-14. The club's informal **Centenary Bar** is also open to visitors. **Burrendale Hotel and Country Club**, on Castlewellan Road in Newcastle, serves a nice fresh salmon and scampi made with locally caught shrimp and offers rooms for overnight stays, with outstanding facilities, including a swimming pool and sauna.

Forest parks are well laid out at **Tollymore**, 3 km (2 miles) west of Newcastle, and **Rostrevor**, 16 km (10 miles) west of Kilkeel on the north shore of Carlingford Lough near the border with the Republic of Ireland.

Notable gardens are at **Castle Ward**, 3 km (2 miles) west of the village of **Strangford** on the shores of Strangford Lough opposite Portaferry; **Mountstewart House**, 8 km (5 miles) south of Newtownards, also on Strangford Lough; and **Rowallane House**, at Saintfield, 18 km (11 miles) southeast of Belfast.

The **Glassdrumman Lodge** at **Annalong**, down the coast from Newcastle, is an exclusive eight-room hotel and restaurant with a deservedly high reputation. In the restaurant beef and pork dishes are made from the stock reared on the grounds; seafood comes fresh from the port of Annalong, only yards away. Especially popular are the home-cooked granary wheaten bread and walnut bread. A seven-course weekend meal in the Memories restaurant will run from about £25; five courses are available from £19.50 during the week. Guests at the hotel enjoy the luxury of a butler and 24-hour room service as well as overnight laundry and secretarial services.

Farther up the coast, at **Portaferry** on the southern tip of the Ards Peninsula, is the **Portaferry Hotel**, run by John and Marie Herlihy. Seafood is the specialty here, and after extensive refurbishment, 14 suites are available. Not far from the hotel is the **Northern Ireland Aquarium**. One of only two public aquariums in Ireland, it displays the variety of marine life in Strangford Lough and is staffed by marine biology experts. The aquarium may be closed occasionally in 1993 due to extensive building work.

The **Ards Peninsula** is an essential excursion, if only to experience a part of the country almost completely untouched by political difficulties (Portaferry provides the perfect base). The scenery is as spectacular as the Mournes and the Antrim Coast, and the peninsula, bordered by Strangford Lough on one side and the Irish Sea on the other, offers deep-sea fishing, all water sports and sailing, golf, horseback riding, and walking. As the first and most peacefully planted area of Ireland, the Ards Peninsula is the ideal choice for the historian. Ireland's history is in microcosm here, from Neolithic burial grounds through Early Christian farmsteads and holy wells to Norman abbeys and castles. A ten-minute car-ferry ride links Portaferry with Strangford and the rest of Down. This trip is enjoyable in itself, the strong tidal currents showing the traveller why the Norsemen gave the area its name, Strang Fiord (Strong River).

If you plan to spend some time in County Down,

O'Hara's Royal Hotel, on the seafront at **Bangor**, at the top of the Ards Peninsula east of Belfast, is a good-quality establishment. Rooms at the front of the hotel cost more than those at the side because of the lovely views across the Irish Sea to Scotland, but special weekend rates are offered on all rooms. Five kilometers (3 miles) west of Bangor you will find **Crawfordsburn**, a beautifully preserved village; the **Old Inn** here, built in 1614, is well worth a stop for dinner or an overnight stay. **Cottage Crafts**, opposite, offers knitwear, Tyrone crystal, and local pottery.

COUNTY ARMAGH

County Armagh, characterized by gentle hills, is sometimes referred to as the Garden (or Orchard) of Ulster, with scenery in marked contrast to the rough mountains and woodlands of Down. This is the ancient cultural and religious capital of Ireland, and **Armagh City**, 136 km (84 miles) north of Dublin and 59 km (37 miles) southwest of Belfast, houses the Catholic Primate, who has his palace here. Nearby in town is the Anglican **Cathedral of St. Patrick**, reputed to be the burial place of Ireland's high king Brian Boru, who was killed in the battle of Clontarf in 1014. The cathedral's library contains a copy of *Gulliver's Travels* corrected in Swift's own hand.

The city of Armagh is small and, although historically important, not the thriving center a visitor might expect. A striking feature of the city is **the Mall**, a tree-lined promenade flanked by gracious Georgian houses, where cricket is often played. The **Armagh Planetarium and Observatory** at College Hill to the northeast of the city center has exciting, computer-aided exhibits and displays; in the Star Theatre viewers travel through time, as the universe puts on its own show; closed Sundays. The **Drumsill House Hotel** on Moy Road in town has a fine restaurant as well as comfortable accommodations, and is probably the best choice for anyone wishing to stay in the area.

Although County Armagh is not known for its fine stores, Market and Scotch streets in Armagh City will meet most shopping demands in the area. **Whitsitt's**, on Market, has a wide range of fine china wares, while Scotch Street has a concentration of smaller fashion shops for women. For jewelry try **Ewart** and **City Jewellers**, both on Scotch.

Armagh currently lacks tourist facilities, but has great plans for the future, including the building of a visitors' center at Navan Fort, just outside of the city. **Navan Fort**, or, in the Irish, Eamhain Mhacha, a huge elliptical earthwork mound about 3 km (2 miles) west of Armagh City, was the site of the chief stronghold of the Celtic kings of Ulster for a thousand years, until its destruction in A.D. 332. The mighty Cuchulain, one of the most heroic figures in Irish mythology—well known to readers of Yeats—practiced feats of arms below the palace in ancient times. Today it is a grassy 16-acre mound but it has an atmosphere rivalled only by Newgrange across the border in Meath. It is worth seeing now, before the heritage experts have tamed it.

There is a fine forest park at **Gosford**, 10 km (6 miles) southeast of Armagh City, an estate that has associations with Dean Swift. Swift (who wrote *Gulliver's Travels*) was a friend of the Earl of Gosford, and often stayed on the estate. Traditional poultry breeds and deer can be seen here. There is another at **Slieve Gullion**, 8 km (5 miles) southwest of **Newry** and about 30 km (19 miles) southeast of Armagh City, which features an eight-mile drive around dense woodland and two megalithic cairns. Northwest of Newry off B 133 is one of the prettiest villages in County Armagh: **Bessbrook**, founded in 1845 by a Quaker, John Richardson.

In addition to its comfortable accommodations, the **Carngrove Hotel** in **Portadown**, 17 km (11 miles) northeast of Armagh City, also operates a highly recommended restaurant and has excellent fishing facilities close by. The **Silverwood Hotel** on Kiln Lane, Silverwood, Lurgan (near Portadown off the M 1), makes a good, comfortable headquarters from which to plan itineraries in County Armagh and beyond, because of its central position and its proximity to the motorway.

For golfers there is the **Portadown Golf Club** just 5 km (3 miles) southeast of the town at 192 Gilford Road, on the M 1 motorway direct from Belfast center. This is a standard scratch score 70, 70-par course. Visitors are welcome any day except Tuesdays and Saturdays; Tel: (0762) 35-53-56.

GETTING AROUND

Travelling by car is the most efficient way to see the Northeast. There are 70 miles of high-quality motorways, as well as divided highways and very good secondary roads right across Northern Ireland. All major road signs are in English, although in some areas smaller street names may be in the Irish language.

This is the greenest part of Ireland, so it is not surprising that it is also the rainiest. Summer and autumn can be idyllic, but the mist on the mountains that makes this part of Ireland so romantic also makes carrying a light raincoat a sensible idea.

Entry documents are not usually required at border crossing points, for either travellers from the Republic or visitors from Britain. For those coming from the Republic by road or rail there is usually no delay at entry points in Down or Armagh, but on the return south the customs and excise people may ask whether consumer goods such as TV sets or microwave ovens have been purchased during the run north. Prices for many things are slightly cheaper in Northern Ireland than in the Republic.

Away from border districts, only sterling currency is accepted in stores and places of business. In the vicinity of the border, however, Republic of Ireland pounds (punts) are accepted at gas stations, hotels, and stores. Throughout Northern Ireland, banks are generally open from 10:00 A.M. until 3:30 P.M., and many have automatic cash dispensers. Cash is needed at smaller hotels and guest houses, although Access, Barclaycard, and American Express credit cards are accepted more frequently now; Diners' Club cards are not quite as widely accepted.

Belfast International Airport is located inland, in County Antrim, about a 30-minute drive from Belfast. A bus service runs every 30 minutes from the airport to the city center. A small airport specializing in flights between major British cities is situated in the dockside area. Travellers by rail from Dublin arrive at Central Station in the heart of Belfast. For those intending to visit Britain from Ireland and return, the fares from the North, both sea and air, are generally cheaper than those from the Republic. Train fares are cheaper in the North as well, running roughly 30 percent below those in the Republic.

Rathlin Ferry operates daily between Ballycastle and Rathlin Island, weather permitting. Tel: (0265) 76-39-17.

Northern Ireland and Scotland are very close to each other along the Antrim coast; only 35 miles separate them at the port of Larne. There are two ferry companies operating from Larne to Stranraer in Scotland: Sealink Ferries, Tel: (0574) 736-16; and P & O European Ferries, Tel: (0574) 743-21. The scenic route to Larne is on the

coast road through Carrickfergus and Whitehead. Upon
entering the town, signposts direct you to the harbor. No
reservations are necessary except during July and August.
A car-ferry service between Belfast and Liverpool is now
also available. Sailings in both directions leave each evening and arrive the following morning. Contact Norse
Irish Ferries in Belfast; Tel: (0232) 77-91-91. The
Strangford Lough car ferry runs at 30-minute intervals,
leaving Portaferry at 15 minutes and 45 minutes past the
hour, and Strangford on the hour and half hour.

ACCOMMODATIONS REFERENCE
*The telephone country code for the Northeast is 44. When
dialing telephone numbers in Northern Ireland from
outside the country, drop the 0 in the area code. The rates
given below are* projections *for weekday rates for 1993
in pounds sterling; for up-to-the-minute rate information
it is always wise to telephone before booking. Unless
otherwise indicated, rates are per person sharing and
include breakfast but not service.*

County Antrim
▶ **Auberge de Seneirl**. 28 Ballyclough Road, **Bushmills**,
County Antrim BT57 8UZ. Tel: (0265) 74-15-36. £18.50–
£33; breakfast not included. All rooms with bath; some
larger rooms with sitting rooms are available.

▶ **Ballygalley Castle**. 274 Coast Road, **Ballygalley**,
County Antrim BT40 Q2Z. Tel: (0574) 58-32-12; Fax:
(0574) 58-36-81. £33.

▶ **Ballymagarry Country House**. 46 Leeke Road,
Portrush, County Antrim BT56 8NH. Tel: (0265) 82-37-37.
£35. Suites are available.

▶ **Bayview Hotel**. 2 Bayhead Road, **Portballintrae**,
County Antrim BT57 8RZ. Tel: (0265) 73-14-53; Fax:
(0265) 73-23-60. £30.

▶ **Dunadry Inn**. 2 Islandreagh Road, **Templepatrick**,
County Antrim BT41 2HA. Tel: (08494) 324-74; Fax:
(08494) 333-89. £50.

▶ **Europa Hotel**. Great Victoria Street, **Belfast**, County
Antrim BT2 7AP. Tel: (0232) 32-70-00; Fax: (0232) 32-78-
00. £47.50, breakfast not included.

▶ **Forte Crest Hotel**. 300 Kingsway, **Dunmurry**, County
Antrim BT17 9ES. Tel: (0232) 61-21-01; Fax: (0232) 62-65-
46. £35.

▶ **Londonderry Arms**. 20 Harbour Road, **Carnlough**,

County Antrim BT44 0EU. Tel: (0574) 88-52-55; Fax: (0574) 88-52-63. £26.

▶ **Plaza Hotel.** 15 Brunswick Street, **Belfast,** County Antrim BT2 7GE. Tel: (0232) 33-35-55; Fax: (0232) 23-29-99. £42.50.

▶ **Royal Court Hotel.** Whiterocks, **Portrush,** County Antrim BT56 8NF. Tel: (0265) 82-22-36; Fax: (0265) 82-44-91. £40.

▶ **Stormont Hotel.** 587 Upper Newtownards Road, **Belfast,** County Antrim BT4 3LP. Tel: (0232) 65-86-21; Fax: (0232) 48-02-40. £55.

▶ **Wellington Park Hotel.** 21 Malone Road, **Belfast,** County Antrim BT9 6RU. Tel: (0232) 38-11-11; Fax: (0232) 66-54-10. £45.

County Down

▶ **Abbey Lodge Hotel.** Belfast Road, **Downpatrick,** County Down BT30 9AV. Tel: (0396) 61-45-11. £26.

▶ **Burrendale Hotel and Country Club.** Castlewellan Road, **Newcastle,** County Down BT33 0JY. Tel: (03967) 225-99; Fax: (03967) 223-28. £109, breakfast not included.

▶ **Culloden Hotel.** 142 Bangor Road, **Holywood,** County Down BT18 0EX. Tel: (0232) 42-52-23; Fax: (0232) 42-67-77. £170.

▶ **Glassdrumman Lodge.** 85 Mill Road, **Annalong,** County Down BT34 4RH. Tel: (03967) 685-85 or 51; Fax: (03967) 670-41. £75; large double, £85, breakfast not included.

▶ **O'Hara's Royal Hotel.** Seafront, **Bangor,** County Down BT20 5ED. Tel: (0247) 27-18-66. £32.50–£37.50.

▶ **Old Inn.** 15 Main Street, **Crawfordsburn,** County Down BT19 1JH. Tel: (0247) 85-32-55; Fax: (0247) 85-27-75. £40.

▶ **Portaferry Hotel.** 10 The Strand, **Portaferry,** County Down BT22 1PE. Tel: (02477) 282-31; Fax: (02477) 289-99. £37.50.

County Armagh

▶ **Carngrove Hotel.** 2 Charlestown Road, **Portadown,** County Armagh BT63 5PW. Tel: (0762) 33-92-22; Fax: (0762) 33-28-99. £26.

▶ **Drumsill House Hotel.** 35 Moy Road, **Armagh City,** County Armagh BT61 8DN. Tel: (0861) 52-20-09; Fax: (0861) 52-56-24. £30.

▶ **Silverwood Hotel.** Kiln Lane, **Lurgan,** County Armagh BT66 6NF. Tel: (0762) 32-77-22; Fax: (0762) 32-52-90. £26.

CHRONOLOGY OF THE HISTORY OF IRELAND

The Mesolithic Era

Human activity in Ireland, as established at present, dates to the arrival in the country's northeast of hunters and fishermen from Scotland in the Mesolithic Era. These Middle Stone Age people, who crossed to Ireland some time after 8000 B.C., are thought to have originated in Scandinavia and probably arrived by boat, though they may have taken advantage of land bridges, which still appeared intermittently and which were responsible for the arrival of many plants and animals in the country. Worked flints from this Mesolithic culture have been found on the Antrim coast, but few other traces have been discovered.

The Neolithic Age

The period from c. 4000–2000 B.C. gave rise to houses and field patterns, as excavated at Lough Gur, County Limerick, the Céide Fields, north County Mayo, and near Boyle, County Roscommon. From this period came the impressive and massive portal tombs in the Boyne Valley, County Meath, Carrowkeel, County Sligo, and elsewhere. These monuments, known as megaliths, were built by a new race of immigrants who were organized in agricultural communities and who used massive stones, in many cases decorated with sophisticated designs, in their construction (itself a matter for speculation).

The Bronze Age

The arrival of the first wave of Celtic-speaking peoples from France, roughly contemporaneous with the Middle

Kingdom of Egypt, marks the transition to the Bronze Age in Ireland. Some time before 2000 B.C. a new style of burial, the "wedge tomb," was introduced, possibly by these same peoples, whose weapons and tools were produced in bronze and objects for personal and ritual use in gold (small decorated discs, crescent-shaped necklets—*lunulae*—such as that in the National Museum, Dublin, dated to 1800–1500 B.C.). Though during the later Bronze Age (1000–200 B.C.) and after these gold artifacts became more widely diversified, still there was a virtual absence of any representational art.

The Celtic Era

With the arrival of Celtic people from central Europe c. 500 B.C., the impact of La Tène culture (named for a Celtic site in Switzerland) made itself evident in the transformation of Irish art, as evidenced in a surviving wealth of gold objects, sculpture, and bronze ware. The coming of Christianity brought the flowering of the art of manuscript illumination of which the *Book of Kells* (Trinity College, Dublin) is the outstanding example. From the sixth century the Scotti Peregrini (Wandering Irish) carried their culture and religion to many centers in Britain and on the European mainland.

- c. 500–150 B.C.: Irish language develops from Proto-Celtic roots.
- c. A.D. 130–180: Ptolemy, Roman geographer, makes map of Ireland.
- 297–c. 450: Irish raids on Roman Britain.
- 431: Palladius, first bishop to Irish Christians. Beginning of *Annals of Ulster*.
- 432: Saint Patrick's mission (traditional date).
- c. 526: Death of Saint Brigid, one of three patron saints of Ireland (along with Patrick and Colmcille) and founder of a great religious house at Kildare.
- 546: Foundation of Derry by Saint Colmcille.
- 574–578: Foundation of monastic center of Clonmacnoise by Saint Ciarán.
- c. 650–750: Ossory group of High Crosses.
- c. 750–800: *Book of Kells* and *St. Gall* illuminated manuscripts.

Viking Period

The Vikings of Scandinavia raided many monastic sites (the round towers, with their entrances high off the ground, were built to safeguard precious possessions against such attacks), and founded towns and cities that still preserve their Norse names (Wexford, Dalkey, Howth, Strangford). Their power was broken at the battle of Clontarf, near Dublin, but many remained to intermarry with the native Irish.

- **795**: First Viking raids. Irish settlement in Iceland.
- **837–876**: Semipermanent Viking settlements.
- **841**: Viking settlement at Dyfflin (Dublin).
- **853**: Olaf becomes first Norse king of Dublin.
- **914**: Viking base at Waterford.
- **978**: Brian Boru becomes king of Munster.
- **1002**: Brian Boru becomes high king of Ireland.
- **1014**: Irish defeat Danes at battle of Clontarf. Brian Boru killed and buried at Armagh.
- **c. 1028**: Foundation of Dublin's Christ Church Cathedral.
- **1092**: Beginning of *Annals of Inisfallen* (to continue to the 14th century).
- **1127–1134**: Construction of St. Cormac's Chapel, Cashel.
- **1142**: First Irish Cistercian foundation, Mellifont, County Louth.
- **1152**: Diarmait Mac Murchada (Dermot Mac-Murrough) abducts Dervorgilla, wife of Tighernan Ua Ruairc (Tiernan O'Rourke); events lead to Anglo-Norman invasion and eventual consolidation of British hegemony.
- **1155**: Papal bull approves conquest of Ireland by English king Henry II.

Anglo-Norman Period

- **1169**: Anglo-Normans land at Bannow, County Wexford.
- **1170**: Waterford captured by Normans under Richard de Clare (Strongbow), who marries Aoife, daughter of Mac Murchada. Capture of Dublin.
- **1171**: Henry II receives submission of four Irish kings.

- **1174**: Henry II grants charter to Dublin.
- **c. 1188**: Geraldus Cambrensis (Gerald of Wales) writes *Expugnatio Hibernica,* first tourist guide (generally unflattering) to the island.
- **1207**: First national coinage carrying harp symbol.
- **1224**: Irish Dominican foundations at Dublin and Drogheda.
- **c. 1224–1230**: Irish Franciscan foundations at Youghal and Cork. Opening of Dublin mint.
- **1262–1263**: High kingship offered to Haakon IV of Norway in return for help in expelling English; his death prevents acceptance.
- **1315–1317**: Famine.
- **1348**: Black Death at Howth and Drogheda.
- **1395**: Irish kings submit to England's Richard II.
- **1422**: Proclamation for expulsion of Irish from England.
- **1431**: Establishment of St. Patrick's Cathedral choir in Dublin.
- **1478–1513**: Supremacy of Garrett Fitzgerald, eighth earl of Kildare ("the Great Earl").
- **1487**: First record of firearms in Ireland.

The Tudor Conquest

The English Crown, until now unacknowledged in most parts of Ireland outside the Pale (the area around Dublin), consolidated its power and finally, following the battle of Kinsale, destroyed the old Gaelic order.

- **1539**: Henry VIII, declared king of Ireland in 1541, attempts to introduce the Reformation to Ireland and dissolves monasteries within the Pale.
- **1561–1567**: Rebellion of Shane O'Neill in Ulster.
- **1571**: First printing in Irish in Dublin.
- **1580**: Papal force massacred by British at Dun an Oir (Smerwick).
- **1588**: Ships of Spanish Armada wrecked off Irish coast. Many survivors massacred by Irish.
- **1590**: Foundation at Alcalá de Henares, Spain, of first Irish college for priests on the Continent.
- **1592**: Incorporation of Trinity College, Dublin.
- **1595–1603**: Rising under Hugh O'Neill, earl of Tyrone.
- **1601**: Battle of Kinsale. Spanish force and allies

Tyrone and Tyrconnell defeated. Tyrconnell leaves for Spain.

- **1606**: Foundation of Irish Franciscan college at Louvain, Belgium.
- **1607**: "Flight of the Earls": Tyrone and Tyrconnell lead exodus to European mainland. Gaelic power broken.

Plantation and Colonization

This period saw the colonization of Ulster and the final attempts of the Gaelic families of the province to retrieve their lands and fortunes. The arrival of the lord protector of England, Oliver Cromwell, proved cataclysmic in its impact. Following the collapse of the English commonwealth in 1660 and the restoration of Charles II, the scene was set for the military and political resolution on Irish soil of the confrontation between Charles's successor, James II, and the latter's son-in-law, William of Orange. This culminated in the battle of the Boyne, which resolved the situation for Britain but established deep divisions in Ireland.

- **1610**: Plantation of Derry by Scots and English settlers on land confiscated from Gaelic chiefs.
- **1632–1636**: Compilation of historical work *Annals of the Four Masters* at Donegal.
- **1642**: Catholic Confederation, representative assembly of the rebels, meets in Kilkenny, demanding full recognition of Catholicism and restoration of confiscated lands.
- **1649**: Massacres at Drogheda and Wexford by Oliver Cromwell.
- **1660**: Robert Boyle enunciates Boyle's Law, which concerns the behavior of gases.
- **1681**: Execution in London of archbishop Oliver Plunkett (subsequently canonized).
- **1689**: Jacobite wars: siege of Derry by James II of England.
- **1690**: Battle of the Boyne, near Drogheda, between James II and William III. William is victorious. Though there are Irish on both sides and the pope supports the Protestant William, the event comes to symbolize the religio-political polarization in Ireland.
- **1691**: Treaty of Limerick (subsequently broken by

British) allows Irish soldiers to follow James II to mainland Europe.

- **1695–1709:** Penal laws against Catholics.
- **1713:** Jonathan Swift (*Gulliver's Travels*) becomes dean of St. Patrick's, Dublin.
- **1728:** Oliver Goldsmith born in County Longford.
- **1729:** Irish Parliament's first meeting in College Green, Dublin.
- **1731:** Foundation of Royal Dublin Society.
- **1737:** First issue of *Belfast News Letter,* oldest newspaper in continuous publication in Ireland or Britain.
- **1742:** First performance of Handel's *Messiah,* Dublin.
- **1759:** Arthur Guinness establishes a brewery in Dublin.
- **1771:** Benjamin Franklin in Ireland.
- **1778:** John Paul Jones, American pirate, raids Belfast Lough.
- **1782:** Britain concedes parliamentary independence: Grattan's Parliament. John Field, composer and inventor of the nocturne, born in Dublin.
- **1785:** First meeting of Irish Academy (later "Royal"), founded to advance study of antiquities and Celtic linguistics and science.

The Struggle for Independence

Though the Dublin Parliament of 1729 had a measure of effective independence, it represented only a small segment of the people. The ideals of the French Revolution inspired Wolfe Tone to seek self-determination for all, and to replace the divisions of "Catholic, Protestant and Dissenter" by "the common name of Irishman." There followed through the next century a number of unsuccessful attempts at insurrection culminating in the Rising of 1916 and the birth, in bloodshed and civil war, of the modern Irish state.

- **1791:** United Irishmen founded in Belfast by Wolfe Tone.
- **1792:** Gathering of Irish harpers in Belfast.
- **1796:** Ambrose O'Higgins becomes viceroy of Peru. His son, Bernardo O'Higgins, eventually becomes a leader of the forces that achieved Chile's independence from Spain in 1818.
- **1798:** Rising. Arrest and death of its leader, Lord

Edward Fitzgerald; French force lands in Connacht and is defeated; Tone, who had sought French assistance, is arrested and commits suicide in jail.

- **1801:** Union of Ireland with Great Britain.
- **1803:** Rising of Robert Emmett in Dublin. Emmett executed.
- **1808:** Christian Brothers teaching order founded in Wexford; major force in education through the late 20th century.
- **1829:** Daniel O'Connell ("the Liberator") enters British Parliament.
- **1834:** First railroad in Ireland: Dublin–Kingstown (Dún Laoghaire).
- **1841:** J. P. Holland, inventor of the submarine, born in County Clare.
- **1842:** First issue of *Nation,* organ of Young Ireland movement.
- **1843:** O'Connell addresses mass meetings supporting repeal of Union.
- **1845:** Inauguration of Rosse telescope, the world's largest, at Birr.
- **1845–1849:** Great Famine follows failure of potato crops; millions die and millions more emigrate to New World.
- **1847:** Bram Stoker, creator of Dracula, born in Dublin.
- **1848:** Young Ireland rising. Leaders transported to Tasmania.
- **1853:** Opening of Belfast shipyard: builders of *Titanic.*
- **1856:** Playwright George Bernard Shaw born in Dublin.
- **1858:** Irish Republican Brotherhood (IRB) founded in Dublin; Fenian Brotherhood founded in New York.
- **1865:** William Butler Yeats born.
- **1866:** Fenian raids against British in Canada.
- **1867:** Fenian rising in Ireland; leaders transported.
- **1873:** Home Rule League: constitutional independence movement of moderate reformers advocating limited independence.
- **1874:** Ernest Shackleton, Antarctic explorer, born in County Kildare.
- **1875:** Charles Stuart Parnell elected to British Parliament.

- **1879–1882:** Land War. Founding of Irish National Land League (1879).
- **1880:** Parnell addresses U.S. House of Representatives. "Boycotting" of landlord Captain Charles Boycott, County Mayo.
- **1884:** Gaelic Athletic Association (GAA) founded, Thurles.
- **1892:** Ulster Convention, Belfast, resolves against Home Rule.
- **1895:** First production of Oscar Wilde's *The Importance of Being Earnest*.
- **1896:** Founding of Irish Socialist Republican party: secretary, James Connolly.
- **1899:** Founding of Irish Literary Theatre, forerunner of the Abbey.
- **1906:** First issue of *Sinn Fein* (*We Ourselves*), editor Arthur Griffith. Samuel Beckett born in Dublin.
- **1913:** General strike in Dublin; workers led by James Larkin. Ulster Volunteer Force established to fight Home Rule.
- **1914:** Publication of James Joyce's *Dubliners*.
- **1916:** Easter Rising. Fifteen leaders executed by British.
- **1919–1921:** War of Independence.

"A Nation Once Again"

- **1920:** British Government of Ireland Act sets up separate subordinate parliaments in Dublin and Belfast.
- **1921:** Northern Ireland Parliament convened by George V.
- **1922:** Anglo-Irish Treaty. Civil war between pro- and anti-Treaty forces. Constitution of Irish Free State approved by Dáil Eireann (parliament). First publication, in Paris, of James Joyce's novel *Ulysses*.
- **1926:** Fianna Fail party launched by New York–born Eamon de Valera.
- **1934:** De Valera becomes chairman of League of Nations, Geneva.
- **1937:** Under new constitution approved by referendum, Irish Free State becomes Eire and severs links with British monarchy.
- **1939:** Ireland declares neutrality in Second World War.

- **1949**: Republic of Ireland declared, removing last British links.
- **1960**: Irish troops serve with United Nations in the Congo.
- **1963**: U.S. president John F. Kennedy in Ireland.
- **1969**: Clash between civil rights marchers (largely Catholic) and police in Derry: beginning of Northern Ireland confrontation involving Nationalist and Loyalist paramilitaries and British army. On Nationalist side the Provisional Irish Republican Army (breakaway group from the original IRA, which fought the War of Independence) wage campaign of murder and destruction, reciprocated by Loyalist Ulster Freedom Fighters in ongoing sectarian struggle; Nobel Prize in literature awarded to Dublin-born Samuel Beckett.
- **1973**: Ireland joins European Economic Community.
- **1977–1982**: "Treasures of Ireland" exhibition of Irish art, 1500 B.C.–A.D. 1500, tours United States and Continental Europe.
- **1979**: Ireland joins European Monetary System (EMS) and breaks link with sterling. Visit of Pope John Paul II.
- **1981**: Death of ten IRA hunger strikers in Long Kesh (Maze) prison, Belfast.
- **1983**: First session of New Ireland Forum to seek solution to Northern situation.
- **1985**: Signature of Anglo-Irish agreement, allowing Dublin a voice in Northern affairs, particularly those relating to the Nationalist minority.
- **1990**: Ireland holds presidency of the European Community. Mary Robinson becomes Ireland's first woman president.
- **1991**: Museum of Modern Art opens in restored 17th-century Royal Hospital, Dublin.
- **1992**: Talks involving Irish and British governments and Northern Ireland parties (excluding Sinn Féin) seek new political solutions.

—Bernard Share

INDEX

*H*ere's what others say...

"As a longtime reader of *Passport*, I trust it as a source of intelligence and ideas on independent travel."

Alan Deutschman
Associate Editor
Fortune Magazine

"The best little newsletter in America."
Crain's Chicago Business

"*Passport* has been appearing for more than 20 years with a brisk, colorful roundup of travel information. Substance prevails over style."
National Geographic Traveler

"In *Passport*, I consistently find the kind of information I want from a travel newsletter—sophisticated, concise and straightforward, without a lot of ego to get in the way."
Travel Editor
Town and Country Magazine

"*T*he first and unquestionably the best luxury travel newsletter."

Alan Tucker, General Editor
Berlitz Travellers Guides

*S*ince 1965, *Passport*, the monthly letter for discriminating travelers, has revealed hard-to-find information about the world's best destinations. Return this card for a free issue or call 800-542-6670. Available worldwide!

Please send a free issue of *Passport* to:

Name

Address

City   State   Zip

" *This* is the granddaddy of travel letters... *Passport* emphasizes culture, comfort, and quality...it can glow with praise, or bite with disapproval."

Condé Nast Traveler